D0384032

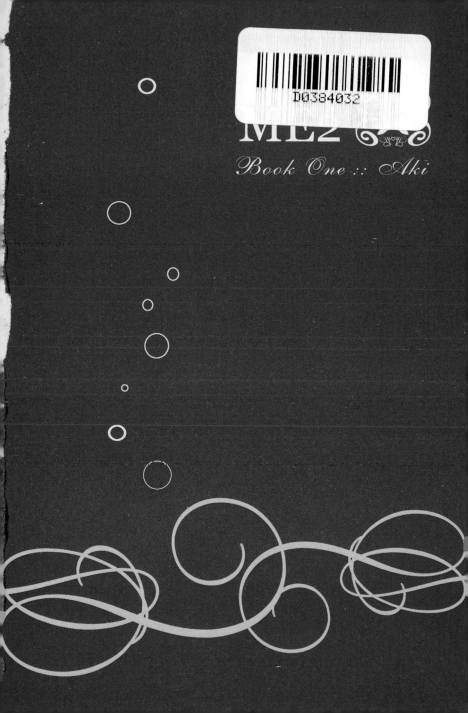

ME2

Book One :: Aki

Me 2 Vol. 1
Written by Sho Murase and Matt Anderson
Illustrated by Sho Murase

Lettering - Lucas Rivera
Development Editor - Jodi Bryson
Cover Art - Sho Murase
Cover Design - Al-Insan Lashley

Editor - Troy Lewter
Digital Imaging Manager - Chris Buford
Pre-Production Supervisor - Erika Terriquez
Art Director - Anne Marie Horne
Production Manager - Elisabeth Brizzi
VP of Production - Ron Klamert
Editor-in-Chief - Rob Tokar
Publisher - Mike Kiley
President and C.O.O. - John Parker
C.E.O. and Chief Creative Officer - Stuart Levy

A **TOKYOPOP**® Manga

TOKYOPOP and ◉ are trademarks or registered trademarks of TOKYOPOP Inc.

TOKYOPOP Inc.
5900 Wilshire Blvd. Suite 2000
Los Angeles, CA 90036

E-mail: info@TOKYOPOP.com
Come visit us online at www.TOKYOPOP.com

ISBN: 978-1-4278-0063-3

First TOKYOPOP printing: July 2007
10 9 8 7 6 5 4 3 2 1
Printed in the USA

Table of contents :

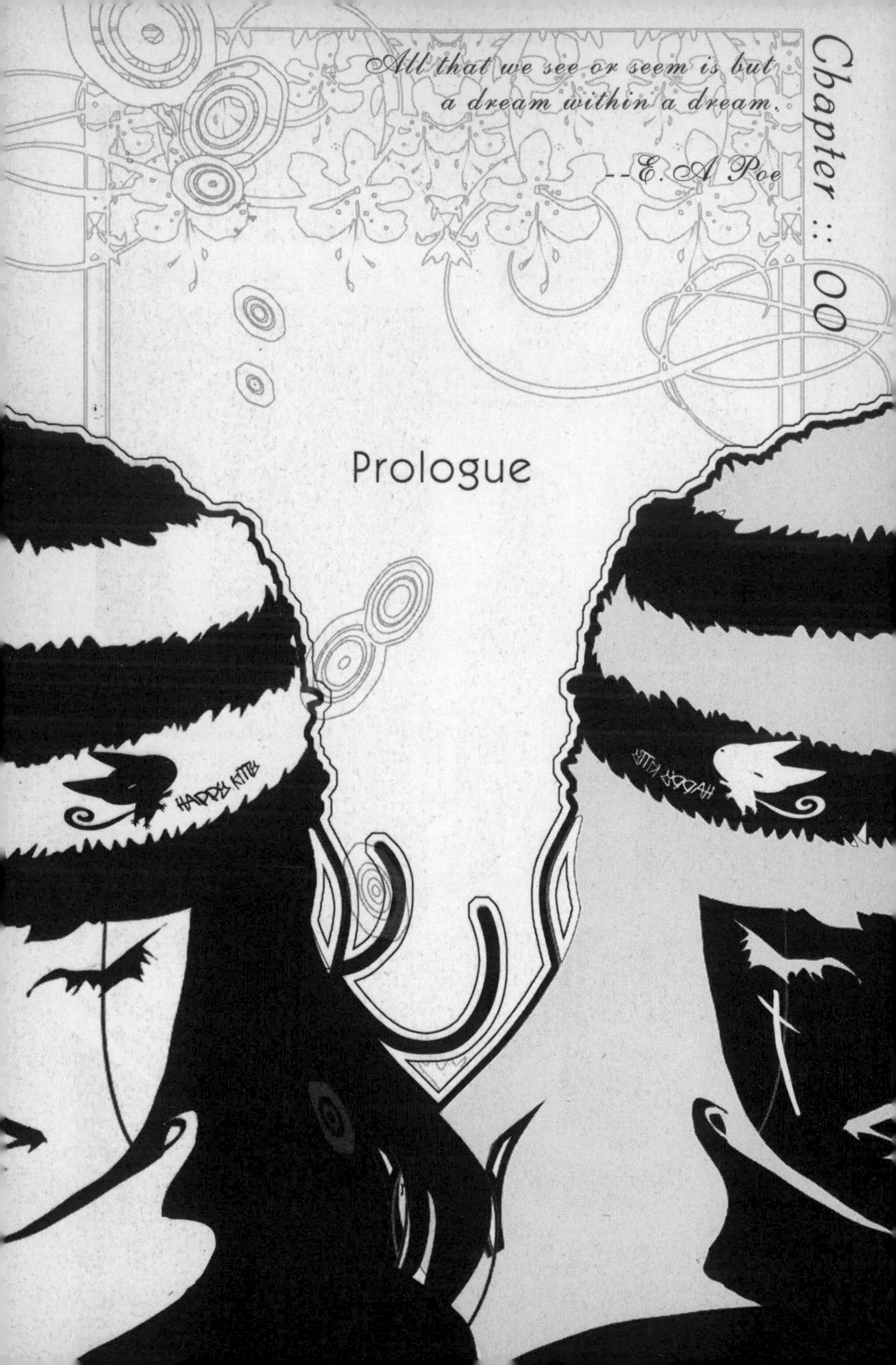
Chapter :: 00
All that we see or seem is but
a dream within a dream.
--E. A Poe
Prologue

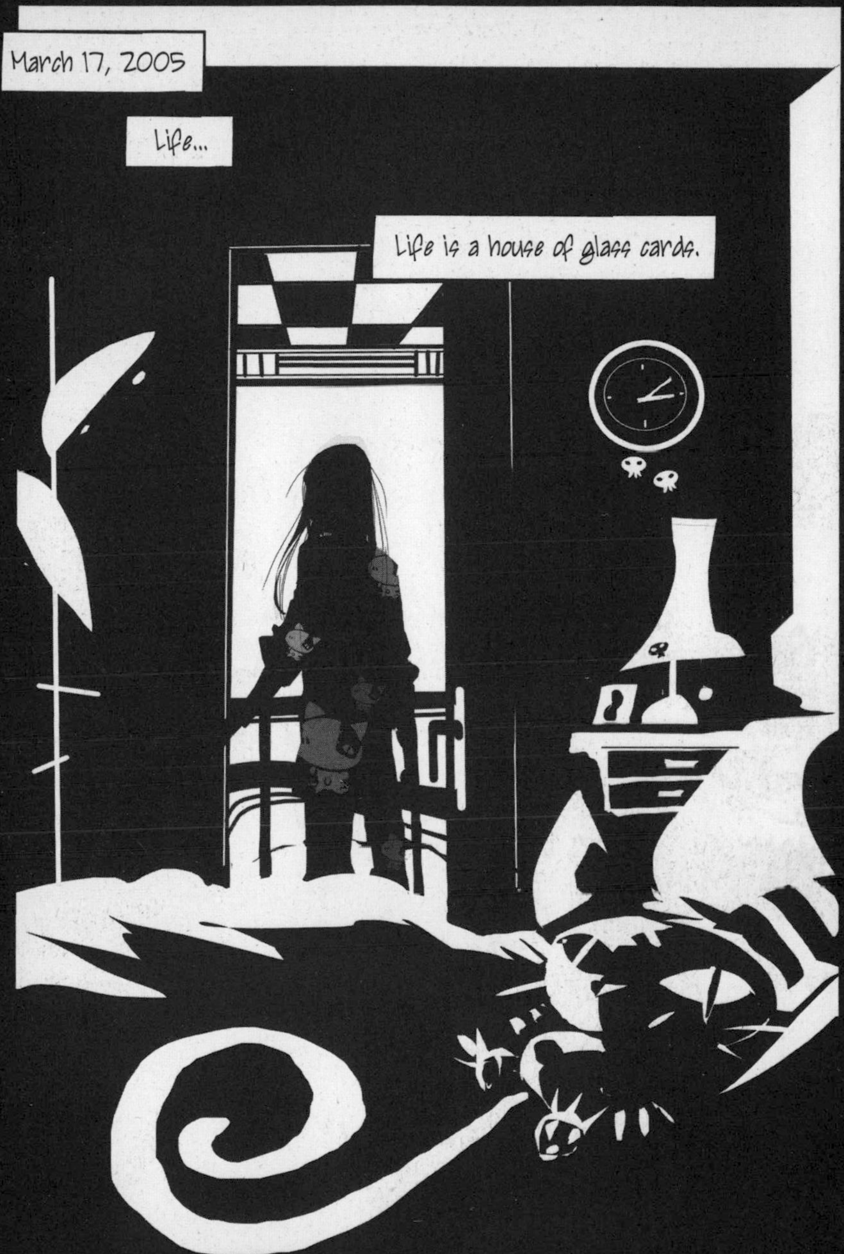
March 17, 2005
Life...
Life is a house of glass cards.

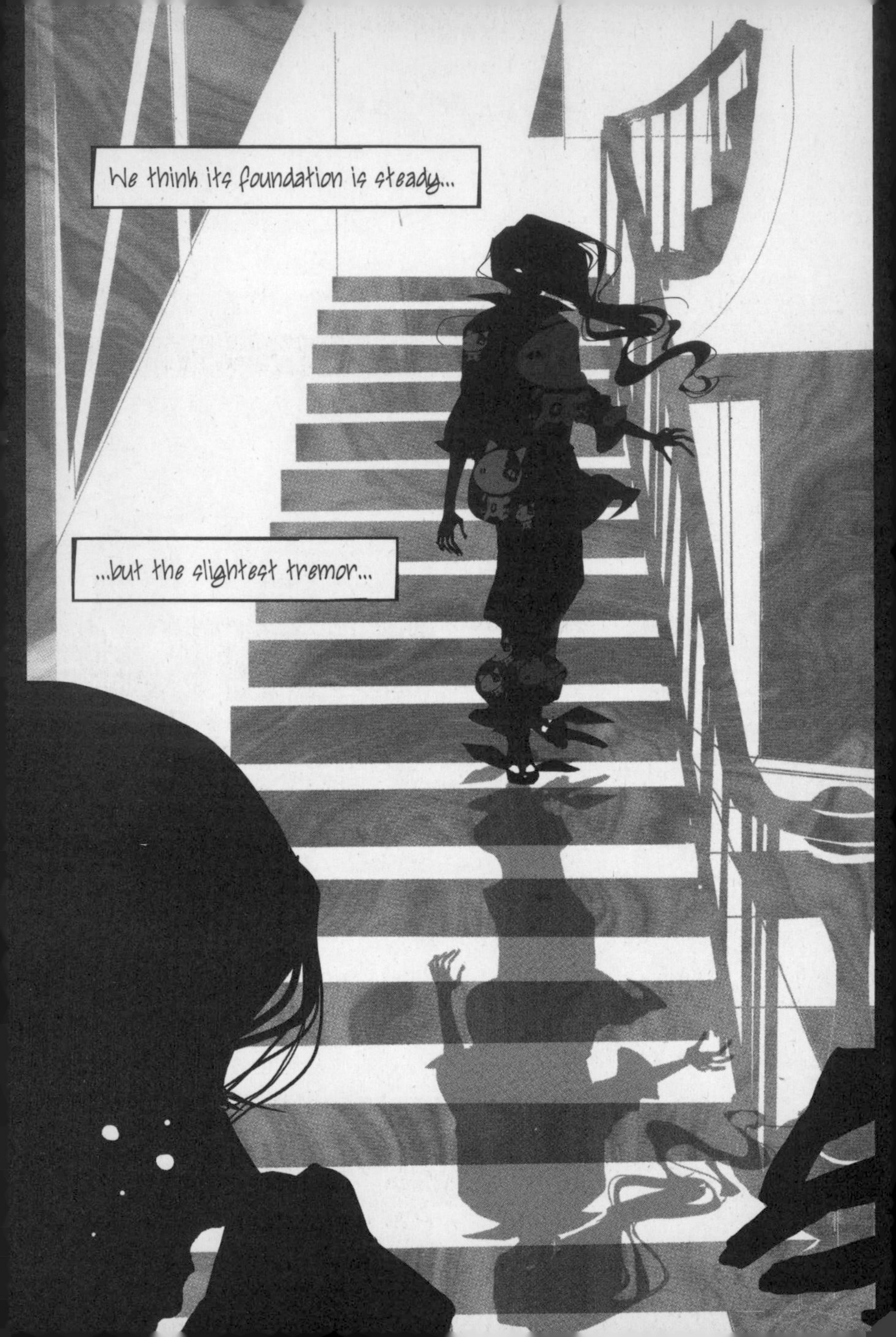
We think its foundation is steady...
...but the slightest tremor...

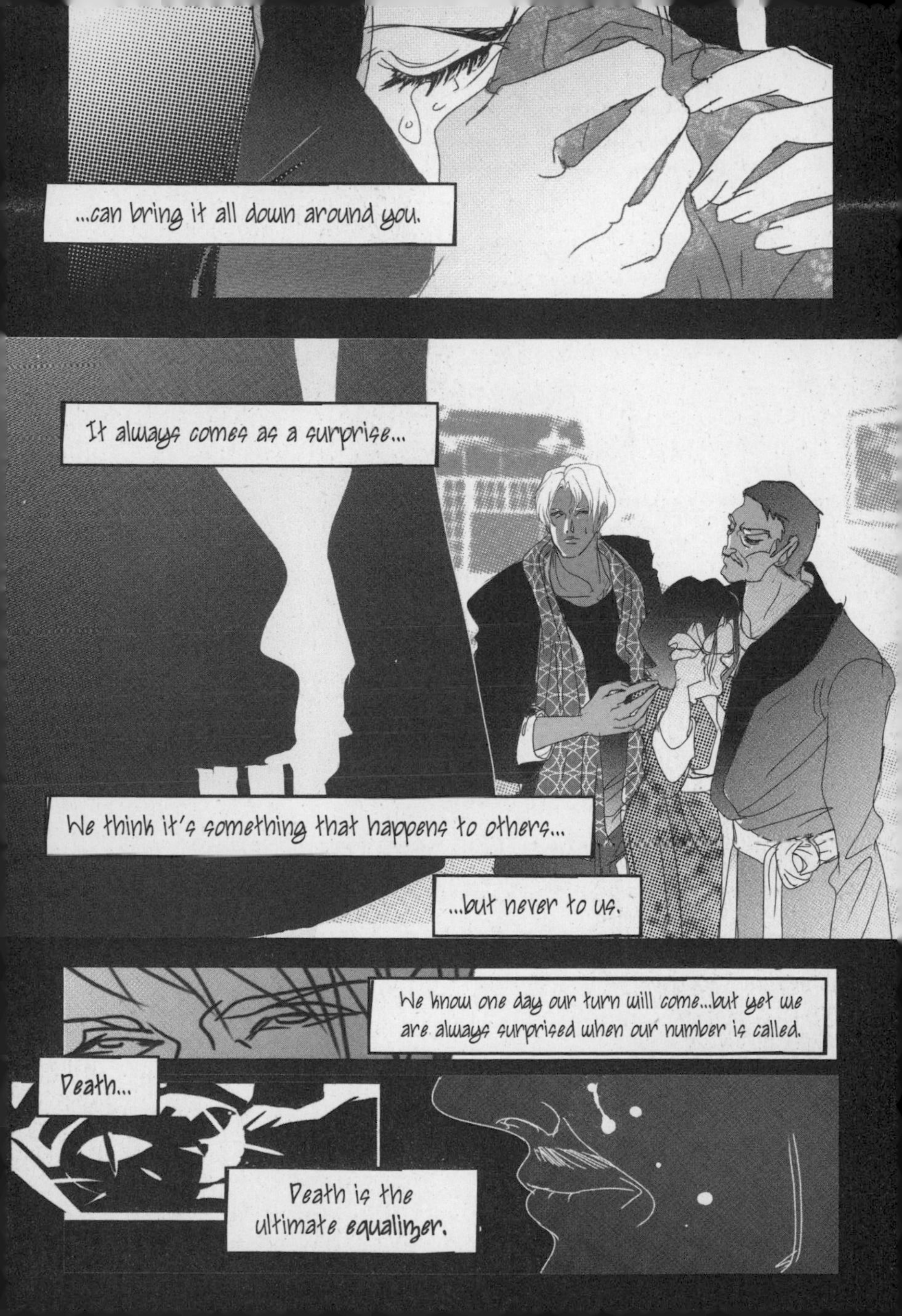
...can bring it all down around you.
It always comes as a surprise...
We think it's something that happens to others...
...but never to us.
We know one day our turn will come...but yet we are always surprised when our number is called.
Death...
Death is the ultimate equalizer.

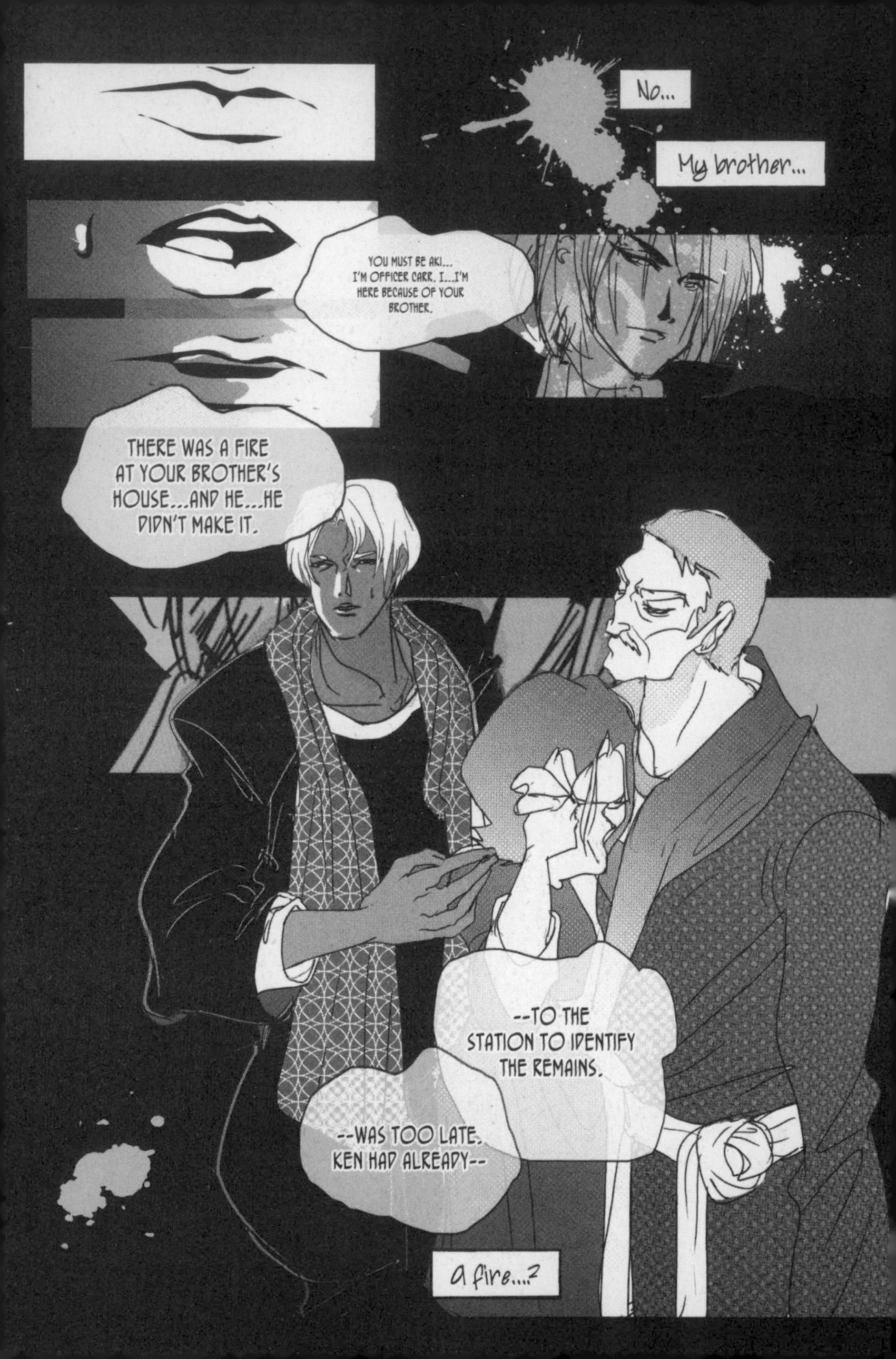
YOU MUST BE AKI... I'M OFFICER CARR. I...I'M HERE BECAUSE OF YOUR BROTHER.
THERE WAS A FIRE AT YOUR BROTHER'S HOUSE...AND HE...HE DIDN'T MAKE IT.
No...
My brother...
a fire...?
--WAS TOO LATE. KEN HAD ALREADY--
--TO THE STATION TO IDENTIFY THE REMAINS.

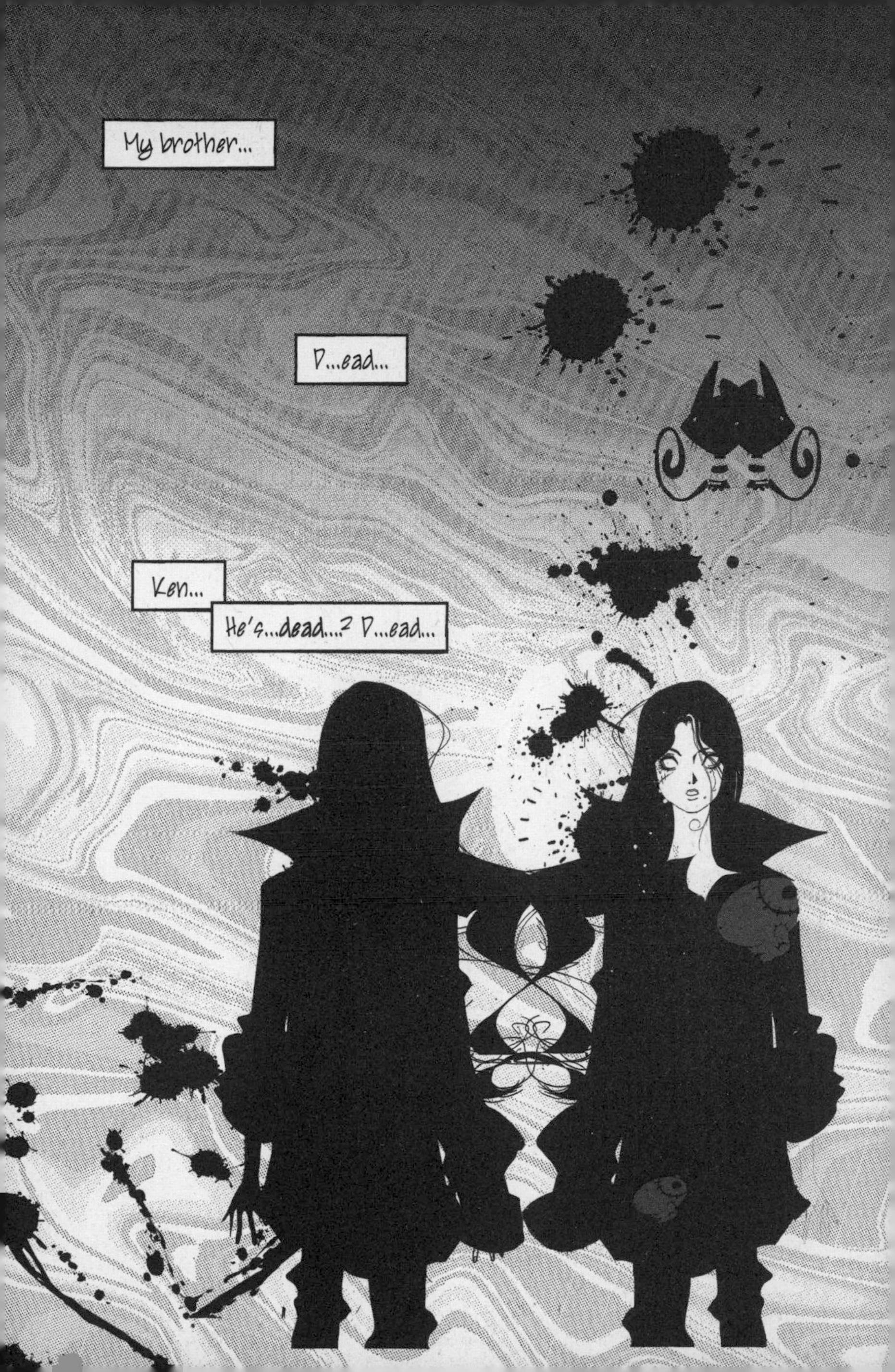
My brother...
D...ead...
Ken...
He's...dead...? D...ead...

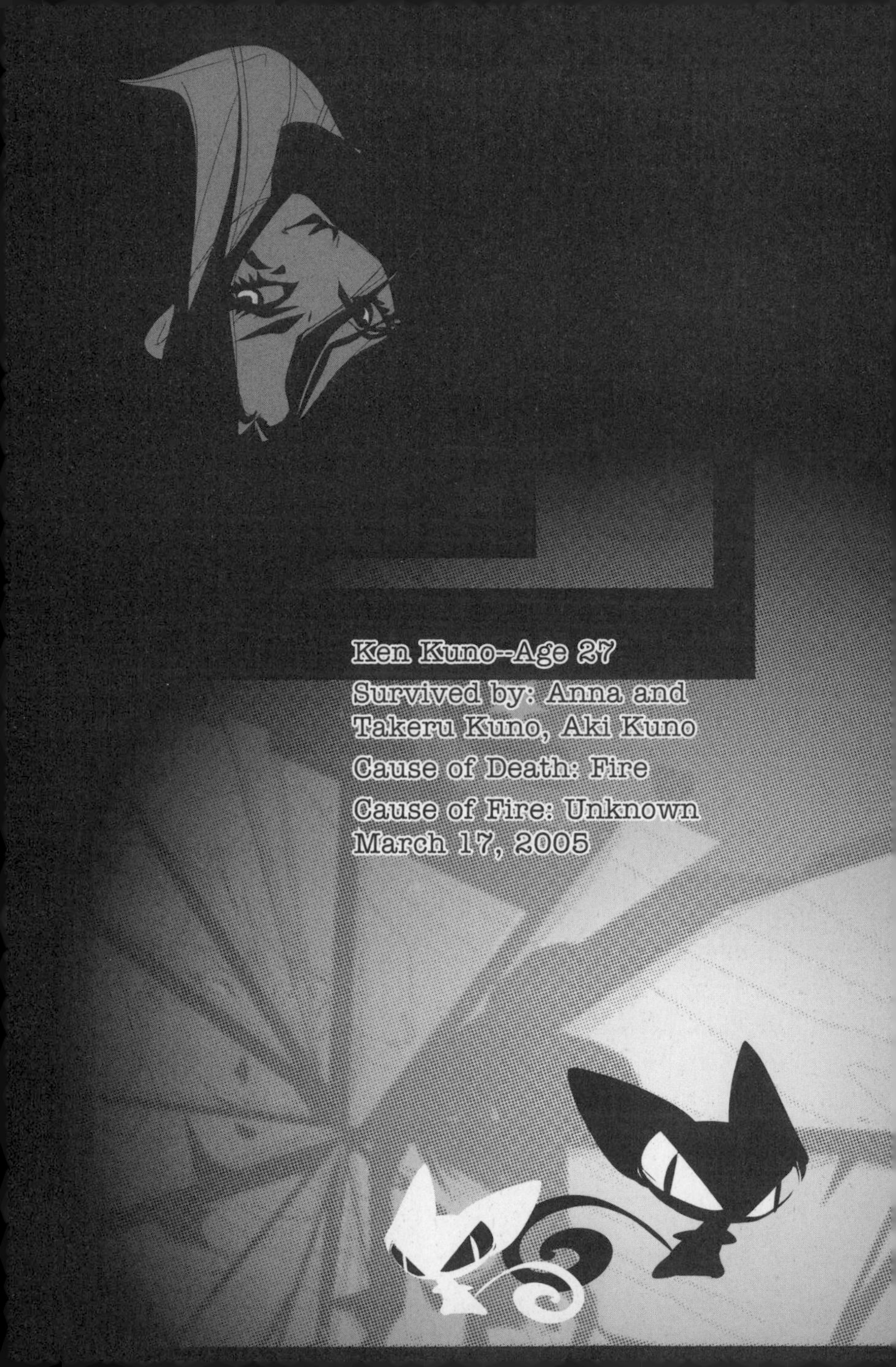
Ken Kuno--Age 27
Survived by: Anna and
Takeru Kuno, Aki Kuno
Cause of Death: Fire
Cause of Fire: Unknown
March 17, 2005

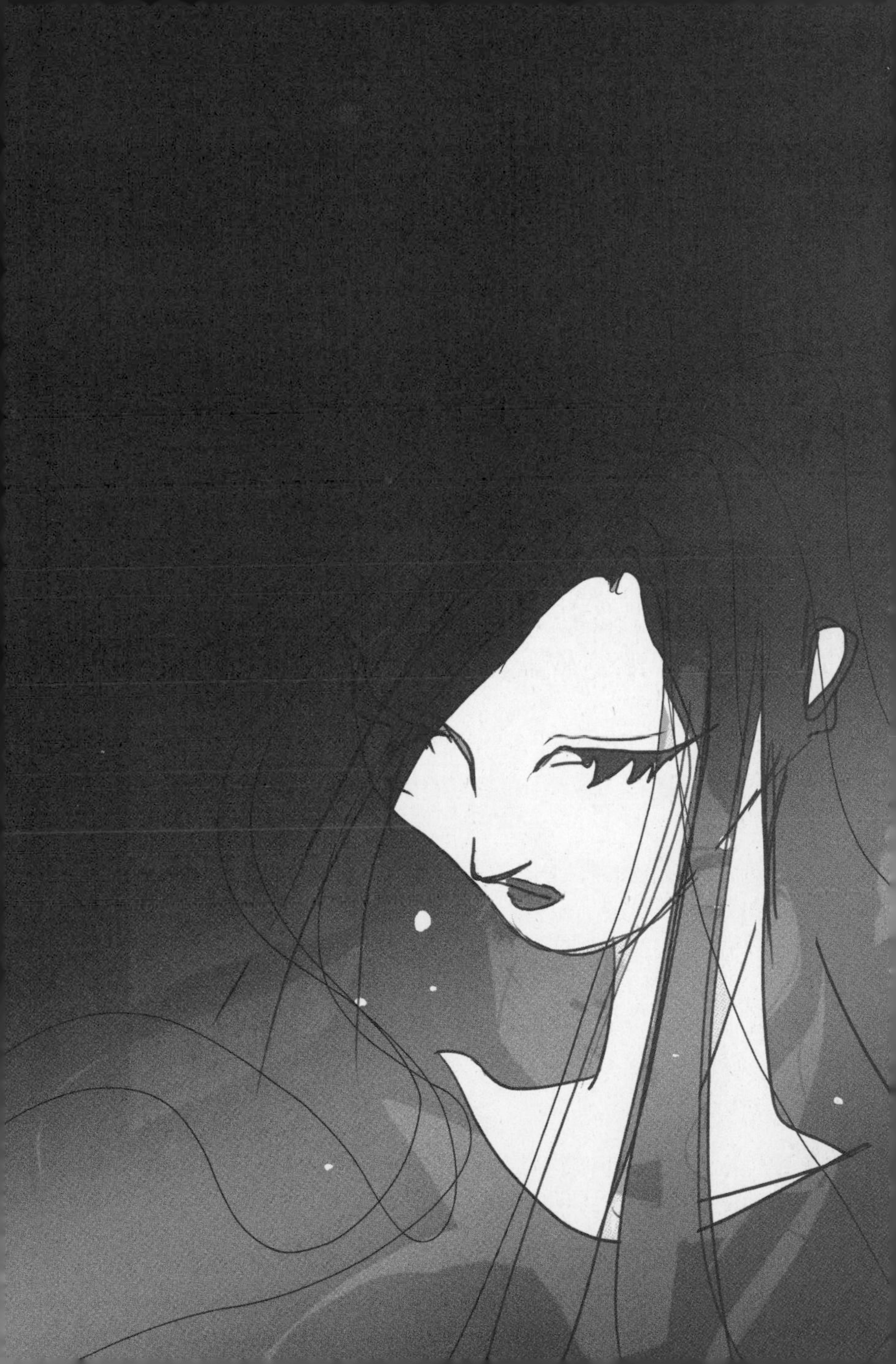

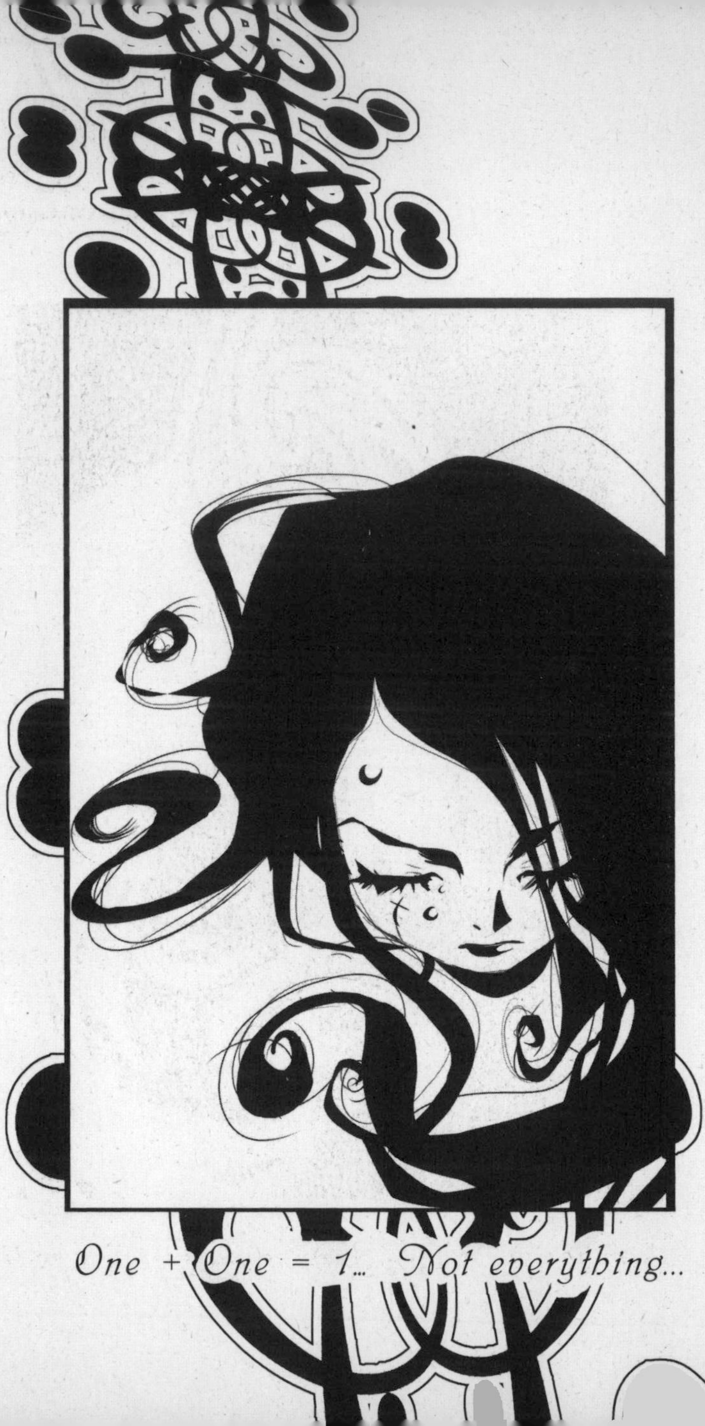
One + One = 1... Not everything...

Chapter ::01

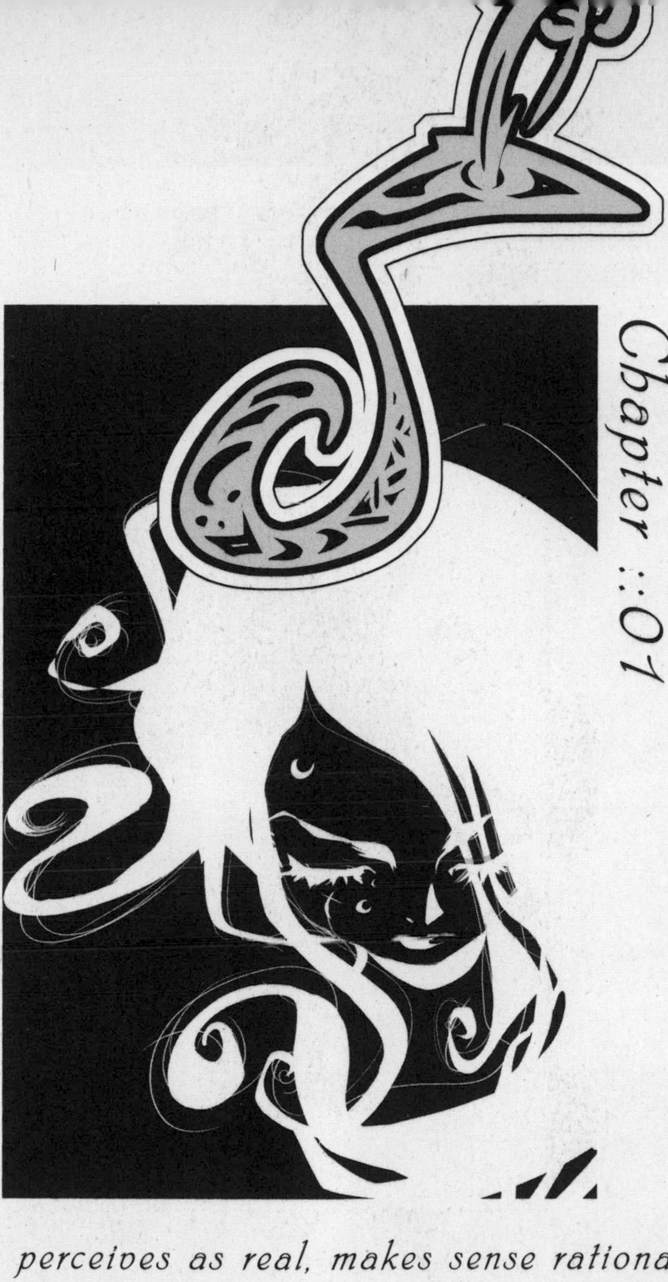

...One perceives as real, makes sense rationally.

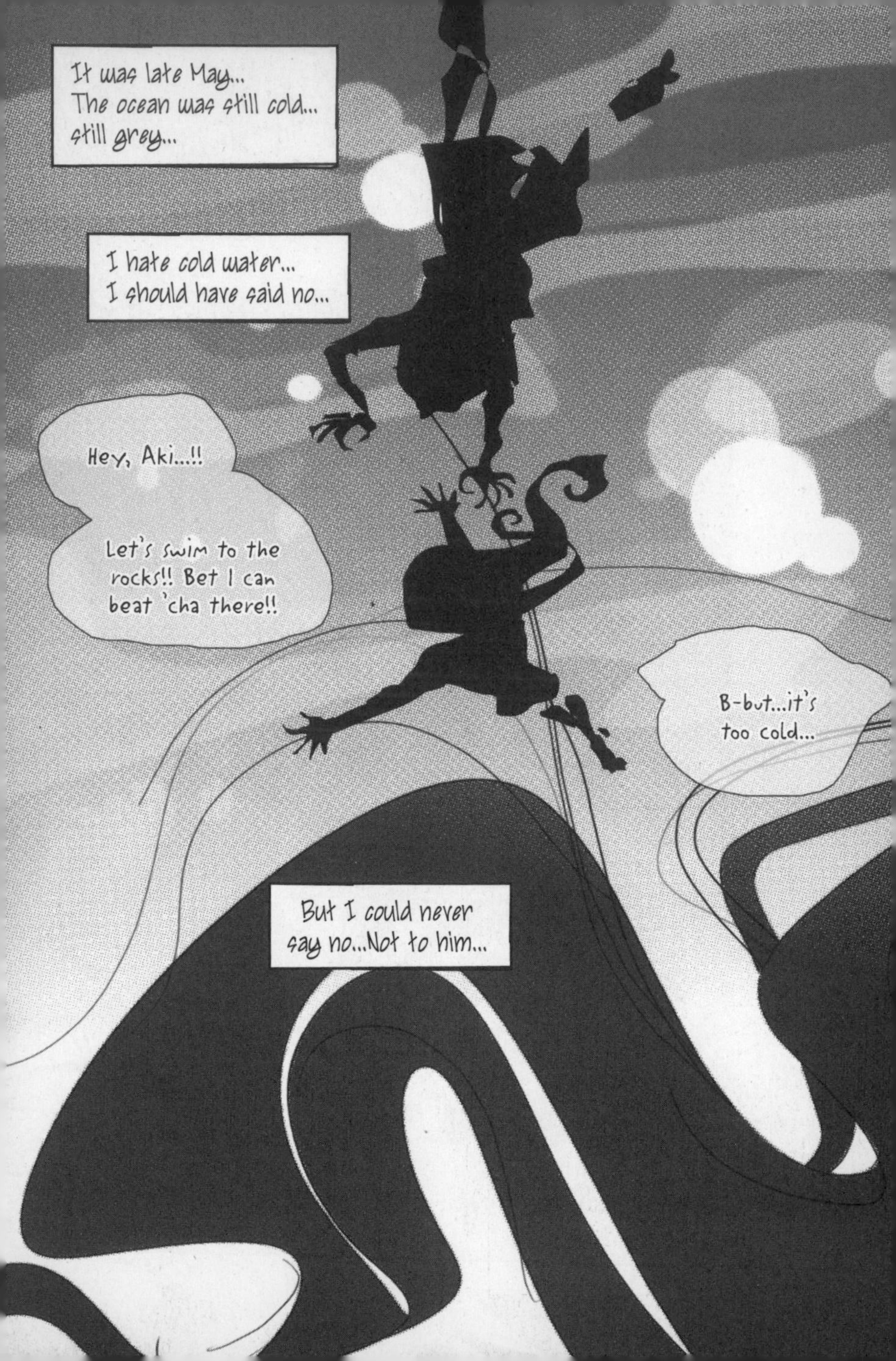
It was late May...
The ocean was still cold...
still grey...
I hate cold water...
I should have said no...
Hey, Aki...!!
Let's swim to the rocks!! Bet I can beat 'cha there!!
B-but...it's too cold...
But I could never say no...Not to him...

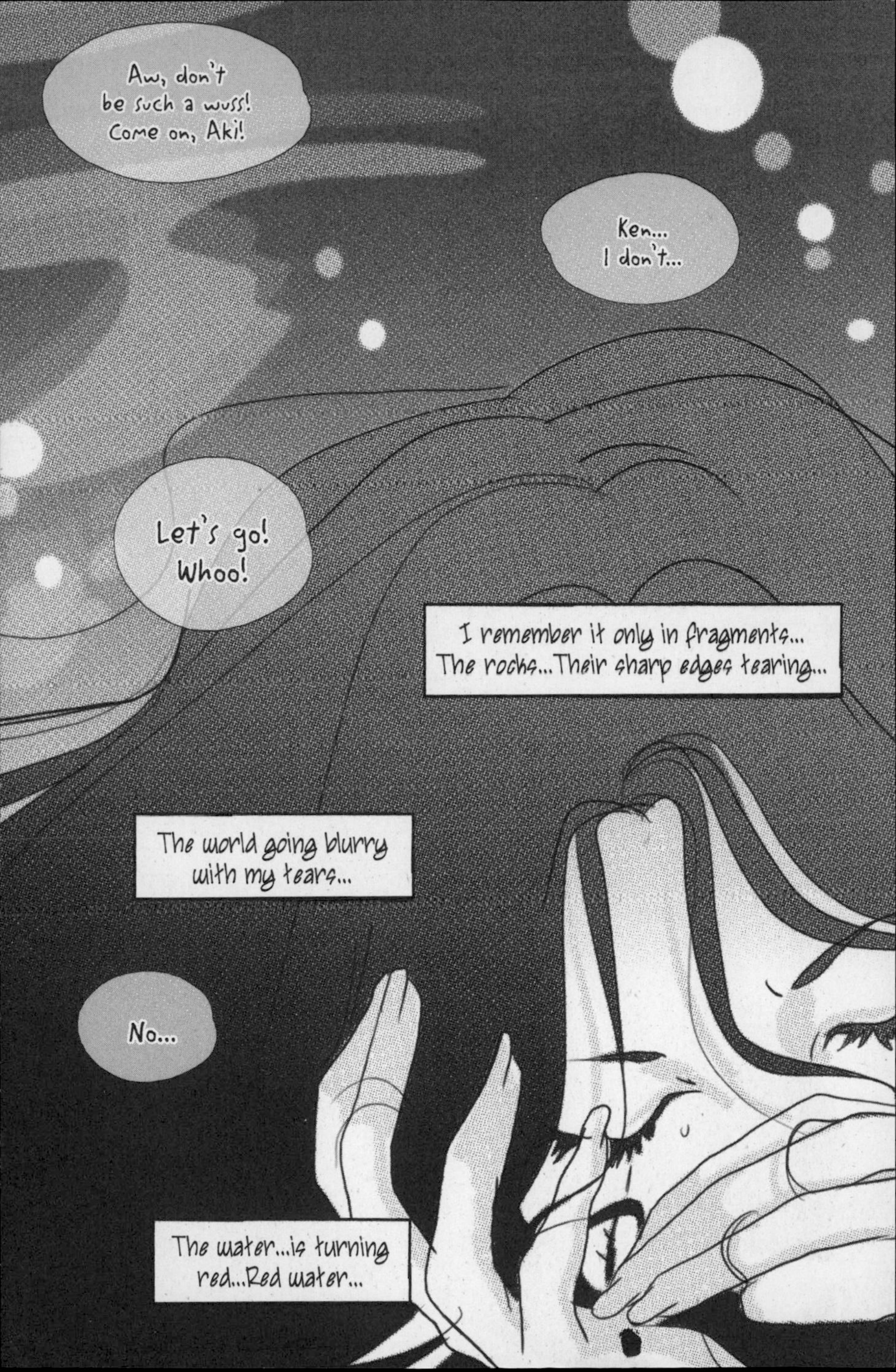
Aw, don't be such a wuss! Come on, Aki!
Ken... I don't...
Let's go! Whoo!
I remember it only in fragments... The rocks...Their sharp edges tearing...
The world going blurry with my tears...
No...
The water...is turning red...Red water...

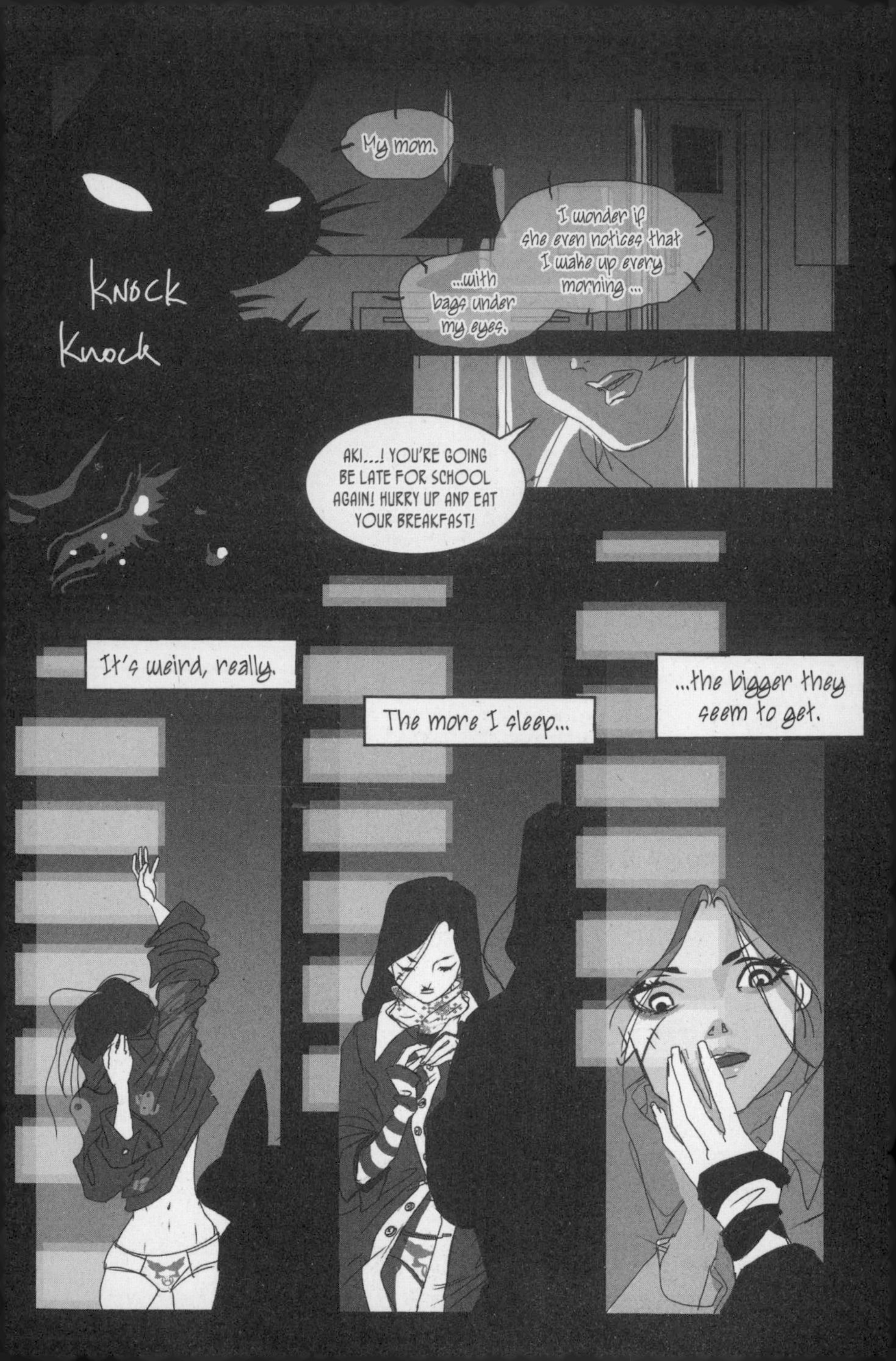

KNOCK
Knock
My mom.
I wonder if she even notices that I wake up every morning ...
...with bags under my eyes.
AKI...! YOU'RE GOING BE LATE FOR SCHOOL AGAIN! HURRY UP AND EAT YOUR BREAKFAST!
It's weird, really.
The more I sleep...
...the bigger they seem to get.

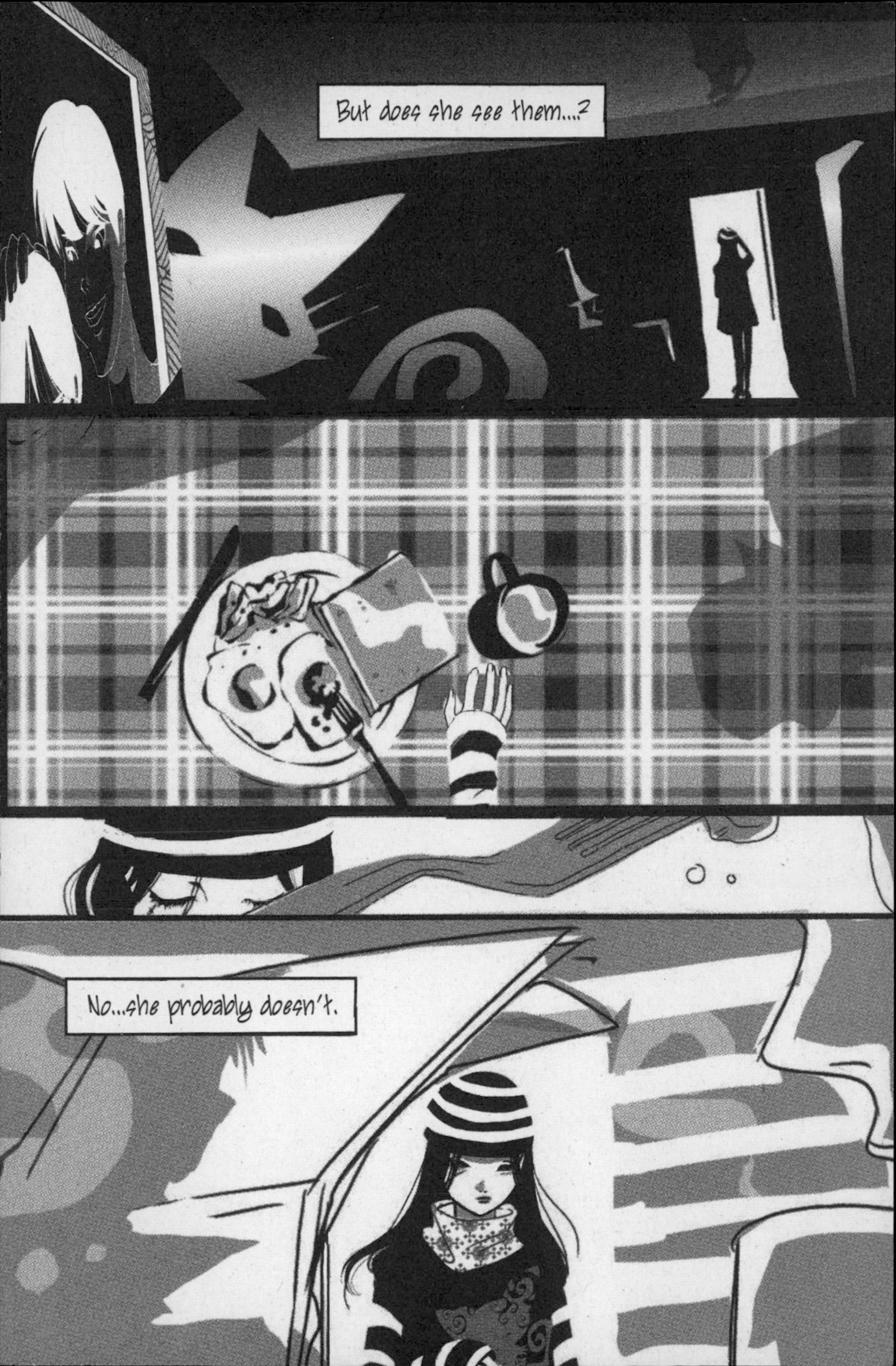
But does she see them...?
No...she probably doesn't.

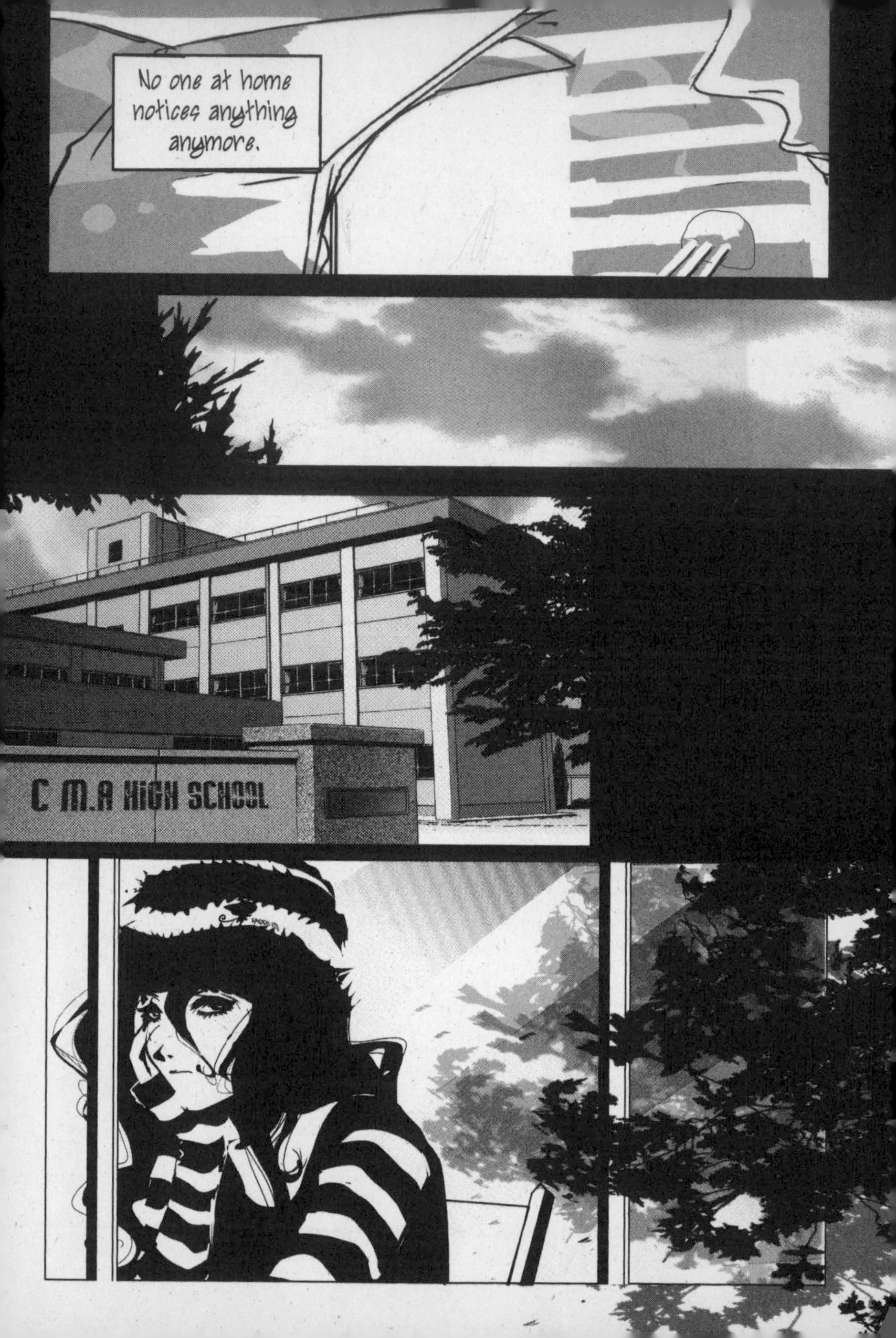
No one at home notices anything anymore.
C M.A HIGH SCHOOL

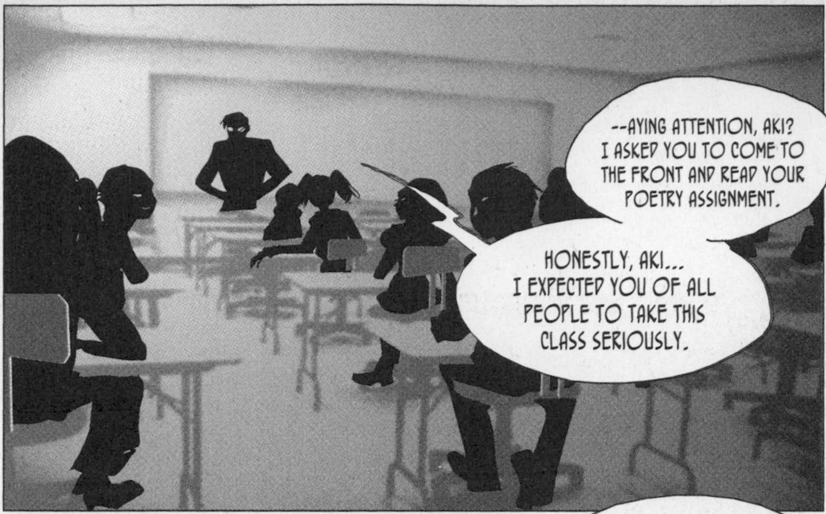
--AYING ATTENTION, AKI? I ASKED YOU TO COME TO THE FRONT AND READ YOUR POETRY ASSIGNMENT.
HONESTLY, AKI... I EXPECTED YOU OF ALL PEOPLE TO TAKE THIS CLASS SERIOUSLY.

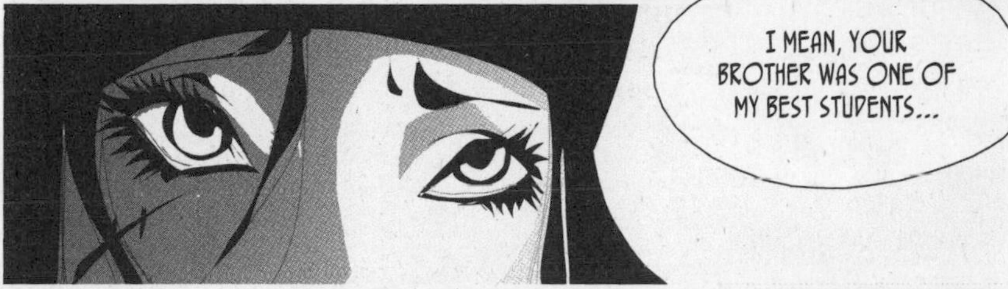
I MEAN, YOUR BROTHER WAS ONE OF MY BEST STUDENTS...

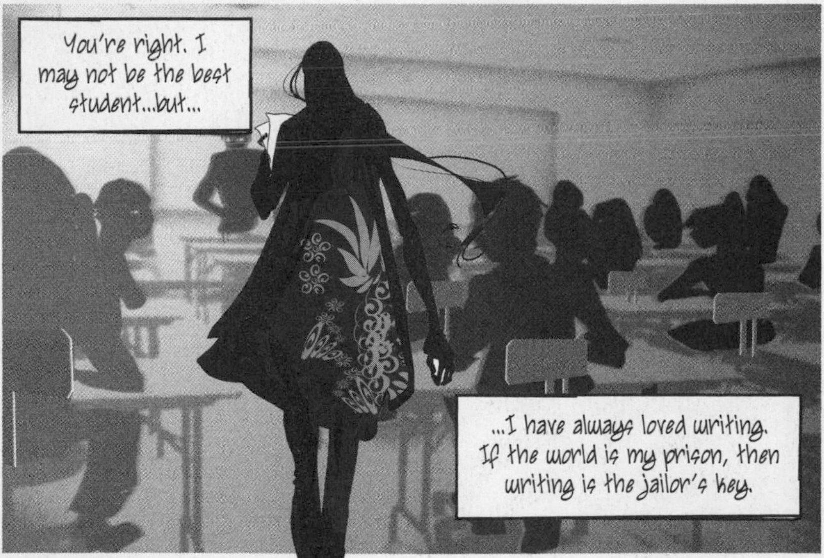
You're right. I may not be the best student...but...
...I have always loved writing. If the world is my prison, then writing is the jailor's key.

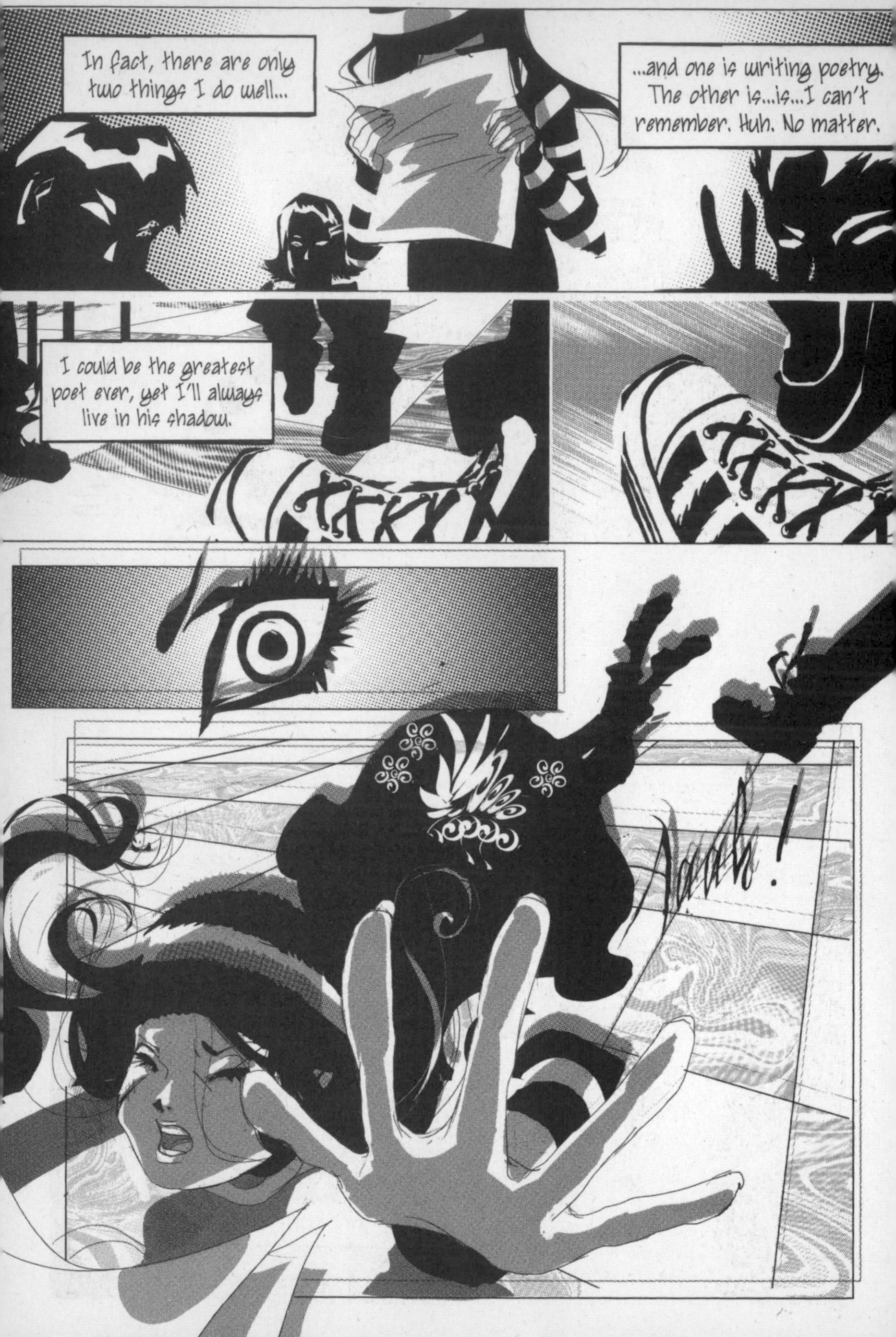
In fact, there are only two things I do well...
...and one is writing poetry. The other is...is...I can't remember. Huh. No matter.
I could be the greatest poet ever, yet I'll always live in his shadow.
Aaah!

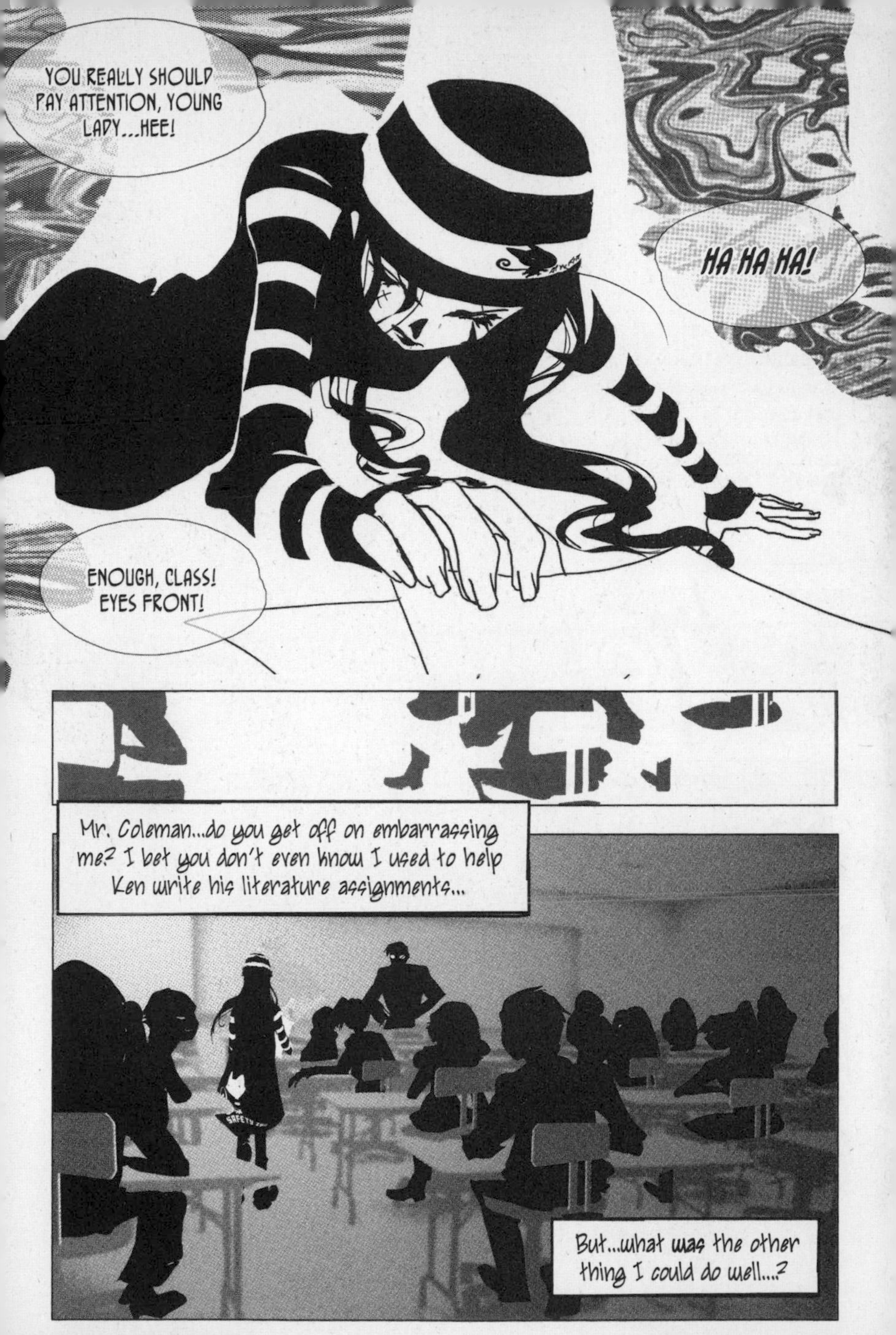
YOU REALLY SHOULD PAY ATTENTION, YOUNG LADY...HEE!
HA HA HA!
ENOUGH, CLASS! EYES FRONT!
Mr. Coleman...do you get off on embarrassing me? I bet you don't even know I used to help Ken write his literature assignments...
But...what was the other thing I could do well...?

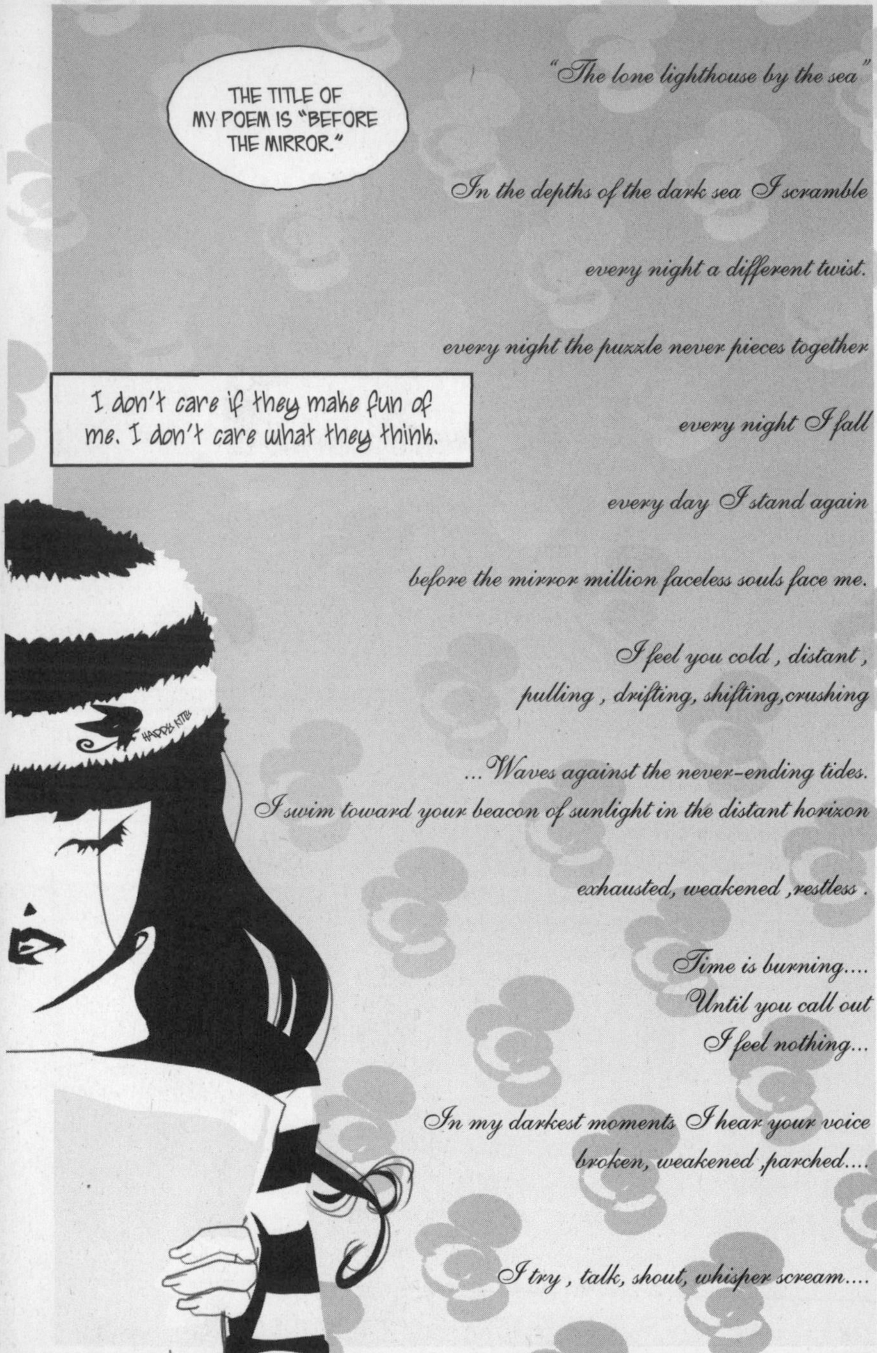
THE TITLE OF MY POEM IS "BEFORE THE MIRROR."
I don't care if they make fun of me. I don't care what they think.
"The lone lighthouse by the sea"
In the depths of the dark sea I scramble
every night a different twist.
every night the puzzle never pieces together
every night I fall
every day I stand again
before the mirror million faceless souls face me.
I feel you cold , distant ,
pulling , drifting, shifting,crushing
...Waves against the never-ending tides.
I swim toward your beacon of sunlight in the distant horizon
exhausted, weakened ,restless .
Time is burning....
Until you call out
I feel nothing...
In my darkest moments I hear your voice
broken, weakened ,parched....
I try , talk, shout, whisper scream....

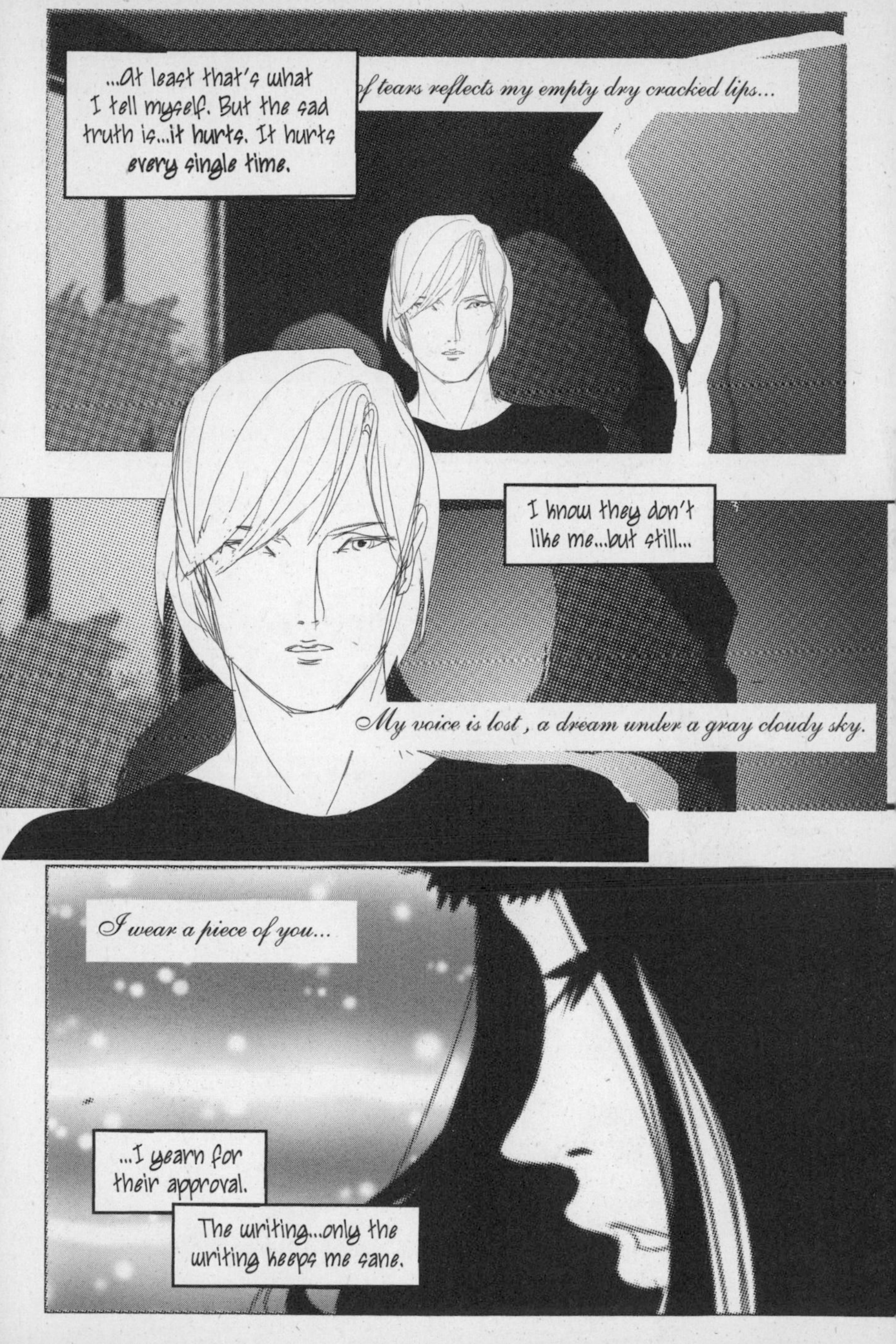
of tears reflects my empty dry cracked lips...
...At least that's what I tell myself. But the sad truth is...it hurts. It hurts every single time.
I know they don't like me...but still...
My voice is lost , a dream under a gray cloudy sky.
I wear a piece of you...
...I yearn for their approval.
The writing...only the writing keeps me sane.

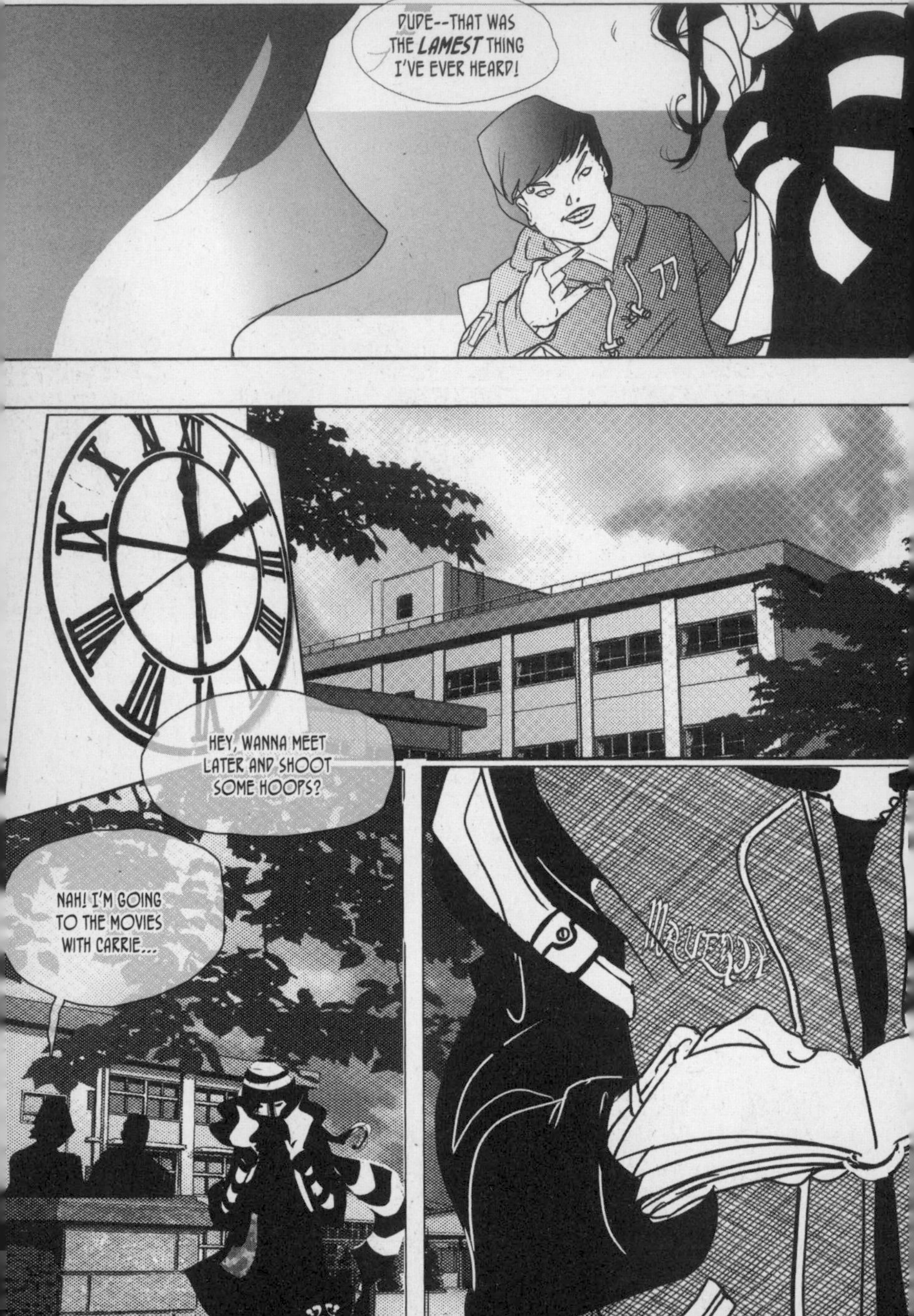
DUDE--THAT WAS THE *LAMEST* THING I'VE EVER HEARD!
HEY, WANNA MEET LATER AND SHOOT SOME HOOPS?
NAH! I'M GOING TO THE MOVIES WITH CARRIE...

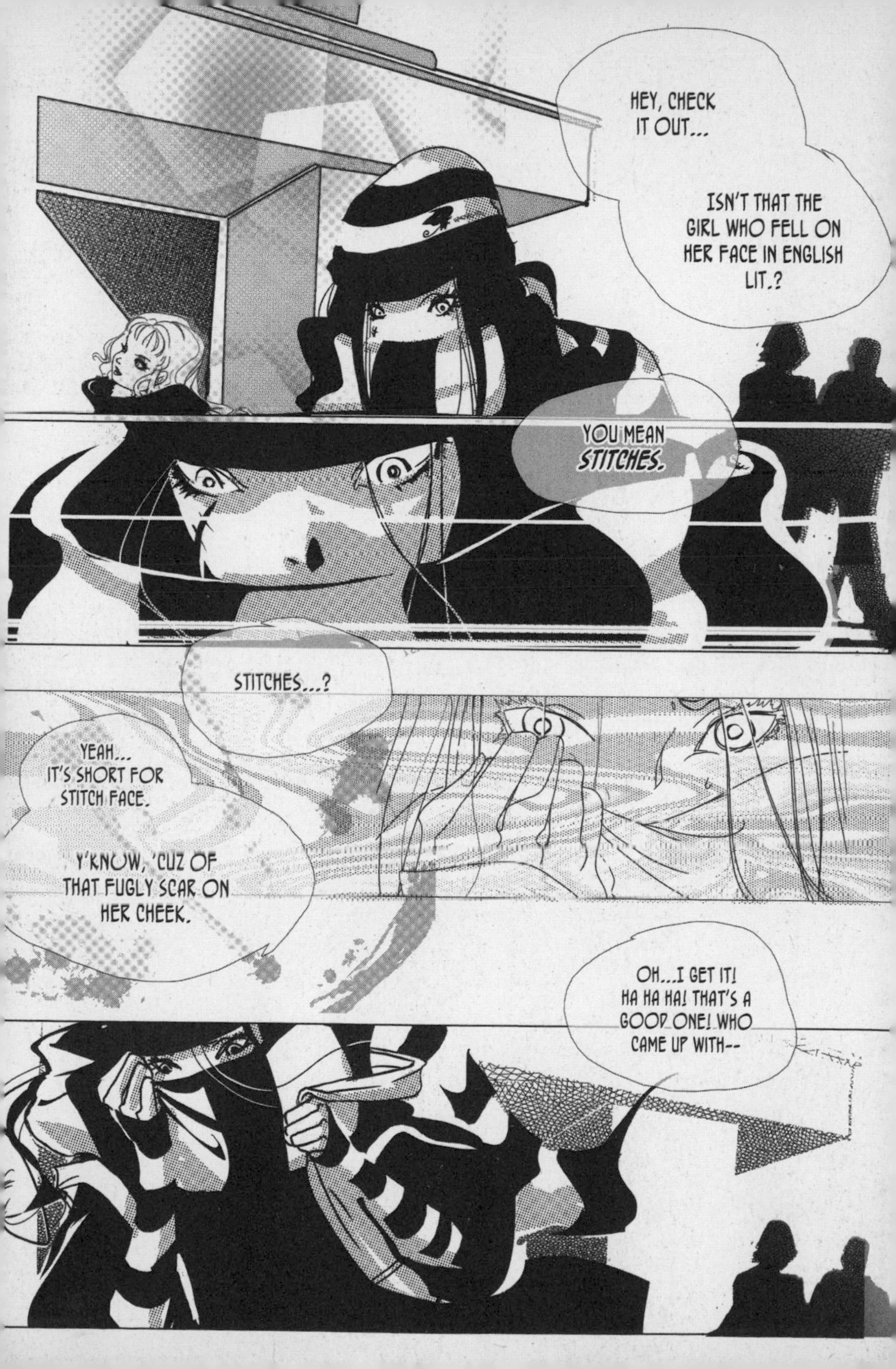
HEY, CHECK IT OUT...
ISN'T THAT THE GIRL WHO FELL ON HER FACE IN ENGLISH LIT.?
YOU MEAN STITCHES.
STITCHES...?
YEAH... IT'S SHORT FOR STITCH FACE.
Y'KNOW, 'CUZ OF THAT FUGLY SCAR ON HER CHEEK.
OH...I GET IT! HA HA HA! THAT'S A GOOD ONE! WHO CAME UP WITH--

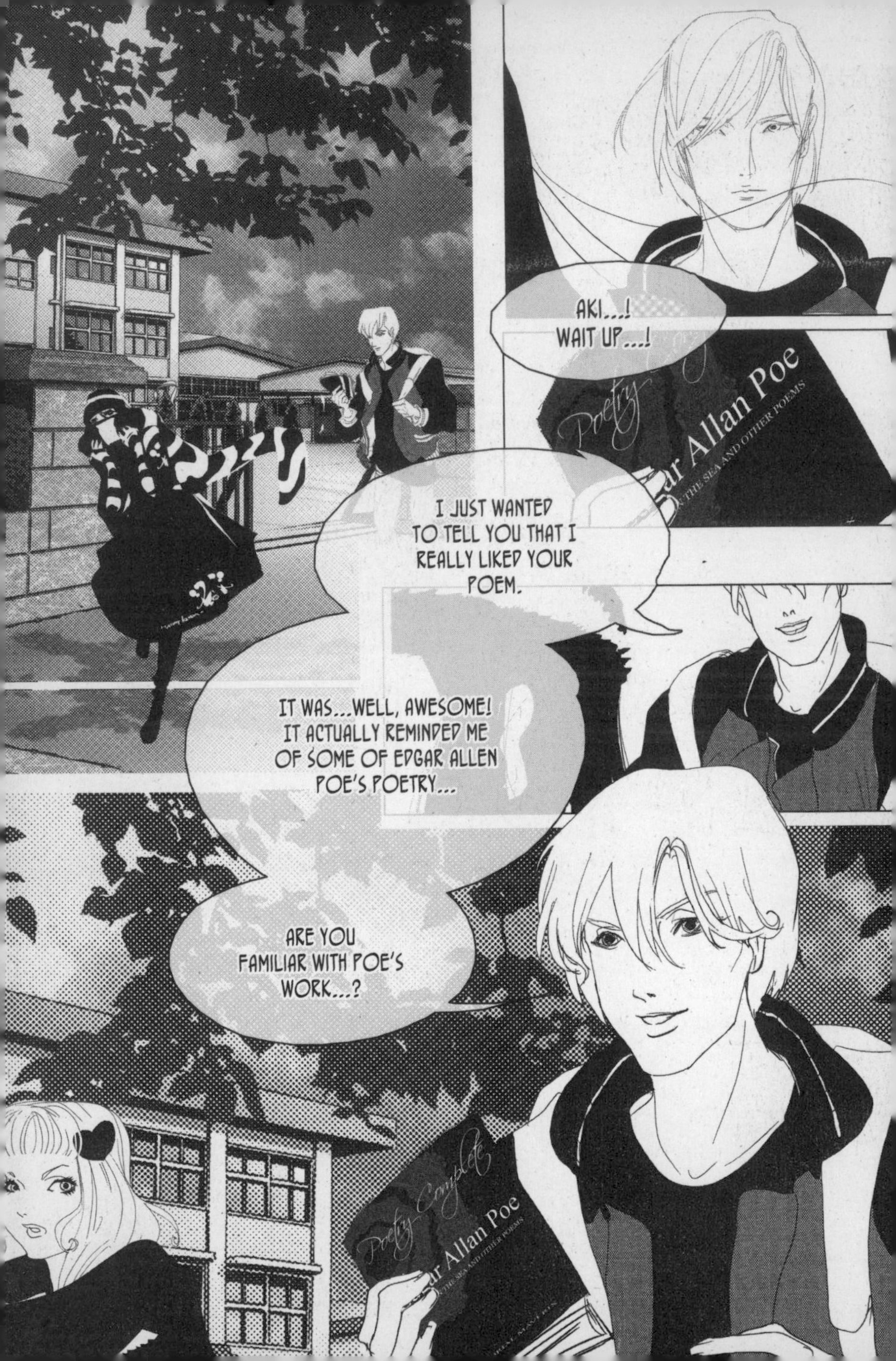
AKI...! WAIT UP...!
I JUST WANTED TO TELL YOU THAT I REALLY LIKED YOUR POEM.
IT WAS...WELL, AWESOME! IT ACTUALLY REMINDED ME OF SOME OF EDGAR ALLEN POE'S POETRY...
ARE YOU FAMILIAR WITH POE'S WORK...?

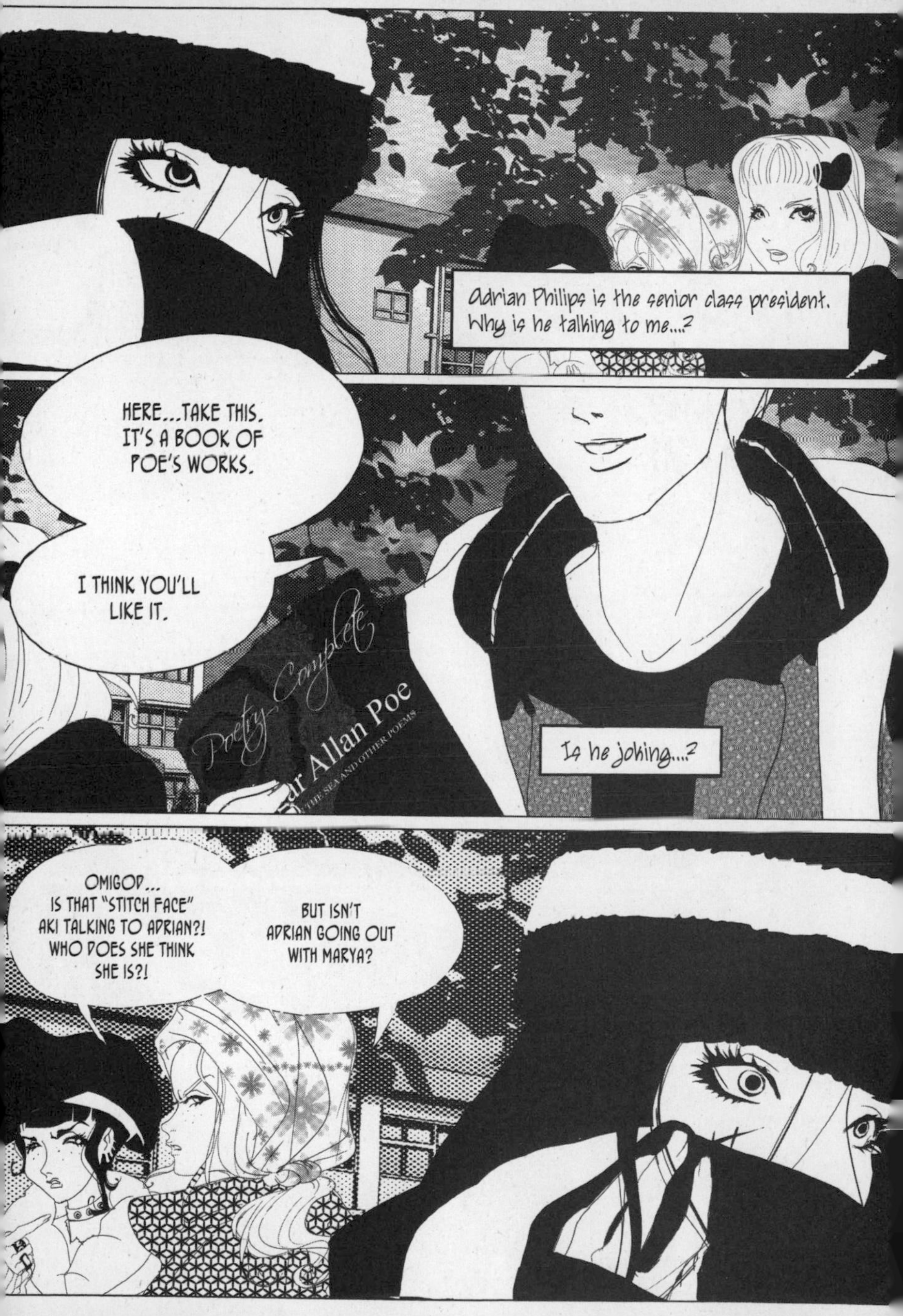
Adrian Philips is the senior class president. Why is he talking to me...?
HERE...TAKE THIS. IT'S A BOOK OF POE'S WORKS.
I THINK YOU'LL LIKE IT.
Poetry Complete
Is he joking...?
OMIGOD... IS THAT "STITCH FACE" AKI TALKING TO ADRIAN?! WHO DOES SHE THINK SHE IS?!
BUT ISN'T ADRIAN GOING OUT WITH MARYA?

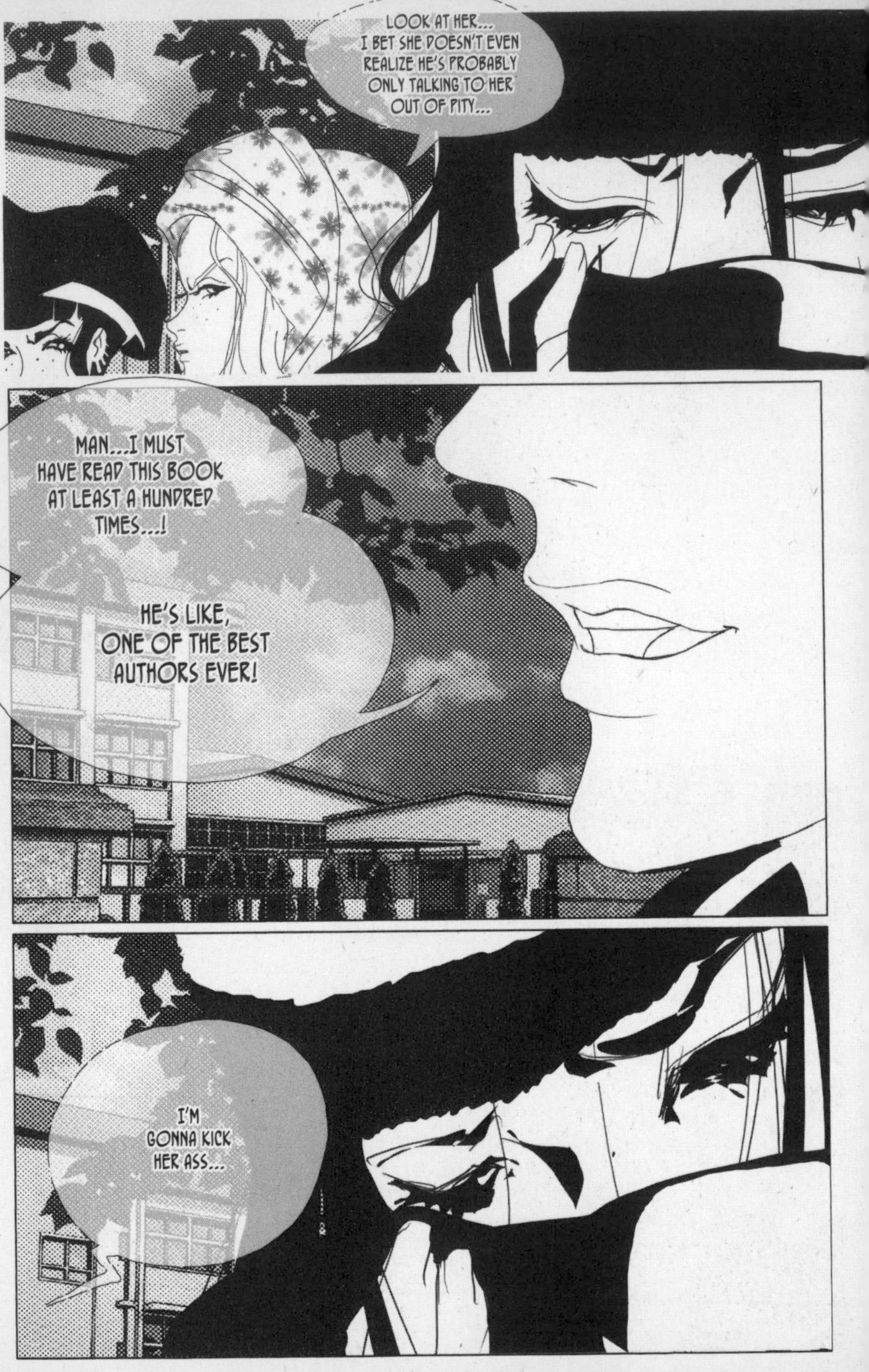
LOOK AT HER... I BET SHE DOESN'T EVEN REALIZE HE'S PROBABLY ONLY TALKING TO HER OUT OF PITY...
MAN...I MUST HAVE READ THIS BOOK AT LEAST A HUNDRED TIMES...!
HE'S LIKE, ONE OF THE BEST AUTHORS EVER!
I'M GONNA KICK HER ASS...

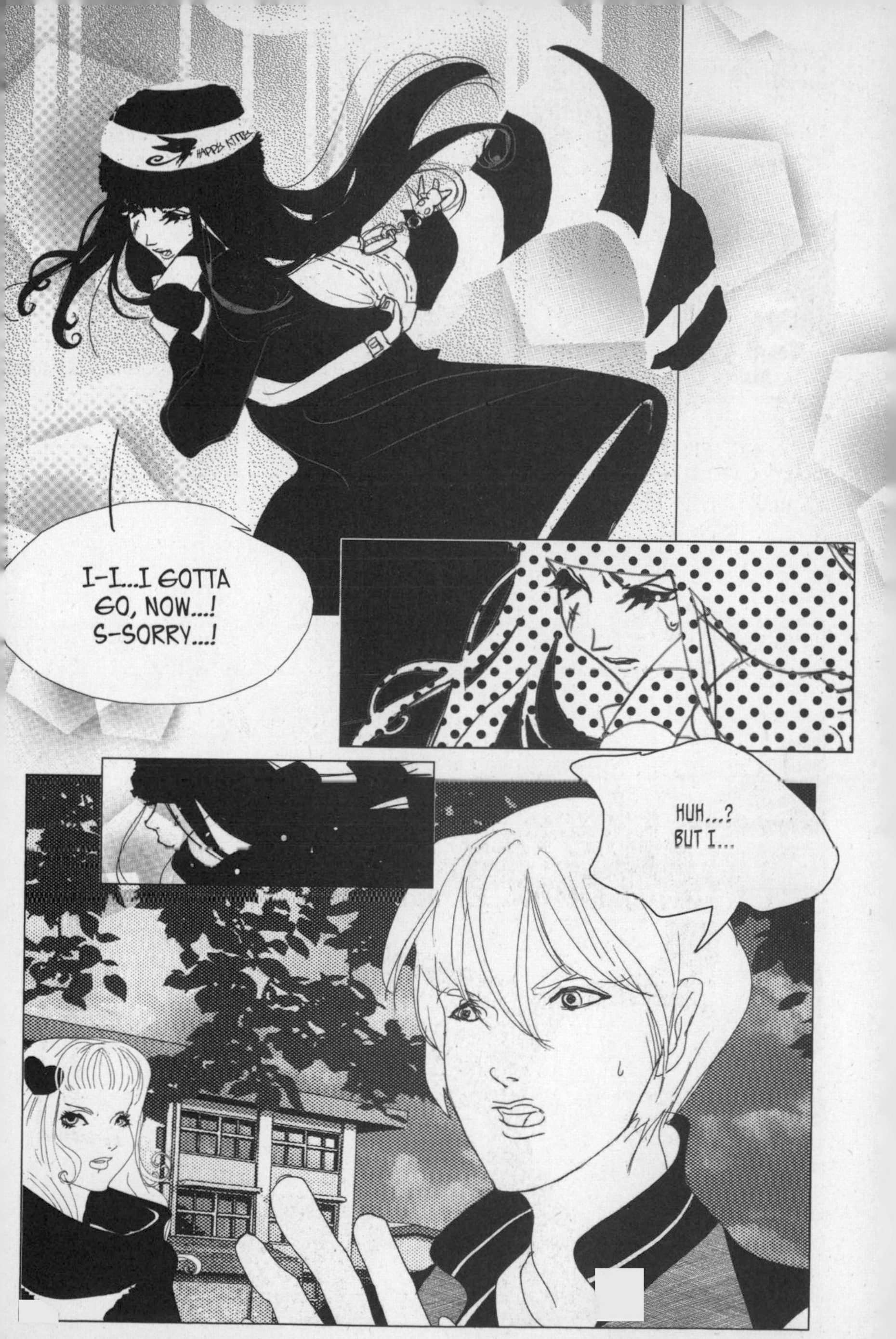
I-I...I GOTTA GO, NOW...! S-SORRY...!
HUH...? BUT I...

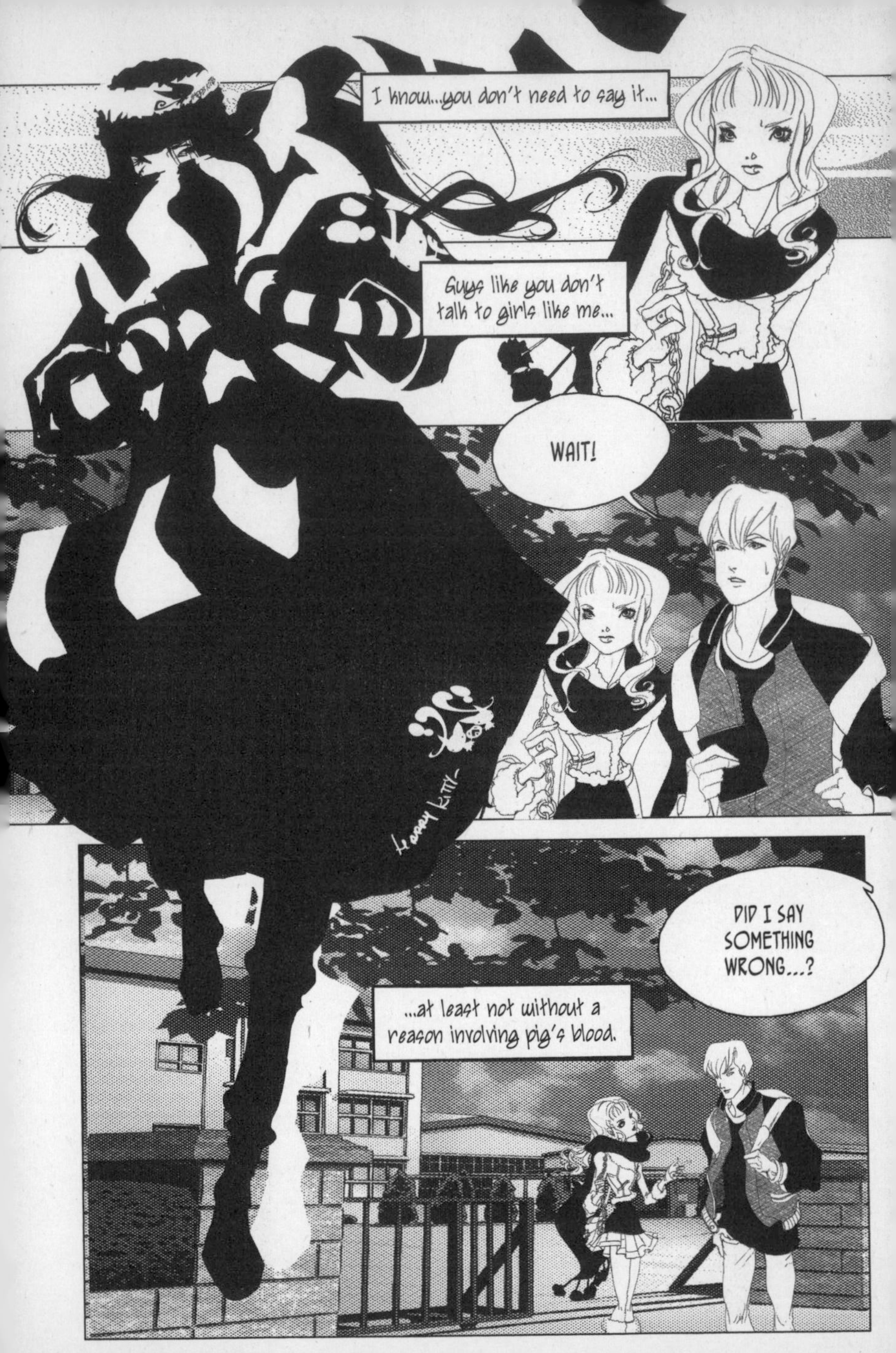
I know...you don't need to say it...
Guys like you don't talk to girls like me...
WAIT!
...at least not without a reason involving pig's blood.
DID I SAY SOMETHING WRONG...?

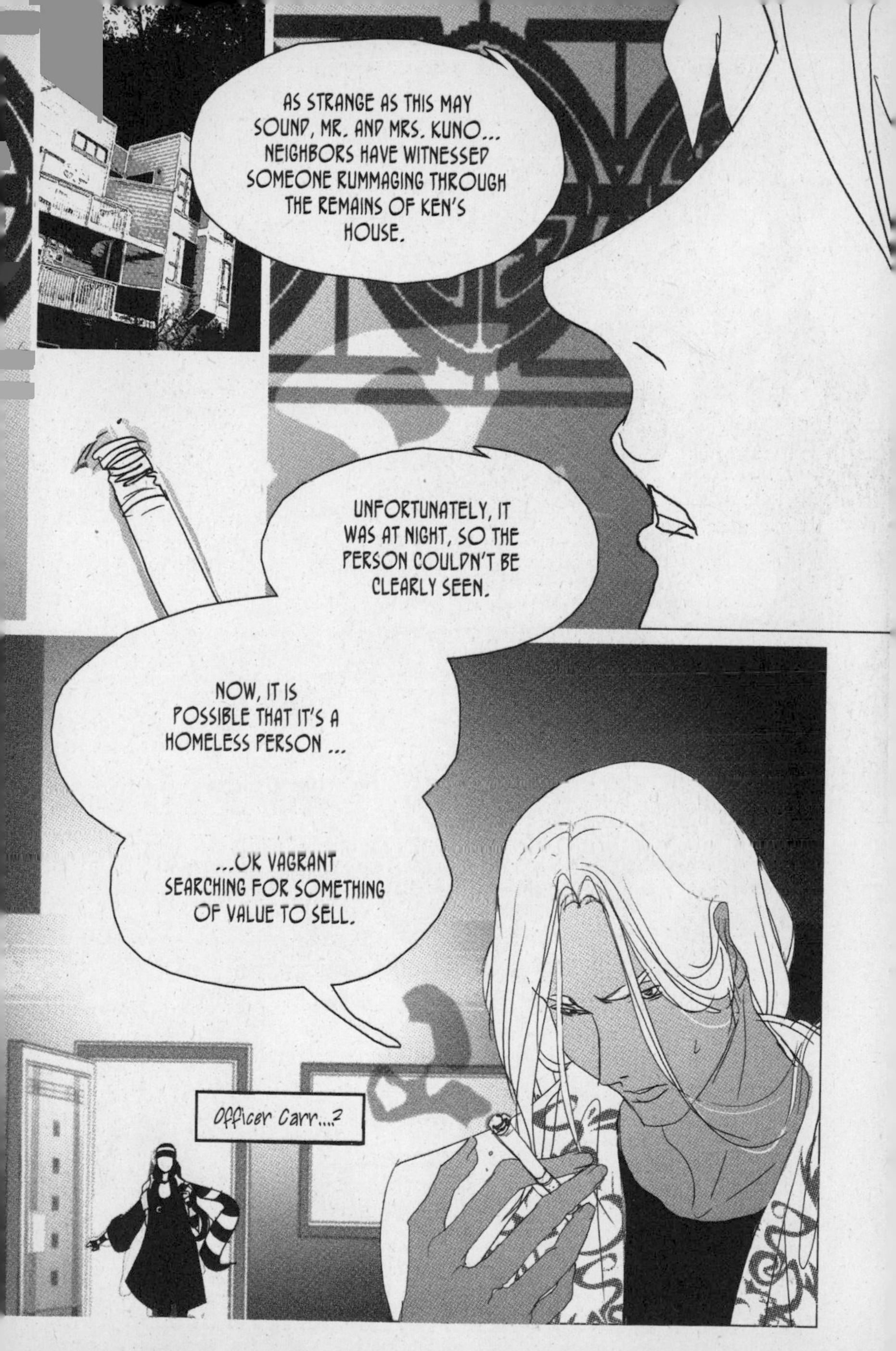
AS STRANGE AS THIS MAY SOUND, MR. AND MRS. KUNO... NEIGHBORS HAVE WITNESSED SOMEONE RUMMAGING THROUGH THE REMAINS OF KEN'S HOUSE.
UNFORTUNATELY, IT WAS AT NIGHT, SO THE PERSON COULDN'T BE CLEARLY SEEN.
NOW, IT IS POSSIBLE THAT IT'S A HOMELESS PERSON ...
...OR VAGRANT SEARCHING FOR SOMETHING OF VALUE TO SELL.
Officer Carr...?

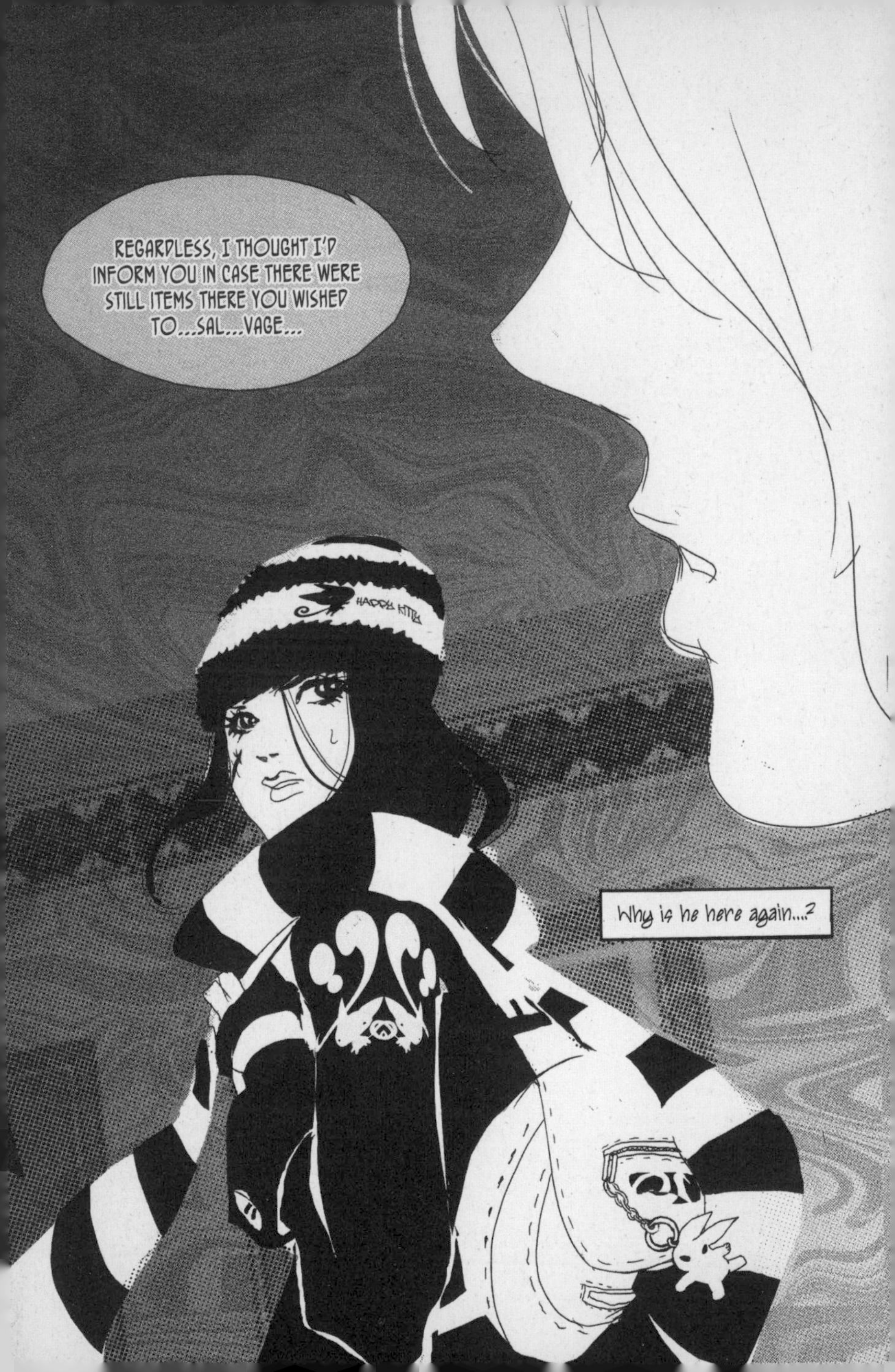
REGARDLESS, I THOUGHT I'D INFORM YOU IN CASE THERE WERE STILL ITEMS THERE YOU WISHED TO...SAL...VAGE...
HAPPY KITTY
Why is he here again...?

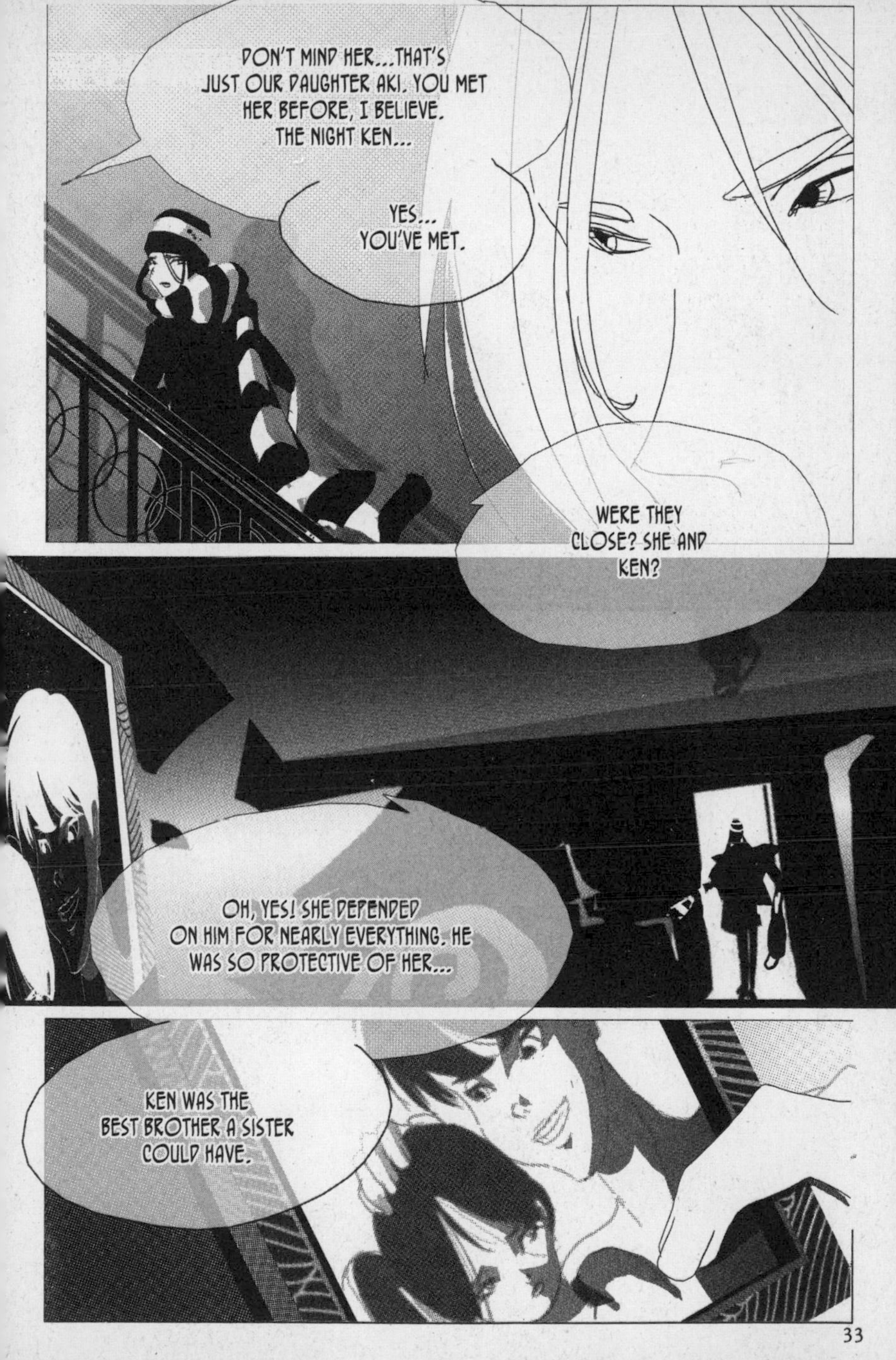

DON'T MIND HER...THAT'S JUST OUR DAUGHTER AKI. YOU MET HER BEFORE, I BELIEVE. THE NIGHT KEN...
YES... YOU'VE MET.
WERE THEY CLOSE? SHE AND KEN?
OH, YES! SHE DEPENDED ON HIM FOR NEARLY EVERYTHING. HE WAS SO PROTECTIVE OF HER...
KEN WAS THE BEST BROTHER A SISTER COULD HAVE.

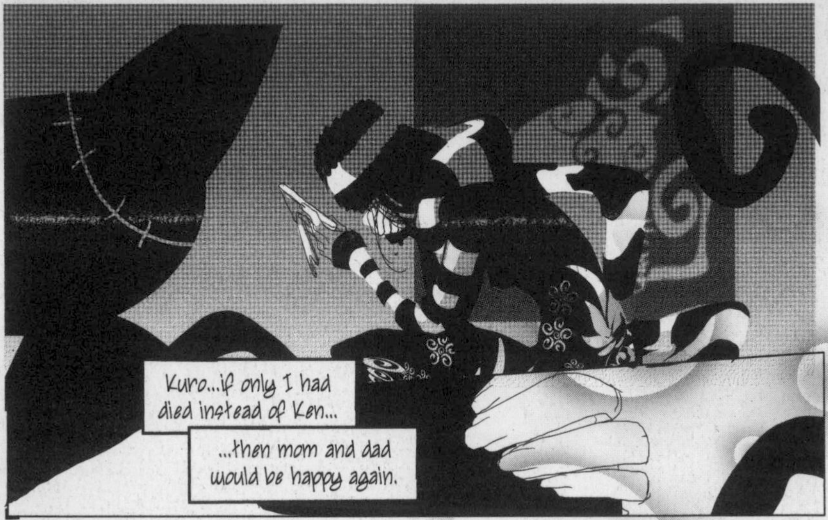
Kuro...if only I had died instead of Ken...
...then mom and dad would be happy again.
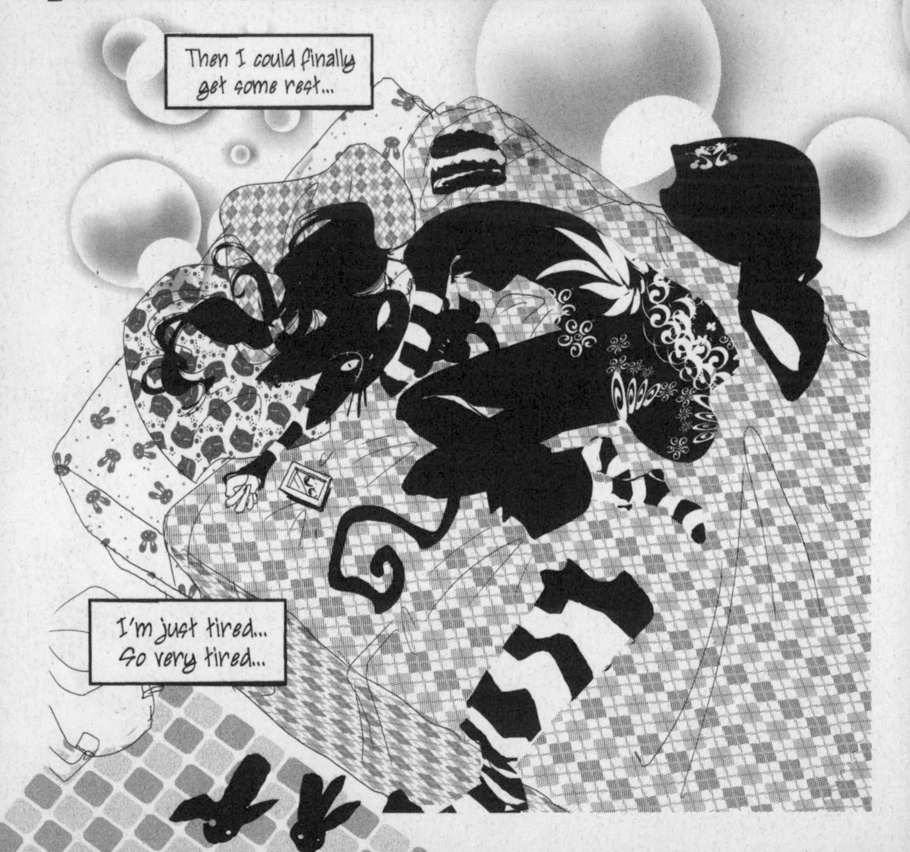
Then I could finally get some rest...
I'm just tired... So very tired...

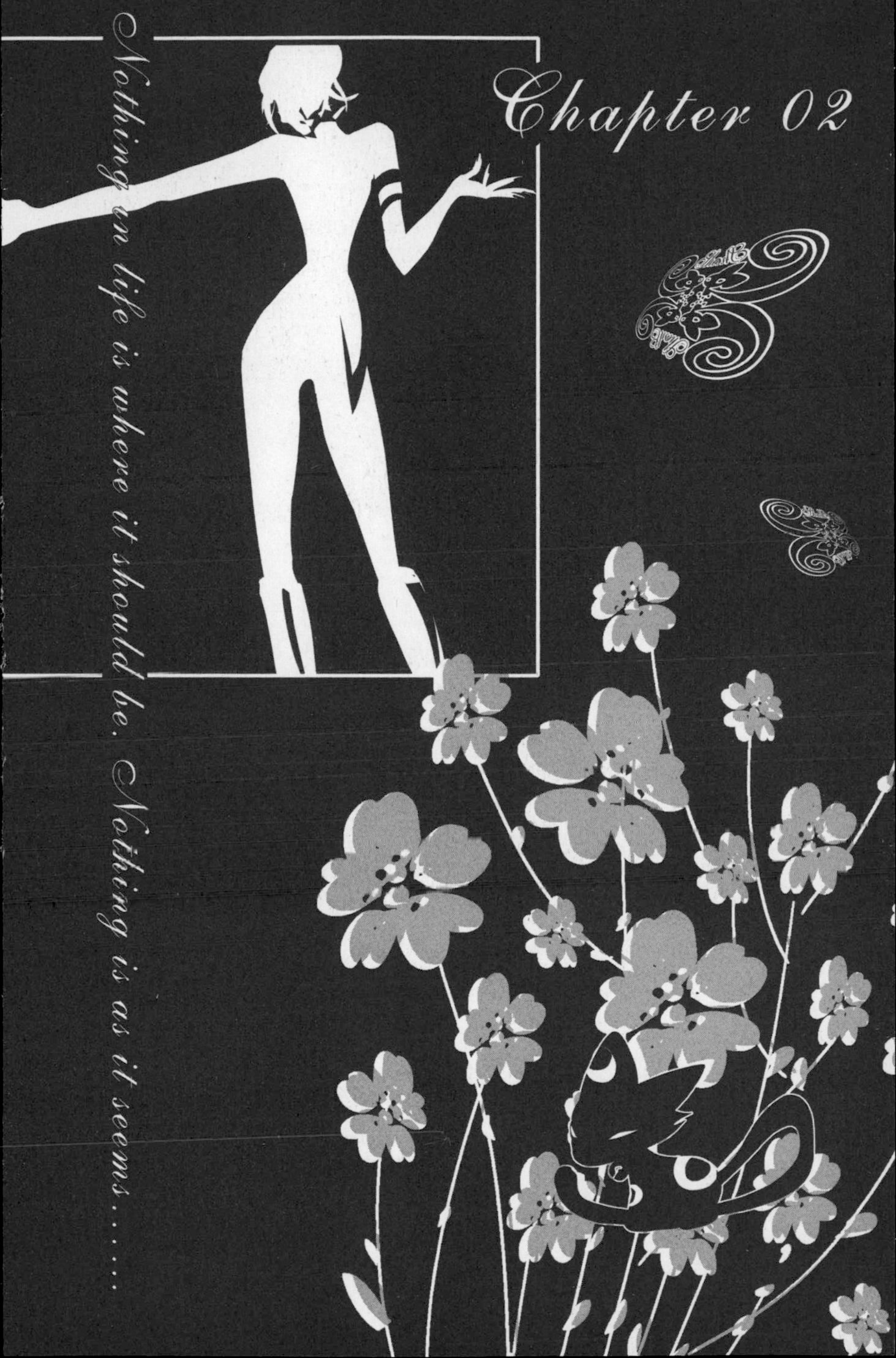
Chapter 02
Nothing in life is where it should be. Nothing is as it seems.....

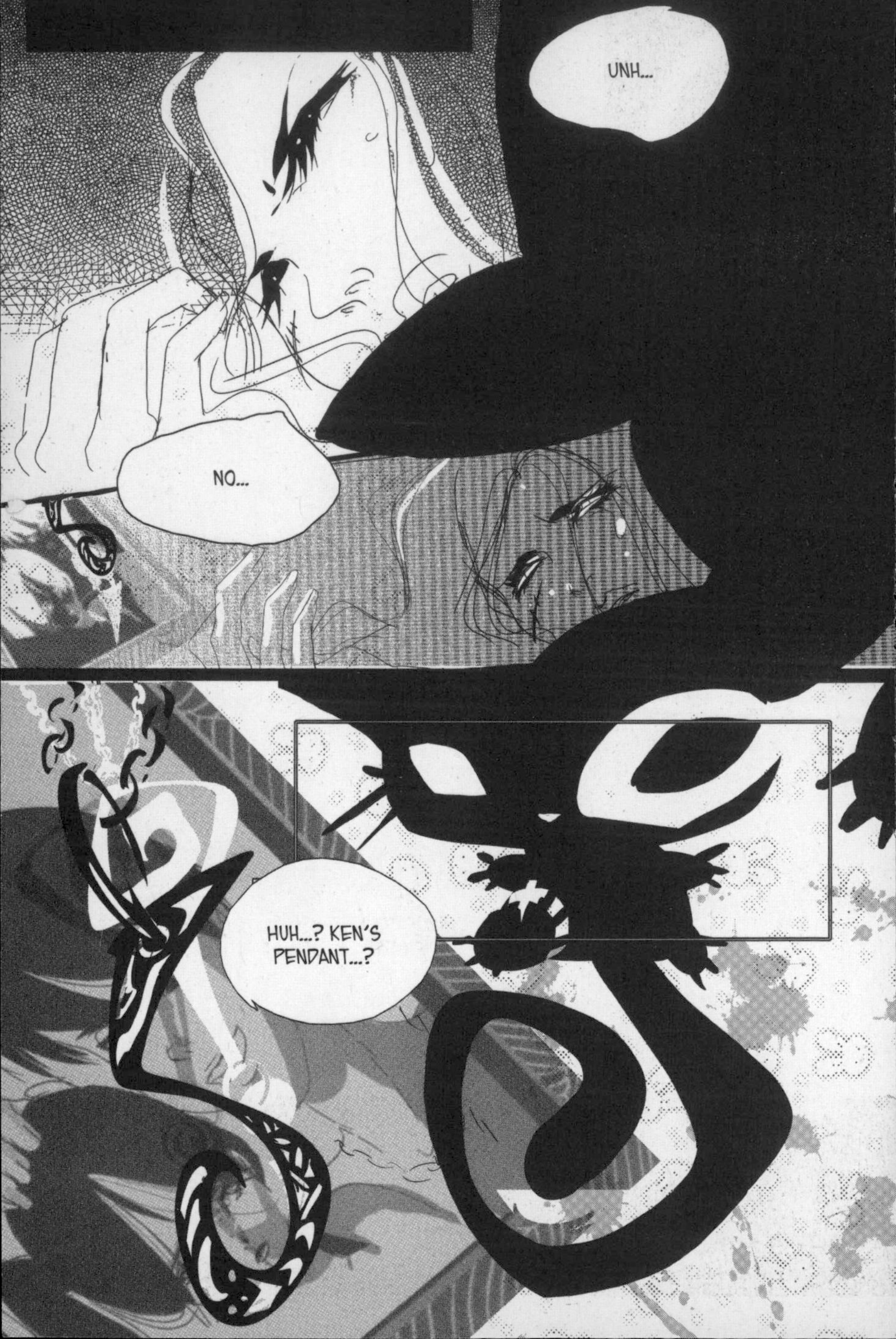
UNH...
NO...
HUH...? KEN'S PENDANT...?

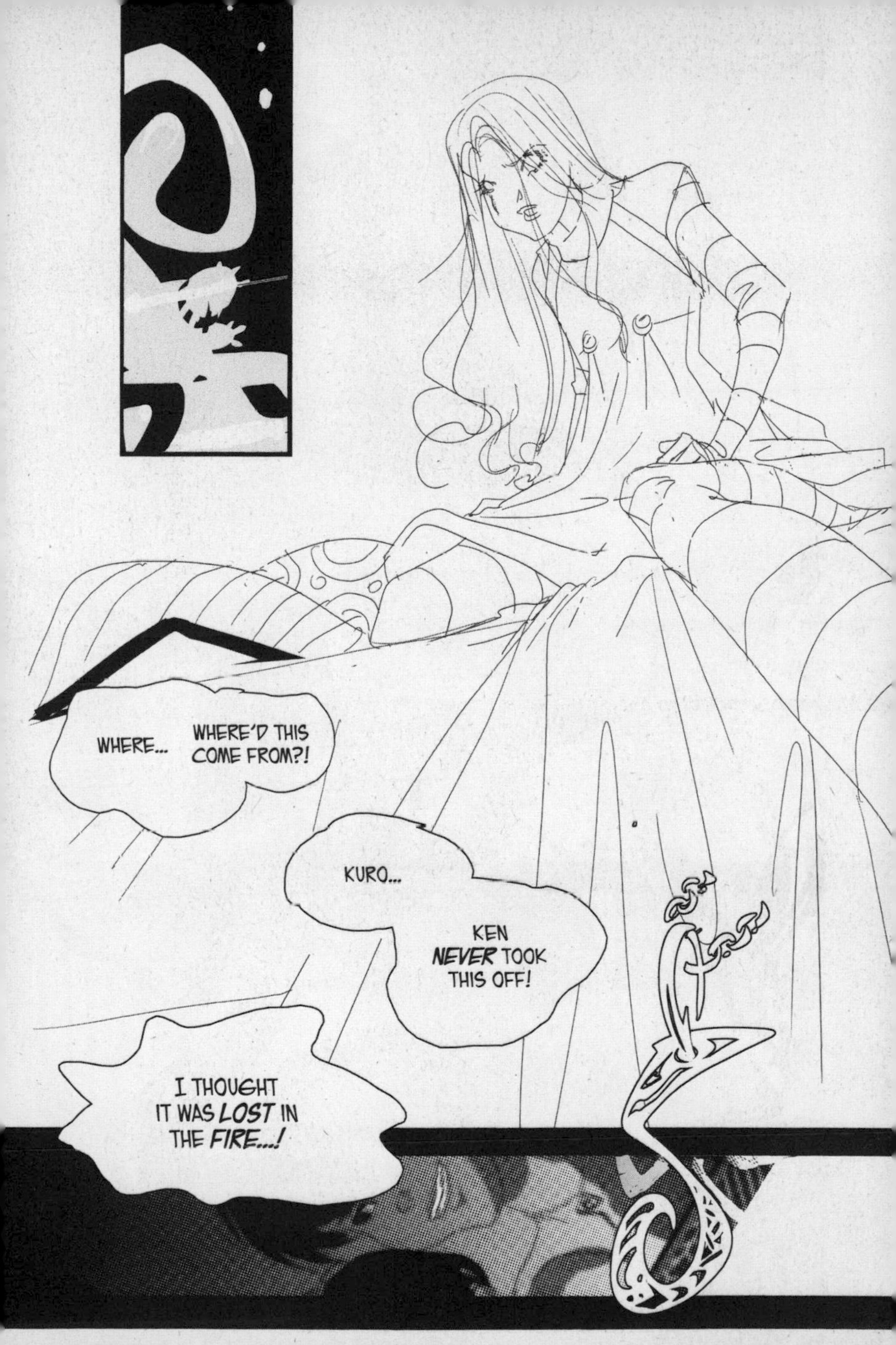
WHERE... WHERE'D THIS COME FROM?!
KURO...
KEN *NEVER* TOOK THIS OFF!
I THOUGHT IT WAS *LOST* IN THE *FIRE*...!

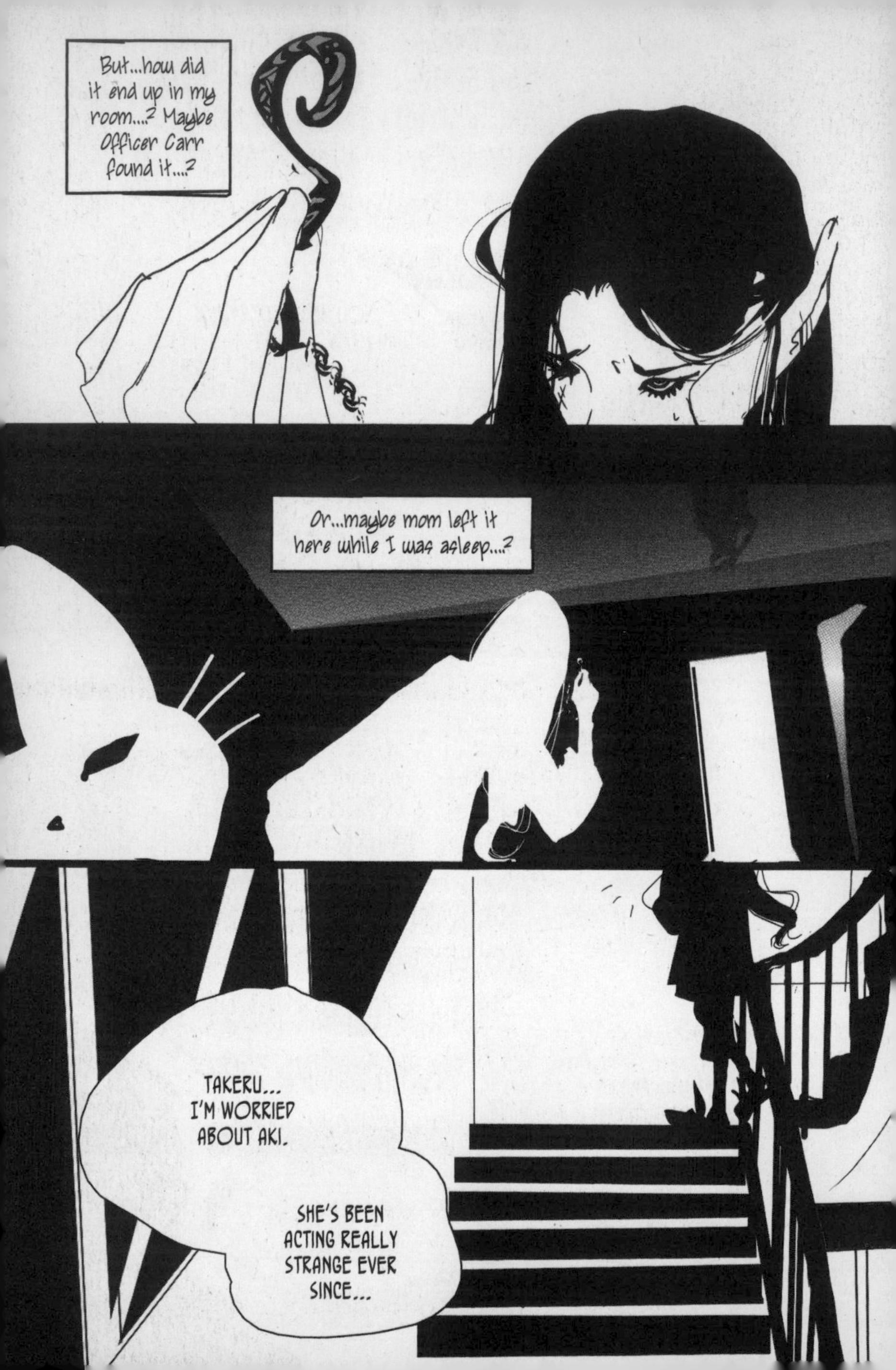
But...how did it end up in my room...? Maybe Officer Carr found it...?
Or...maybe mom left it here while I was asleep...?
TAKERU... I'M WORRIED ABOUT AKI.
SHE'S BEEN ACTING REALLY STRANGE EVER SINCE...

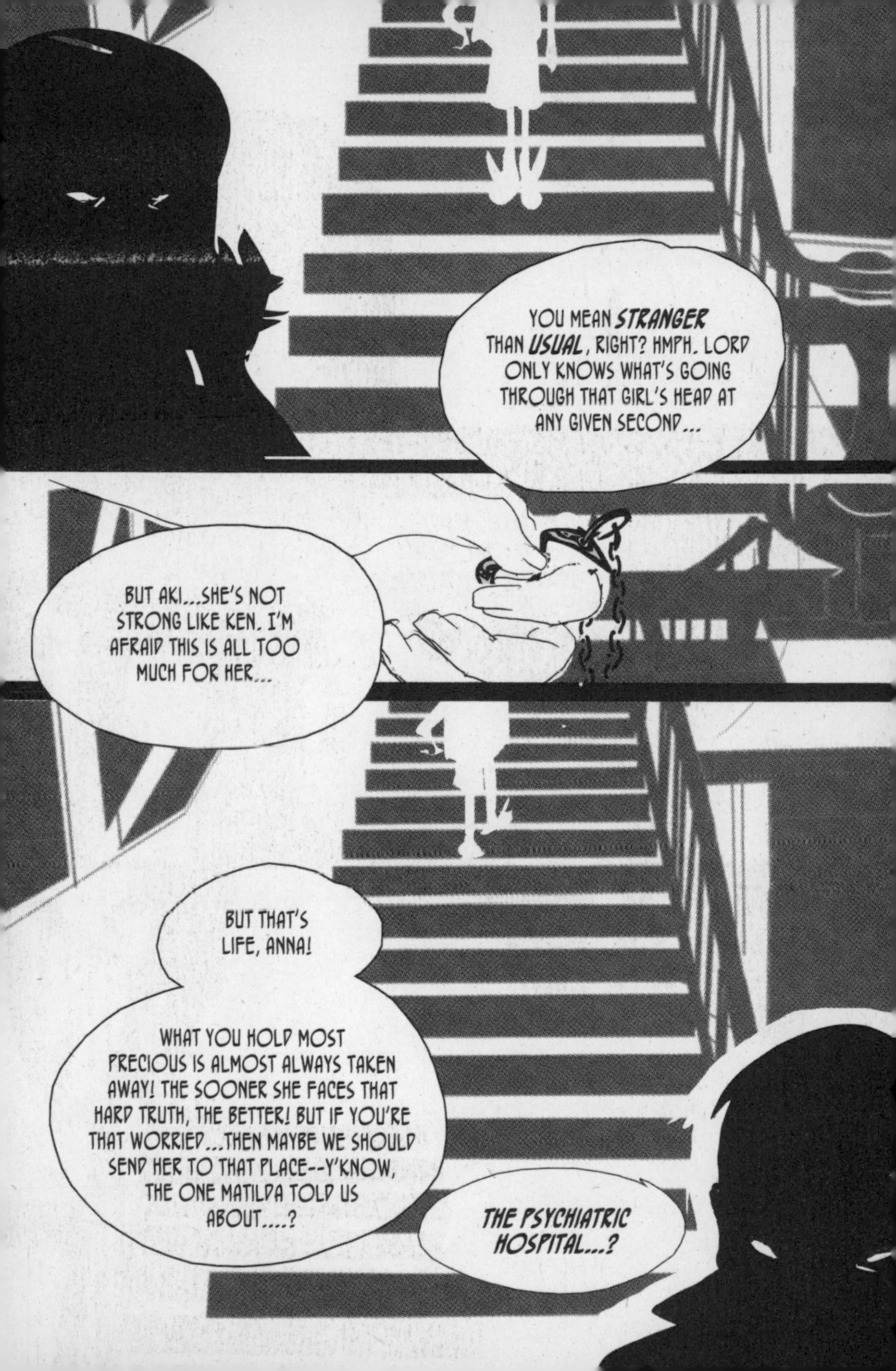
YOU MEAN STRANGER THAN USUAL, RIGHT? HMPH. LORD ONLY KNOWS WHAT'S GOING THROUGH THAT GIRL'S HEAD AT ANY GIVEN SECOND...
BUT AKI...SHE'S NOT STRONG LIKE KEN. I'M AFRAID THIS IS ALL TOO MUCH FOR HER...
BUT THAT'S LIFE, ANNA!
WHAT YOU HOLD MOST PRECIOUS IS ALMOST ALWAYS TAKEN AWAY! THE SOONER SHE FACES THAT HARD TRUTH, THE BETTER! BUT IF YOU'RE THAT WORRIED...THEN MAYBE WE SHOULD SEND HER TO THAT PLACE--Y'KNOW, THE ONE MATILDA TOLD US ABOUT....?
THE PSYCHIATRIC HOSPITAL...?

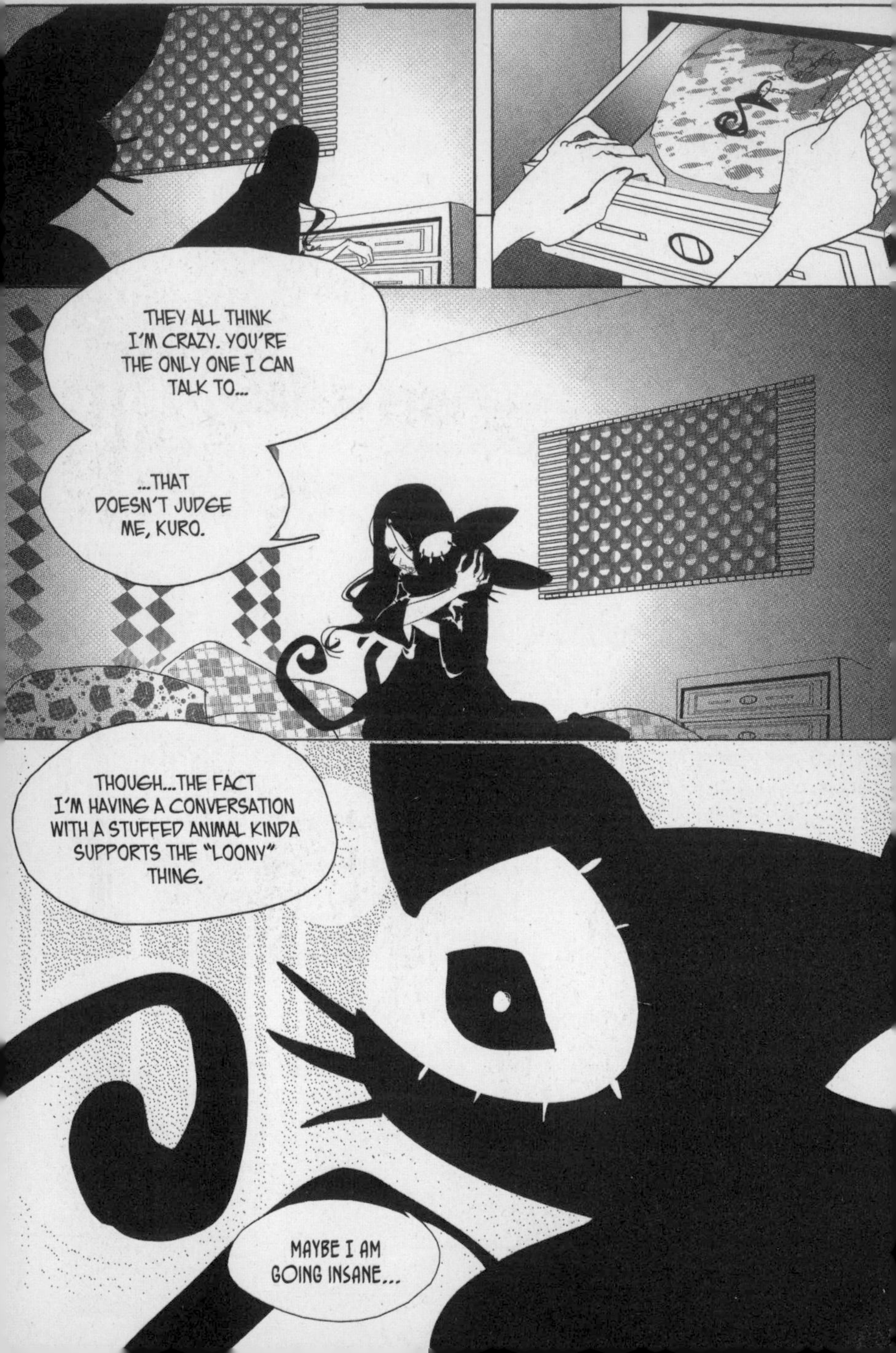
THEY ALL THINK I'M CRAZY. YOU'RE THE ONLY ONE I CAN TALK TO...
...THAT DOESN'T JUDGE ME, KURO.
THOUGH...THE FACT I'M HAVING A CONVERSATION WITH A STUFFED ANIMAL KINDA SUPPORTS THE "LOONY" THING.
MAYBE I AM GOING INSANE...

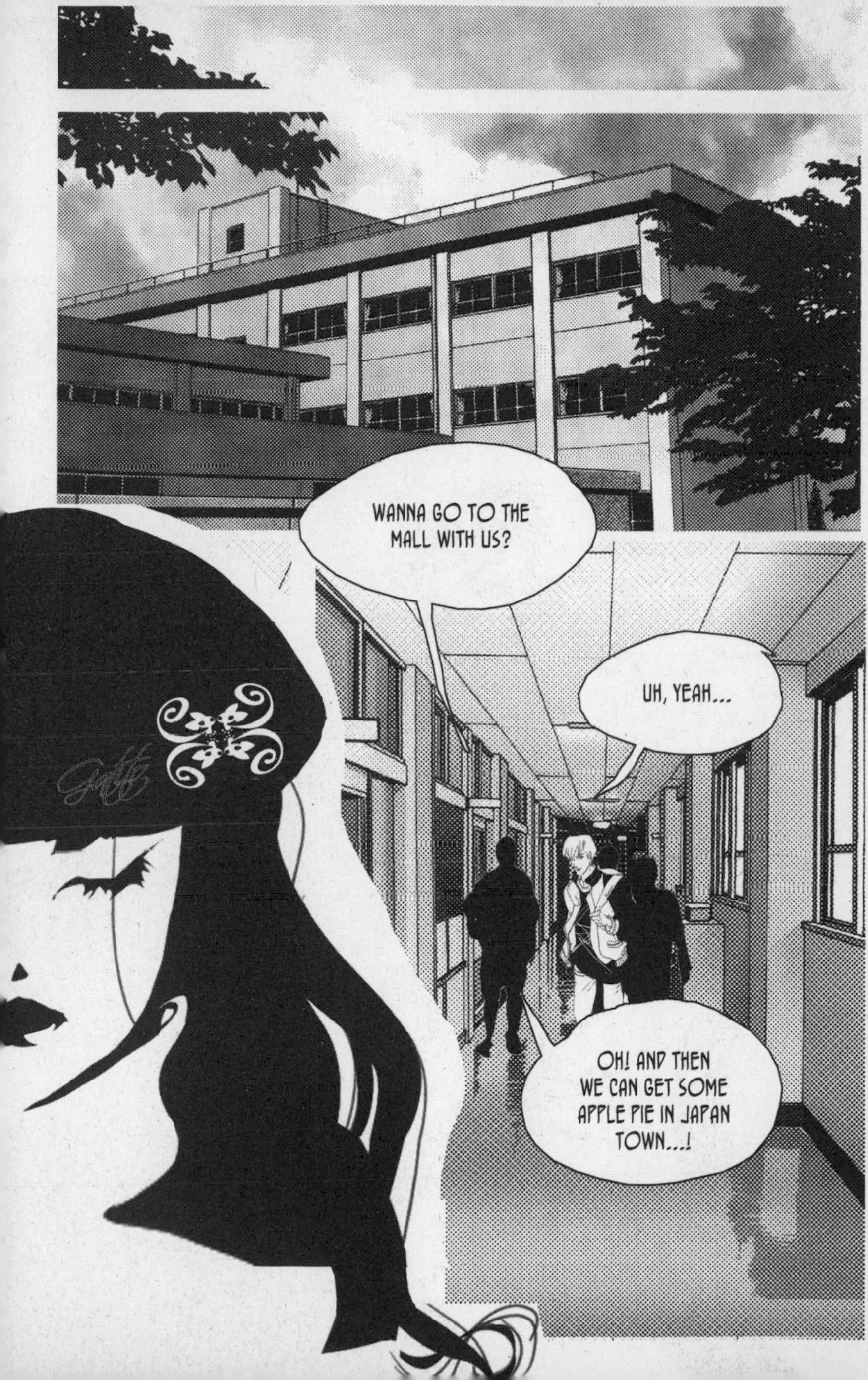
WANNA GO TO THE MALL WITH US?
UH, YEAH...
OH! AND THEN WE CAN GET SOME APPLE PIE IN JAPAN TOWN...!

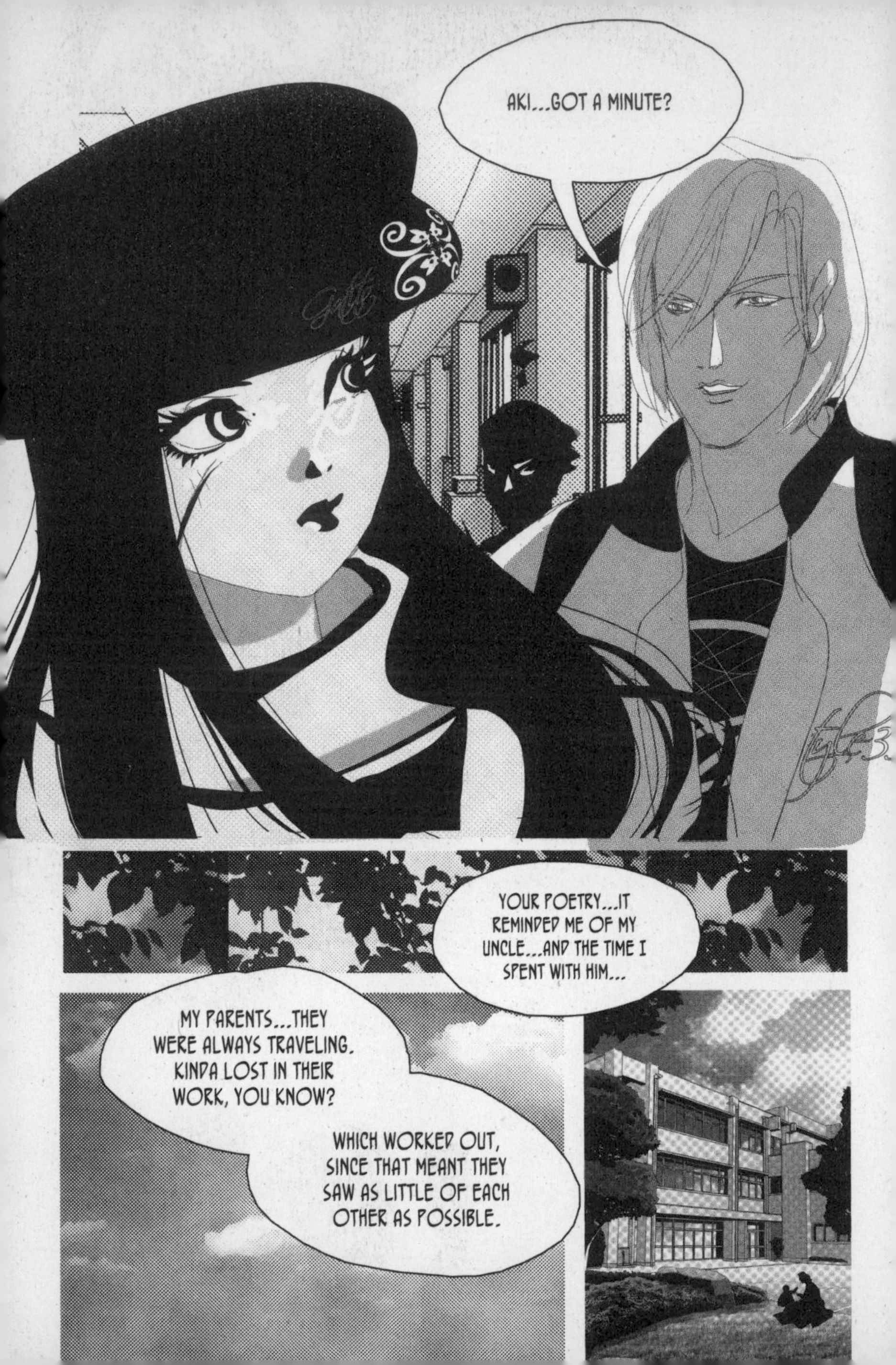
AKI...GOT A MINUTE?
YOUR POETRY...IT REMINDED ME OF MY UNCLE...AND THE TIME I SPENT WITH HIM...
MY PARENTS...THEY WERE ALWAYS TRAVELING. KINDA LOST IN THEIR WORK, YOU KNOW?
WHICH WORKED OUT, SINCE THAT MEANT THEY SAW AS LITTLE OF EACH OTHER AS POSSIBLE.

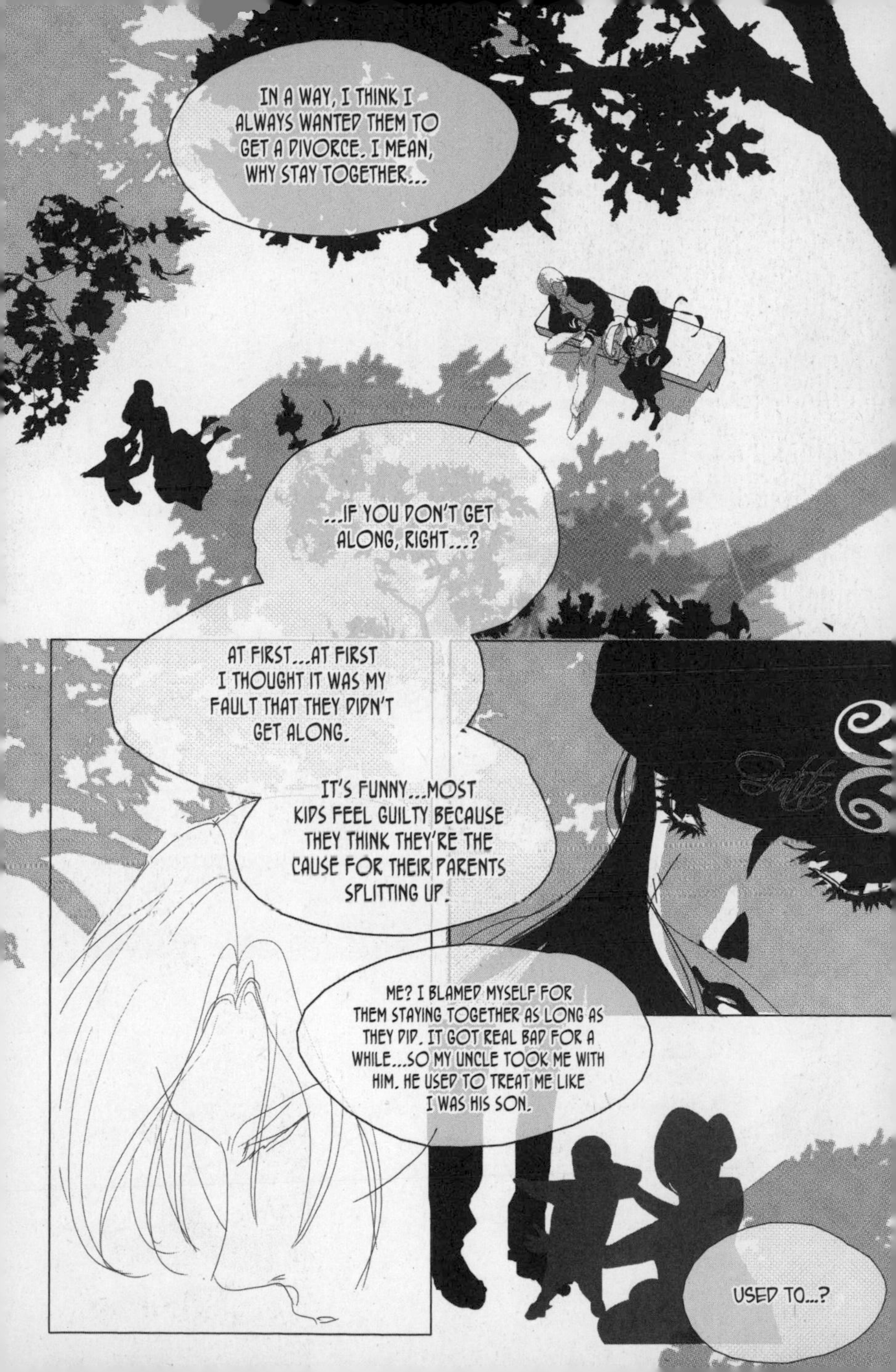
IN A WAY, I THINK I ALWAYS WANTED THEM TO GET A DIVORCE. I MEAN, WHY STAY TOGETHER...
...IF YOU DON'T GET ALONG, RIGHT...?
AT FIRST...AT FIRST I THOUGHT IT WAS MY FAULT THAT THEY DIDN'T GET ALONG.
IT'S FUNNY...MOST KIDS FEEL GUILTY BECAUSE THEY THINK THEY'RE THE CAUSE FOR THEIR PARENTS SPLITTING UP.
ME? I BLAMED MYSELF FOR THEM STAYING TOGETHER AS LONG AS THEY DID. IT GOT REAL BAD FOR A WHILE...SO MY UNCLE TOOK ME WITH HIM. HE USED TO TREAT ME LIKE I WAS HIS SON.
USED TO...?

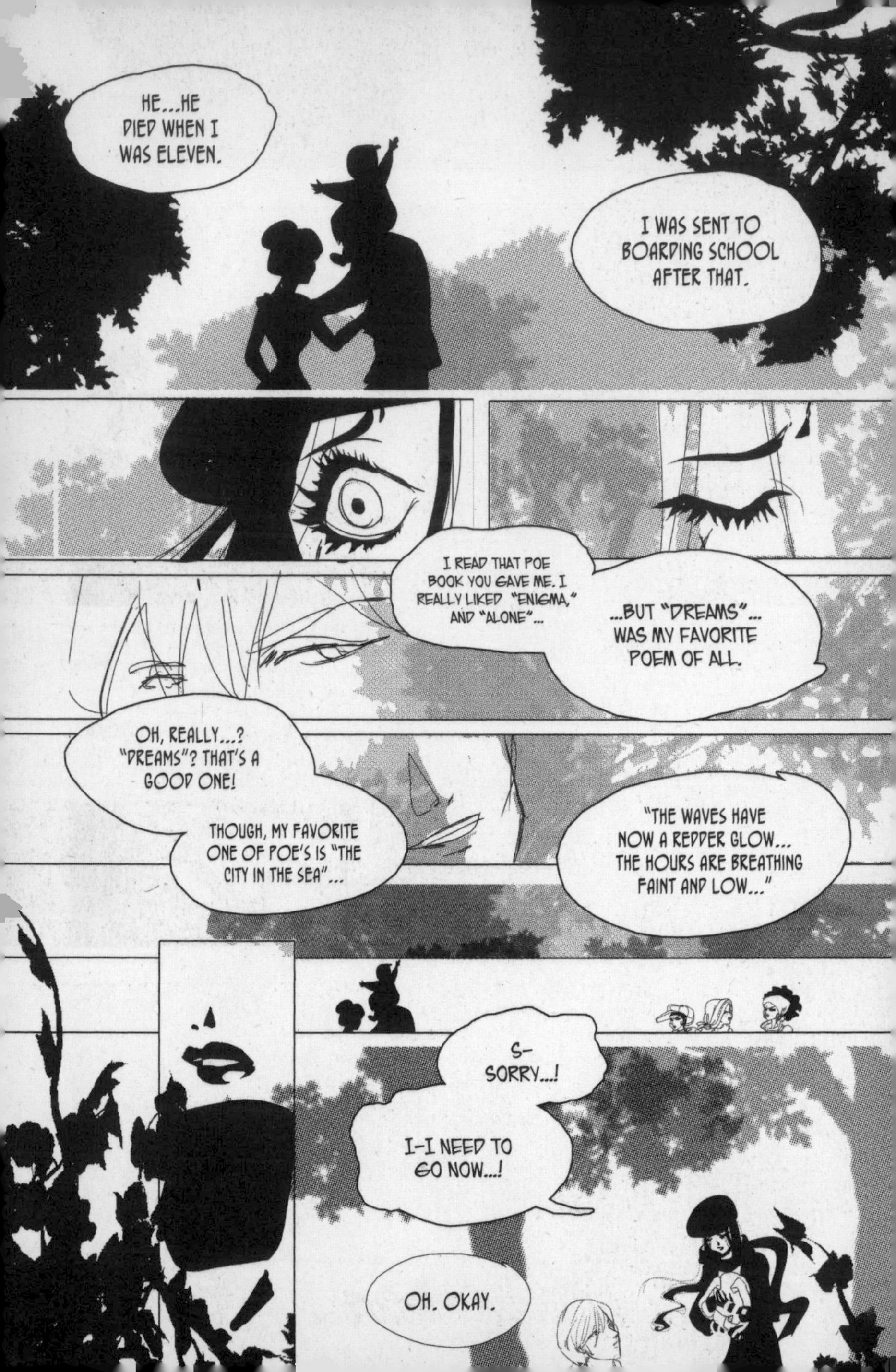
HE...HE DIED WHEN I WAS ELEVEN.
I WAS SENT TO BOARDING SCHOOL AFTER THAT.
I READ THAT POE BOOK YOU GAVE ME. I REALLY LIKED "ENIGMA," AND "ALONE"...
...BUT "DREAMS"... WAS MY FAVORITE POEM OF ALL.
OH, REALLY...? "DREAMS"? THAT'S A GOOD ONE!
THOUGH, MY FAVORITE ONE OF POE'S IS "THE CITY IN THE SEA"...
"THE WAVES HAVE NOW A REDDER GLOW... THE HOURS ARE BREATHING FAINT AND LOW..."
S-SORRY...!
I-I NEED TO GO NOW...!
OH. OKAY.

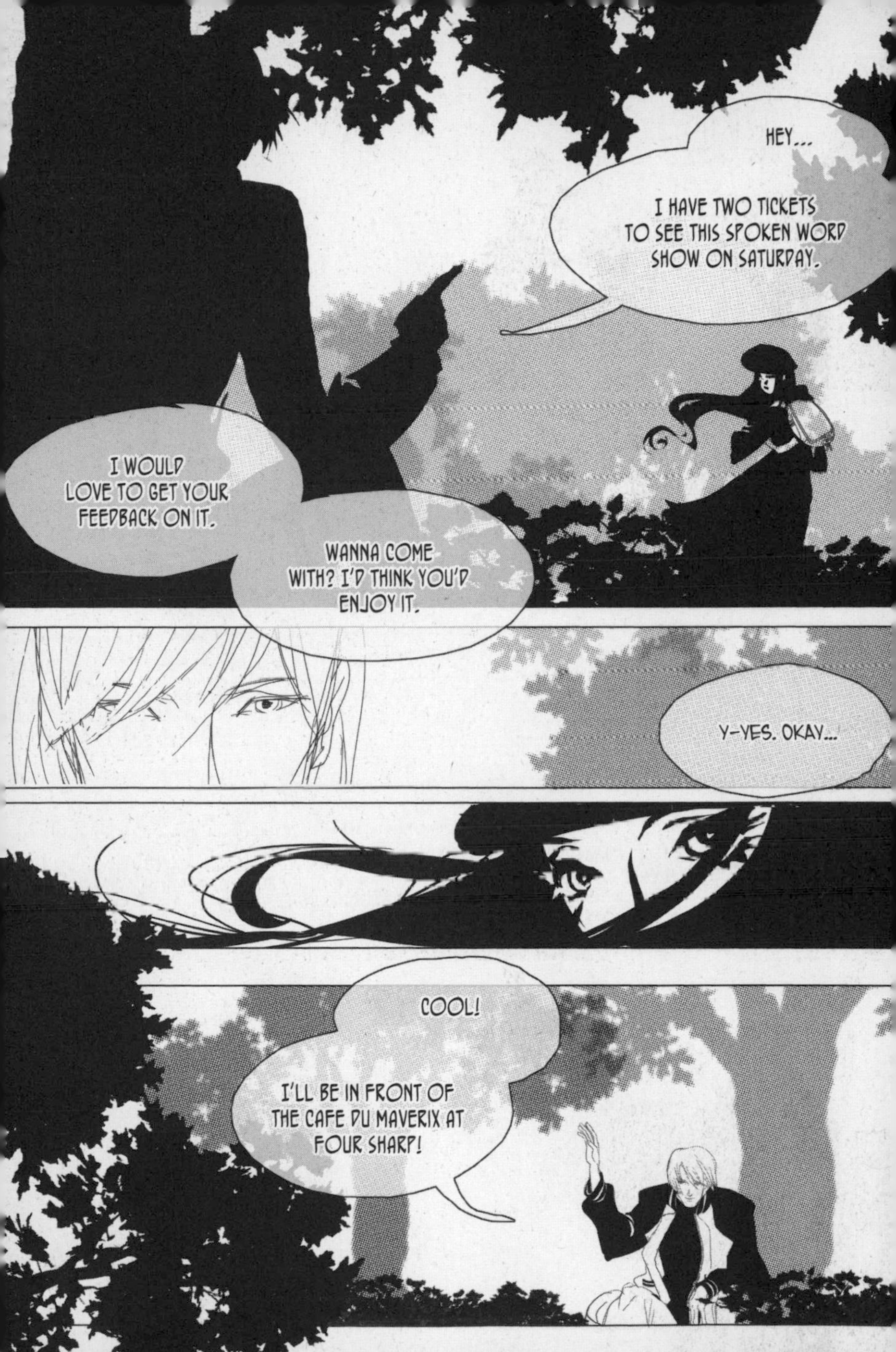
HEY...
I HAVE TWO TICKETS TO SEE THIS SPOKEN WORD SHOW ON SATURDAY.
WANNA COME WITH? I'D THINK YOU'D ENJOY IT.
I WOULD LOVE TO GET YOUR FEEDBACK ON IT.
Y-YES. OKAY...
COOL!
I'LL BE IN FRONT OF THE CAFE DU MAVERIX AT FOUR SHARP!

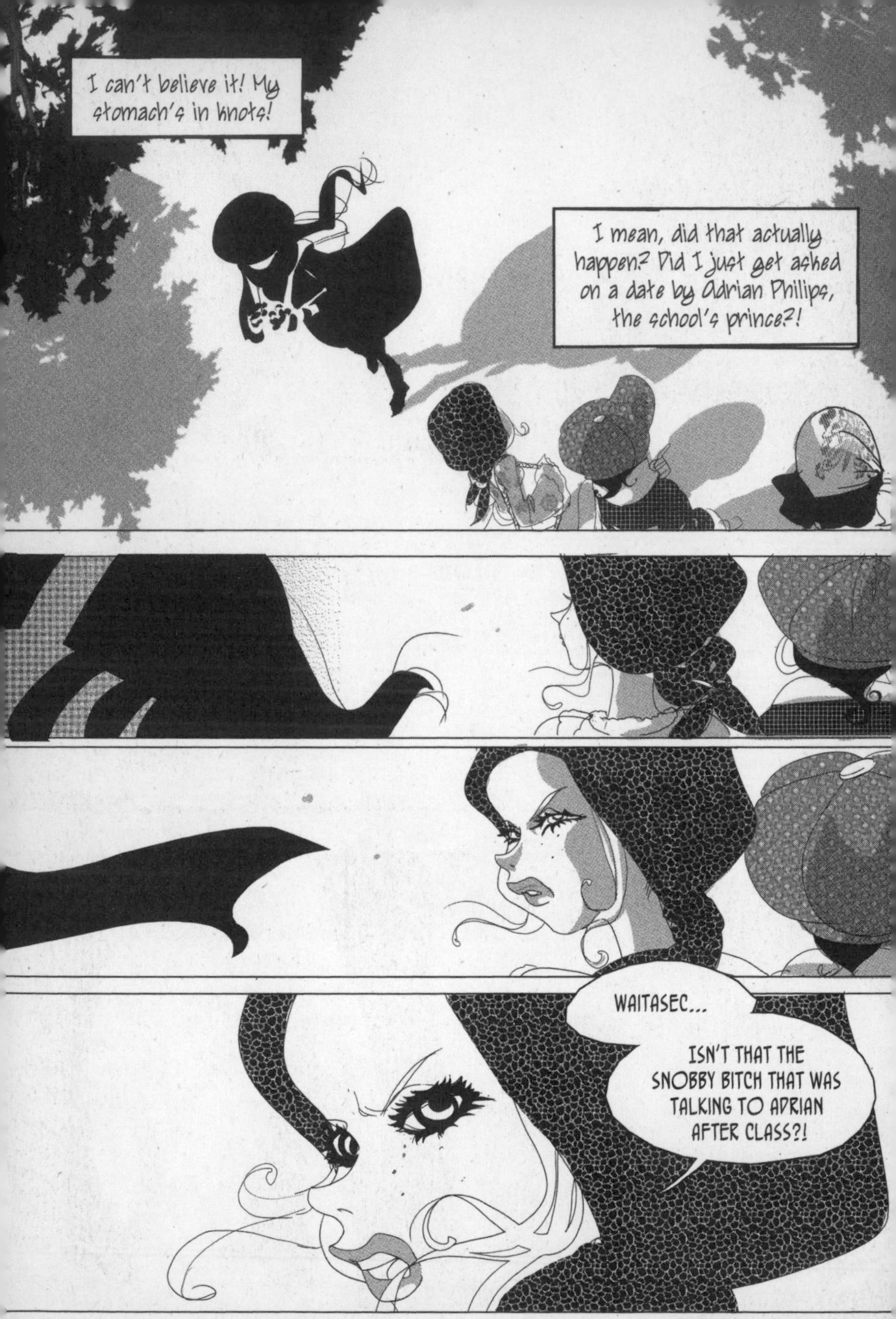
I can't believe it! My stomach's in knots!
I mean, did that actually happen? Did I just get asked on a date by Adrian Philips, the school's prince?!
WAITASEC...
ISN'T THAT THE SNOBBY BITCH THAT WAS TALKING TO ADRIAN AFTER CLASS?!

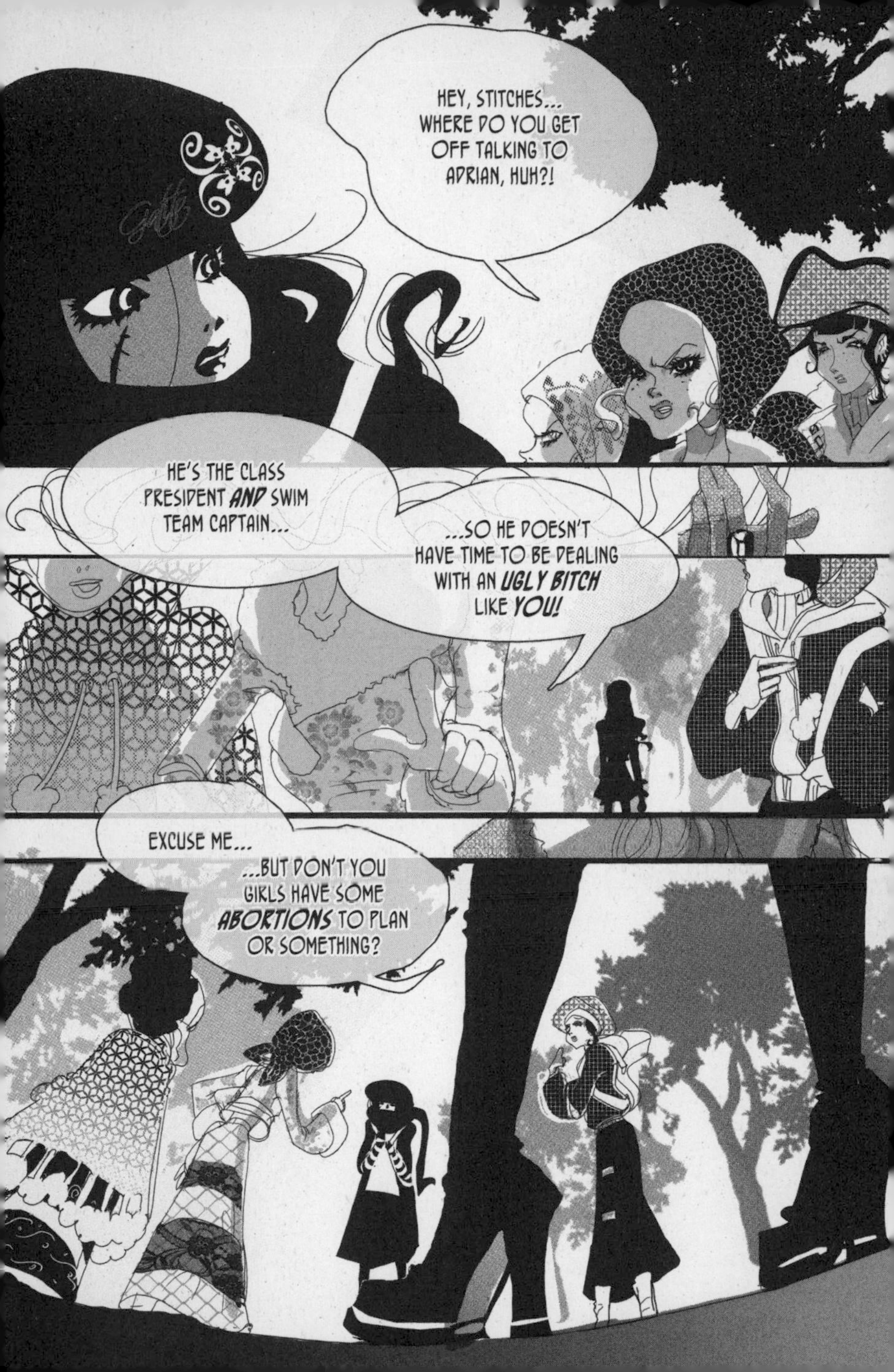
HEY, STITCHES... WHERE DO YOU GET OFF TALKING TO ADRIAN, HUH?!
HE'S THE CLASS PRESIDENT AND SWIM TEAM CAPTAIN...
...SO HE DOESN'T HAVE TIME TO BE DEALING WITH AN UGLY BITCH LIKE YOU!
EXCUSE ME...
...BUT DON'T YOU GIRLS HAVE SOME ABORTIONS TO PLAN OR SOMETHING?

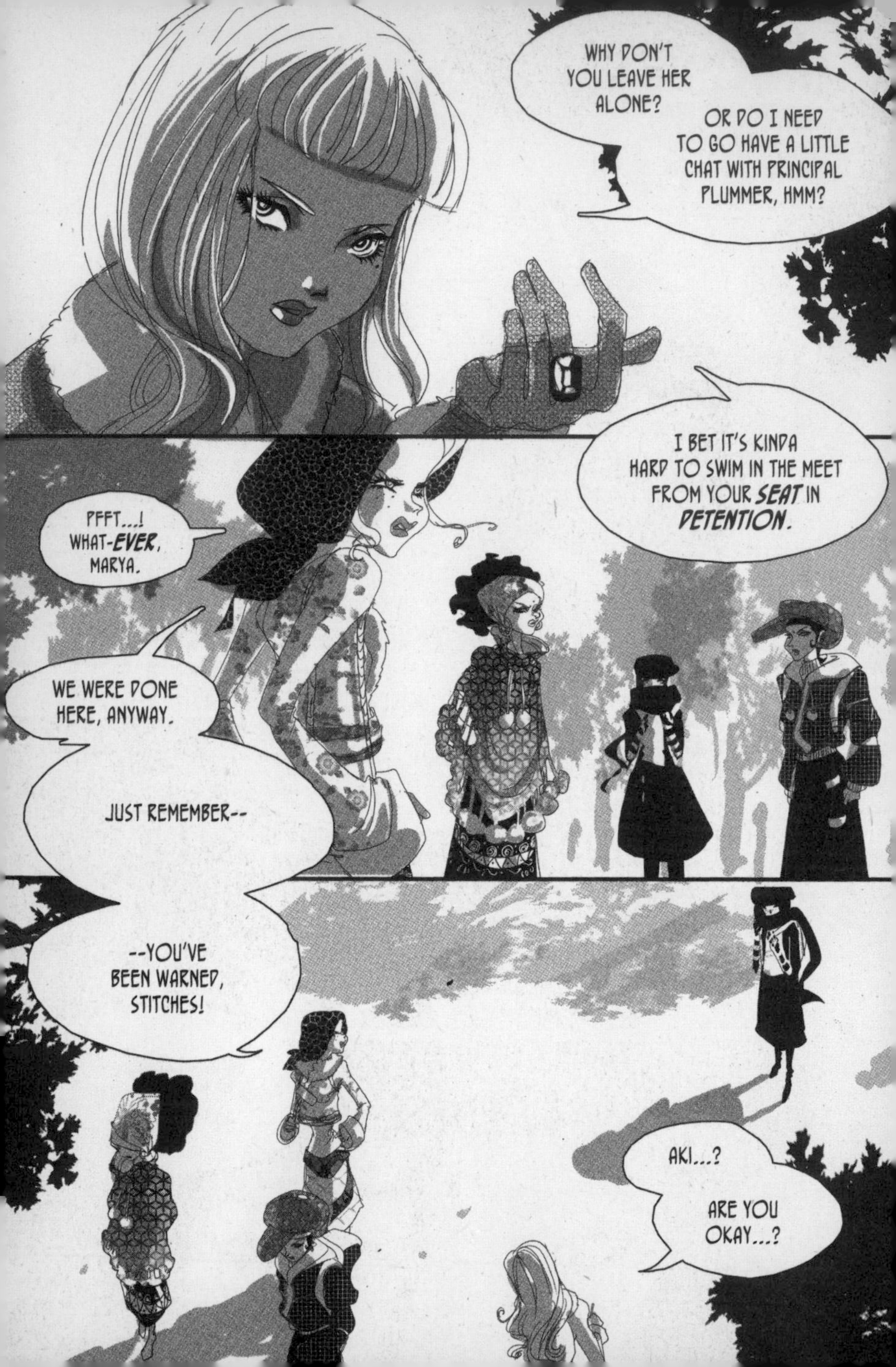
WHY DON'T YOU LEAVE HER ALONE?
OR DO I NEED TO GO HAVE A LITTLE CHAT WITH PRINCIPAL PLUMMER, HMM?
I BET IT'S KINDA HARD TO SWIM IN THE MEET FROM YOUR ***SEAT*** IN ***DETENTION***.
PFFT...! WHAT-***EVER***, MARYA.
WE WERE DONE HERE, ANYWAY.
JUST REMEMBER--
--YOU'VE BEEN WARNED, STITCHES!
AKI...?
ARE YOU OKAY...?

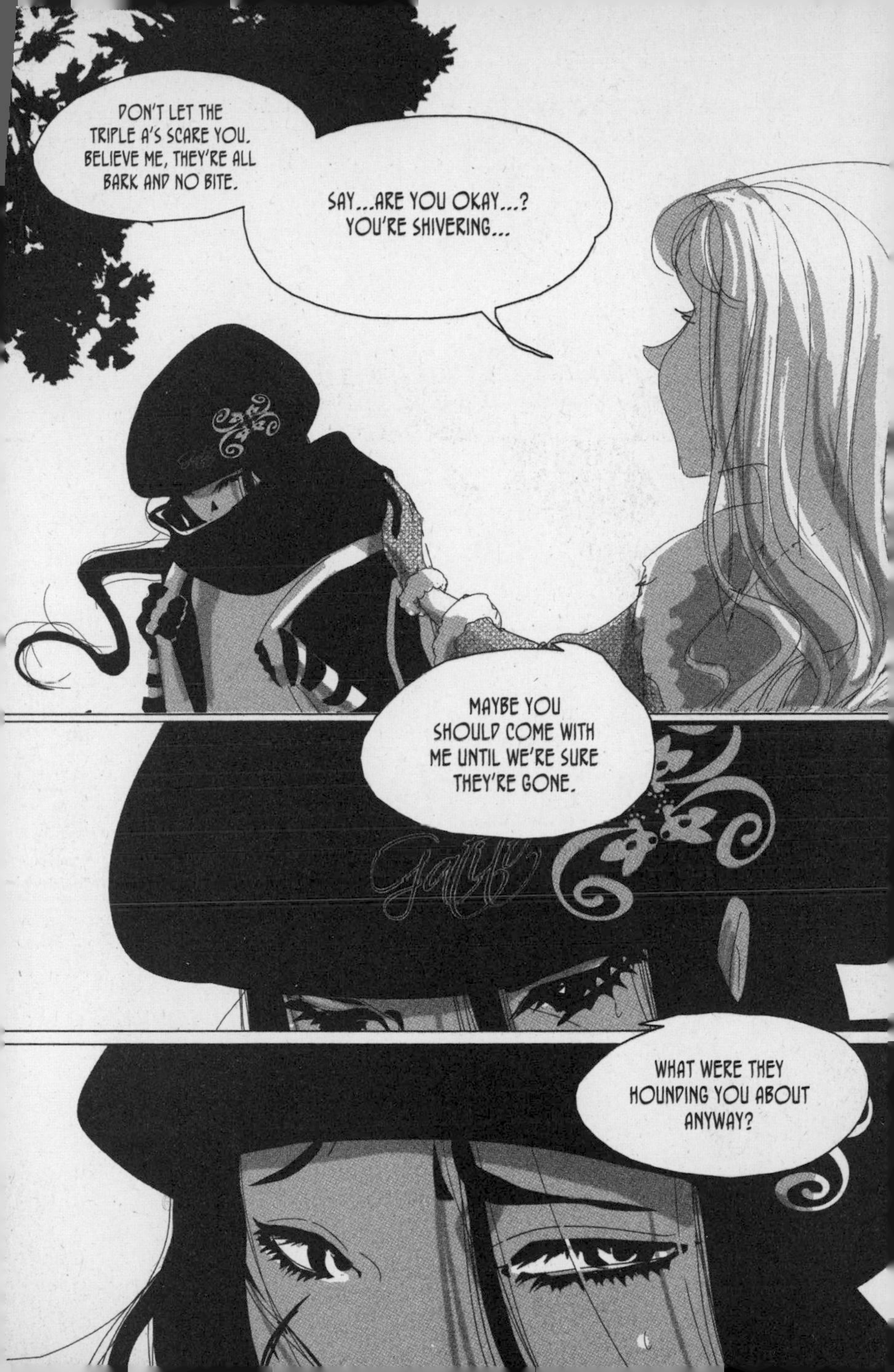
DON'T LET THE TRIPLE A'S SCARE YOU. BELIEVE ME, THEY'RE ALL BARK AND NO BITE.
SAY...ARE YOU OKAY...? YOU'RE SHIVERING...
MAYBE YOU SHOULD COME WITH ME UNTIL WE'RE SURE THEY'RE GONE.
WHAT WERE THEY HOUNDING YOU ABOUT ANYWAY?

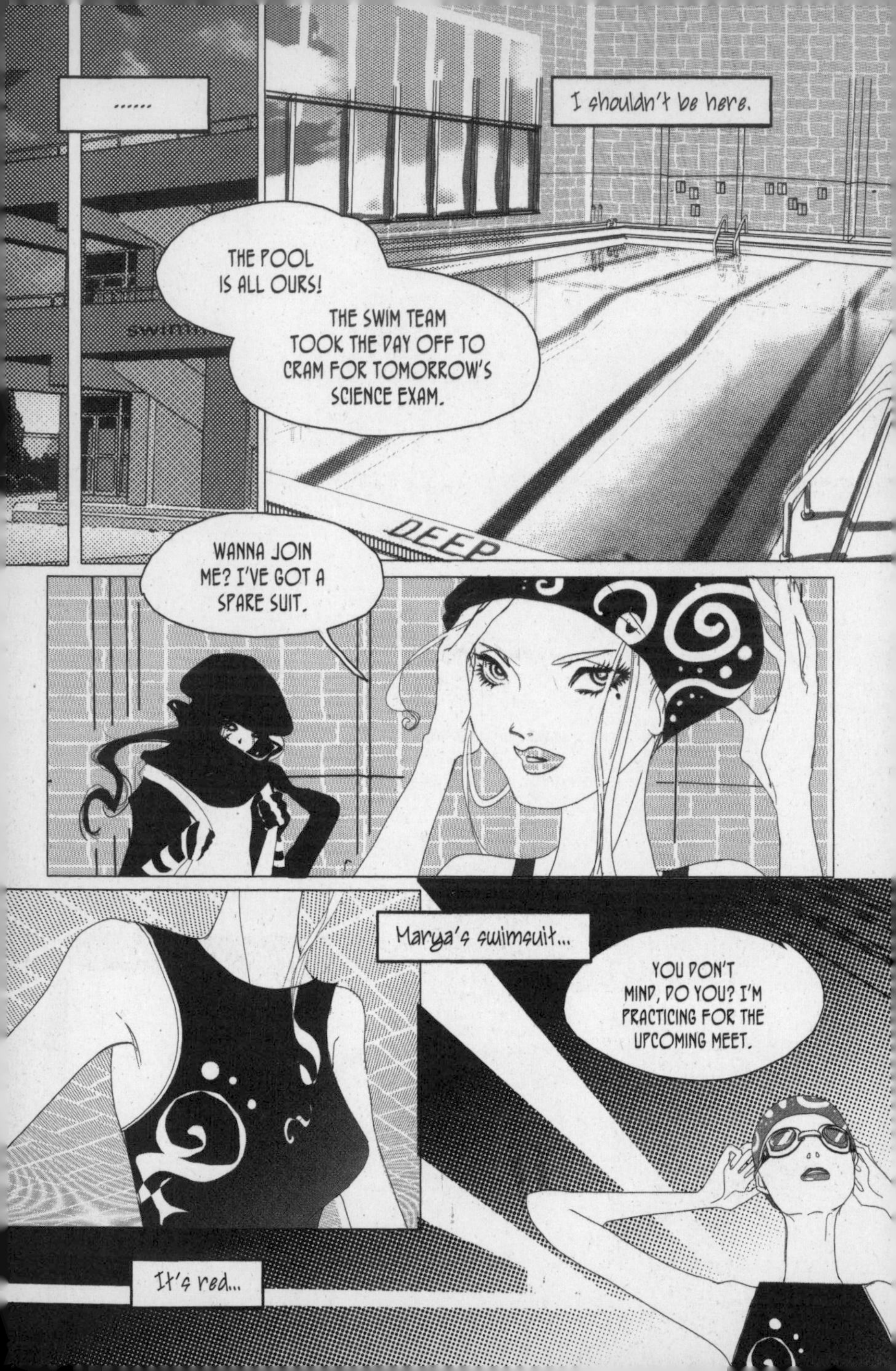
I shouldn't be here.
THE POOL IS ALL OURS!
THE SWIM TEAM TOOK THE DAY OFF TO CRAM FOR TOMORROW'S SCIENCE EXAM.
......
WANNA JOIN ME? I'VE GOT A SPARE SUIT.
YOU DON'T MIND, DO YOU? I'M PRACTICING FOR THE UPCOMING MEET.
Marya's swimsuit...
It's red...

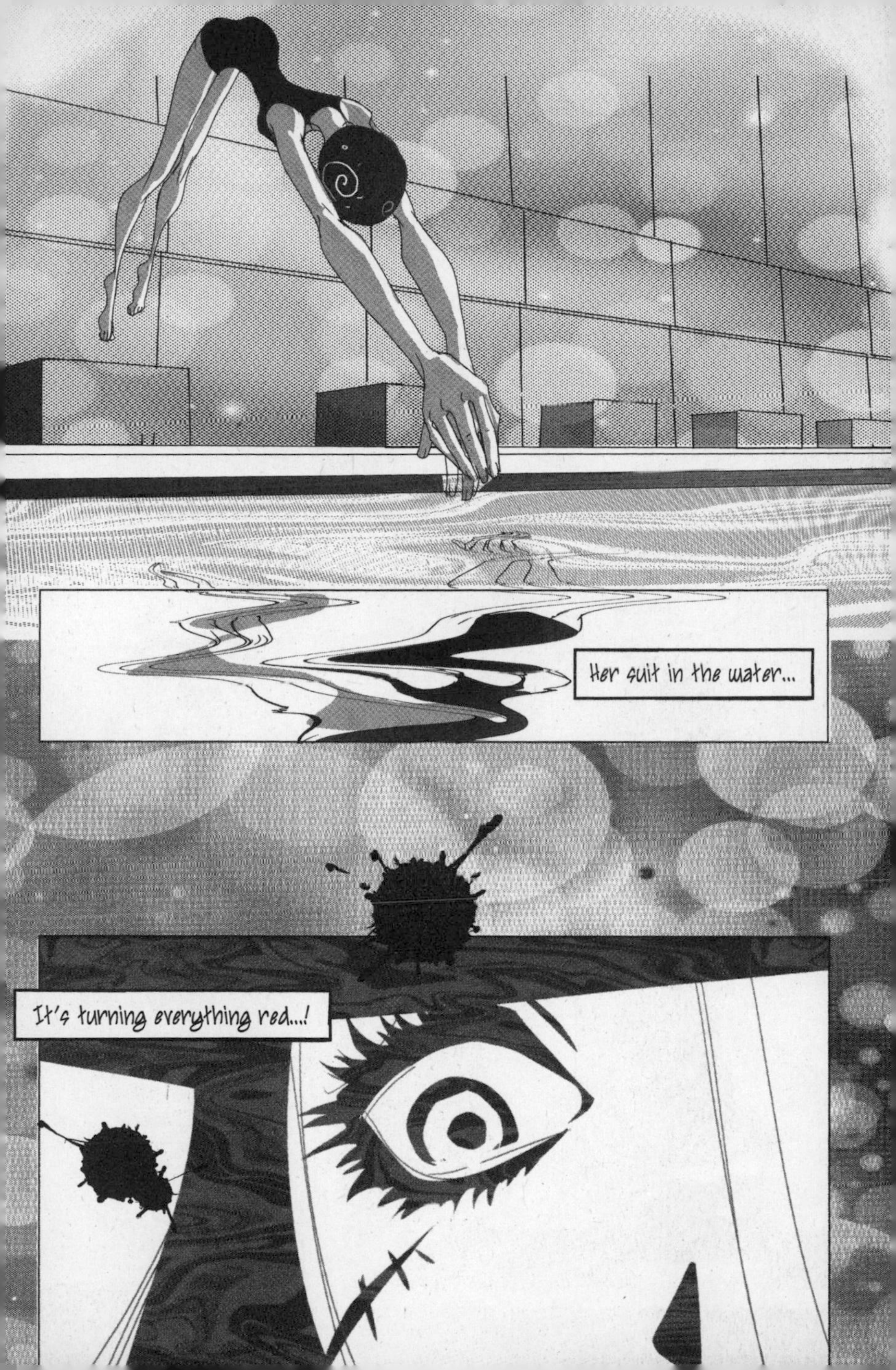
Her suit in the water...
It's turning everything red...!

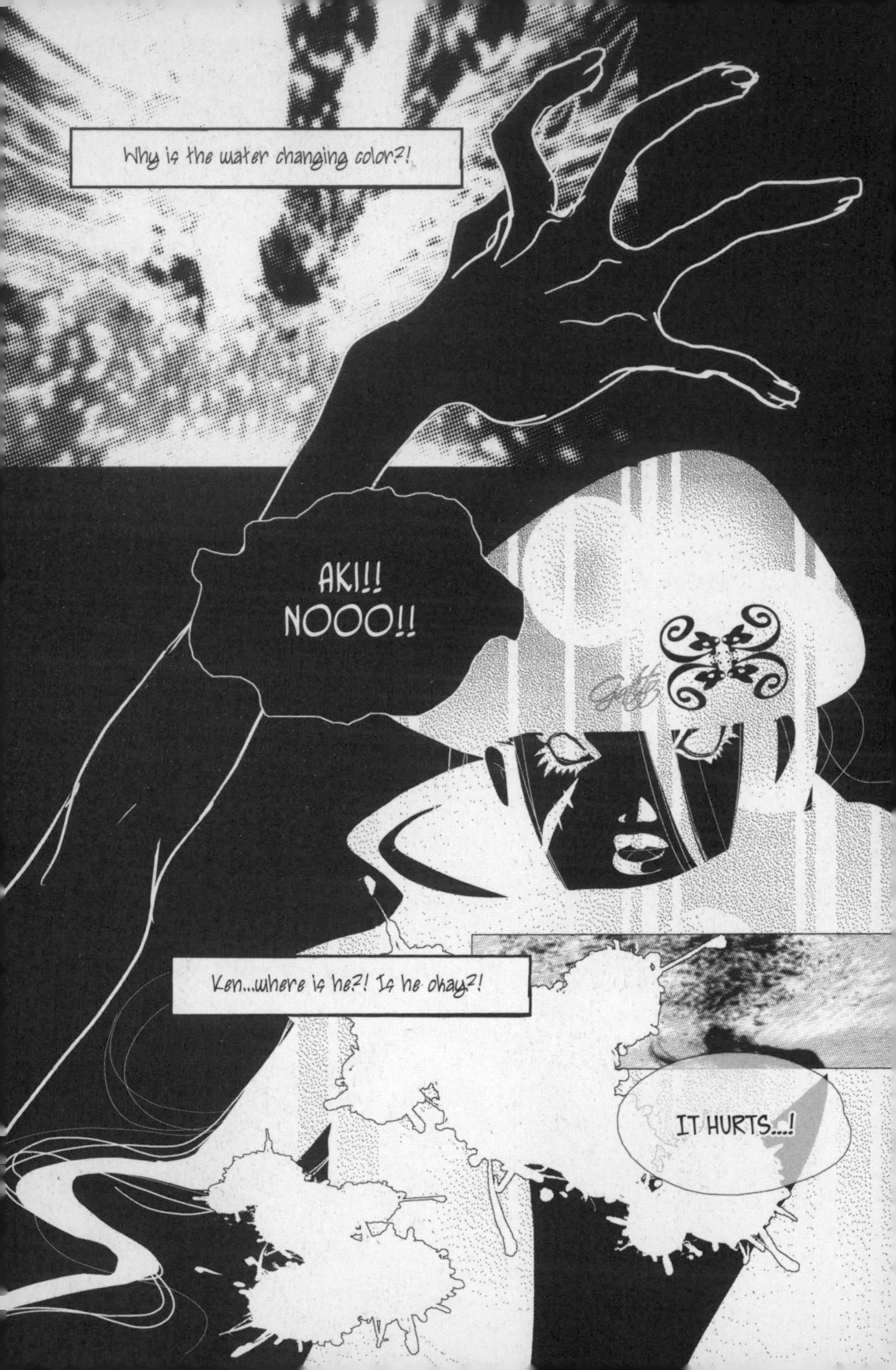
Why is the water changing color?!
AKI!! NOOO!!
Ken...where is he?! Is he okay?!
IT HURTS...!

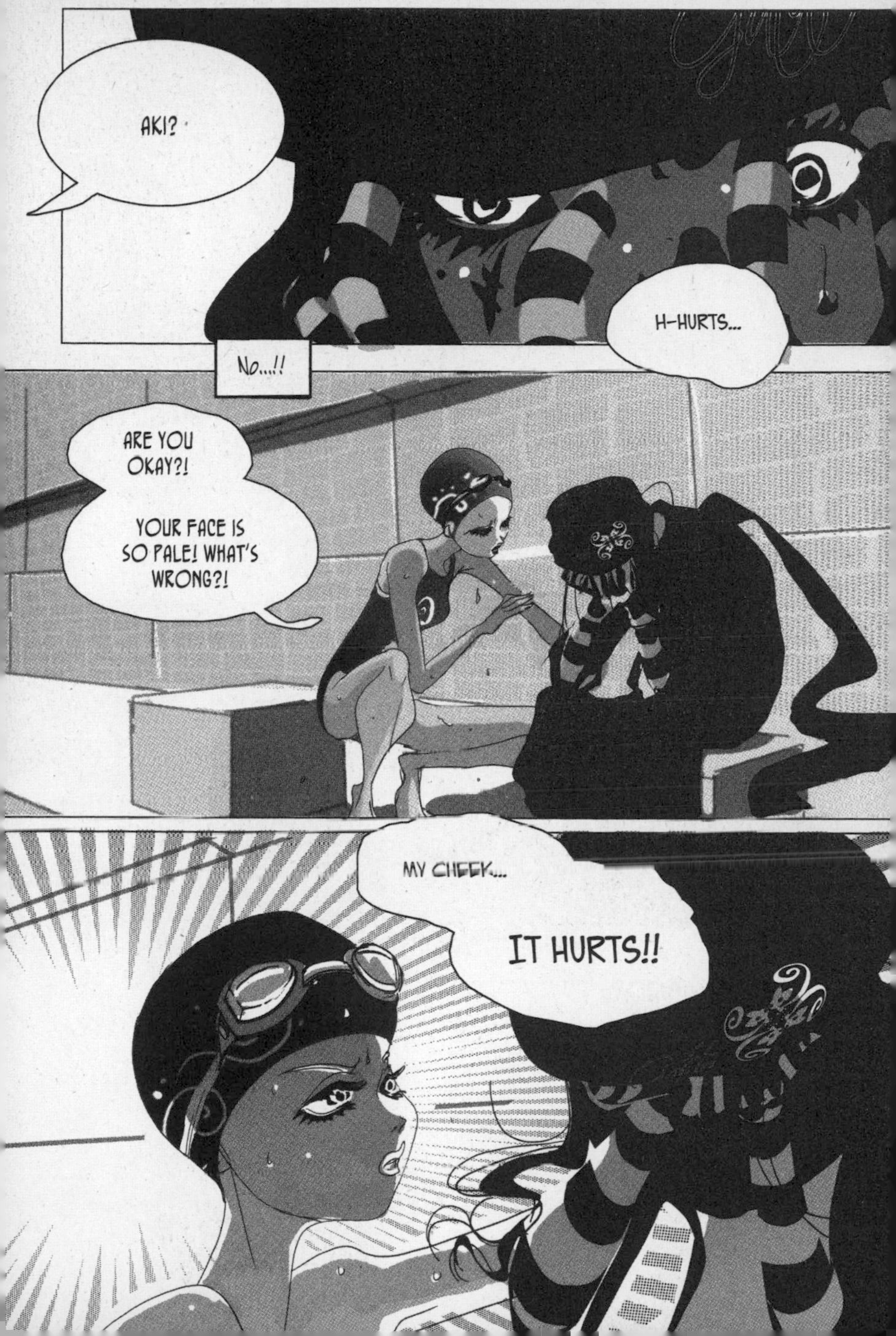
AKI?
H-HURTS...
No...!!
ARE YOU OKAY?!
YOUR FACE IS SO PALE! WHAT'S WRONG?!
MY CHEEK...
IT HURTS!!

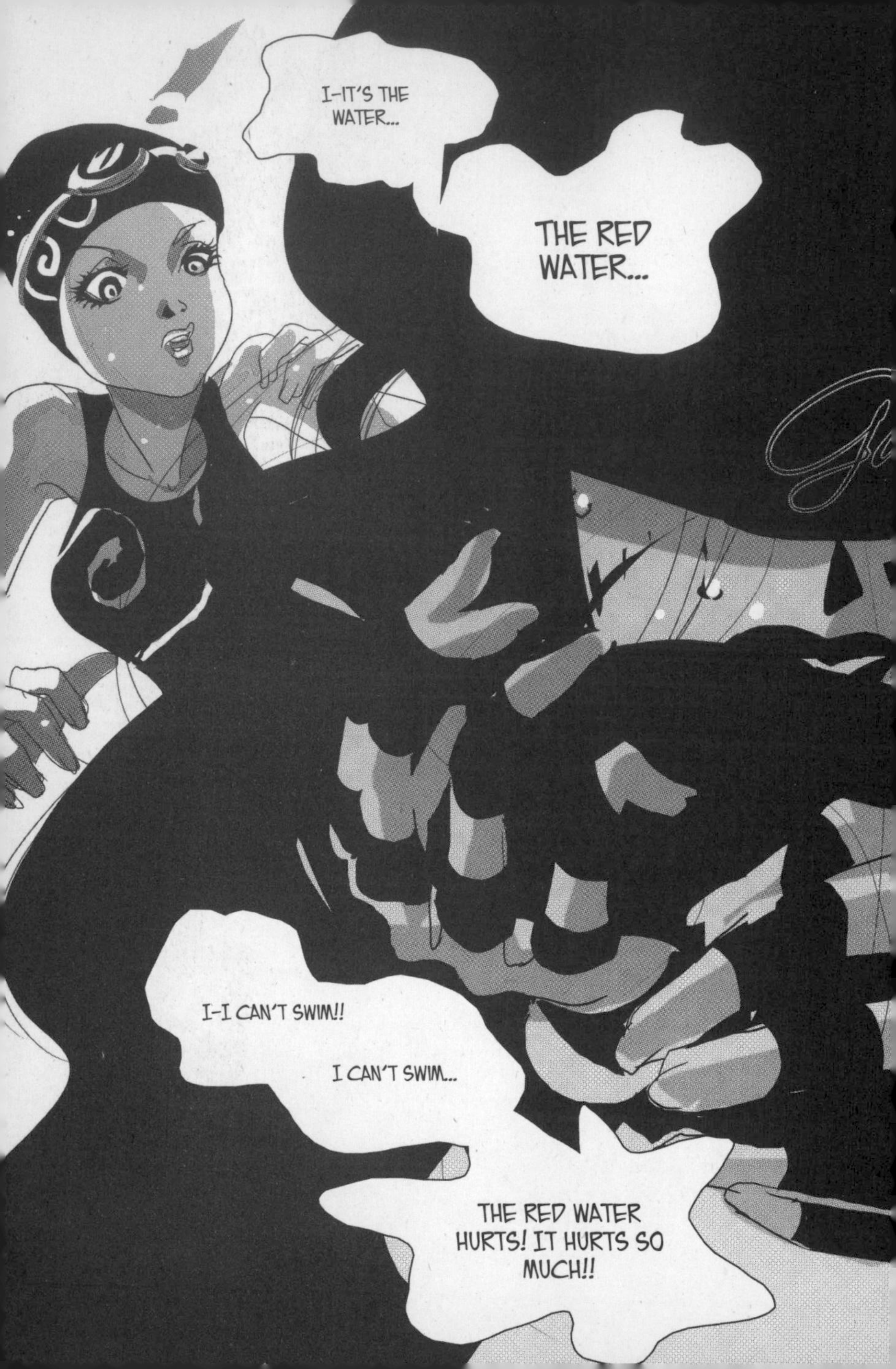
I-IT'S THE WATER...
THE RED WATER...
I-I CAN'T SWIM!!
I CAN'T SWIM...
THE RED WATER HURTS! IT HURTS SO MUCH!!

CHAPTER :: 03

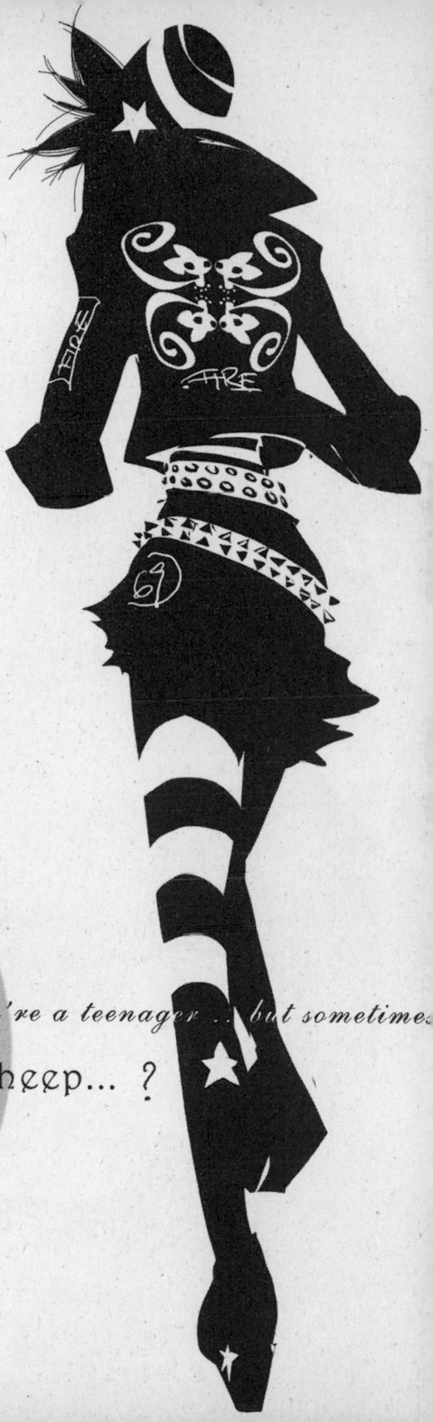

...*Life's* **hard** *when you're a teenager* ... *but sometimes*

etimes it's funner to be the black sheep... ?

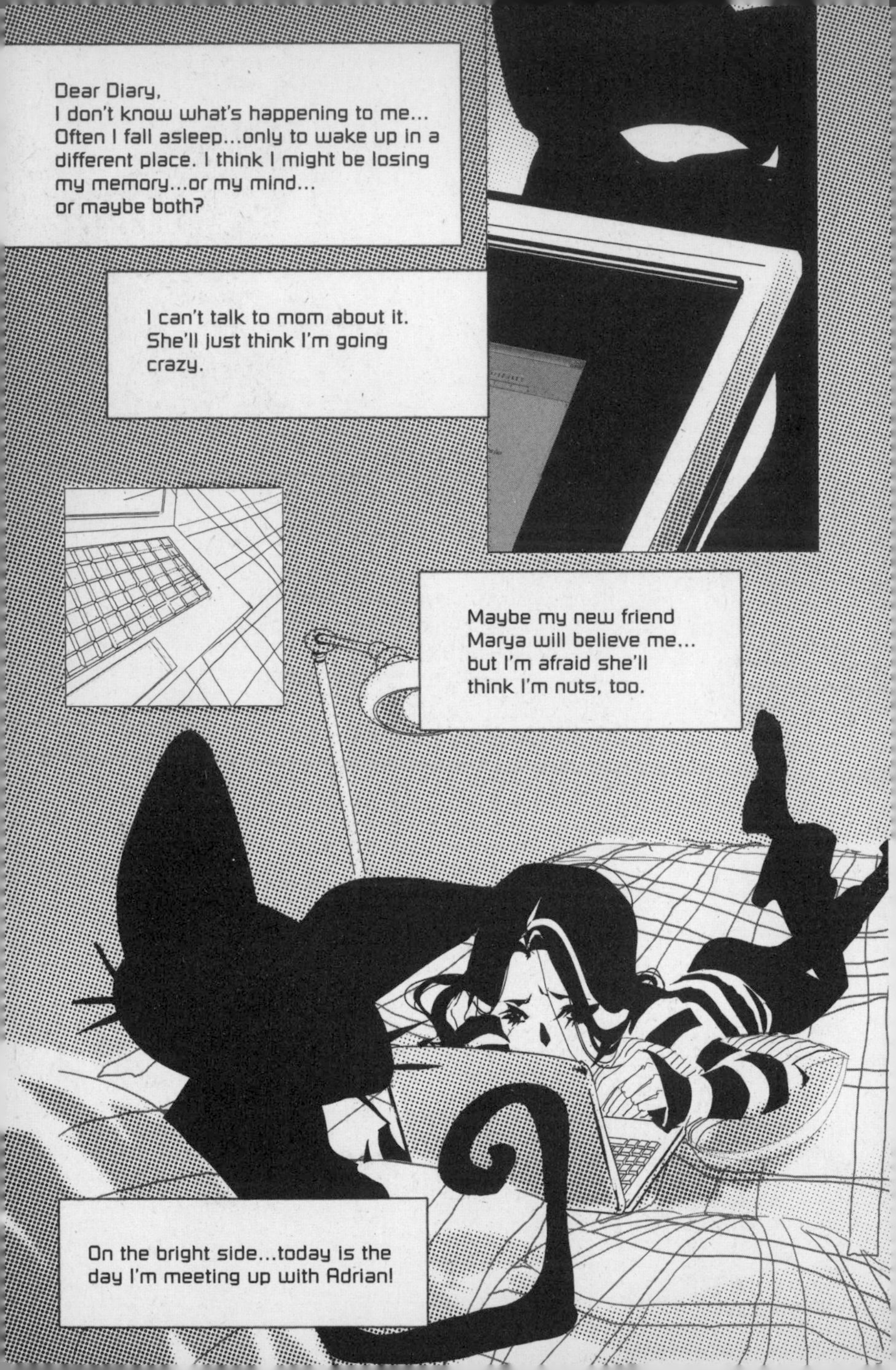
Dear Diary,
I don't know what's happening to me... Often I fall asleep...only to wake up in a different place. I think I might be losing my memory...or my mind... or maybe both?
I can't talk to mom about it. She'll just think I'm going crazy.
Maybe my new friend Marya will believe me... but I'm afraid she'll think I'm nuts, too.
On the bright side...today is the day I'm meeting up with Adrian!

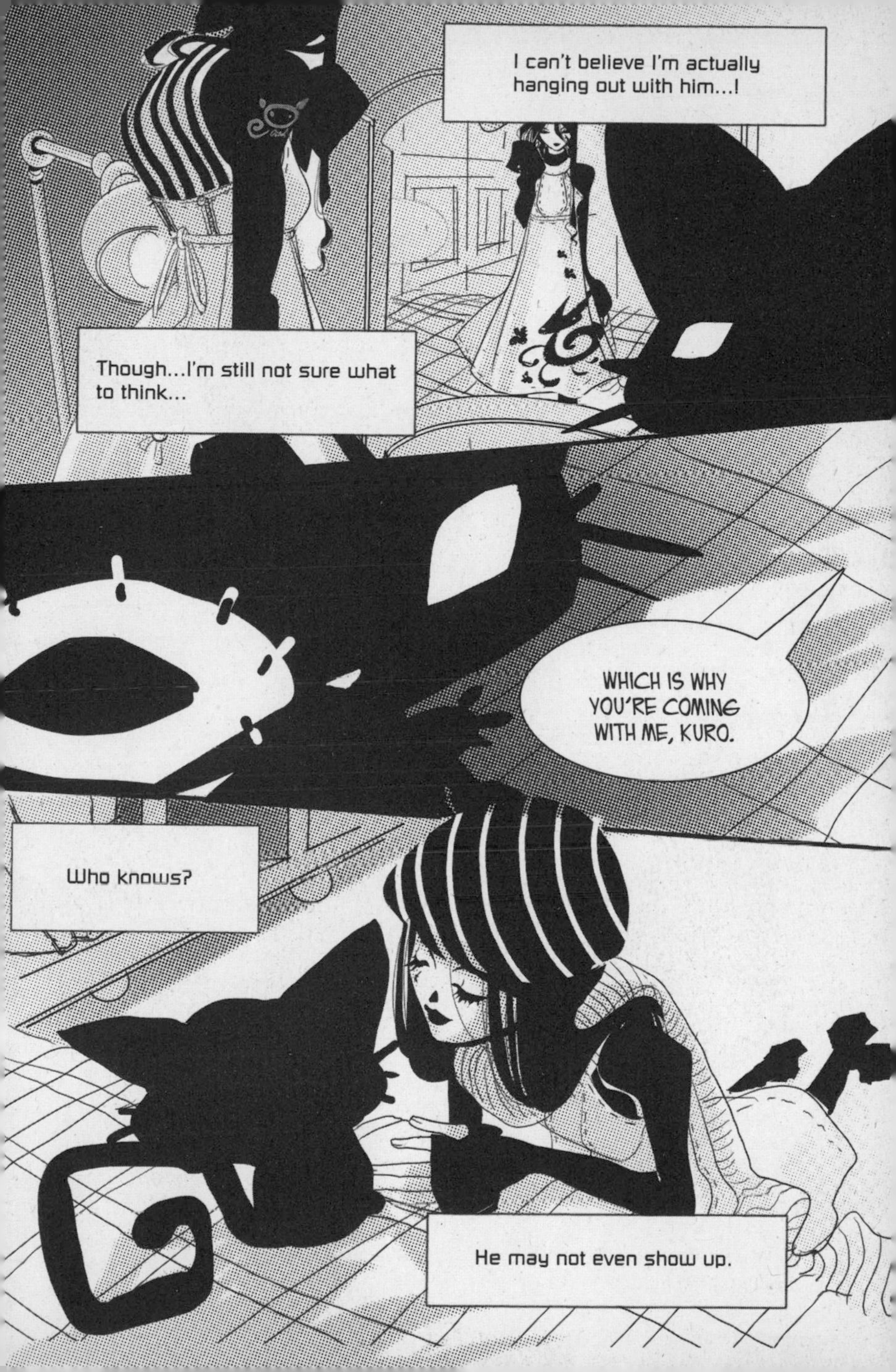
I can't believe I'm actually hanging out with him...!
Though...I'm still not sure what to think...
WHICH IS WHY YOU'RE COMING WITH ME, KURO.
Who knows?
He may not even show up.

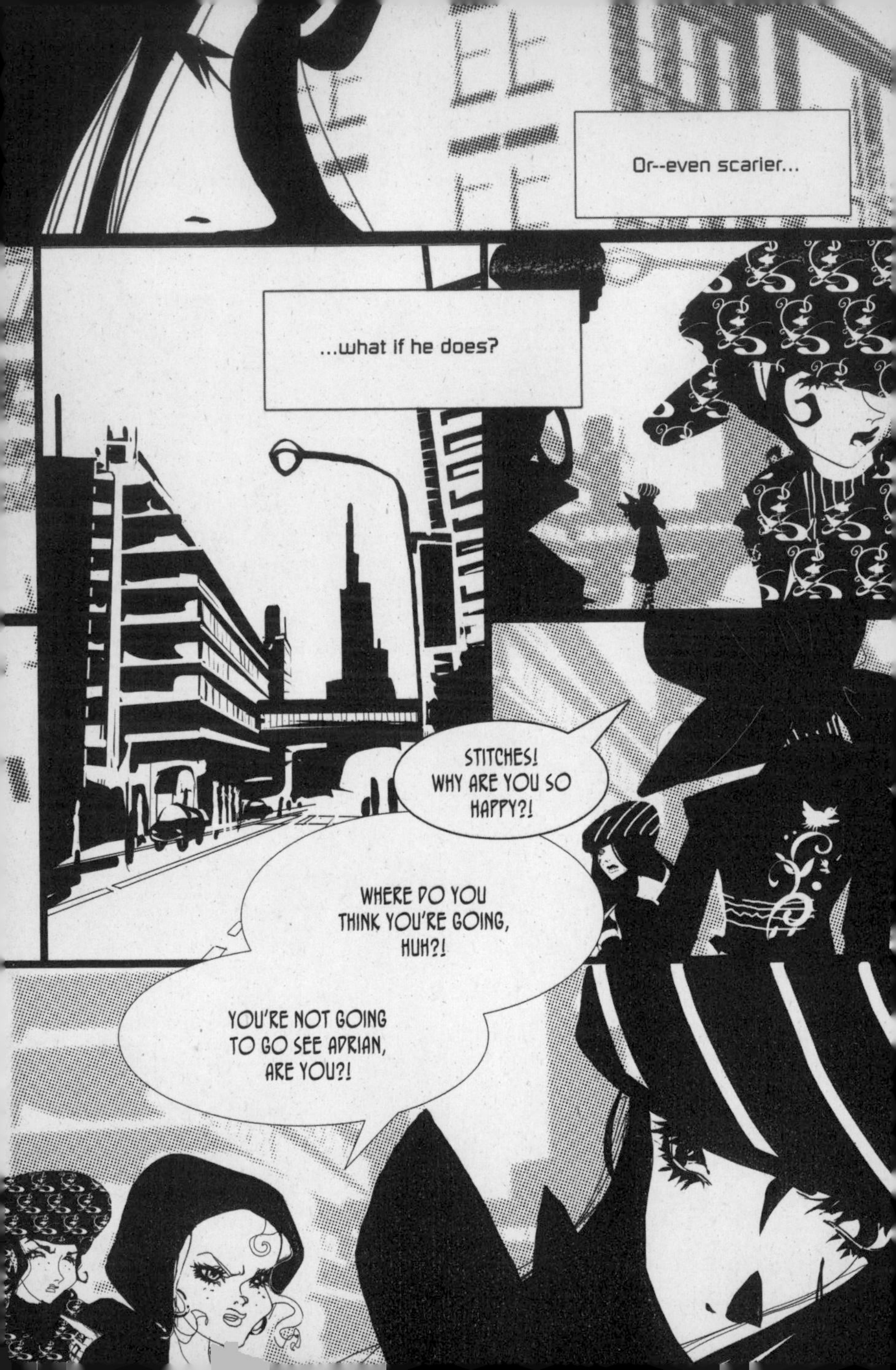
Or--even scarier...
...what if he does?
STITCHES! WHY ARE YOU SO HAPPY?!
WHERE DO YOU THINK YOU'RE GOING, HUH?!
YOU'RE NOT GOING TO GO SEE ADRIAN, ARE YOU?!

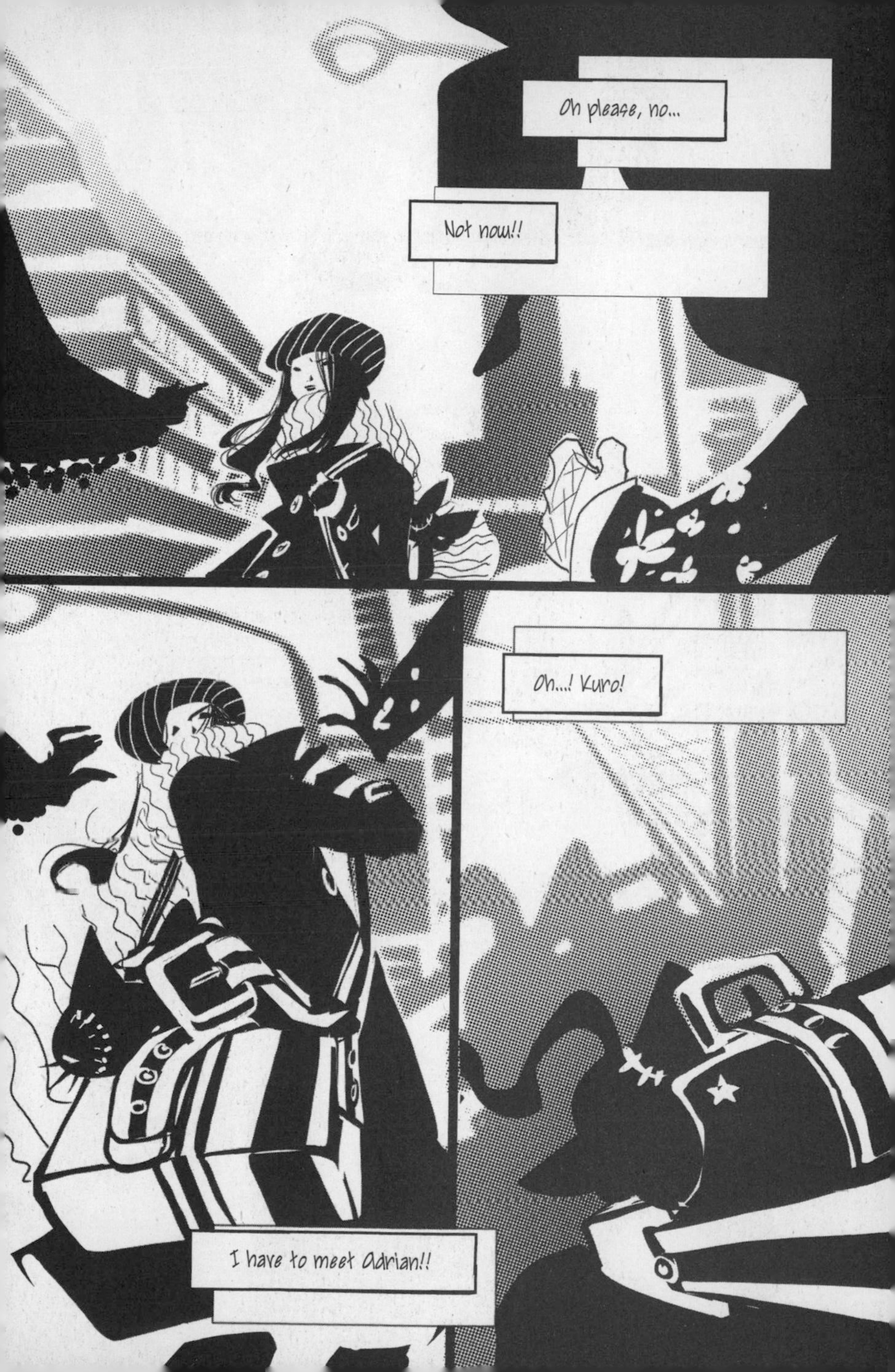
Oh please, no...
Not now!!
Oh...! Kuro!
I have to meet Adrian!!

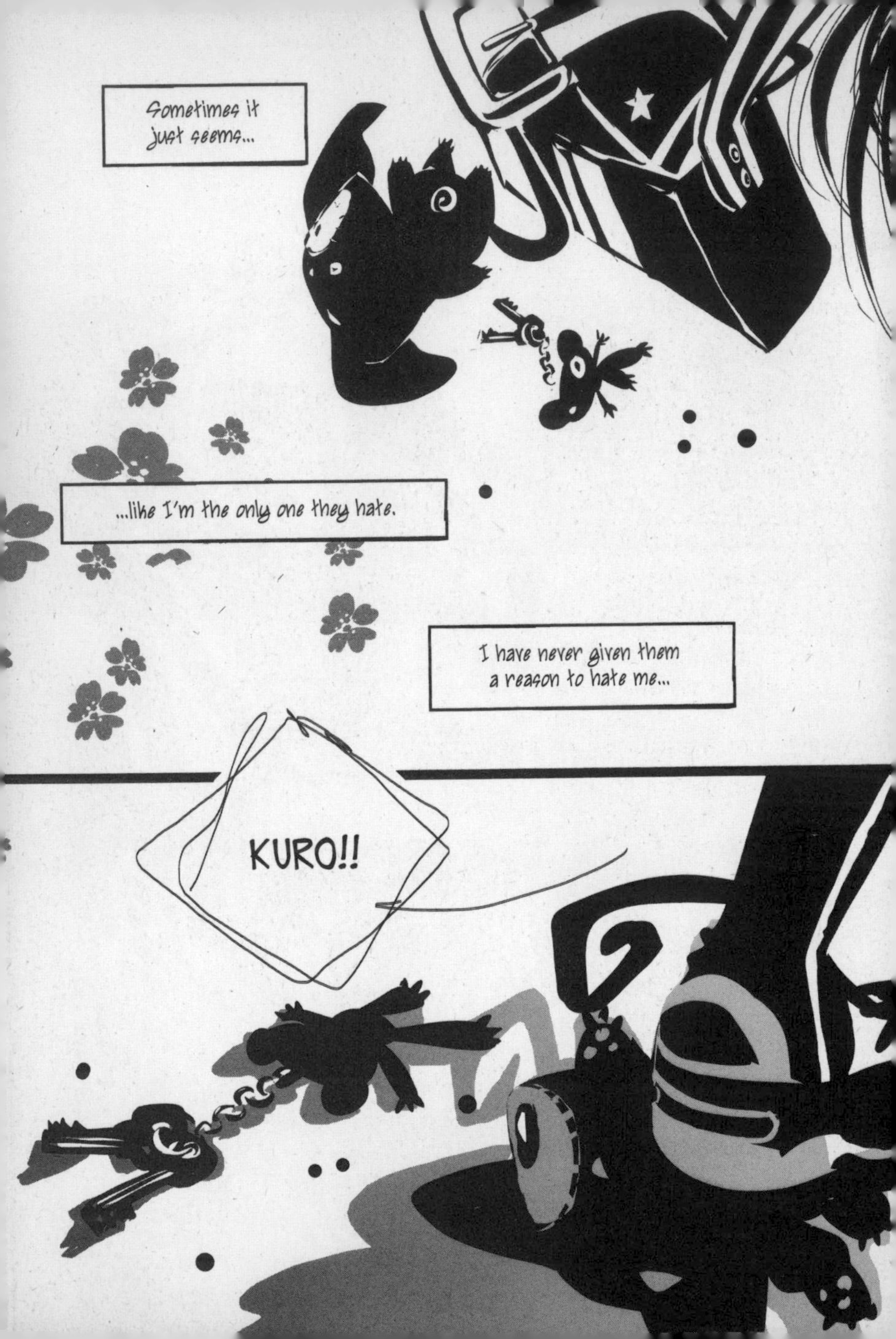
Sometimes it just seems...
...like I'm the only one they hate.
I have never given them a reason to hate me...
KURO!!

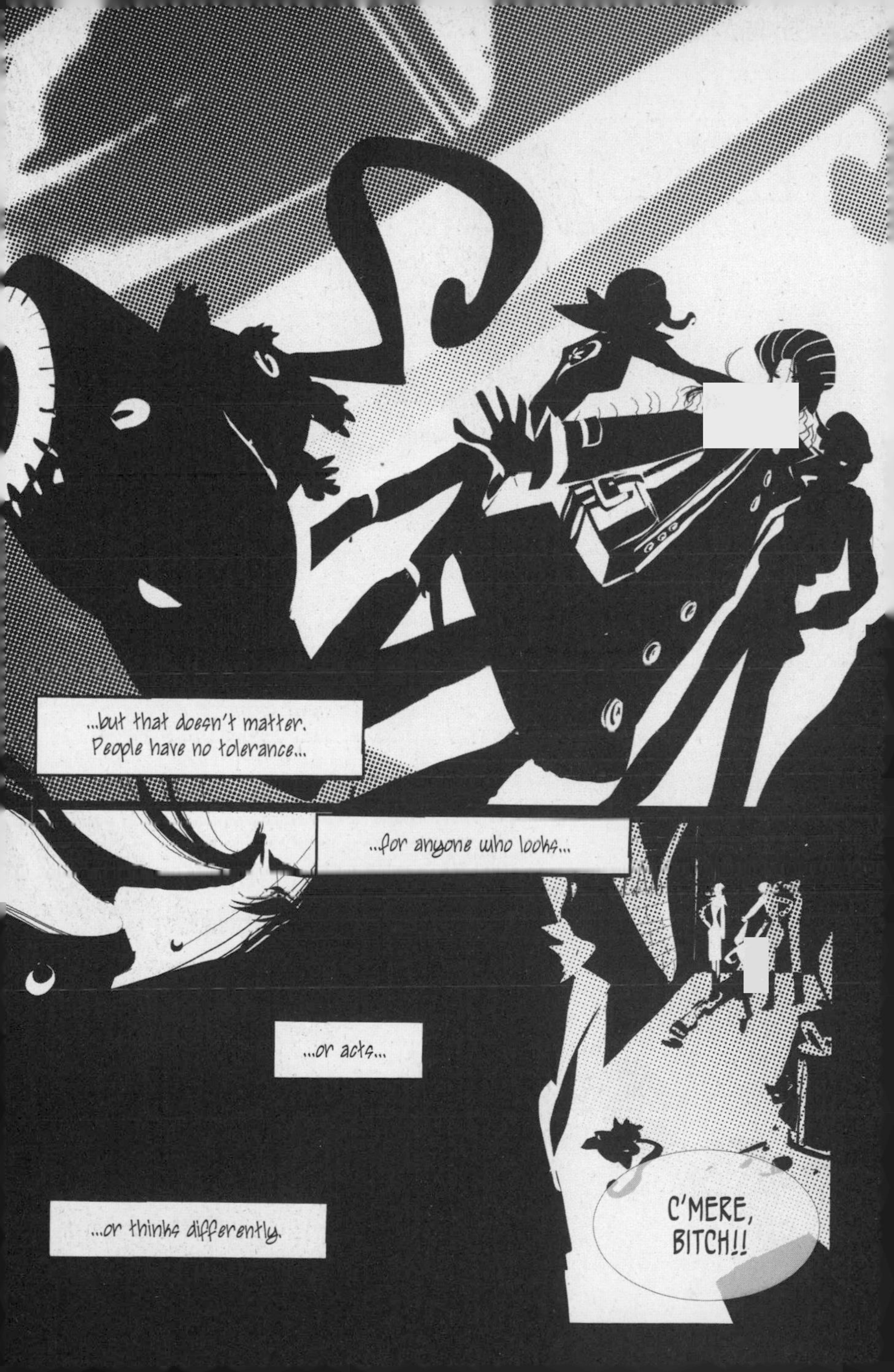
...but that doesn't matter. People have no tolerance...
...for anyone who looks...
...or acts...
...or thinks differently.
C'MERE, BITCH!!

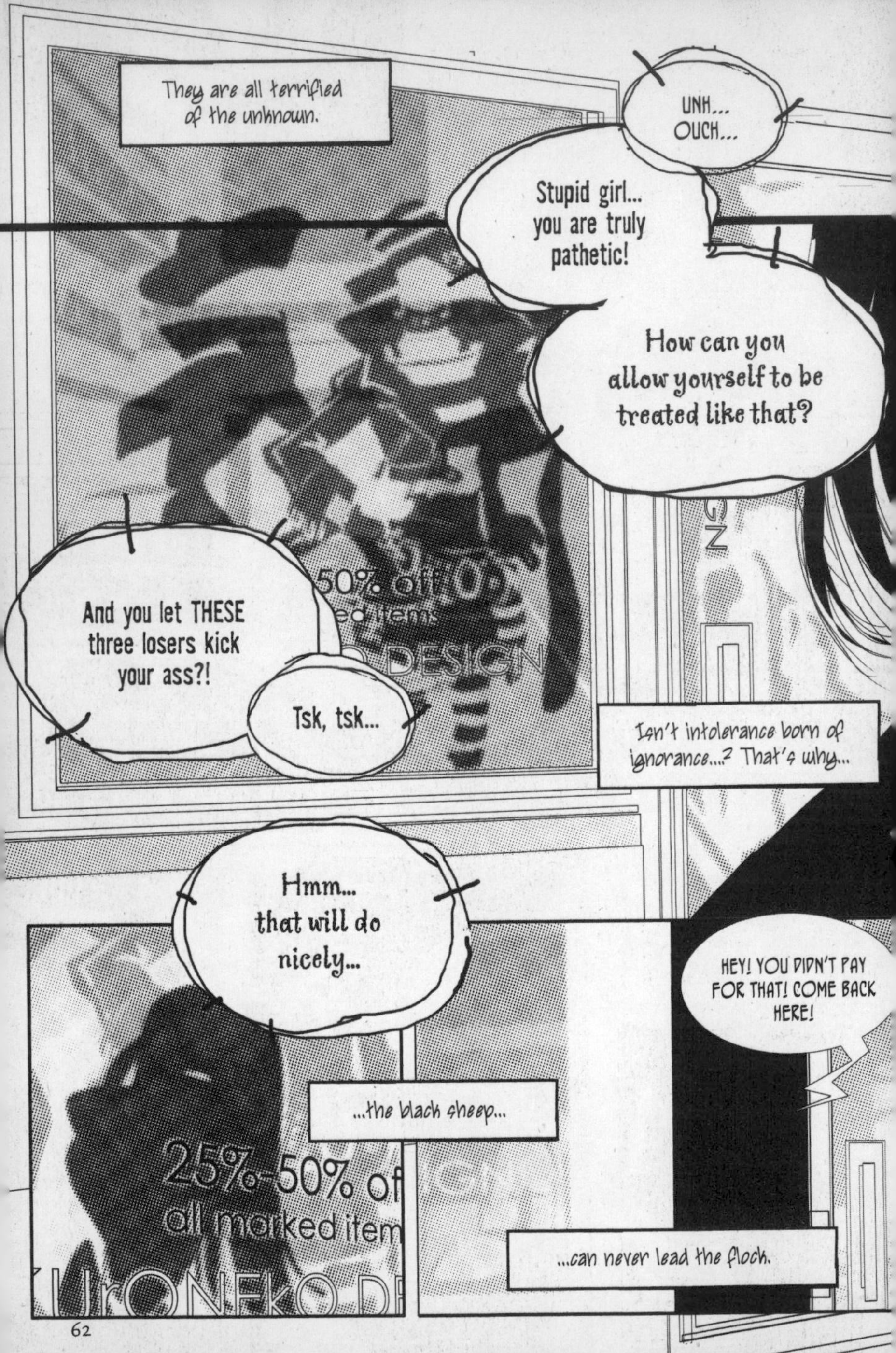
They are all terrified of the unknown.
UNH... OUCH...
Stupid girl... you are truly pathetic!
How can you allow yourself to be treated like that?
And you let THESE three losers kick your ass?!
Tsk, tsk...
Isn't intolerance born of ignorance...? That's why...
Hmm... that will do nicely...
...the black sheep...
HEY! YOU DIDN'T PAY FOR THAT! COME BACK HERE!
...can never lead the flock.

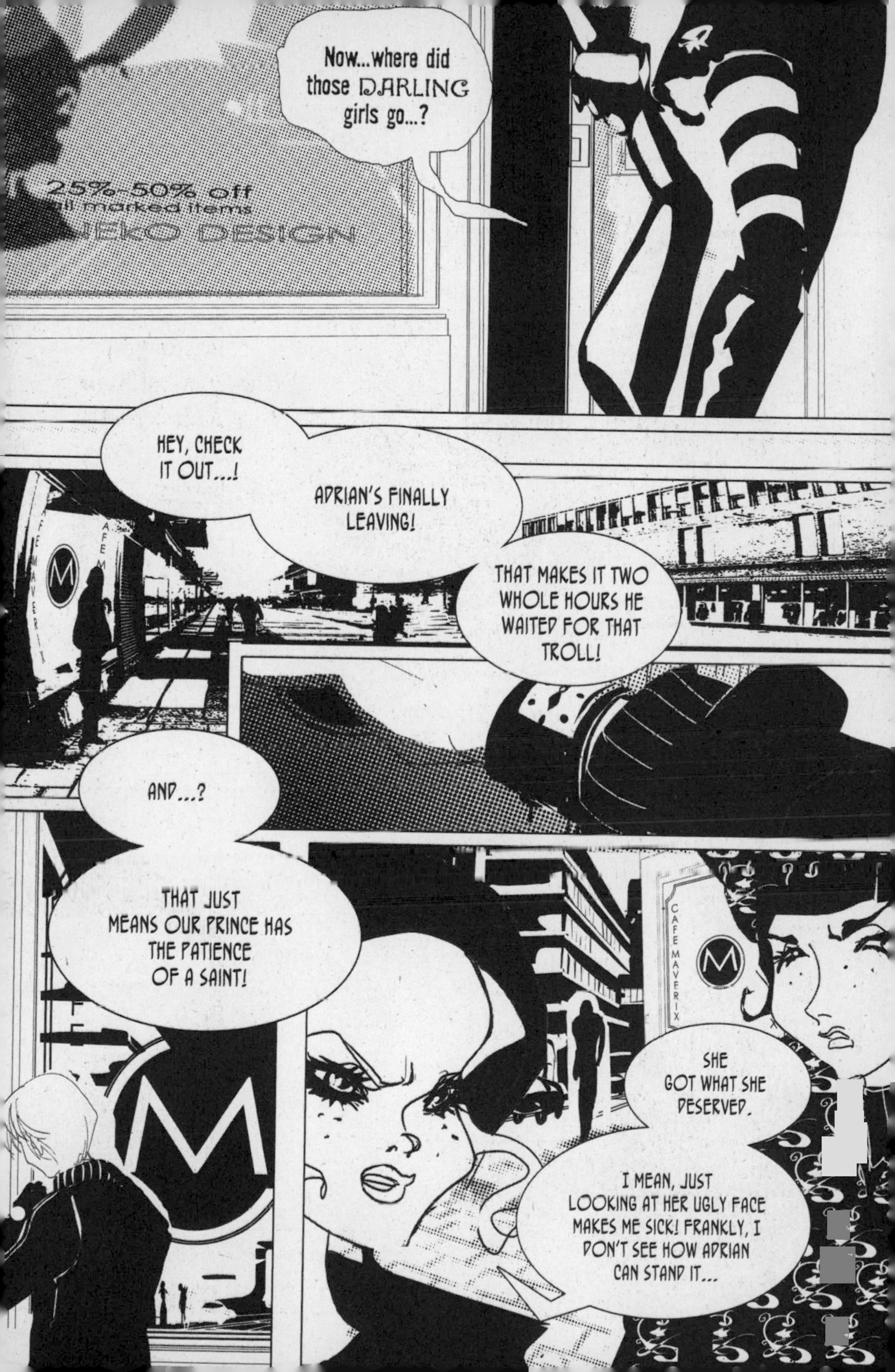
25%-50% off
Now...where did those DARLING girls go...?
HEY, CHECK IT OUT...!
ADRIAN'S FINALLY LEAVING!
THAT MAKES IT TWO WHOLE HOURS HE WAITED FOR THAT TROLL!
AND...?
THAT JUST MEANS OUR PRINCE HAS THE PATIENCE OF A SAINT!
CAFE MAVERIX
SHE GOT WHAT SHE DESERVED.
I MEAN, JUST LOOKING AT HER UGLY FACE MAKES ME SICK! FRANKLY, I DON'T SEE HOW ADRIAN CAN STAND IT...

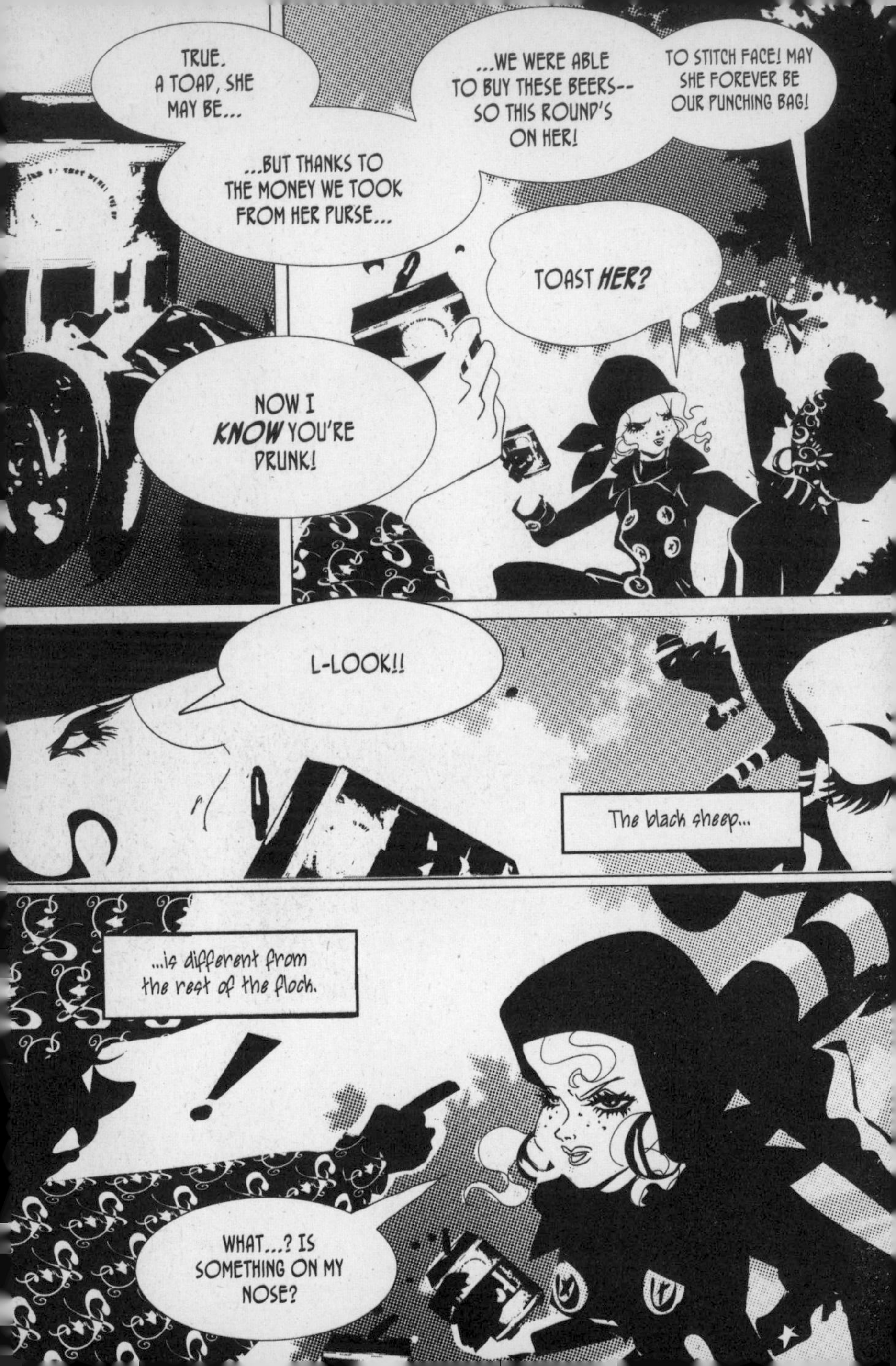
TRUE. A TOAD, SHE MAY BE...
...BUT THANKS TO THE MONEY WE TOOK FROM HER PURSE...
...WE WERE ABLE TO BUY THESE BEERS-- SO THIS ROUND'S ON HER!
TO STITCH FACE! MAY SHE FOREVER BE OUR PUNCHING BAG!
TOAST HER?
NOW I KNOW YOU'RE DRUNK!
L-LOOK!!
The black sheep...
...is different from the rest of the flock.
!
WHAT...? IS SOMETHING ON MY NOSE?

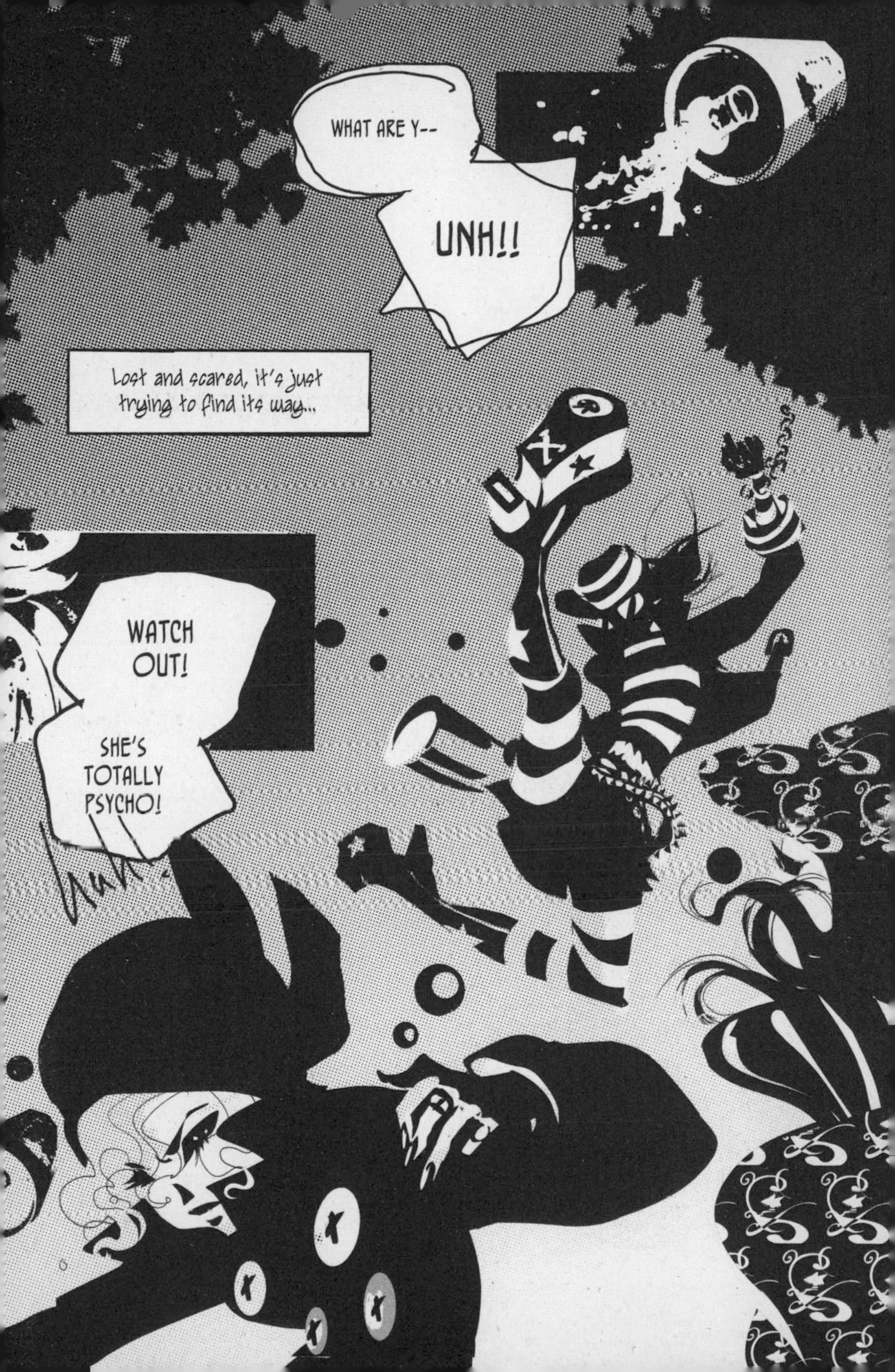
WHAT ARE Y--
UNH!!
Lost and scared, it's just trying to find its way...
WATCH OUT!
SHE'S TOTALLY PSYCHO!

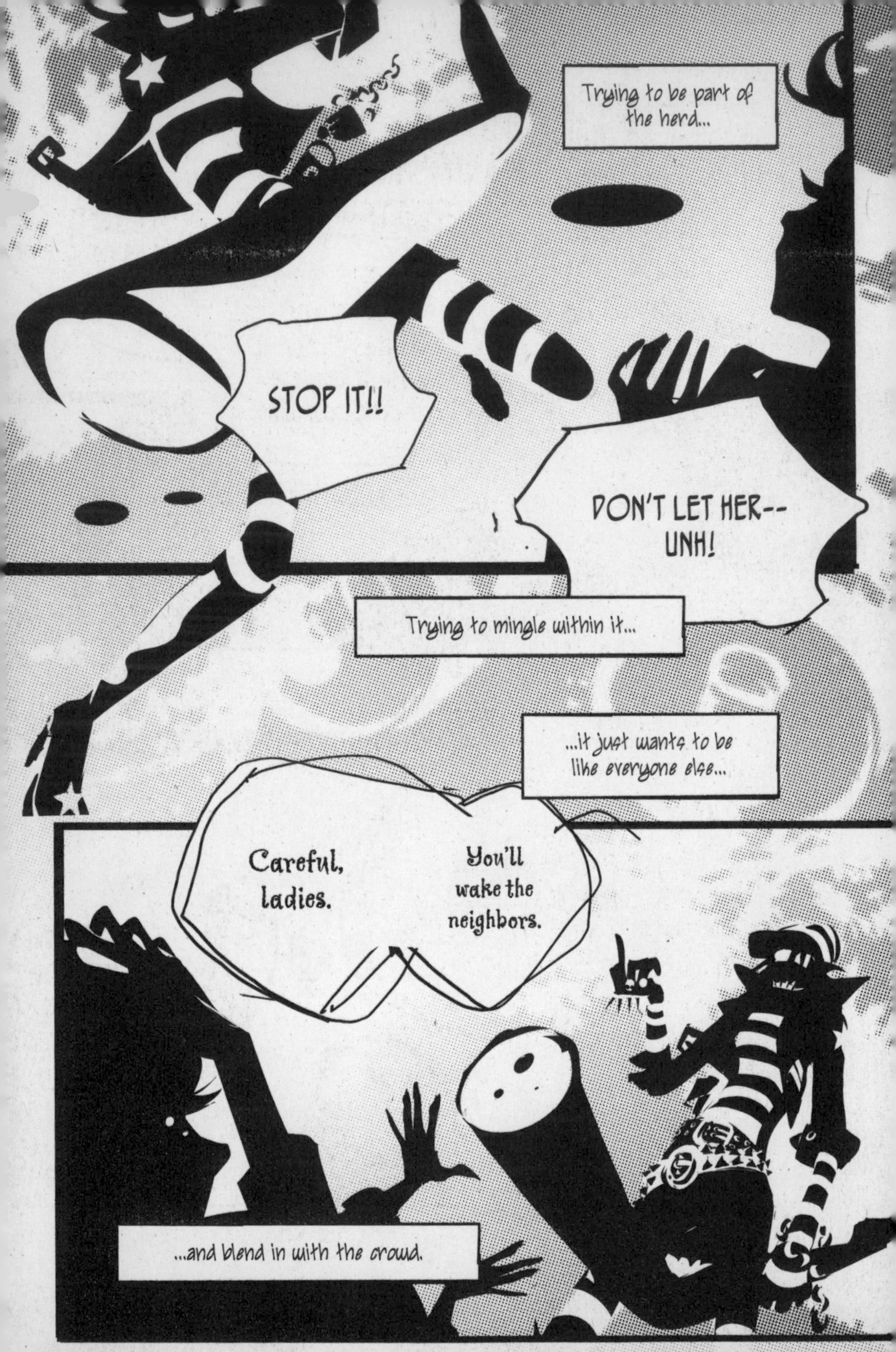
Trying to be part of the herd...
STOP IT!!
DON'T LET HER-- UNH!
Trying to mingle within it...
...it just wants to be like everyone else...
Careful, ladies.
You'll wake the neighbors.
...and blend in with the crowd.

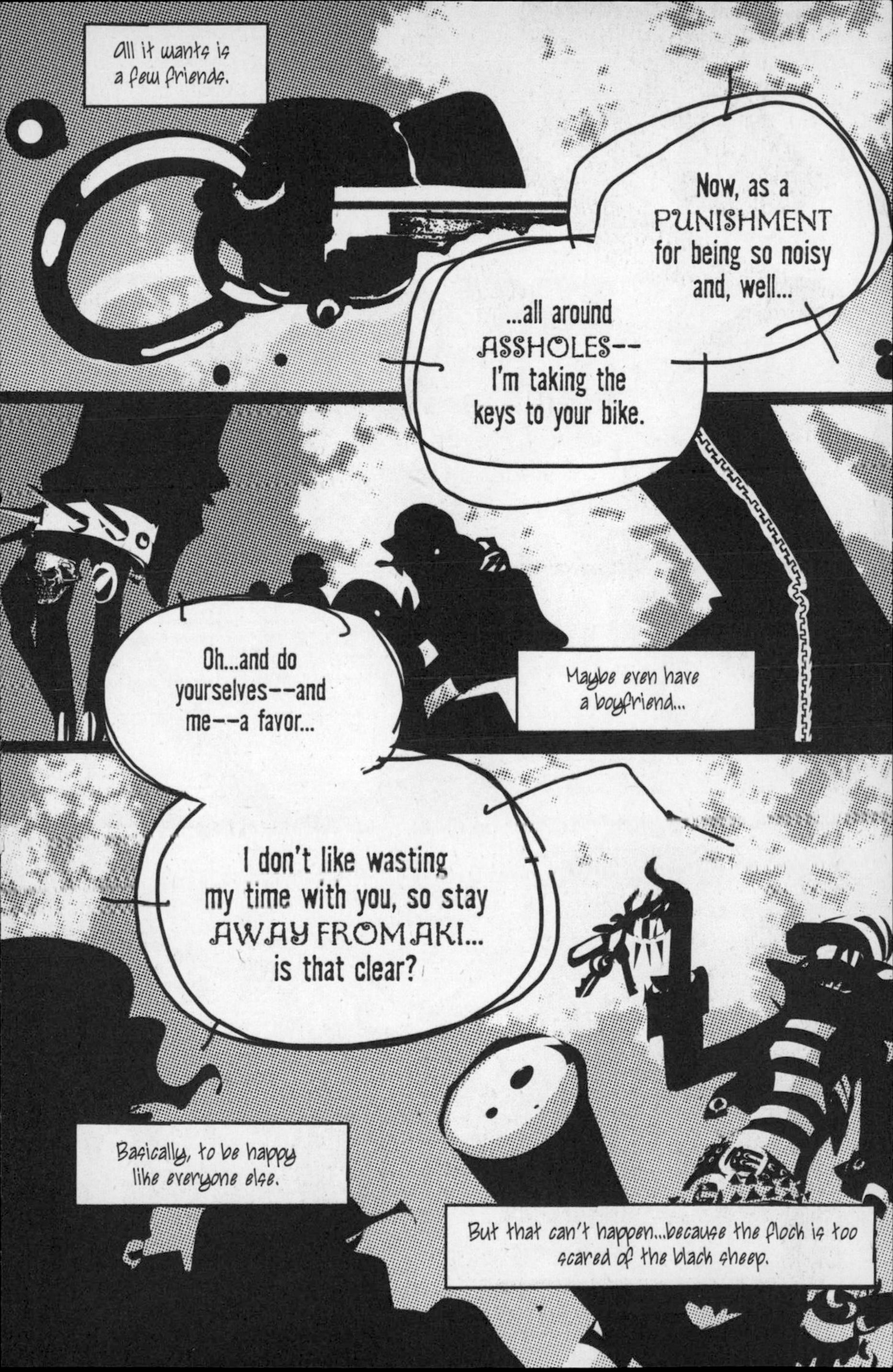
All it wants is a few friends.
Now, as a PUNISHMENT for being so noisy and, well...
...all around ASSHOLES-- I'm taking the keys to your bike.
Maybe even have a boyfriend...
Oh...and do yourselves--and me--a favor...
I don't like wasting my time with you, so stay AWAY FROM AKI... is that clear?
Basically, to be happy like everyone else.
But that can't happen...because the flock is too scared of the black sheep.

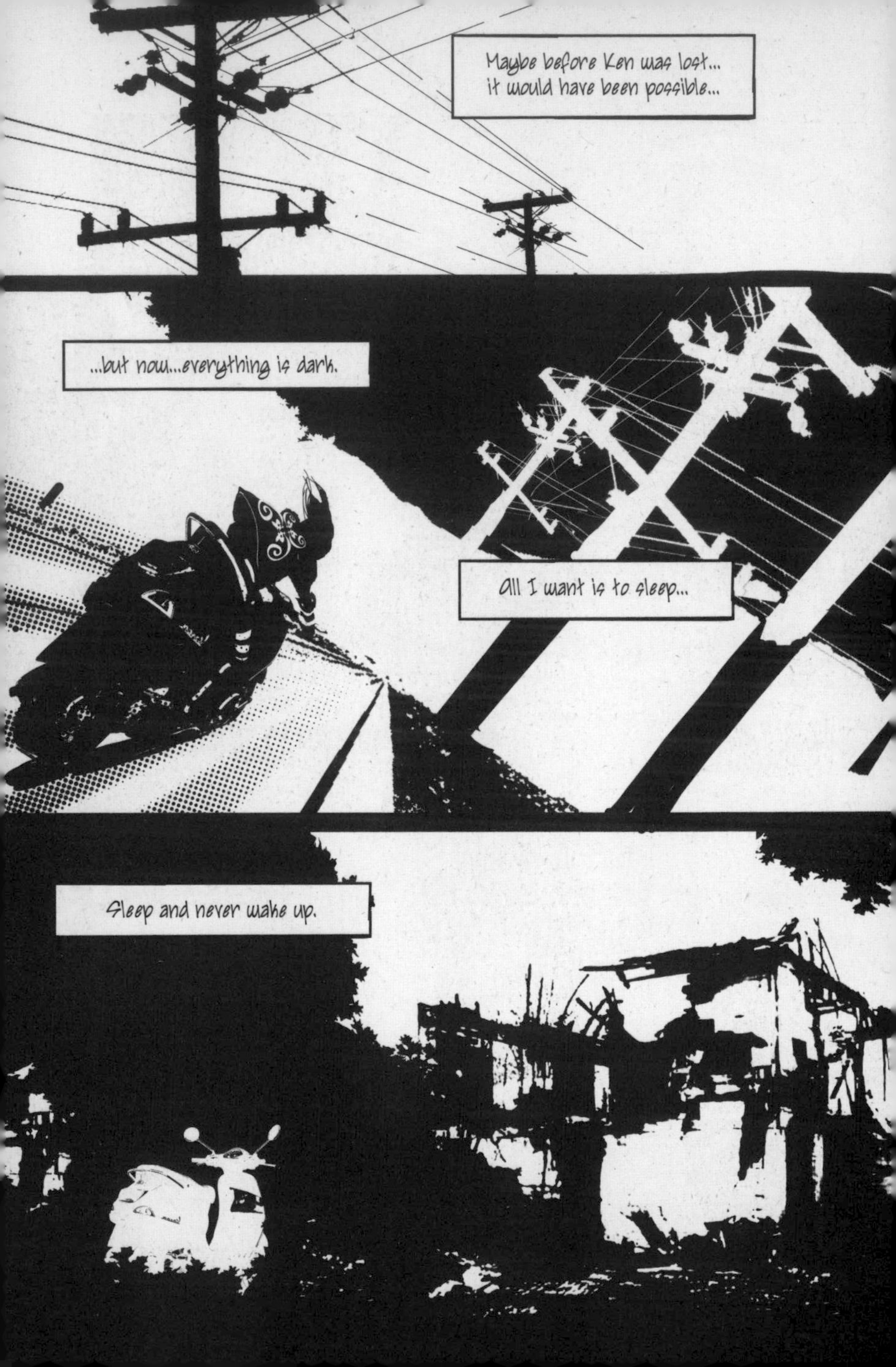
Maybe before Ken was lost...
it would have been possible...
...but now...everything is dark.
All I want is to sleep...
Sleep and never wake up.

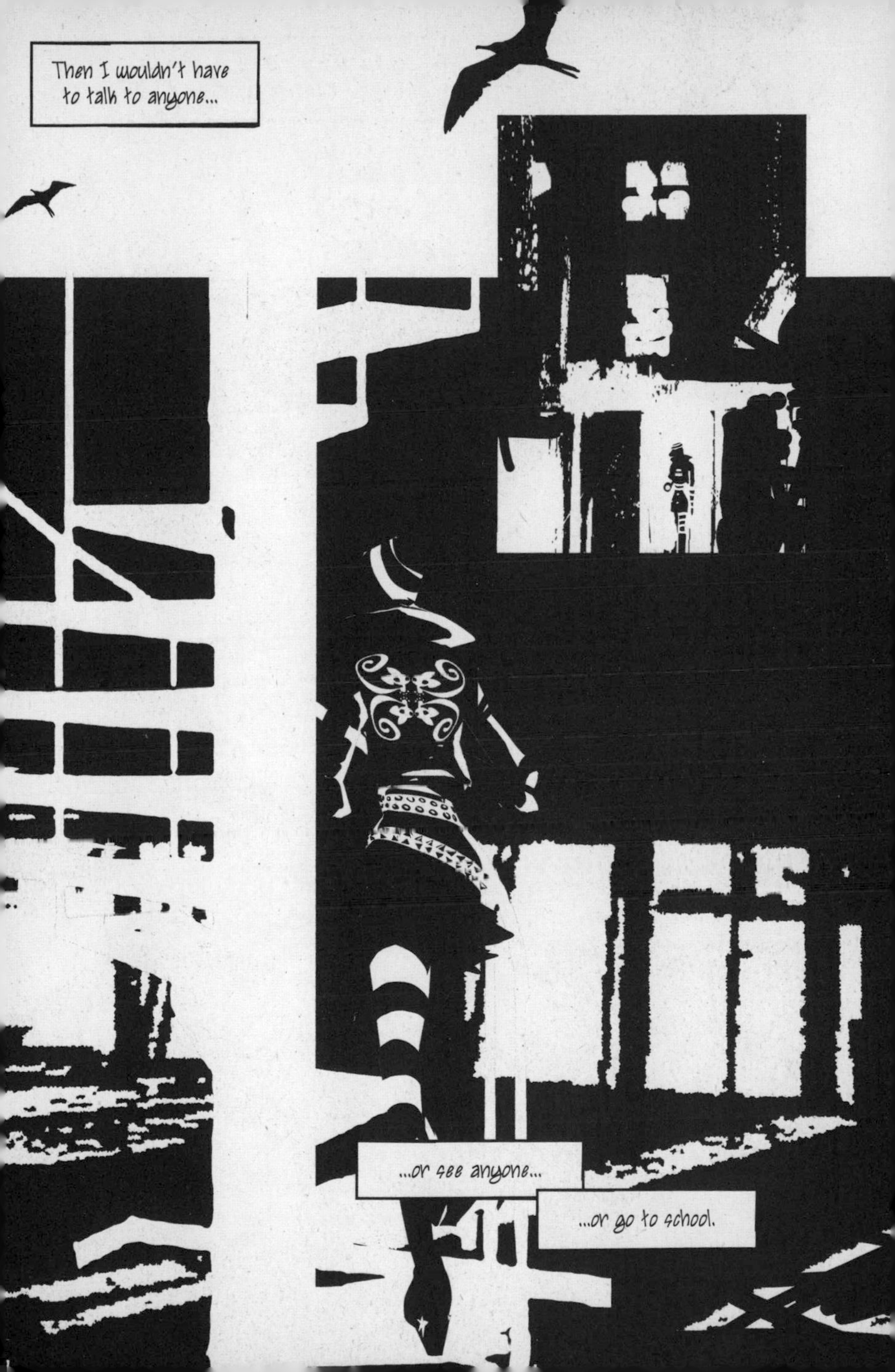
Then I wouldn't have to talk to anyone...
...or see anyone...
...or go to school.

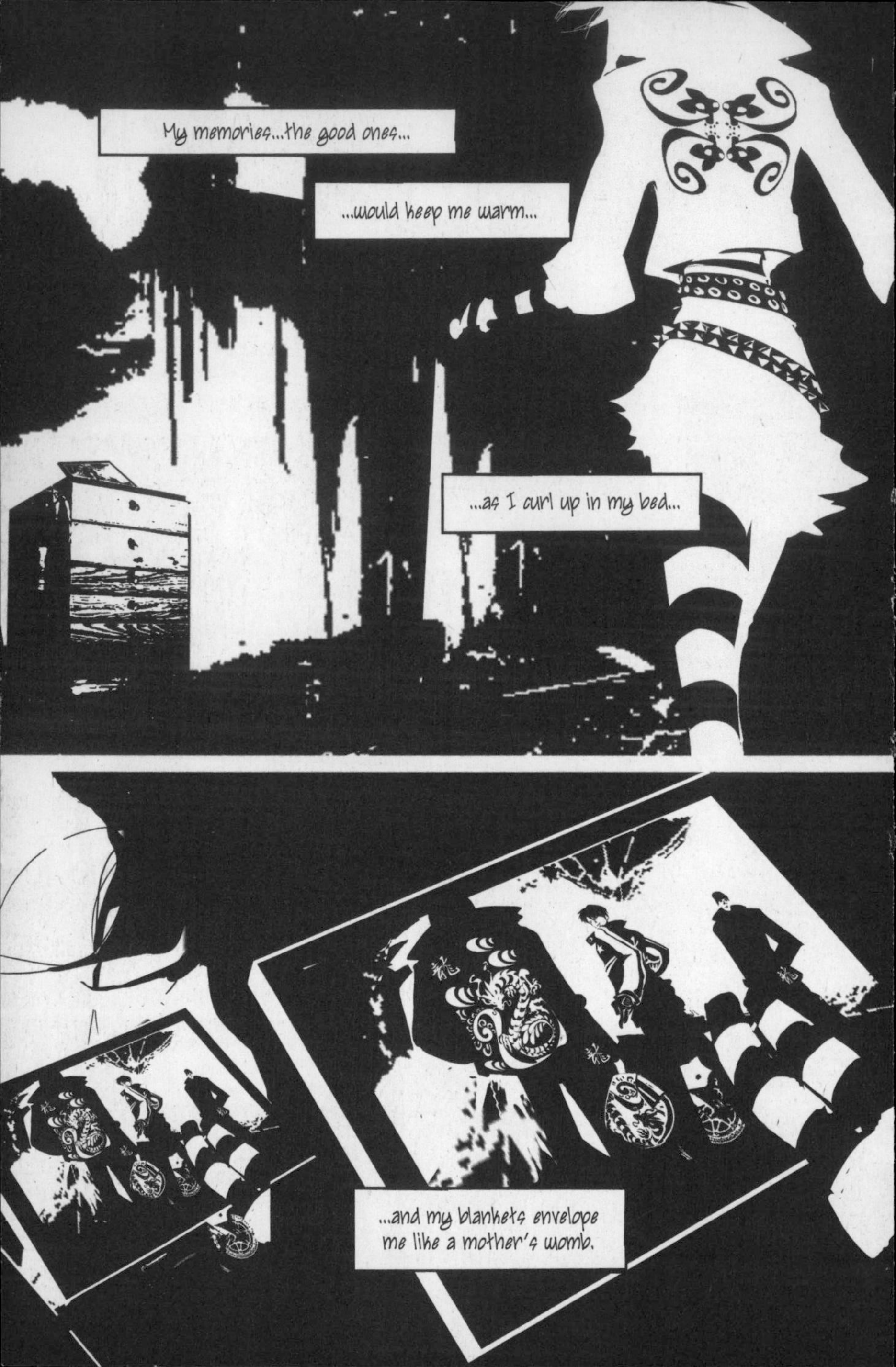
My memories...the good ones...
...would keep me warm...
...as I curl up in my bed...
...and my blankets envelope me like a mother's womb.

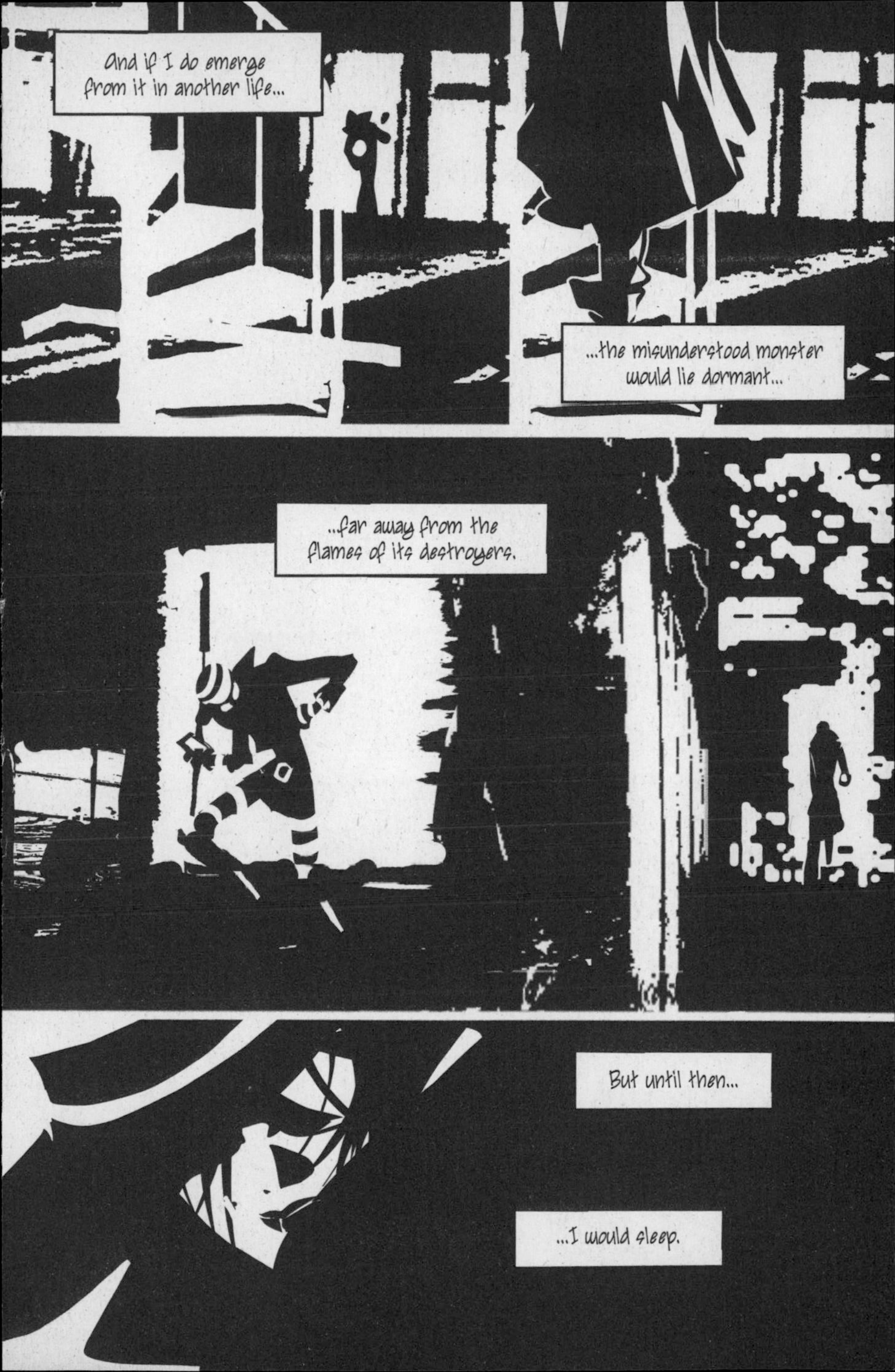
And if I do emerge from it in another life...
...the misunderstood monster would lie dormant...
...far away from the flames of its destroyers.
But until then...
...I would sleep.

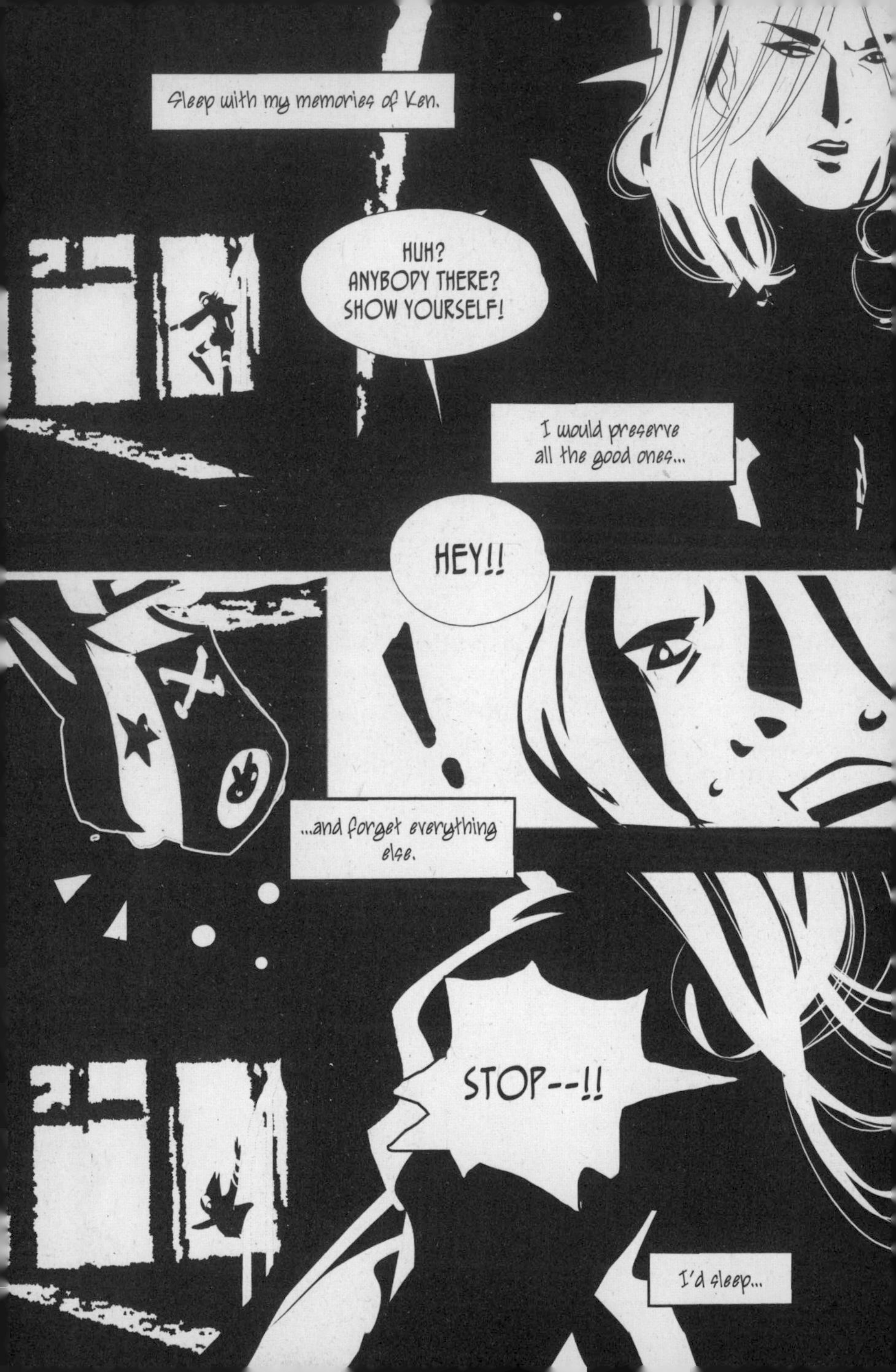
Sleep with my memories of Ken.
HUH? ANYBODY THERE? SHOW YOURSELF!
I would preserve all the good ones...
HEY!!
...and forget everything else.
STOP--!!
I'd sleep...

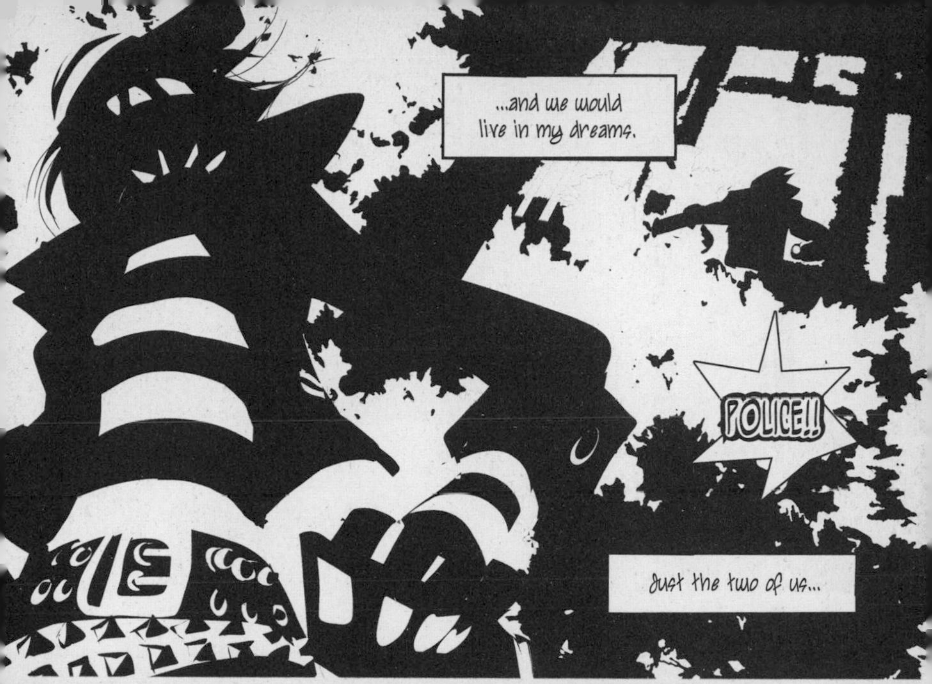
...and we would live in my dreams.
POLICE!!
Just the two of us...
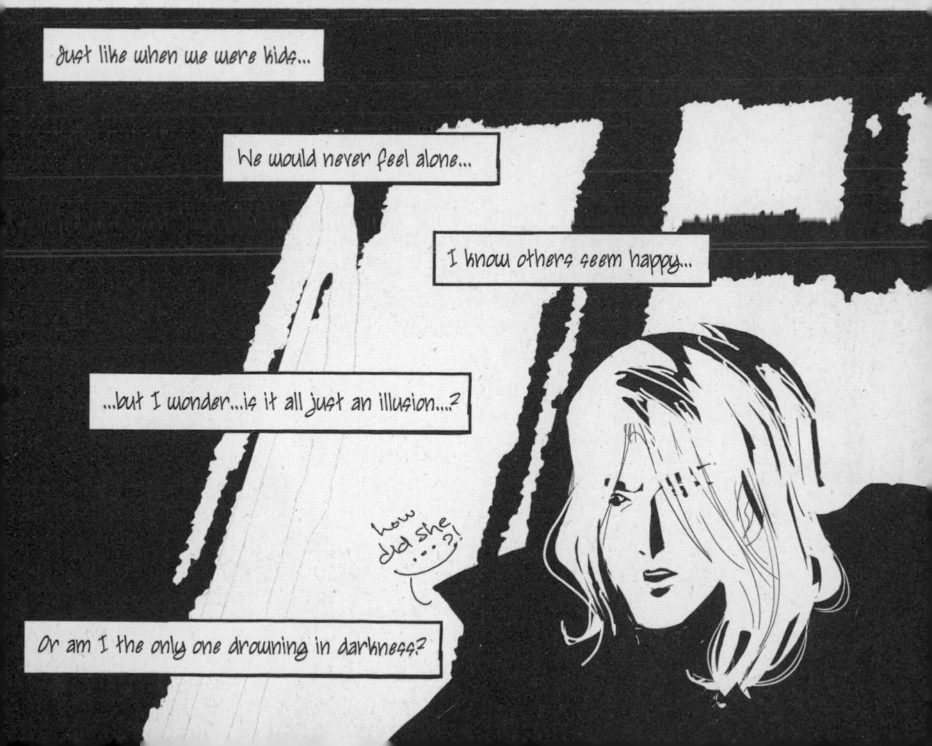
Just like when we were kids...
We would never feel alone...
I know others seem happy...
...but I wonder...is it all just an illusion....?
how did she...?!
Or am I the only one drowning in darkness?

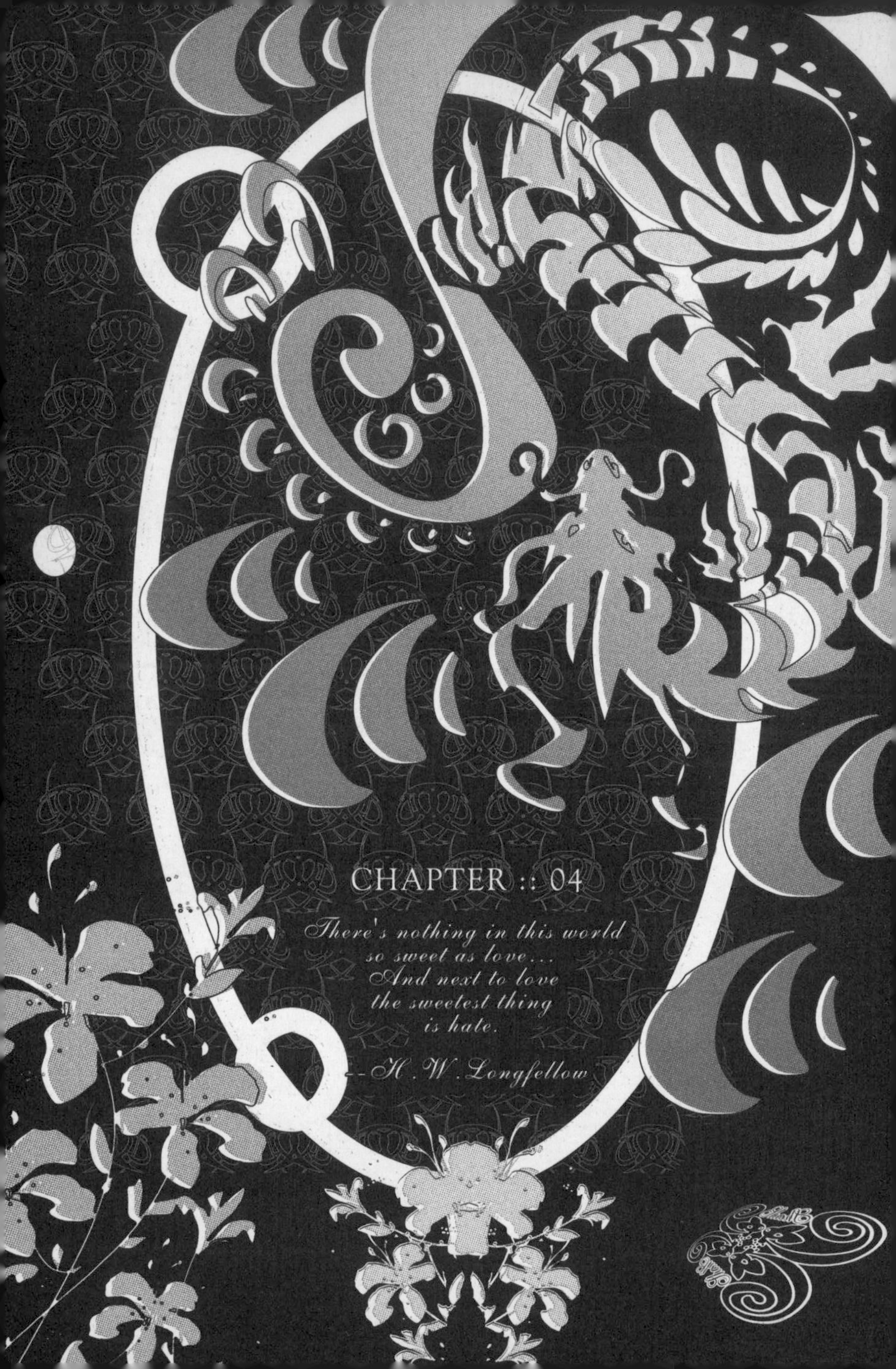
CHAPTER :: 04
There's nothing in this world
so sweet as love...
And next to love
the sweetest thing
is hate.
--H. W. Longfellow

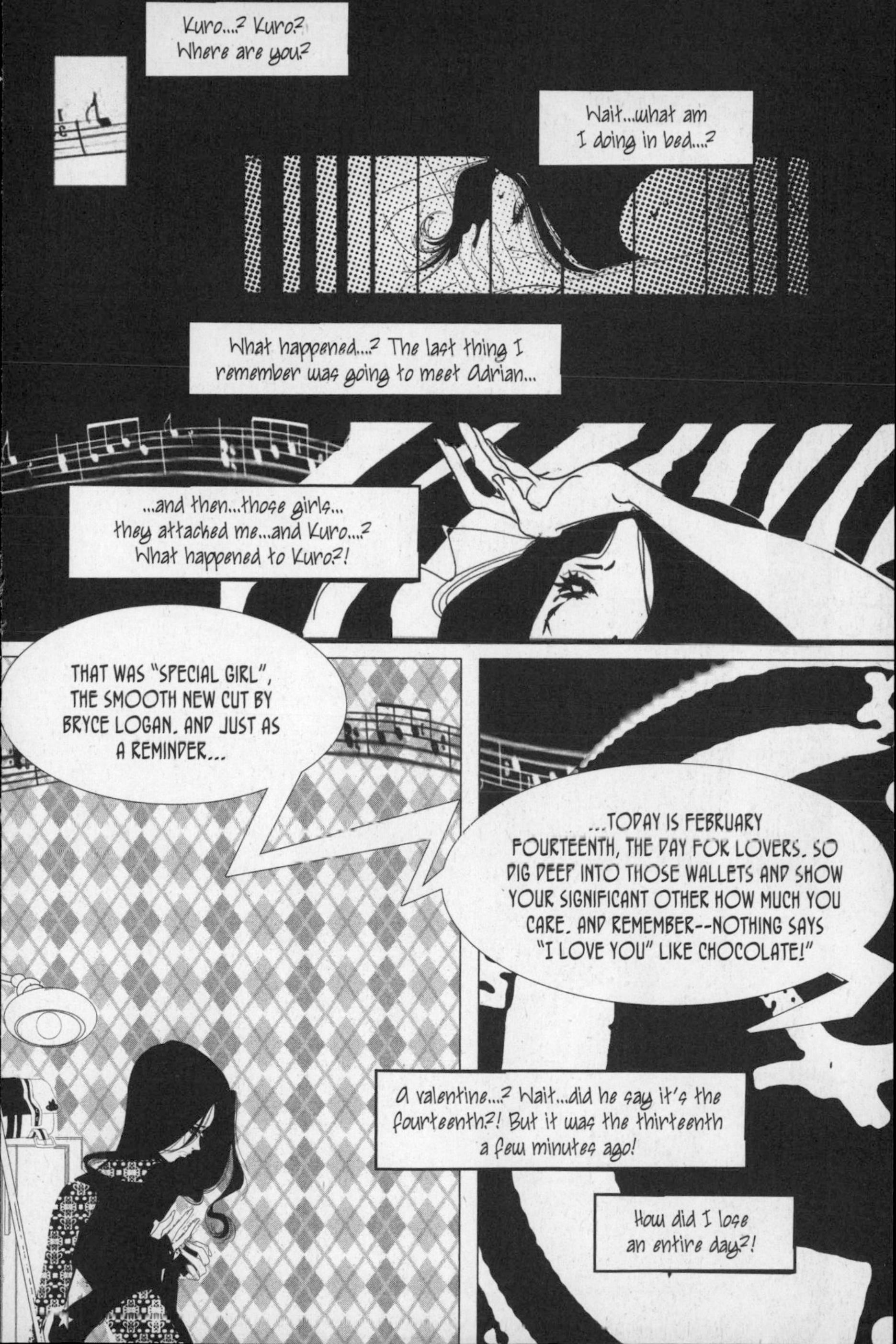
Kuro...? Kuro? Where are you?
Wait...what am I doing in bed...?
What happened...? The last thing I remember was going to meet Adrian...
...and then...those girls... they attached me...and Kuro...? What happened to Kuro?!
THAT WAS "SPECIAL GIRL", THE SMOOTH NEW CUT BY BRYCE LOGAN. AND JUST AS A REMINDER...
...TODAY IS FEBRUARY FOURTEENTH, THE DAY FOK LOVERS. SO DIG DEEF INTO THOSE WALLETS AND SHOW YOUR SIGNIFICANT OTHER HOW MUCH YOU CARE. AND REMEMBER--NOTHING SAYS "I LOVE YOU" LIKE CHOCOLATE!"
A valentine...? Wait...did he say it's the fourteenth?! But it was the thirteenth a few minutes ago!
How did I lose an entire day?!

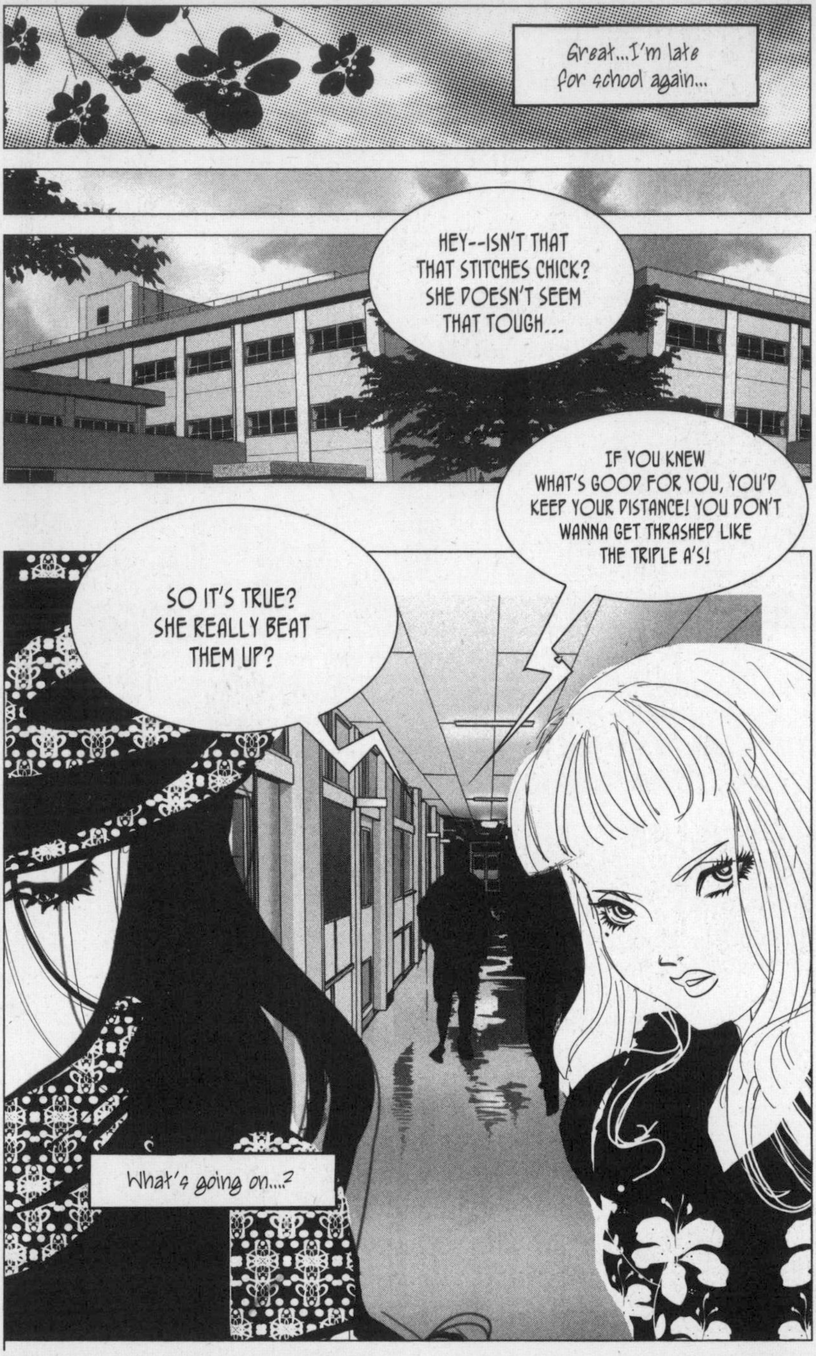
Great...I'm late for school again...
HEY--ISN'T THAT THAT STITCHES CHICK? SHE DOESN'T SEEM THAT TOUGH...
IF YOU KNEW WHAT'S GOOD FOR YOU, YOU'D KEEP YOUR DISTANCE! YOU DON'T WANNA GET THRASHED LIKE THE TRIPLE A'S!
SO IT'S TRUE? SHE REALLY BEAT THEM UP?
What's going on...?

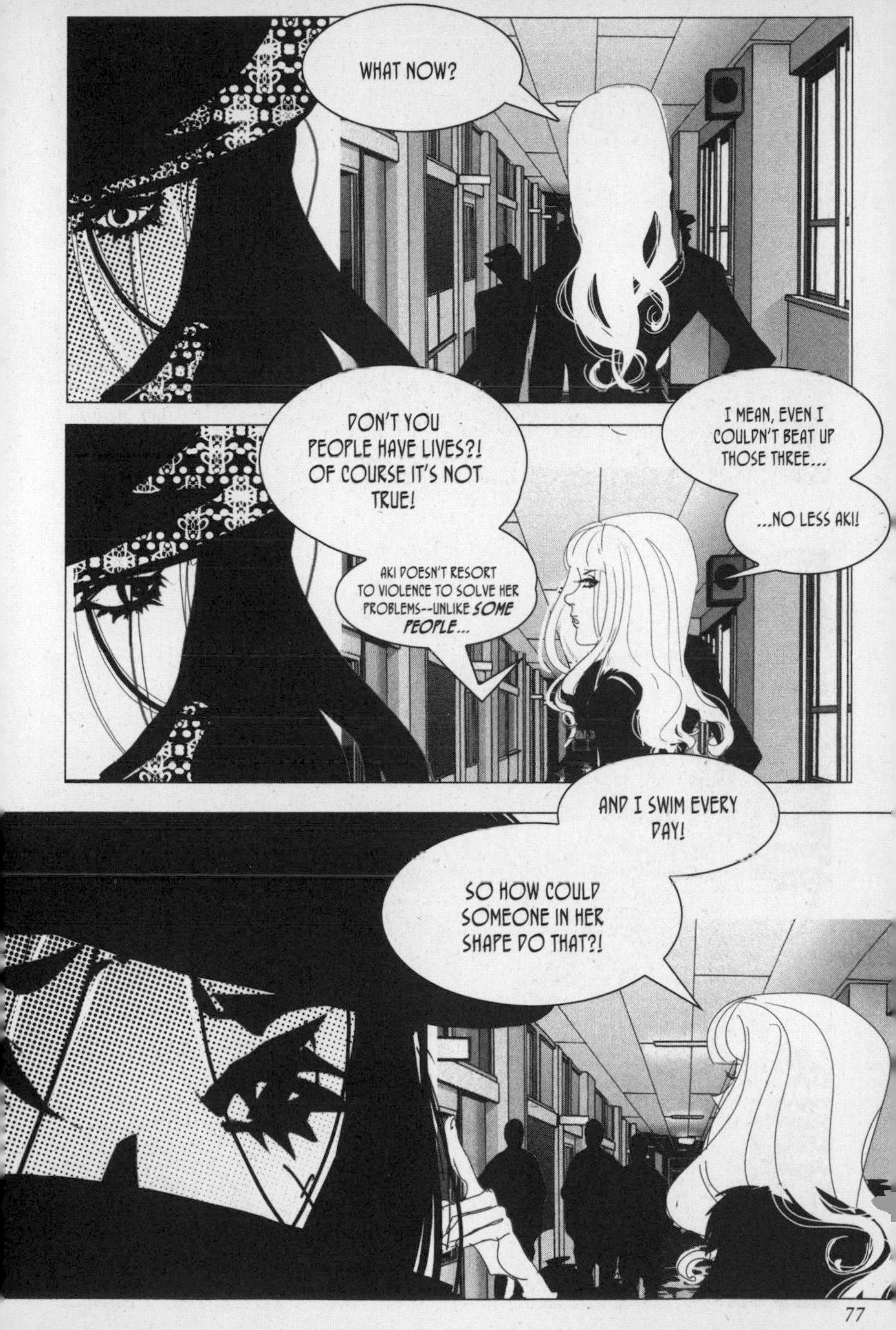
WHAT NOW?
DON'T YOU PEOPLE HAVE LIVES?! OF COURSE IT'S NOT TRUE!
AKI DOESN'T RESORT TO VIOLENCE TO SOLVE HER PROBLEMS--UNLIKE *SOME PEOPLE*...
I MEAN, EVEN I COULDN'T BEAT UP THOSE THREE...
...NO LESS AKI!
AND I SWIM EVERY DAY!
SO HOW COULD SOMEONE IN HER SHAPE DO THAT?!

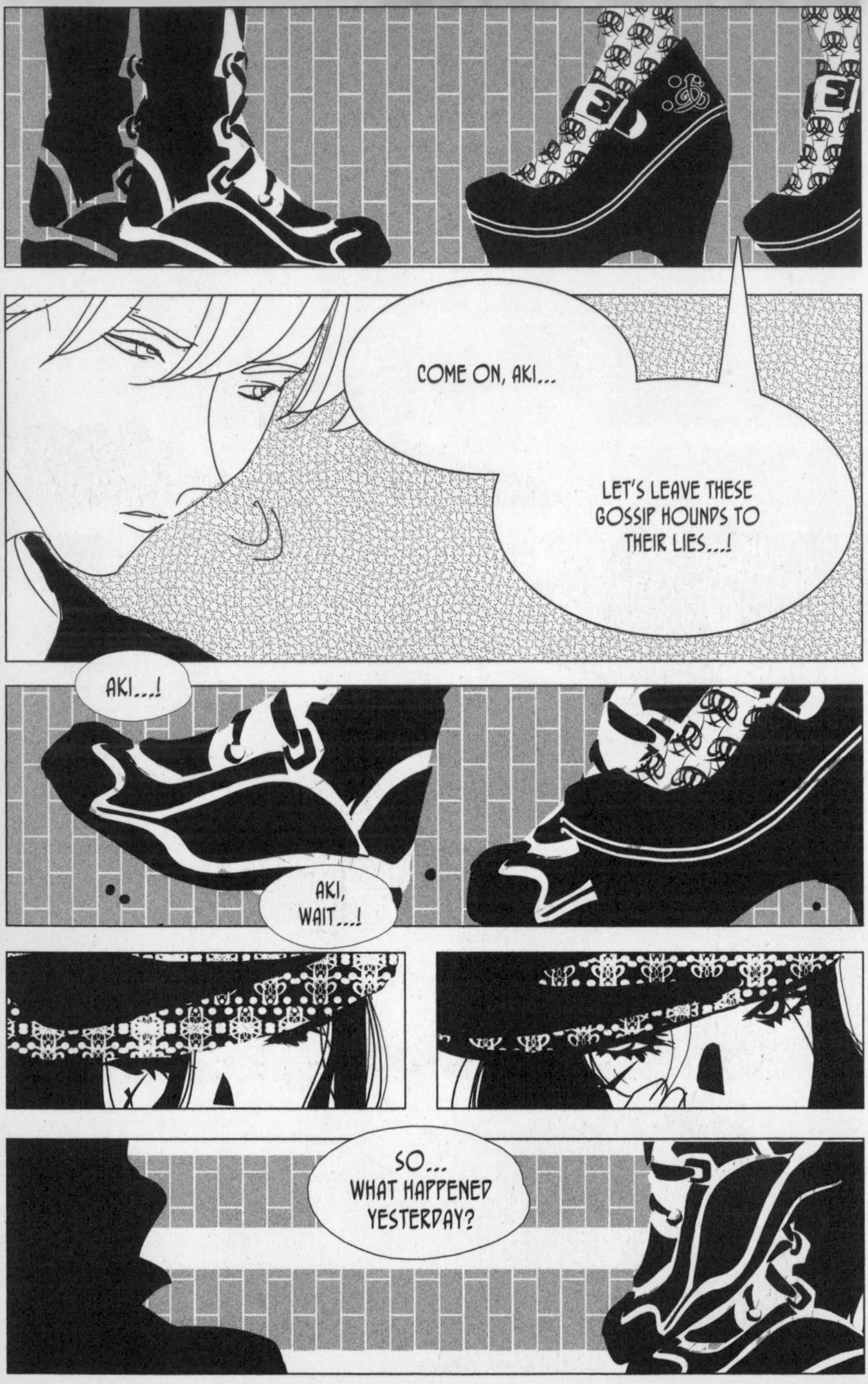
COME ON, AKI...
LET'S LEAVE THESE GOSSIP HOUNDS TO THEIR LIES...!
AKI...!
AKI, WAIT...!
SO... WHAT HAPPENED YESTERDAY?

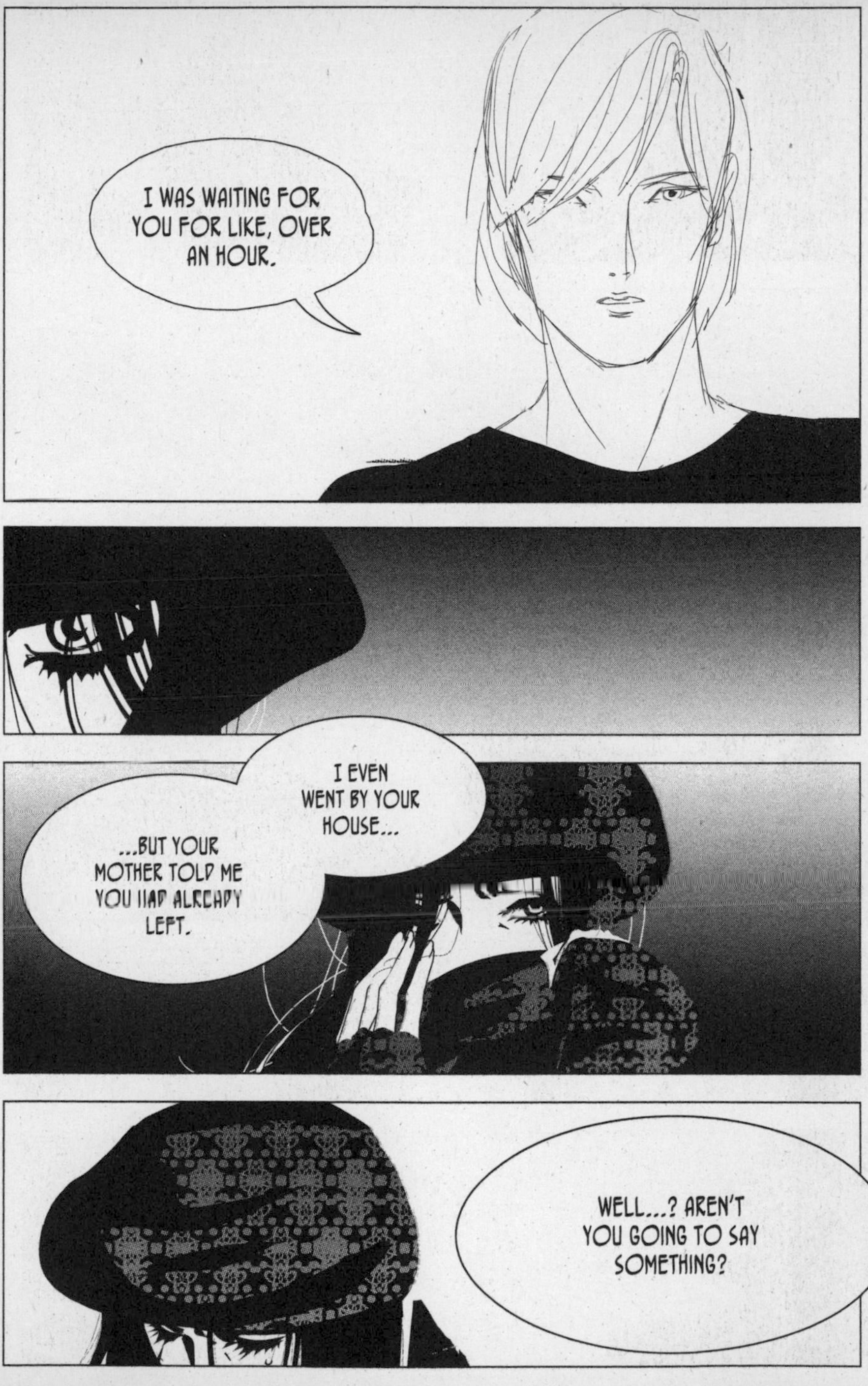
I WAS WAITING FOR YOU FOR LIKE, OVER AN HOUR.
I EVEN WENT BY YOUR HOUSE...
...BUT YOUR MOTHER TOLD ME YOU HAD ALREADY LEFT.
WELL...? AREN'T YOU GOING TO SAY SOMETHING?

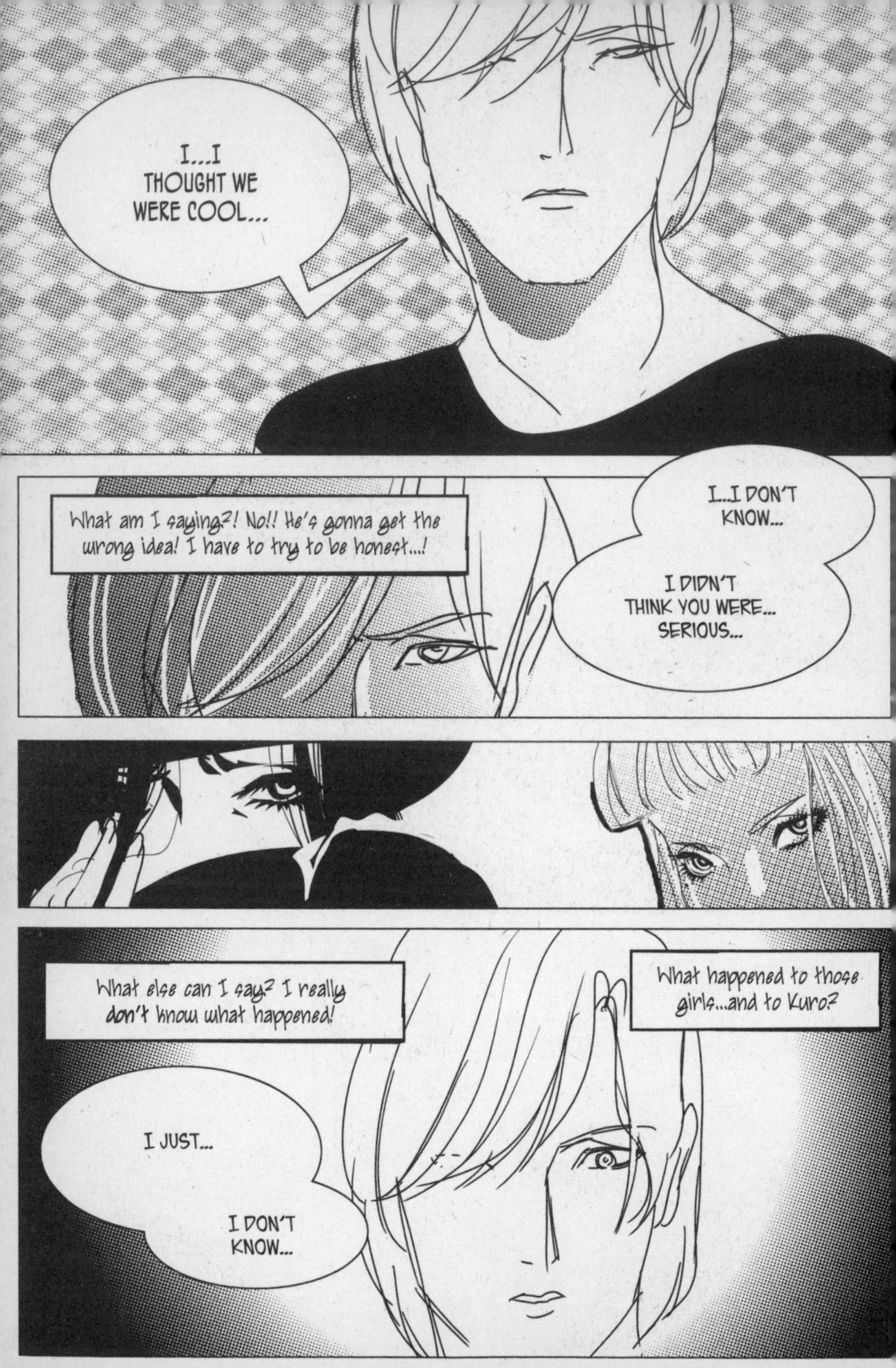
I...I THOUGHT WE WERE COOL...
What am I saying?! No!! He's gonna get the wrong idea! I have to try to be honest...!
I...I DON'T KNOW...
I DIDN'T THINK YOU WERE... SERIOUS...
What else can I say? I really don't know what happened!
What happened to those girls...and to Kuro?
I JUST...
I DON'T KNOW...

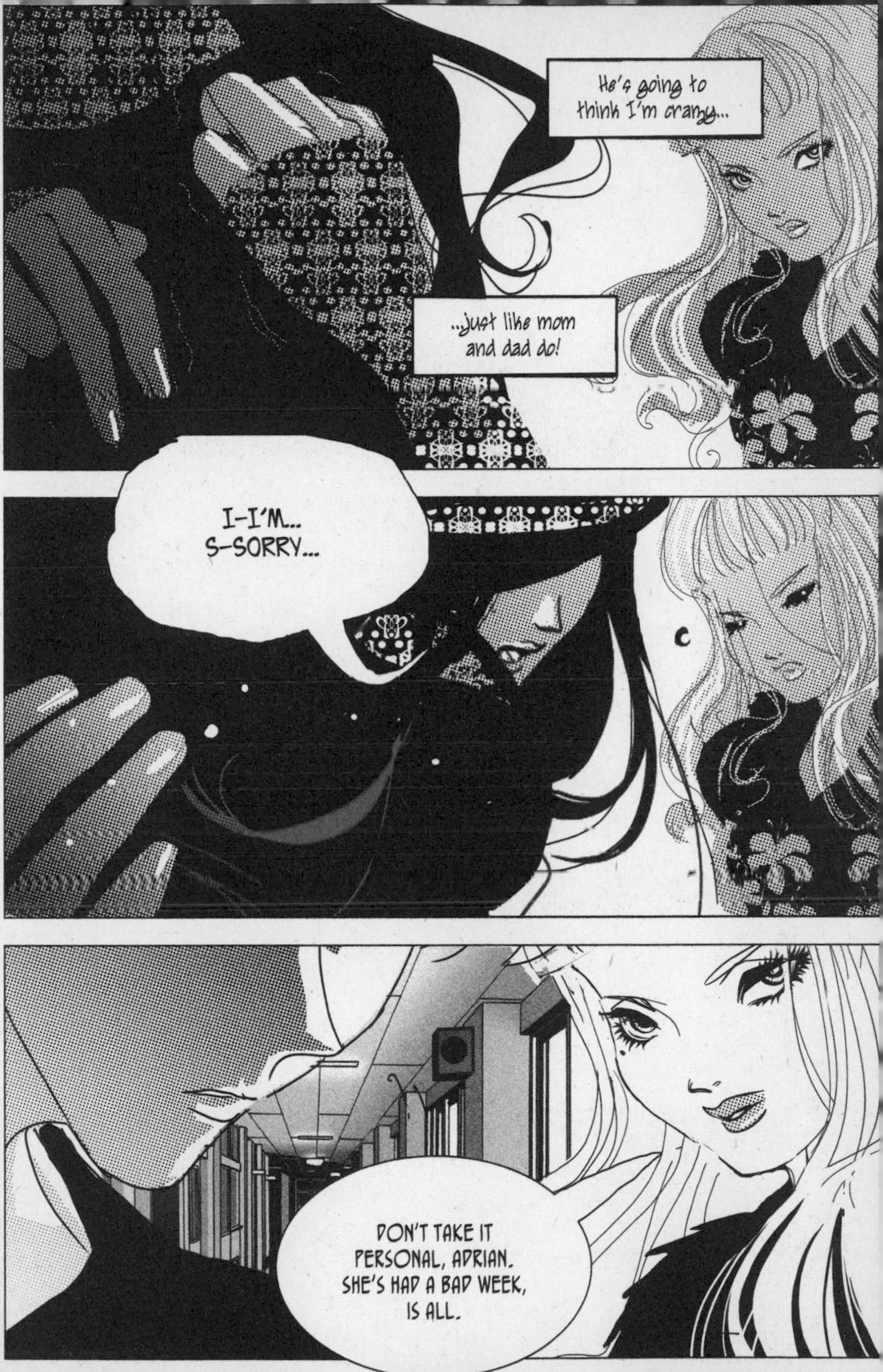
He's going to think I'm crazy...
...just like mom and dad do!
I-I'M... S-SORRY...
DON'T TAKE IT PERSONAL, ADRIAN. SHE'S HAD A BAD WEEK, IS ALL.

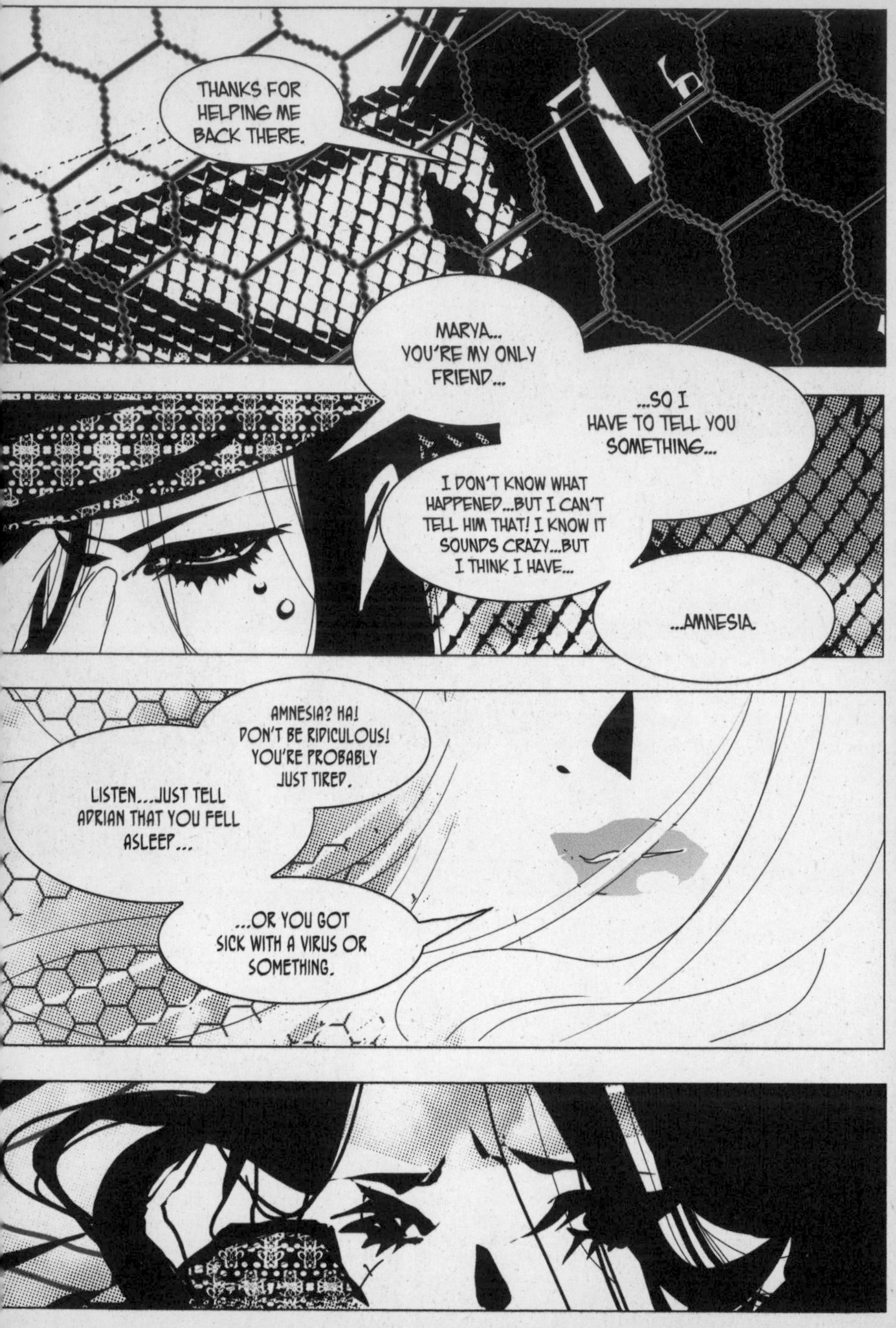
THANKS FOR HELPING ME BACK THERE.
MARYA... YOU'RE MY ONLY FRIEND...
...SO I HAVE TO TELL YOU SOMETHING...
I DON'T KNOW WHAT HAPPENED...BUT I CAN'T TELL HIM THAT! I KNOW IT SOUNDS CRAZY...BUT I THINK I HAVE...
...AMNESIA.
AMNESIA? HA! DON'T BE RIDICULOUS! YOU'RE PROBABLY JUST TIRED.
LISTEN...JUST TELL ADRIAN THAT YOU FELL ASLEEP...
...OR YOU GOT SICK WITH A VIRUS OR SOMETHING.

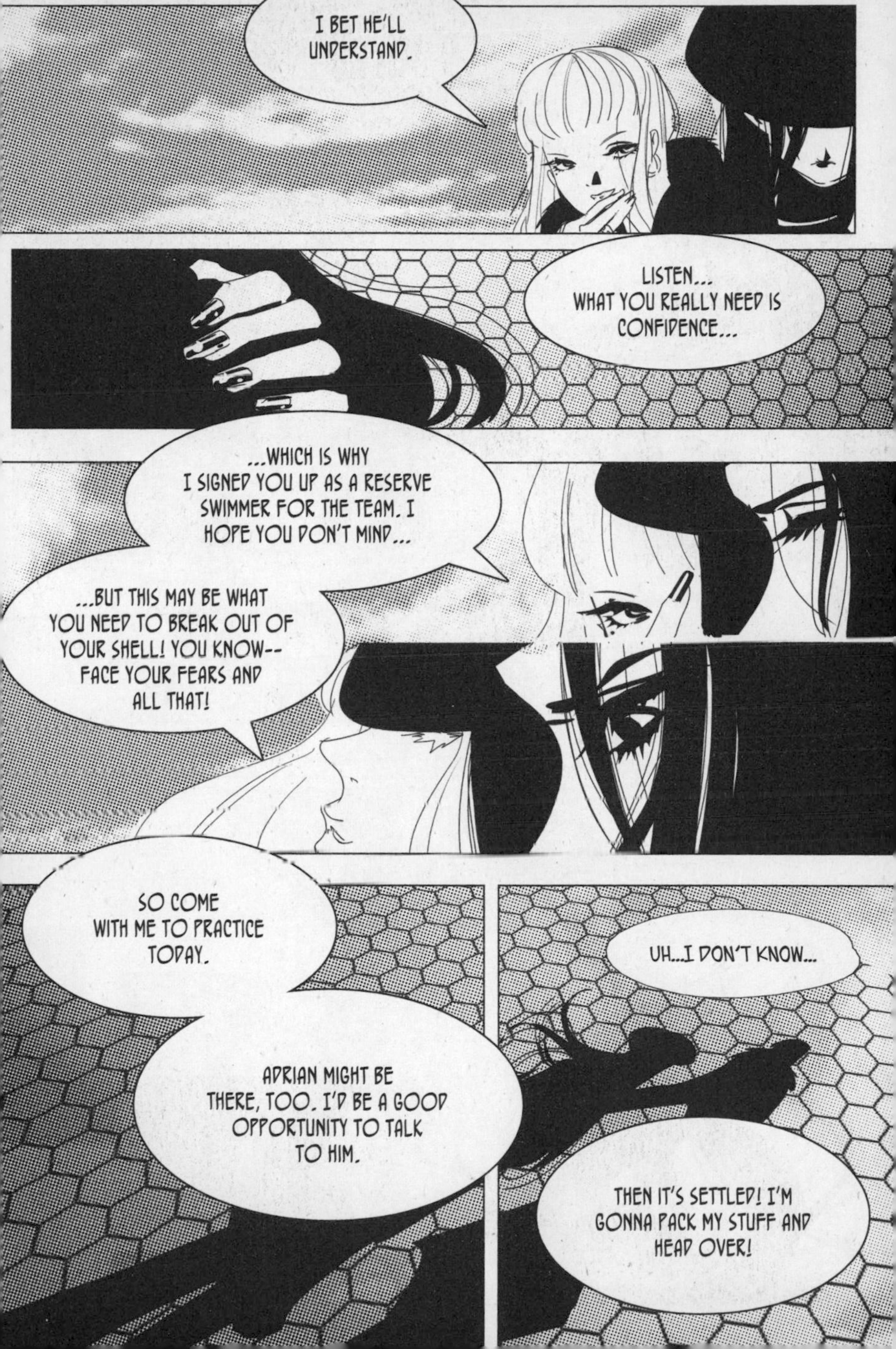
I BET HE'LL UNDERSTAND.
LISTEN... WHAT YOU REALLY NEED IS CONFIDENCE...
...WHICH IS WHY I SIGNED YOU UP AS A RESERVE SWIMMER FOR THE TEAM. I HOPE YOU DON'T MIND...
...BUT THIS MAY BE WHAT YOU NEED TO BREAK OUT OF YOUR SHELL! YOU KNOW-- FACE YOUR FEARS AND ALL THAT!
SO COME WITH ME TO PRACTICE TODAY.
UH...I DON'T KNOW...
ADRIAN MIGHT BE THERE, TOO. I'D BE A GOOD OPPORTUNITY TO TALK TO HIM.
THEN IT'S SETTLED! I'M GONNA PACK MY STUFF AND HEAD OVER!

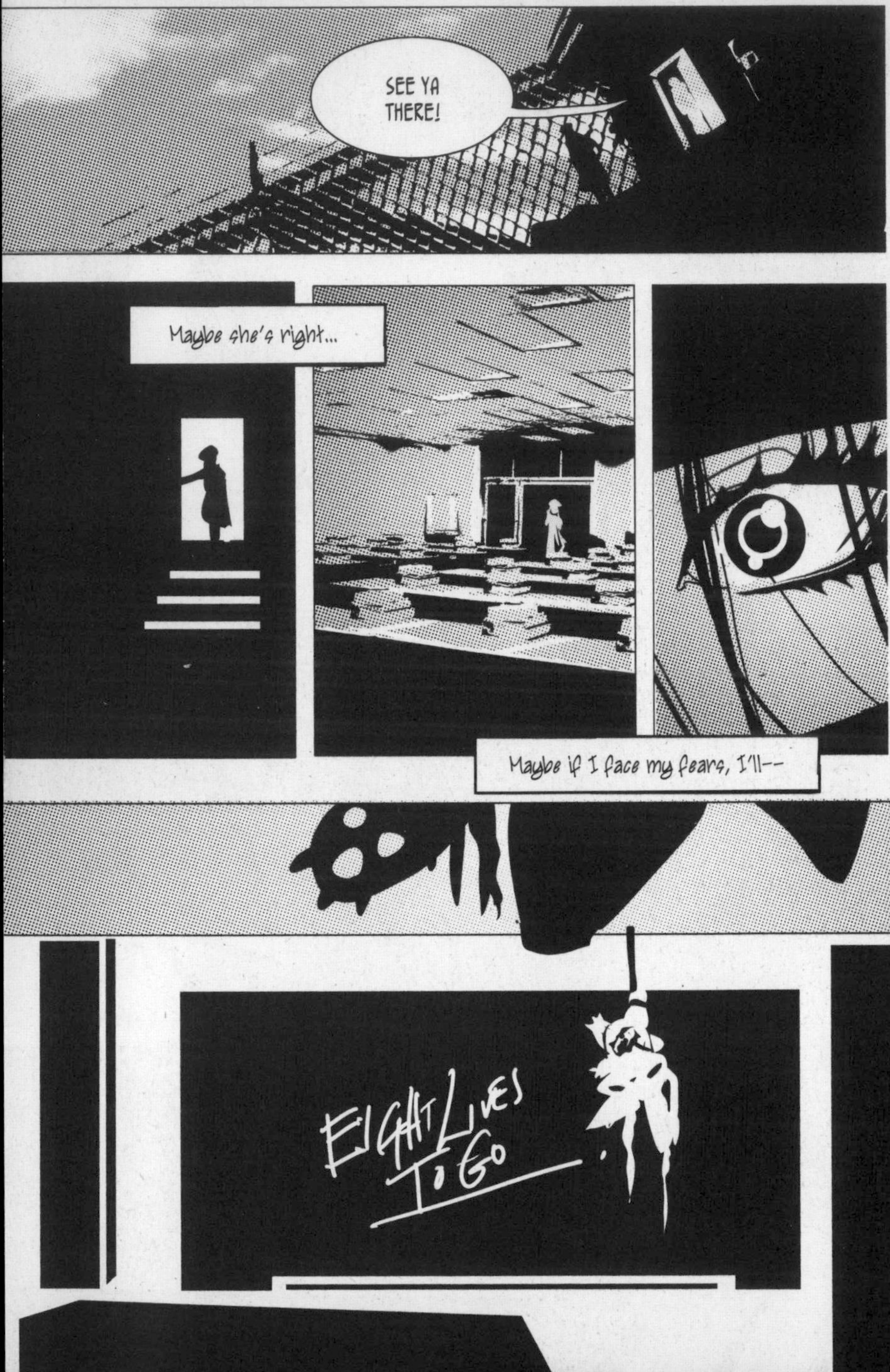
SEE YA THERE!
Maybe she's right...
Maybe if I face my fears, I'll--
EIGHT LIVES TO GO

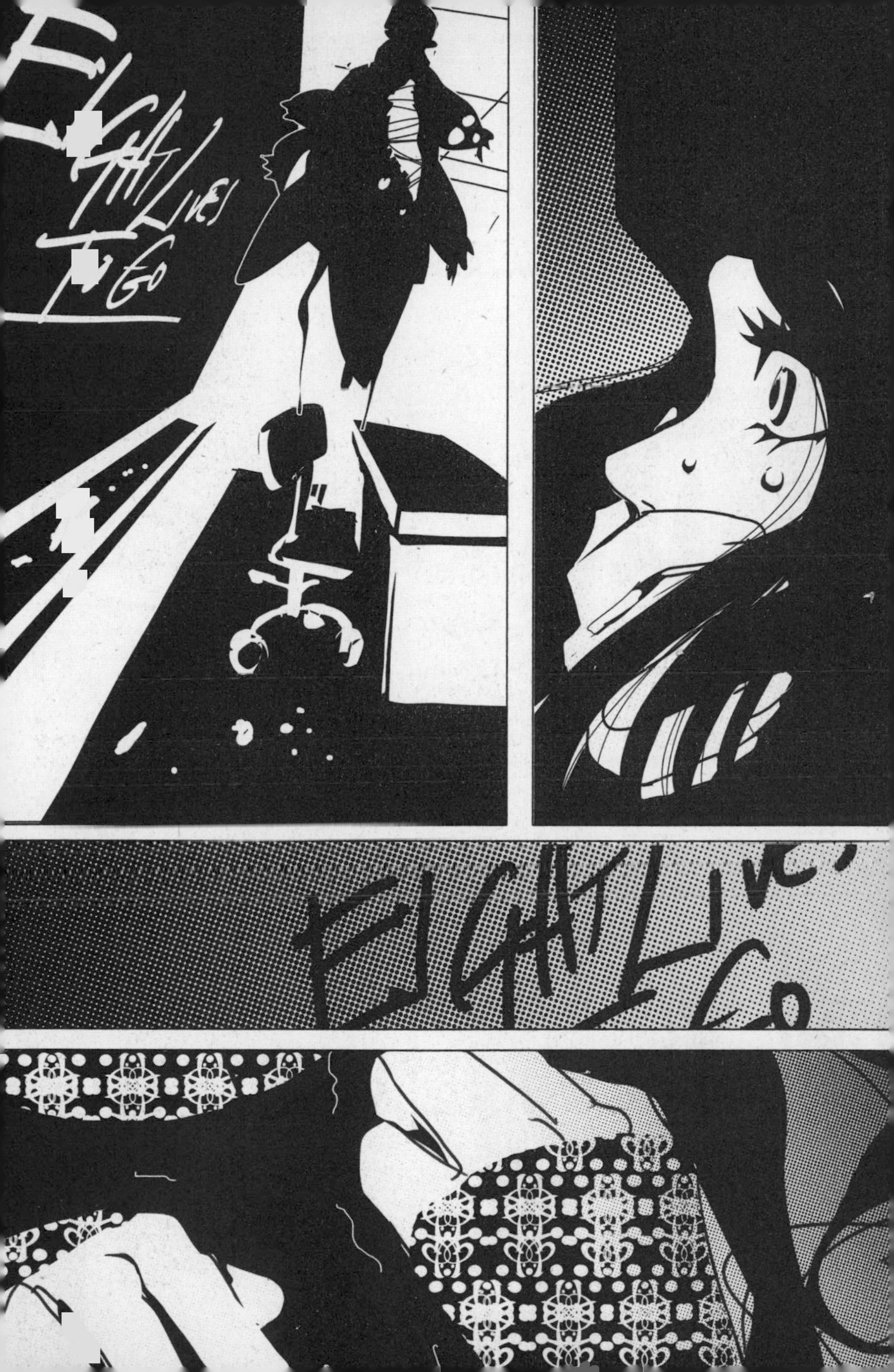
EIGHT LIVES TO GO

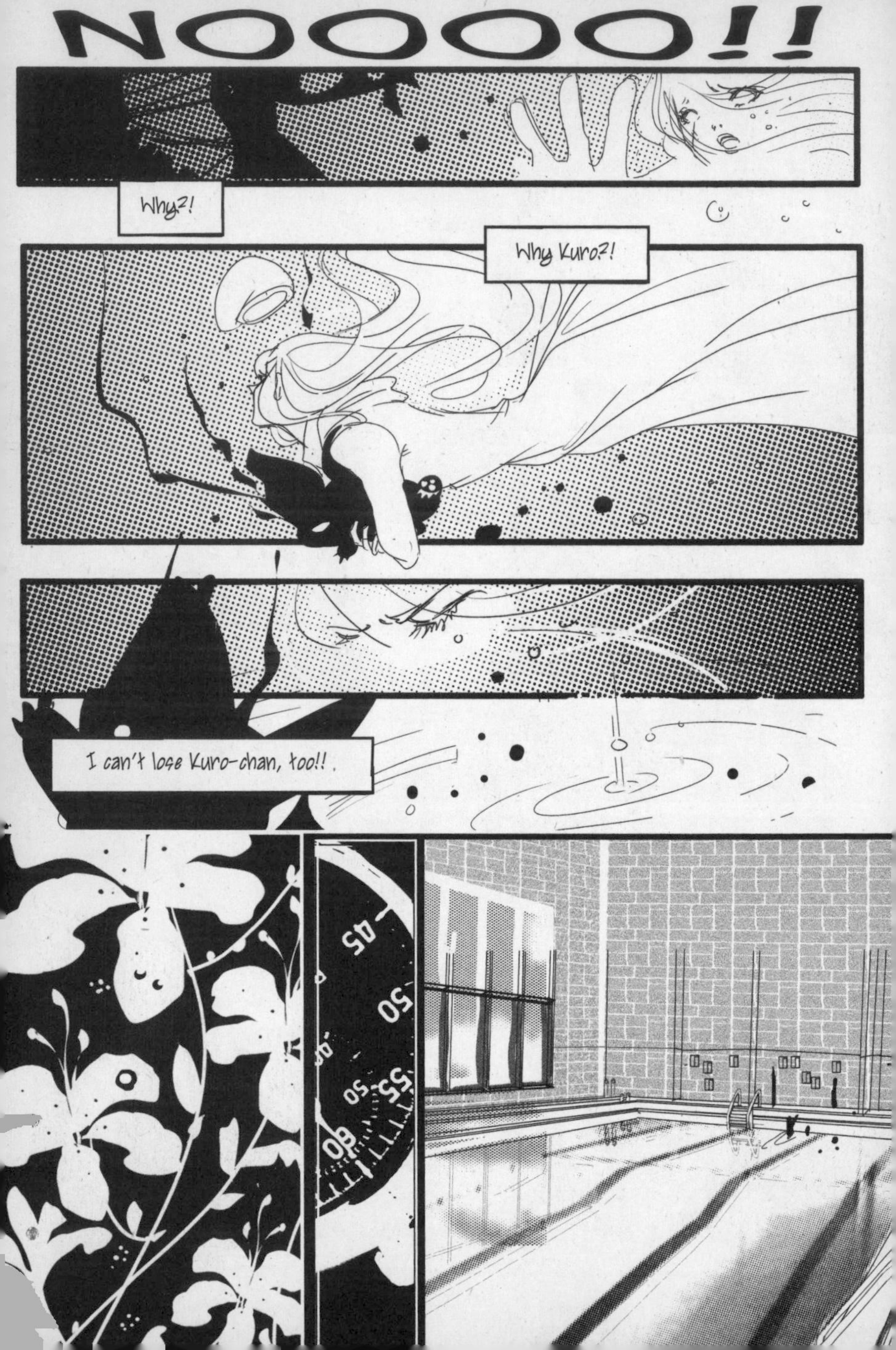
NOOOO!!
Why?!
Why Kuro?!
I can't lose Kuro-chan, too!!
45
50
55
50
60

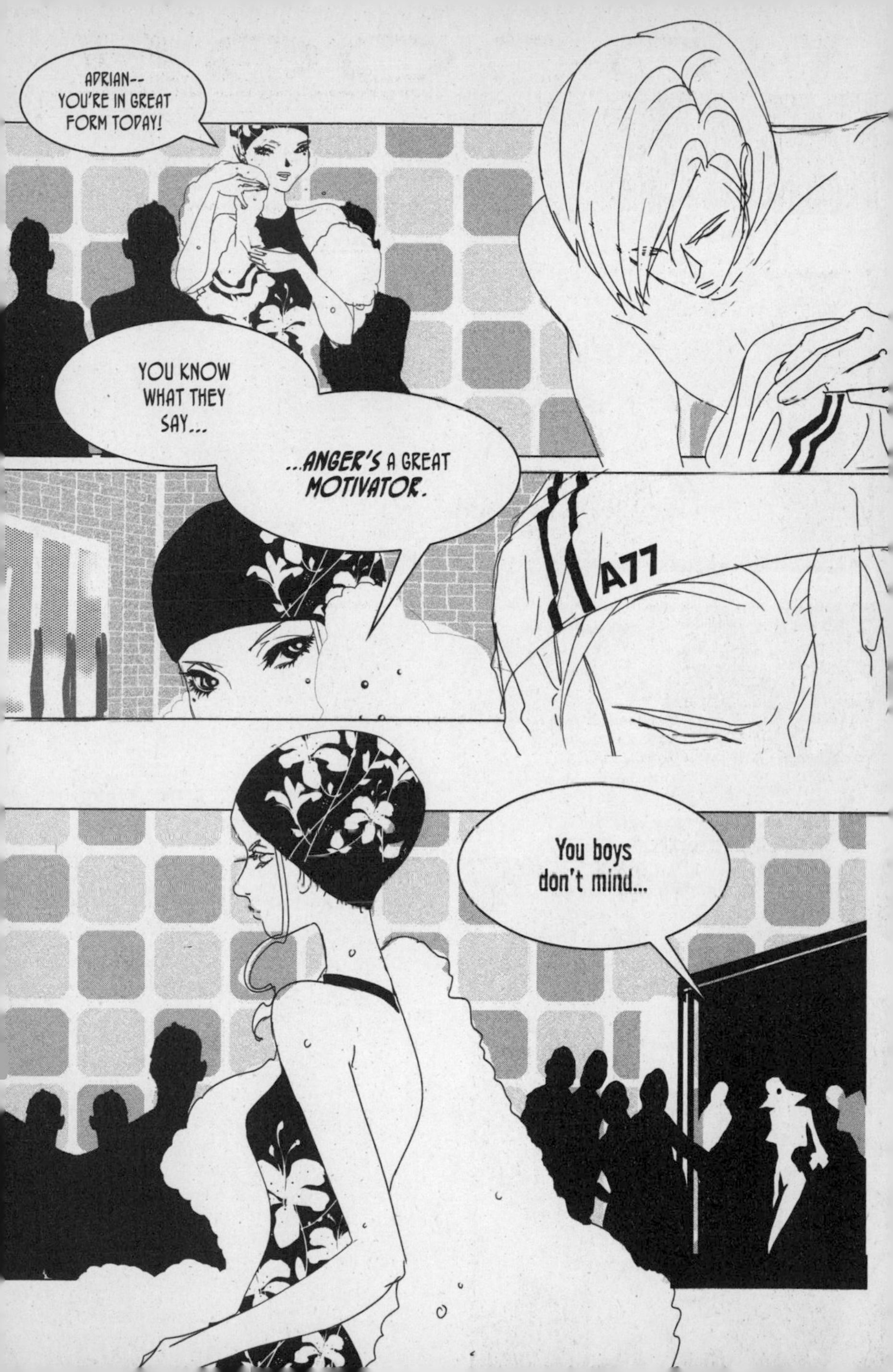
ADRIAN-- YOU'RE IN GREAT FORM TODAY!
YOU KNOW WHAT THEY SAY...
...ANGER'S A GREAT MOTIVATOR.
A77
You boys don't mind...

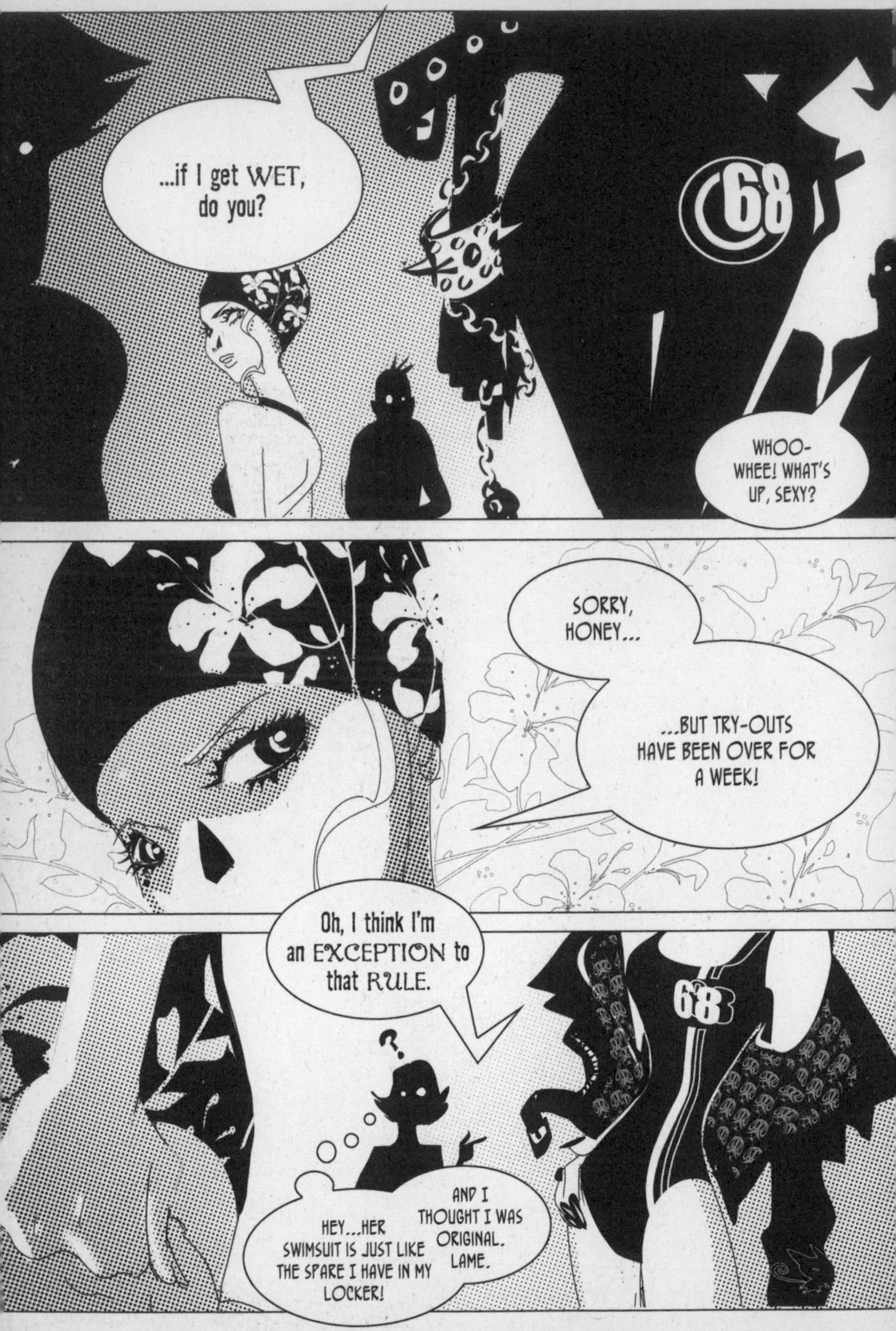
...if I get WET, do you?
WHOO-WHEE! WHAT'S UP, SEXY?
SORRY, HONEY...
...BUT TRY-OUTS HAVE BEEN OVER FOR A WEEK!
Oh, I think I'm an EXCEPTION to that RULE.
?
HEY...HER SWIMSUIT IS JUST LIKE THE SPARE I HAVE IN MY LOCKER!
AND I THOUGHT I WAS ORIGINAL. LAME.

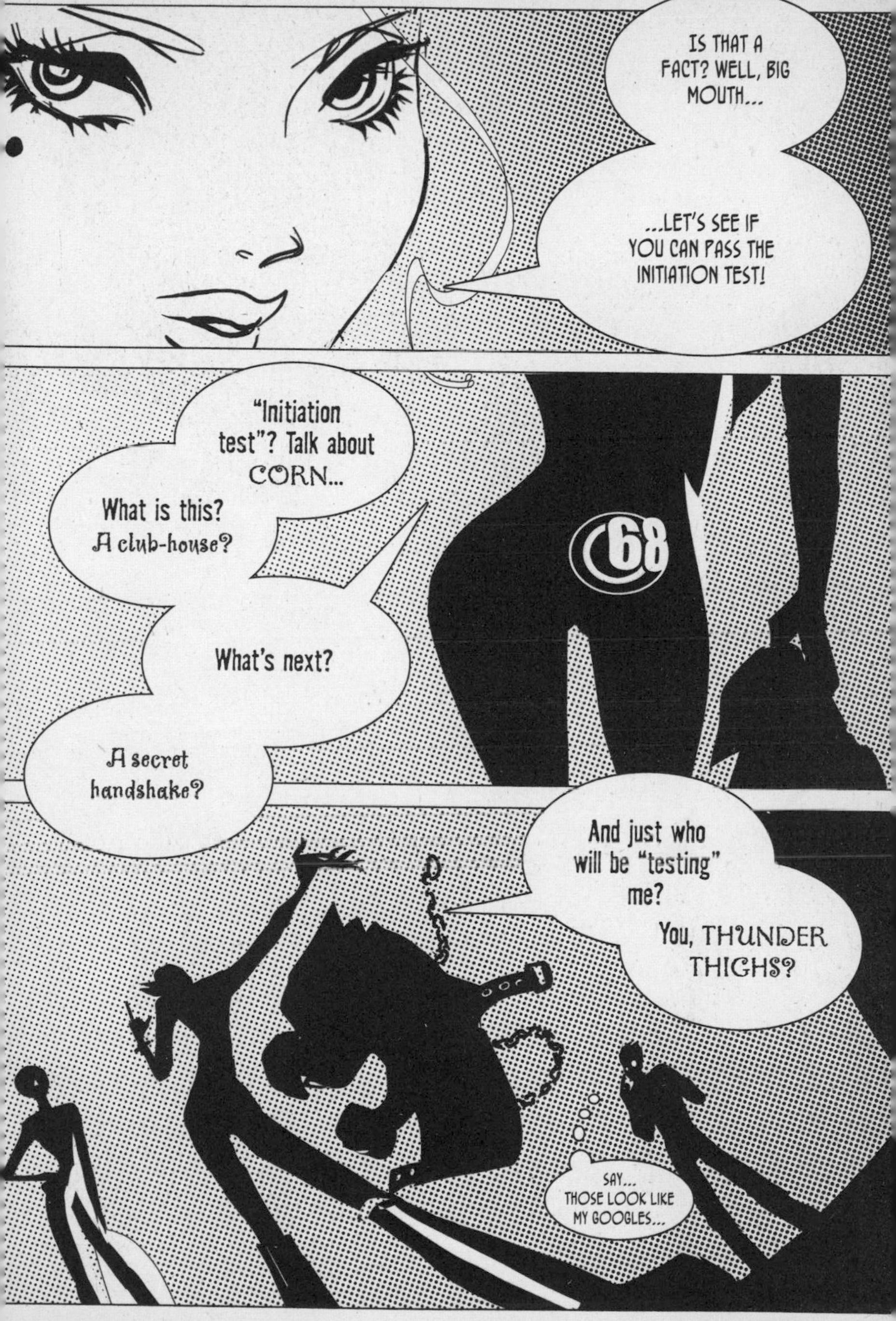
IS THAT A FACT? WELL, BIG MOUTH...
...LET'S SEE IF YOU CAN PASS THE INITIATION TEST!
"Initiation test"? Talk about CORN...
What is this? A club-house?
What's next?
A secret handshake?
68
And just who will be "testing" me?
You, THUNDER THIGHS?
SAY... THOSE LOOK LIKE MY GOOGLES...

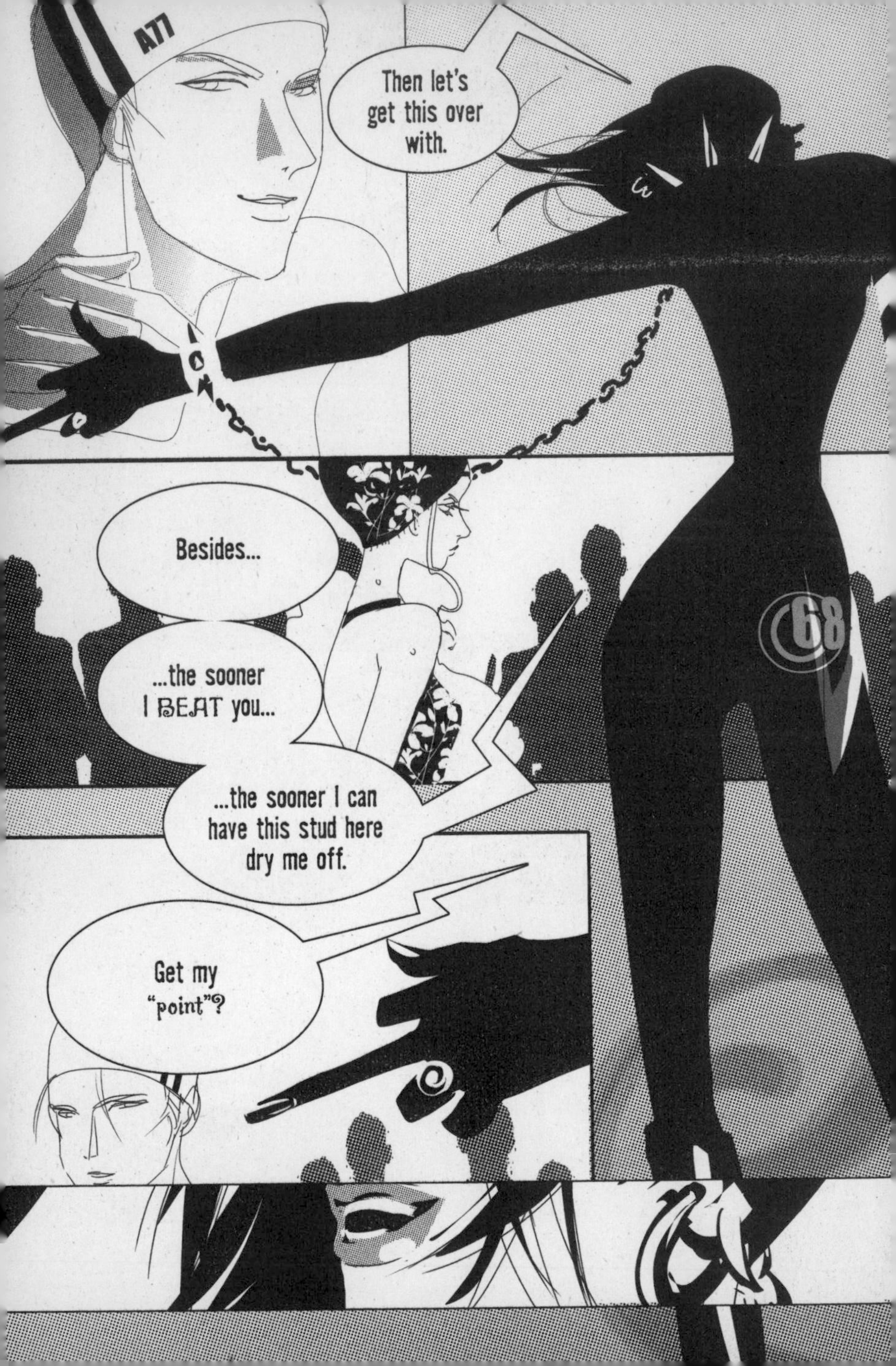
A77
Then let's get this over with.
Besides...
...the sooner I BEAT you...
...the sooner I can have this stud here dry me off.
Get my "point"?
68

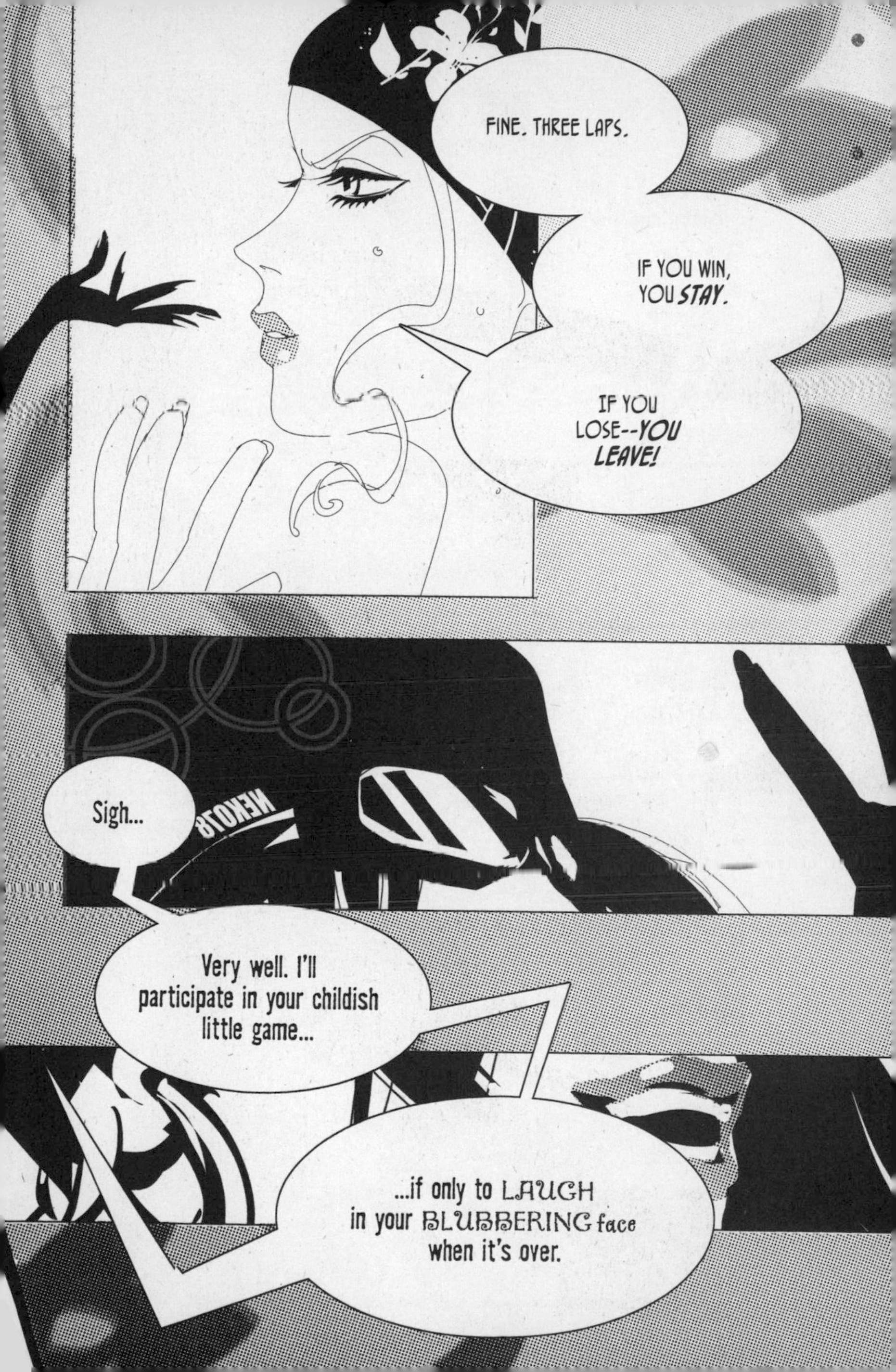
FINE. THREE LAPS.
IF YOU WIN, YOU STAY.
IF YOU LOSE--YOU LEAVE!
Sigh...
Very well. I'll participate in your childish little game...
...if only to LAUGH in your BLUBBERING face when it's over.

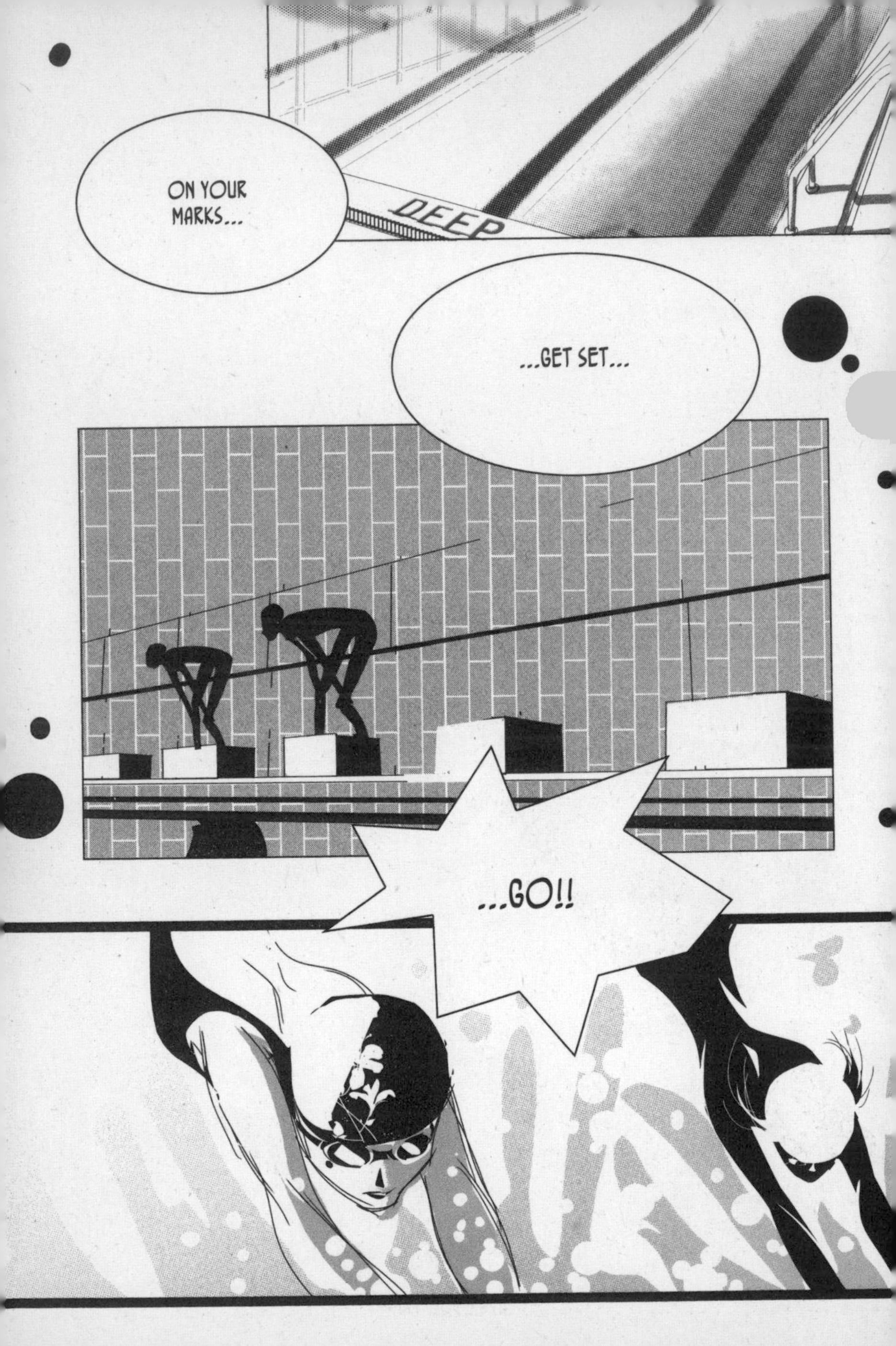
ON YOUR MARKS...
DEEP
...GET SET...
...GO!!

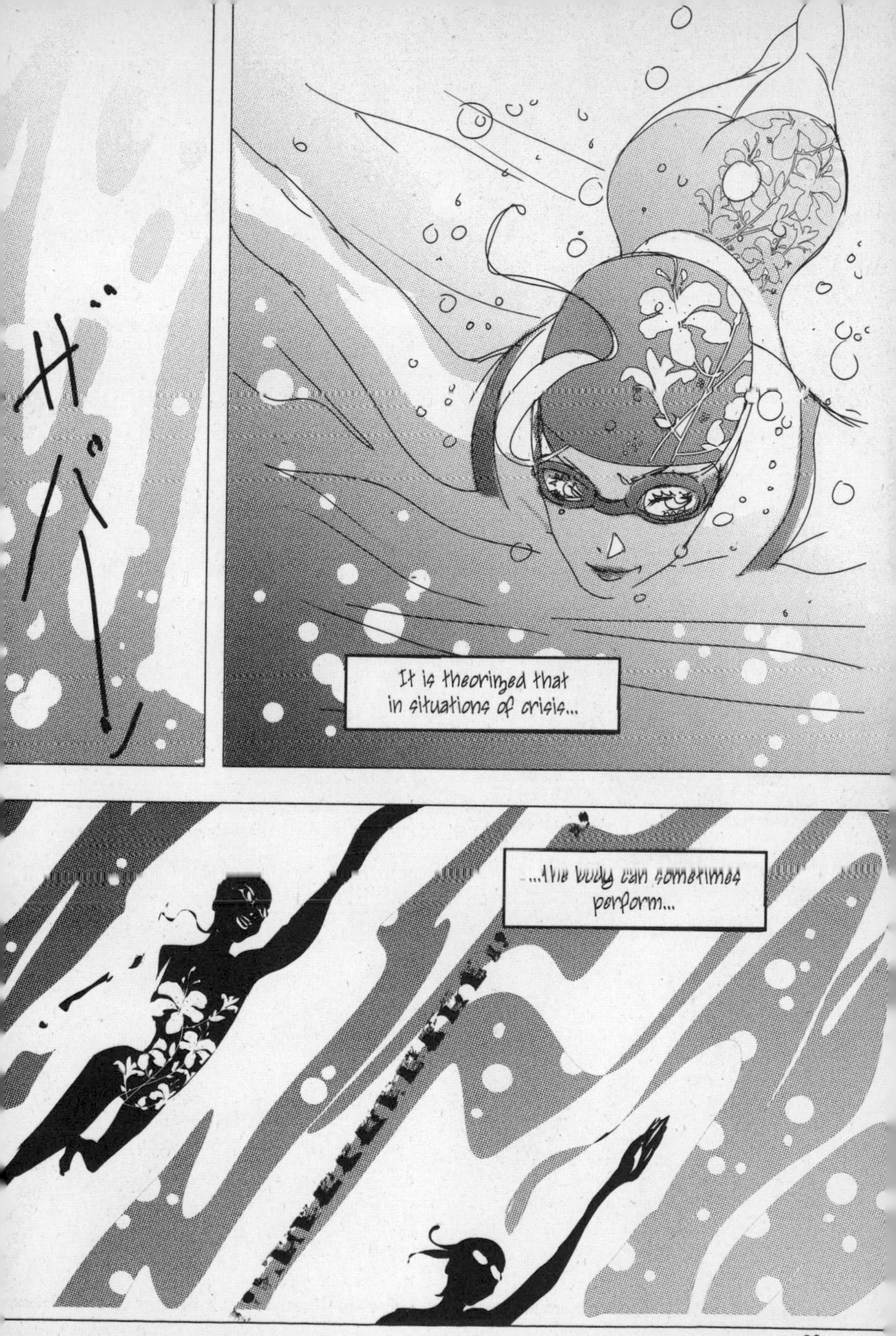
It is theorized that in situations of crisis...
...the body can sometimes perform...

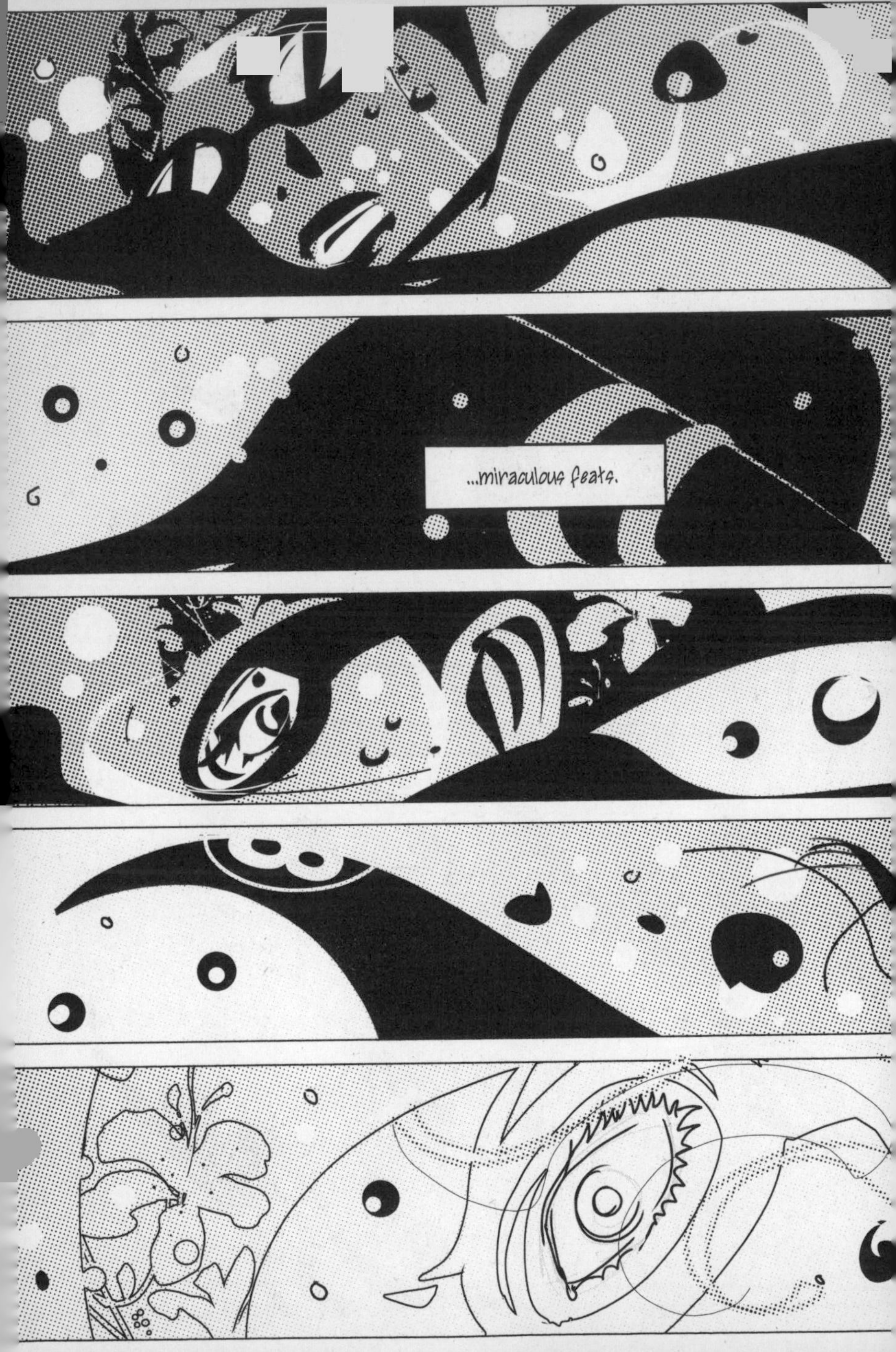
...miraculous feats.

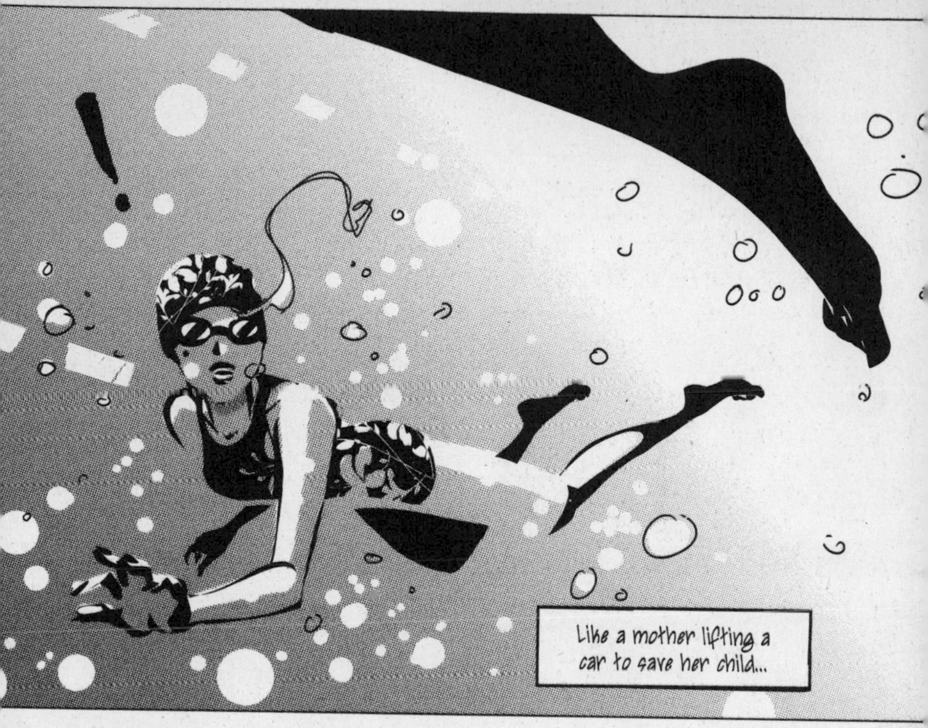
!
Like a mother lifting a car to save her child...
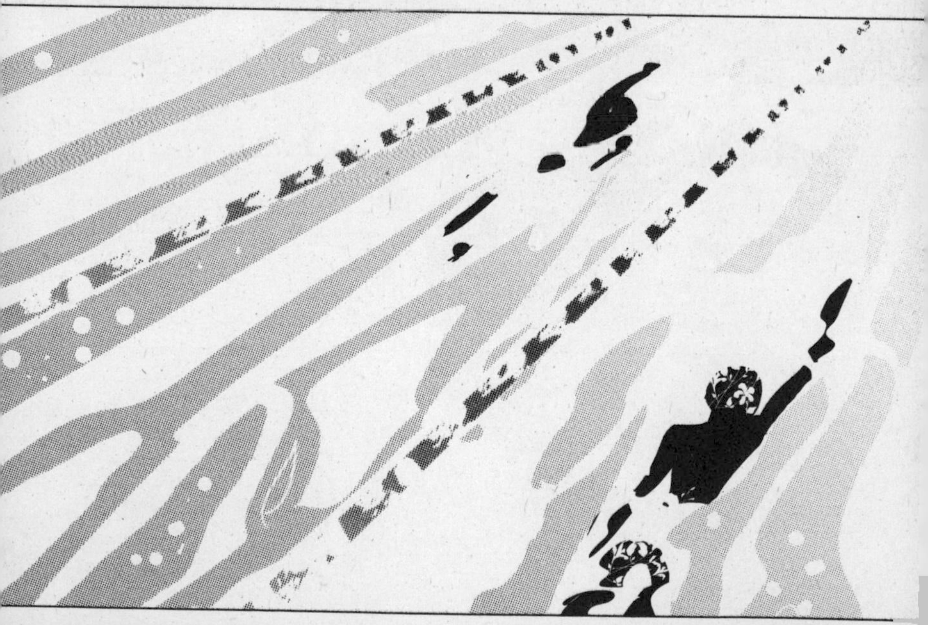

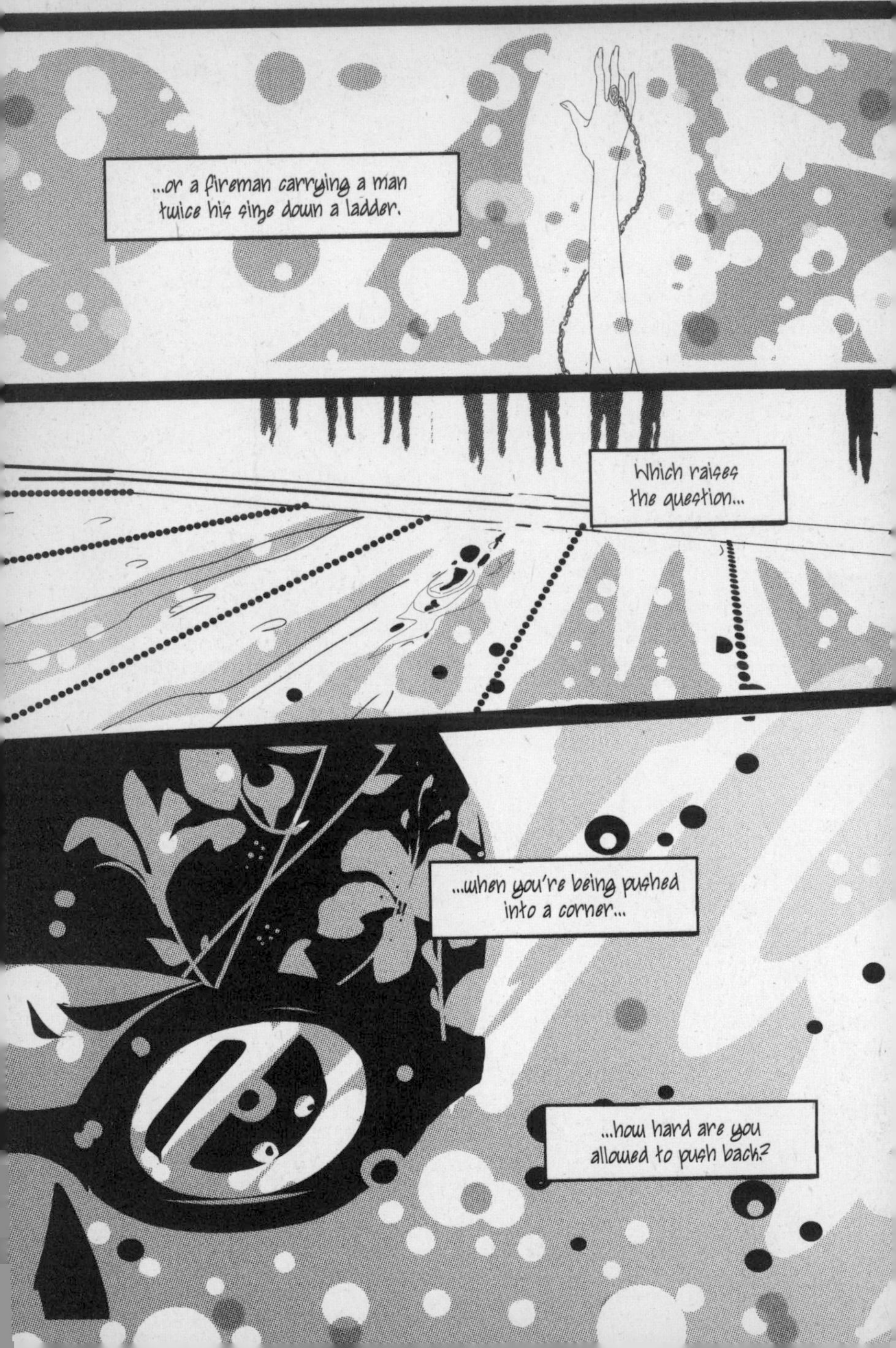
...or a fireman carrying a man twice his size down a ladder.
Which raises the question...
...when you're being pushed into a corner...
...how hard are you allowed to push back?

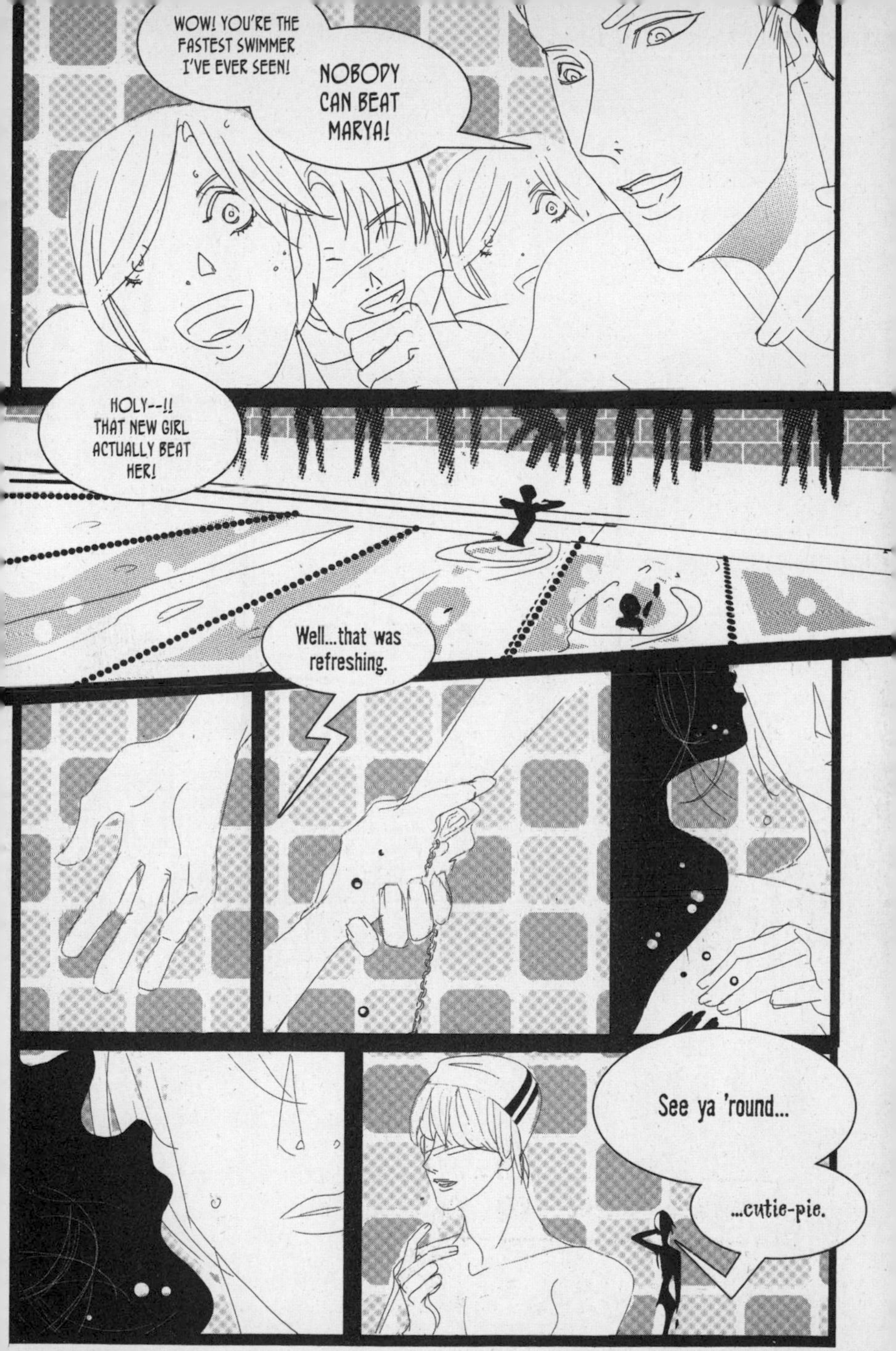
WOW! YOU'RE THE FASTEST SWIMMER I'VE EVER SEEN!
NOBODY CAN BEAT MARYA!
HOLY--!! THAT NEW GIRL ACTUALLY BEAT HER!
Well...that was refreshing.
See ya 'round...
...cutie-pie.

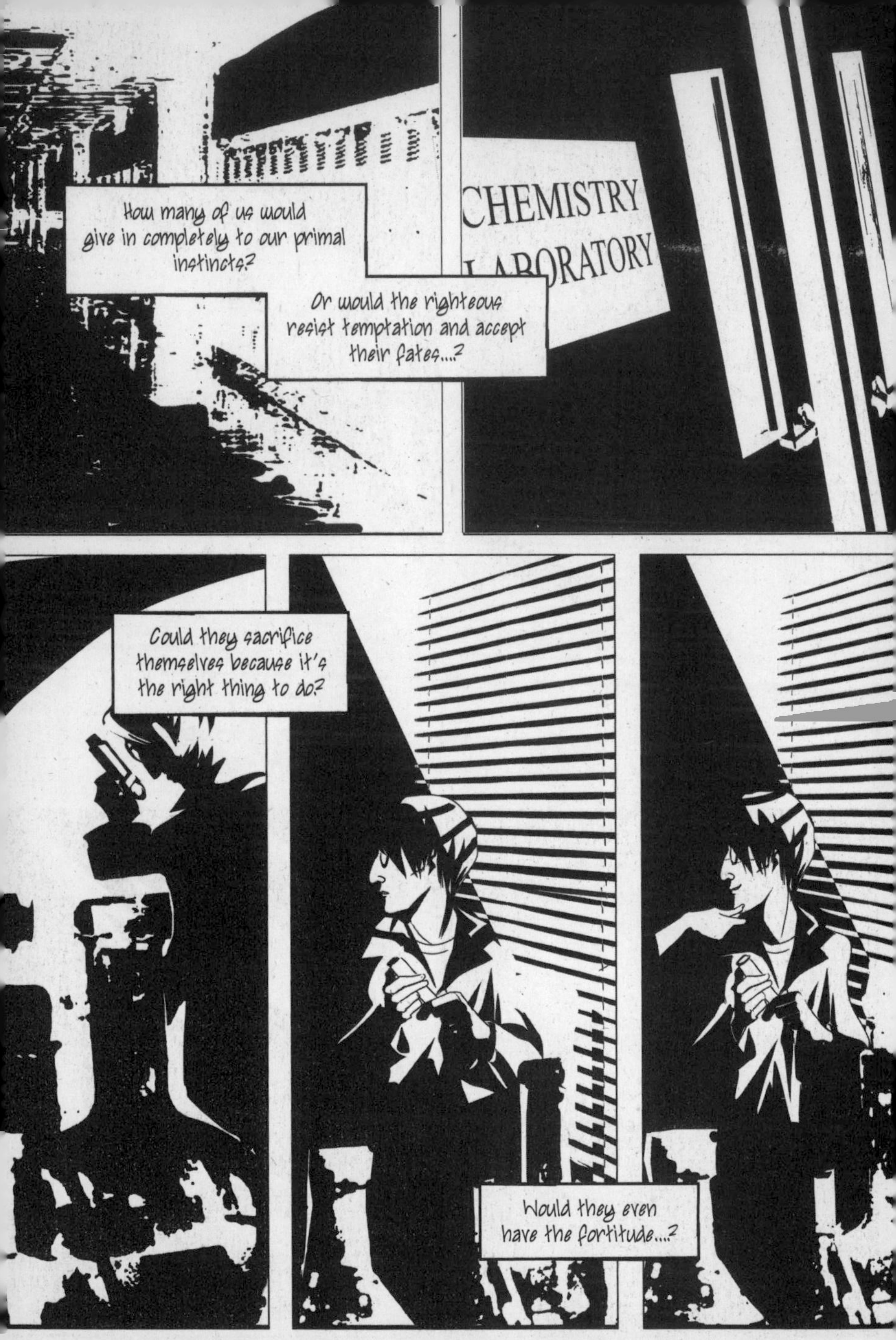
How many of us would give in completely to our primal instincts?
Or would the righteous resist temptation and accept their fates....?
CHEMISTRY LABORATORY
Could they sacrifice themselves because it's the right thing to do?
Would they even have the fortitude....?

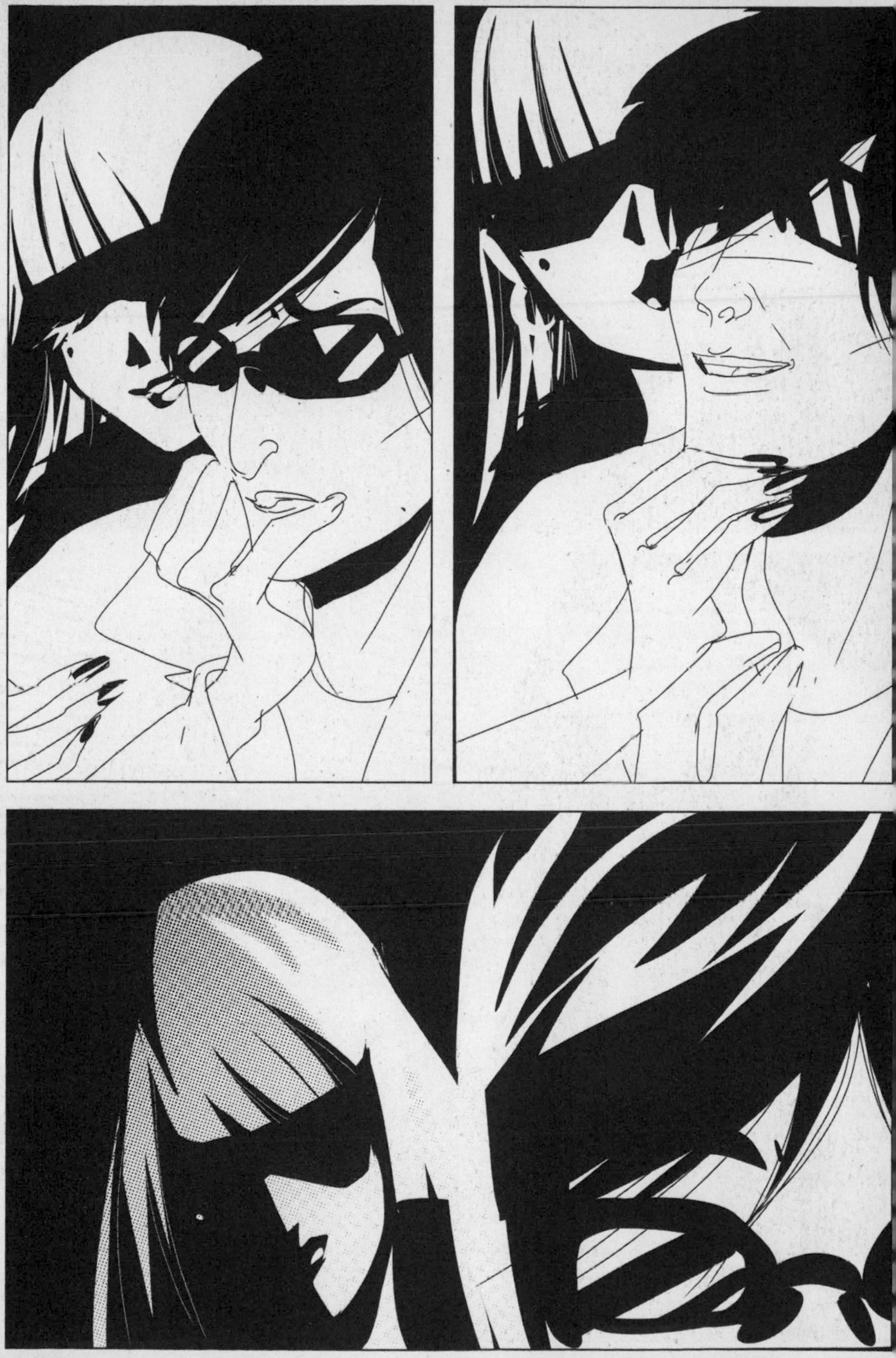

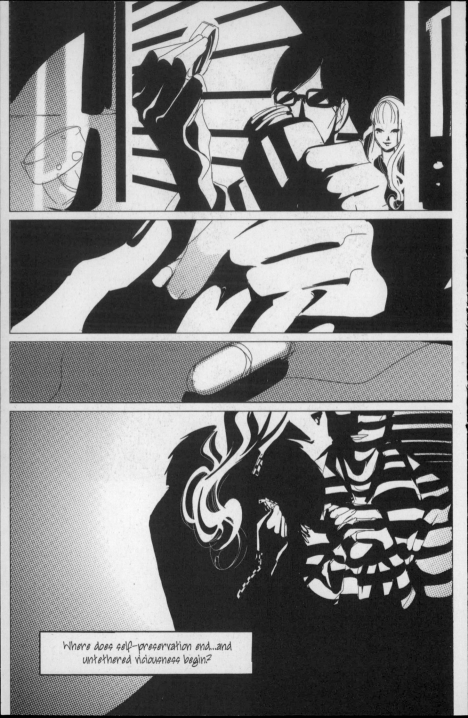

Where does self-preservation end...and untethered viciousness begin?

CHAPTER :: 05

No price is too high to pay for the privilege of owning yourself. *Friedrich Nietzsche*

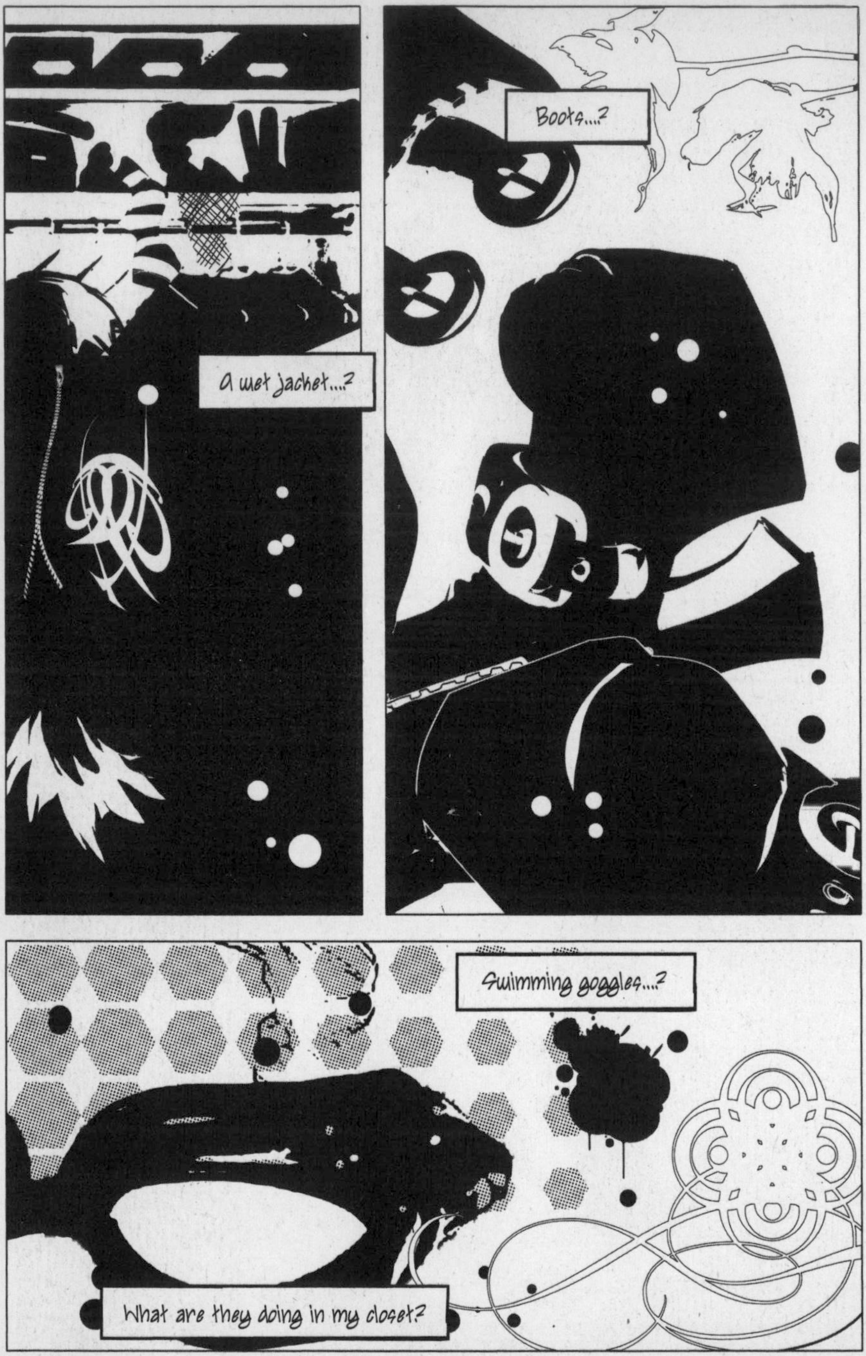
Boots....?
A wet jacket....?
Swimming goggles....?
What are they doing in my closet?

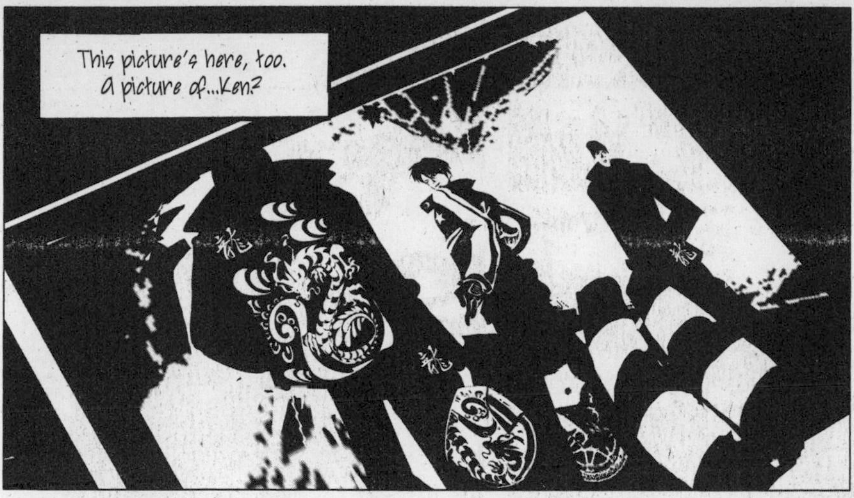
This picture's here, too.
A picture of...Ken?

Who are these other two guys?

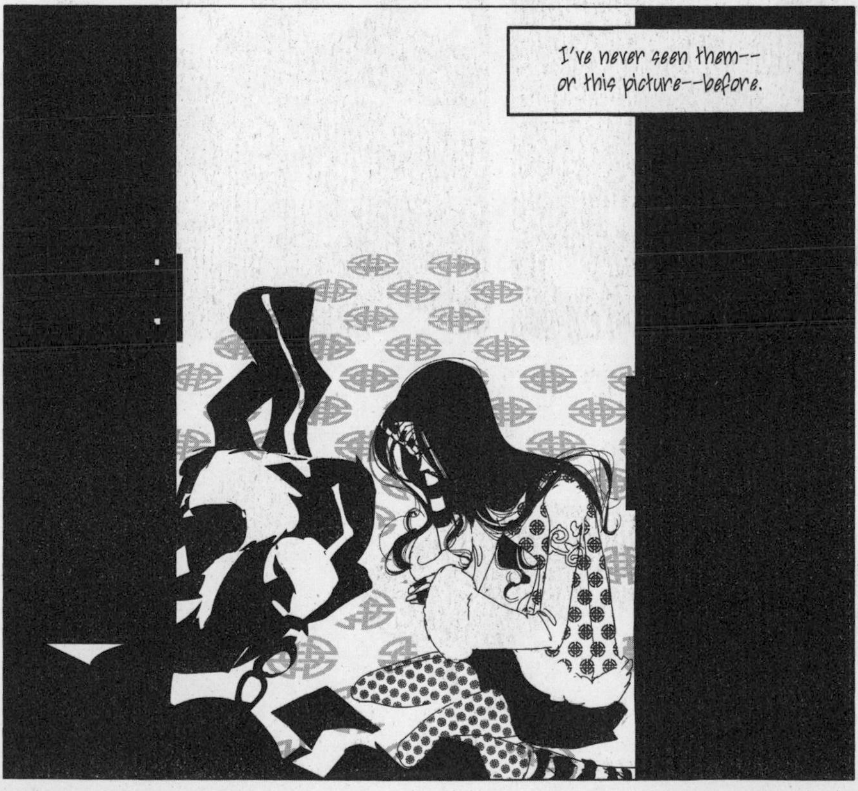
I've never seen them--
or this picture--before.

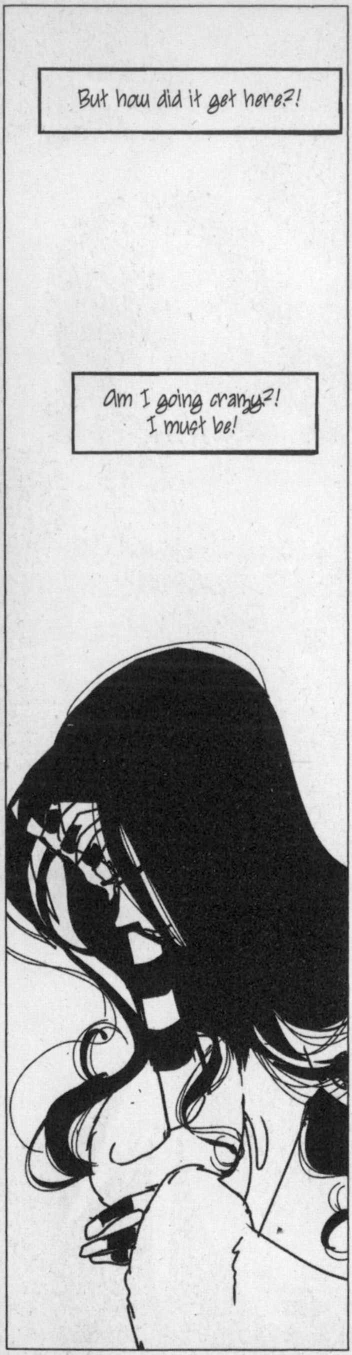
But how did it get here?!
Am I going crazy?! I must be!

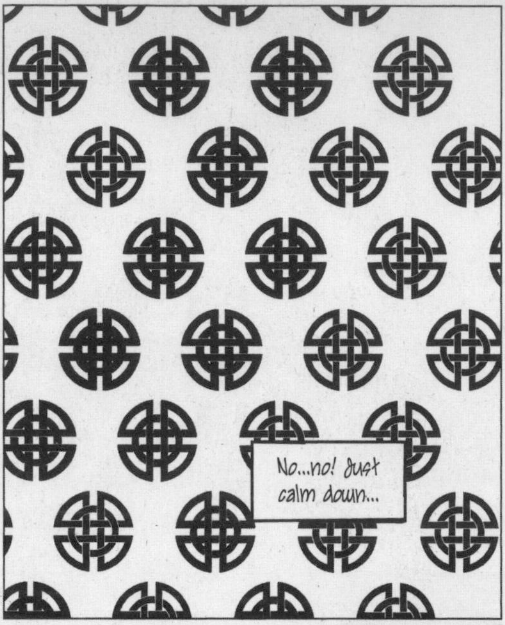
No...no! Just calm down...

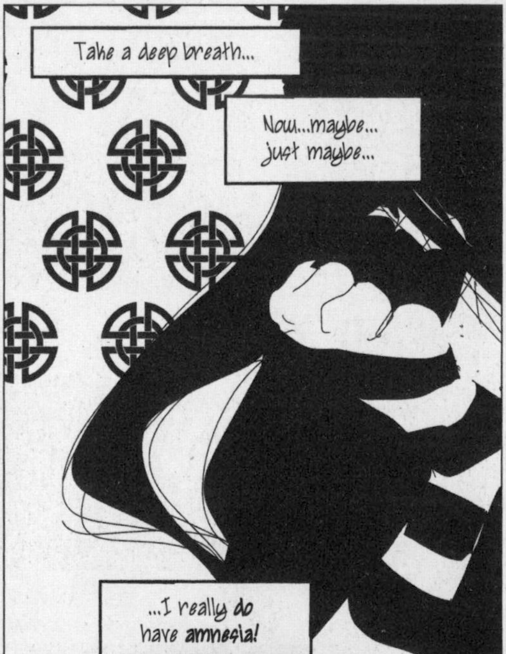
Take a deep breath...
Now...maybe... just maybe...
...I really do have amnesia!

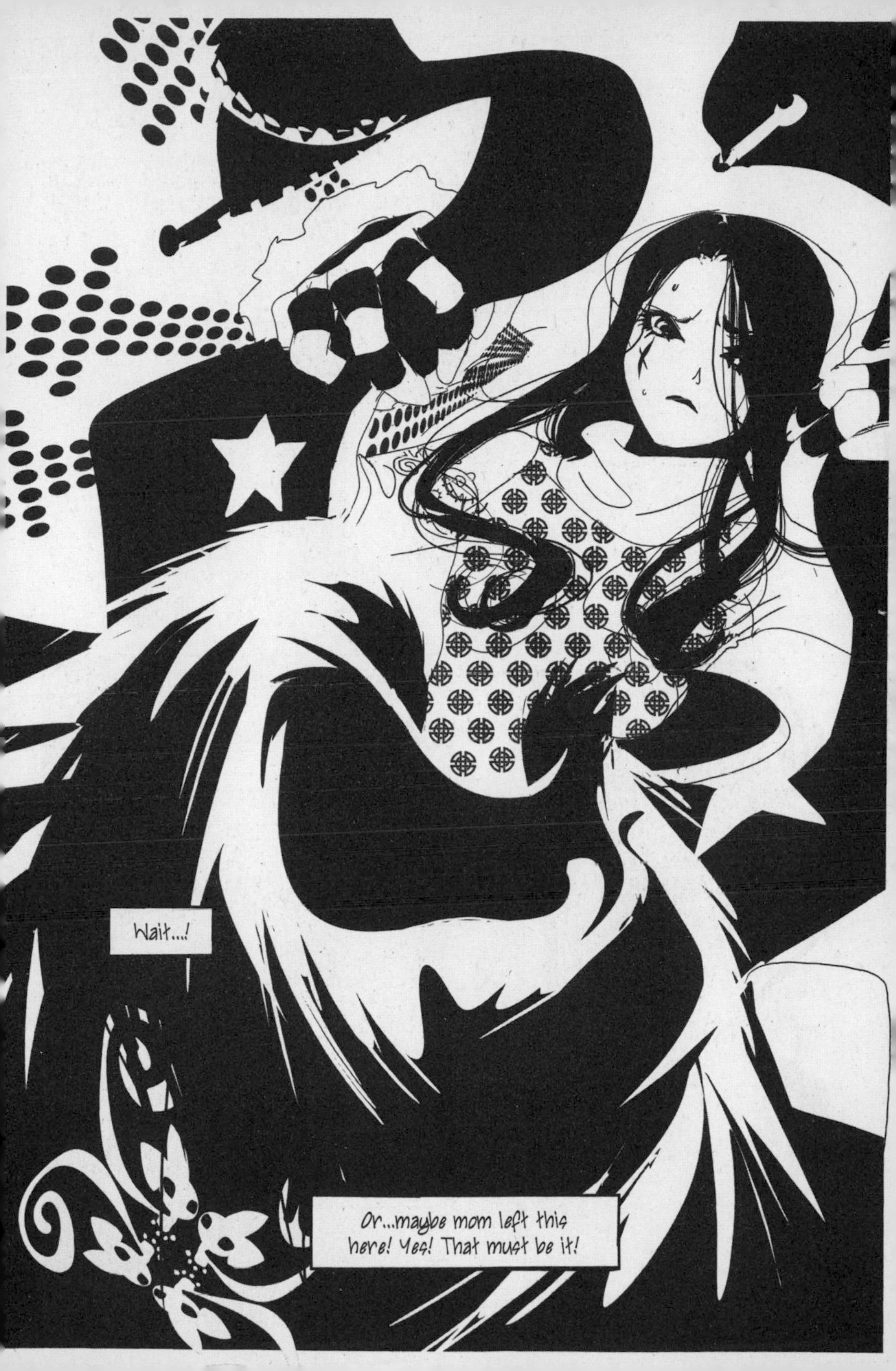
Wait...!
Or...maybe mom left this here! Yes! That must be it!

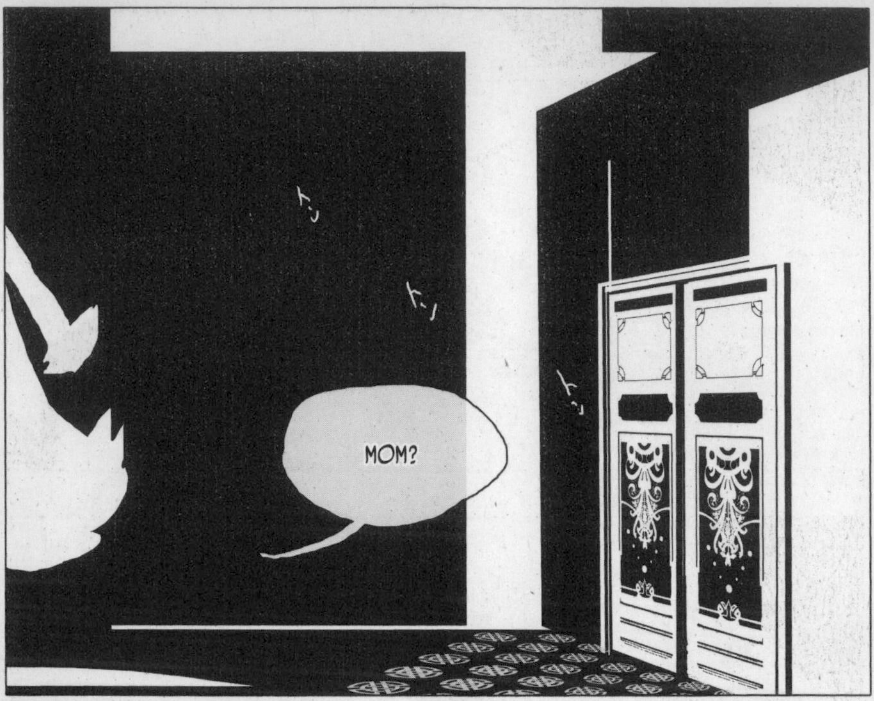
MOM?

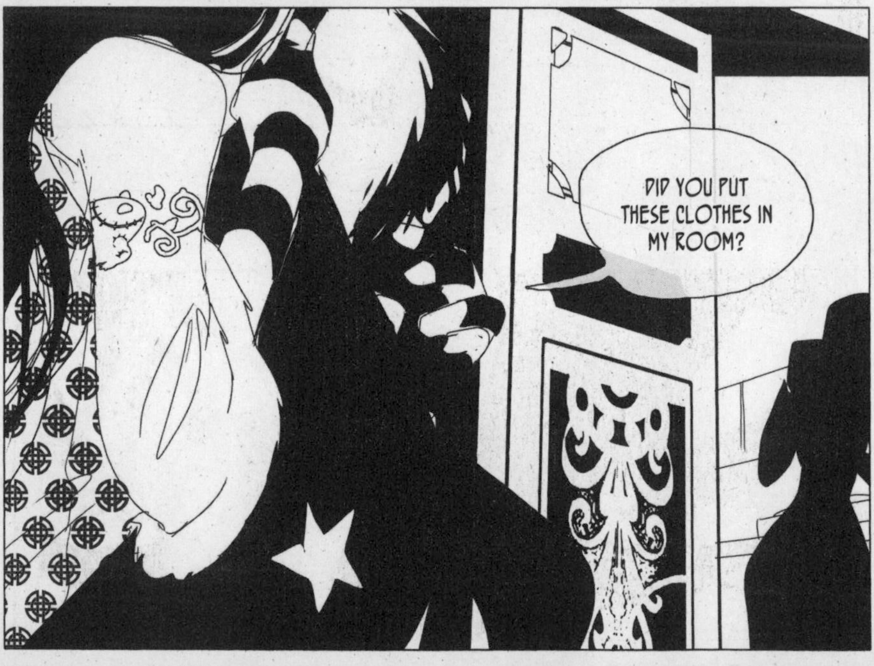
DID YOU PUT THESE CLOTHES IN MY ROOM?

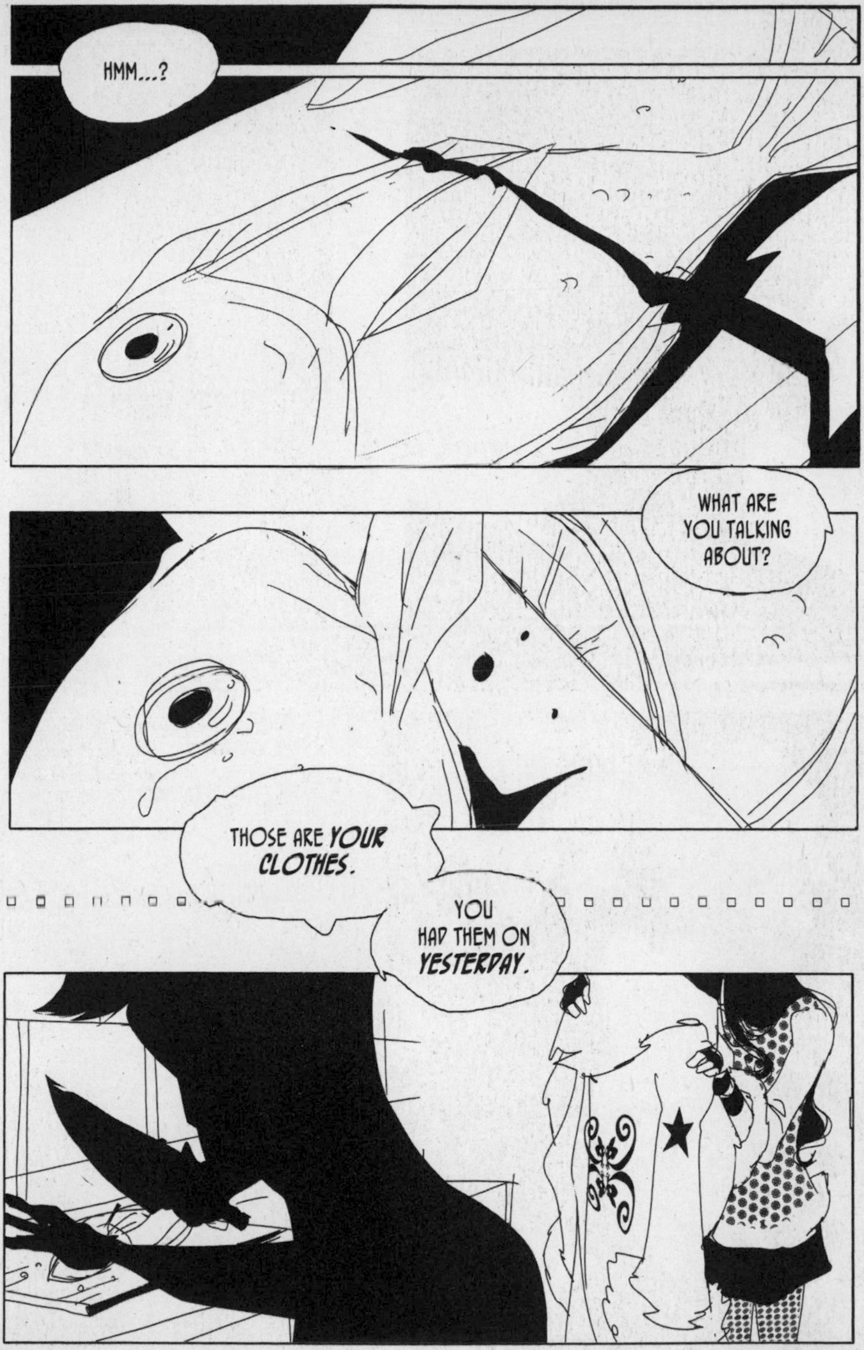
HMM...?
WHAT ARE YOU TALKING ABOUT?
THOSE ARE *YOUR* *CLOTHES*.
YOU HAD THEM ON *YESTERDAY*.

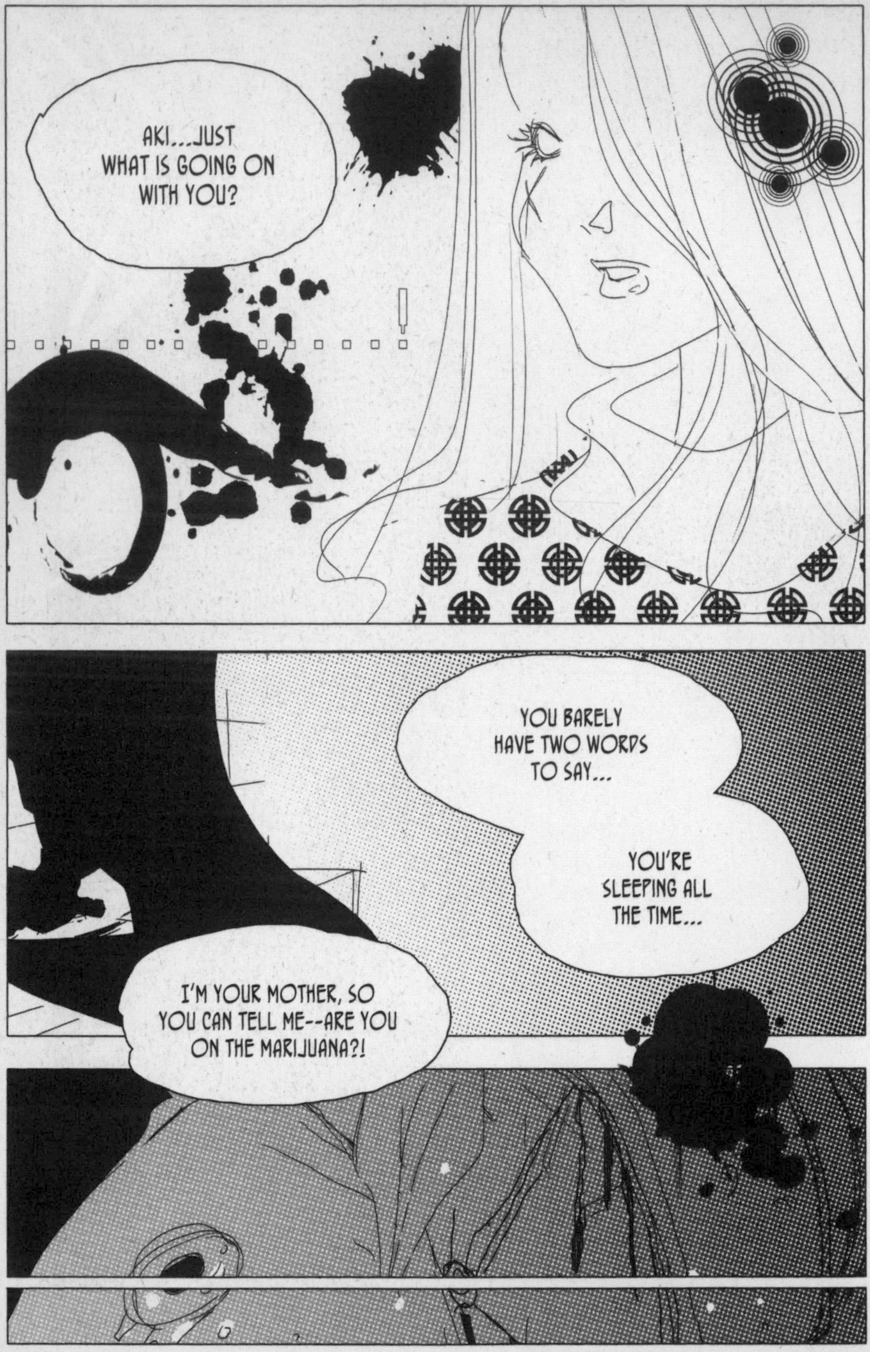
AKI...JUST WHAT IS GOING ON WITH YOU?
YOU BARELY HAVE TWO WORDS TO SAY...
YOU'RE SLEEPING ALL THE TIME...
I'M YOUR MOTHER, SO YOU CAN TELL ME--ARE YOU ON THE MARIJUANA?!

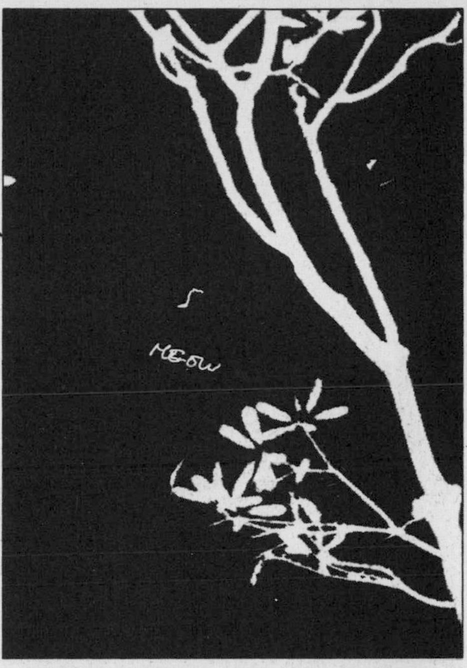
MEOW
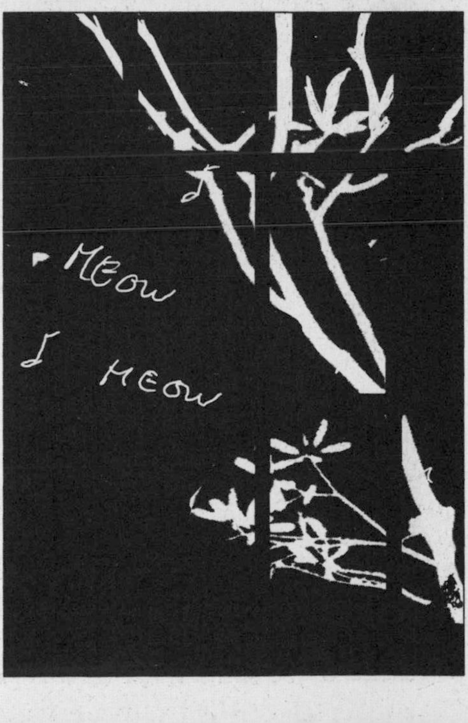
MEOW
MEOW
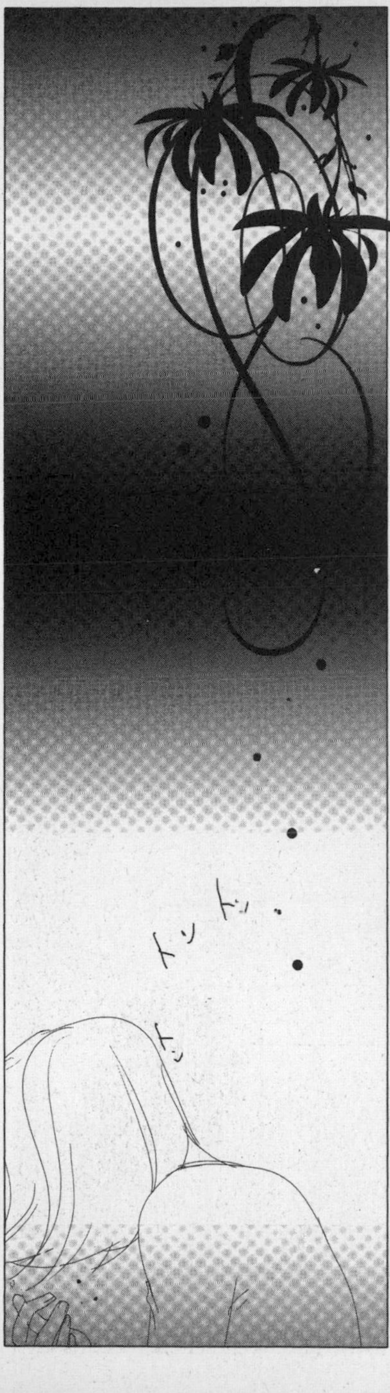
トットッ..
トッ

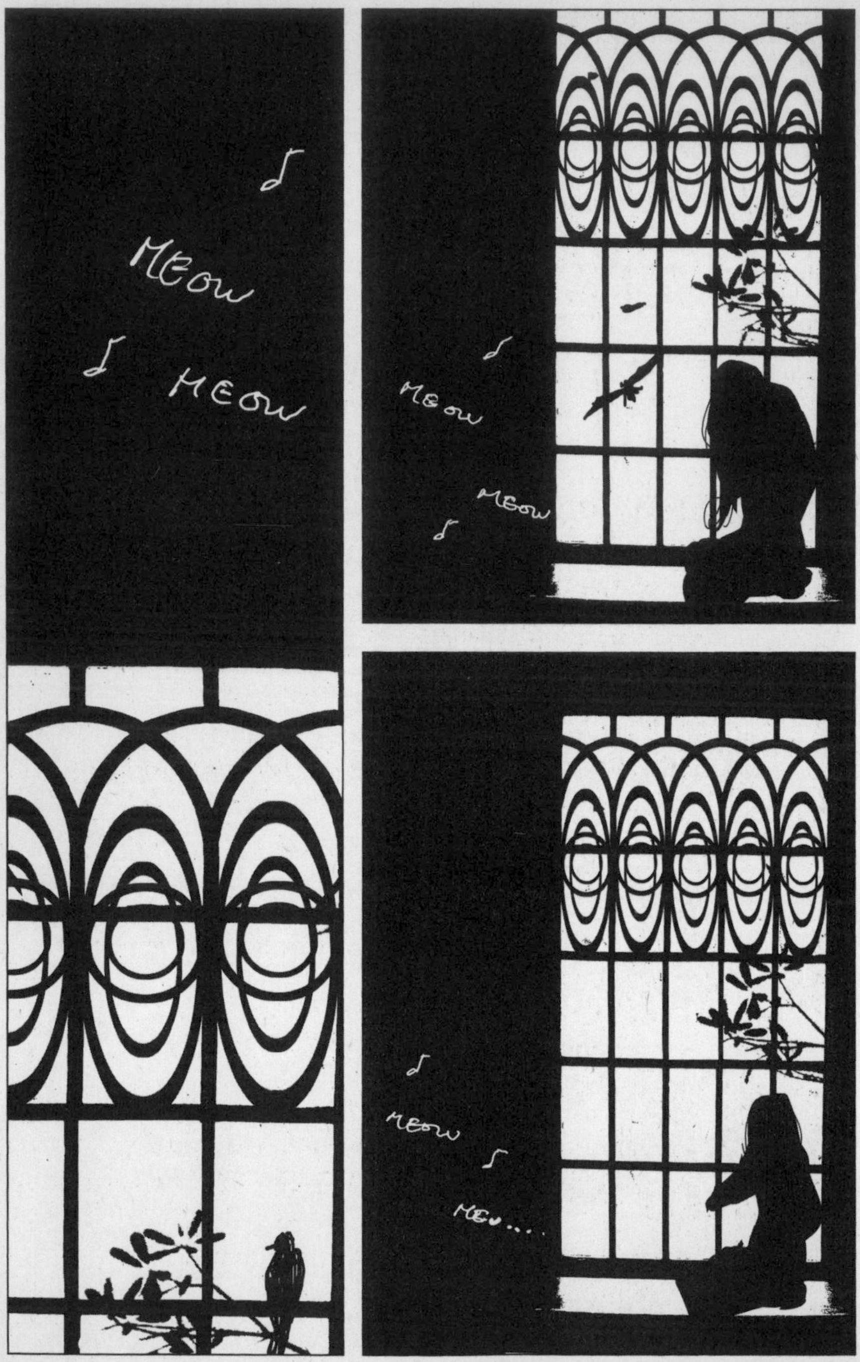
MEOW
MEOW
MEOW
MEOW
MEOW
MEW....

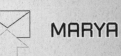

Remember WHAT DAY IS 2DAY?

Swim meet day!

We're up against a longtime rival of ours

Plz don't b late! I'm the first one up!

I need u there 4 moral support! Counting on u

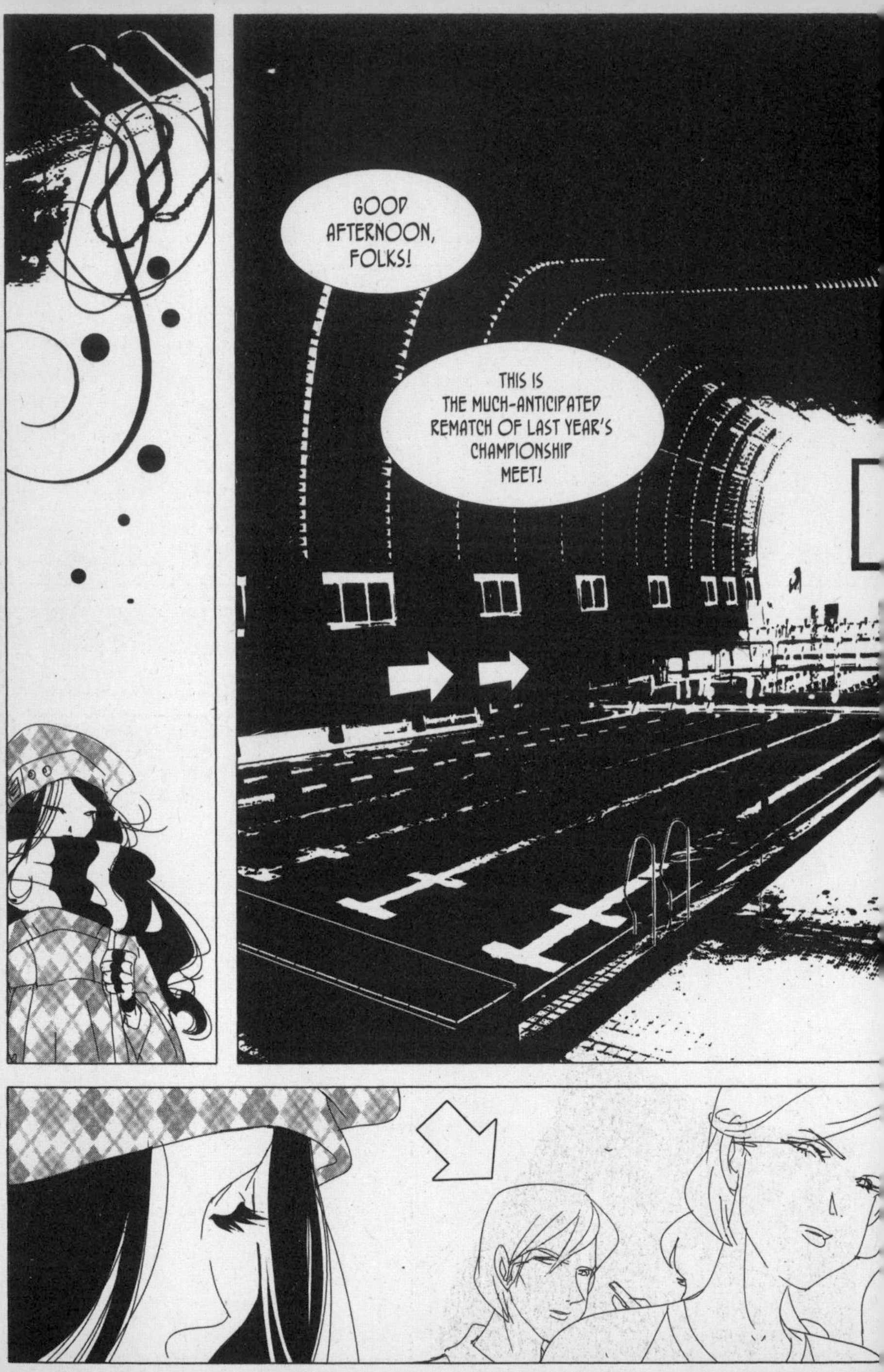
GOOD AFTERNOON, FOLKS!
THIS IS THE MUCH-ANTICIPATED REMATCH OF LAST YEAR'S CHAMPIONSHIP MEET!

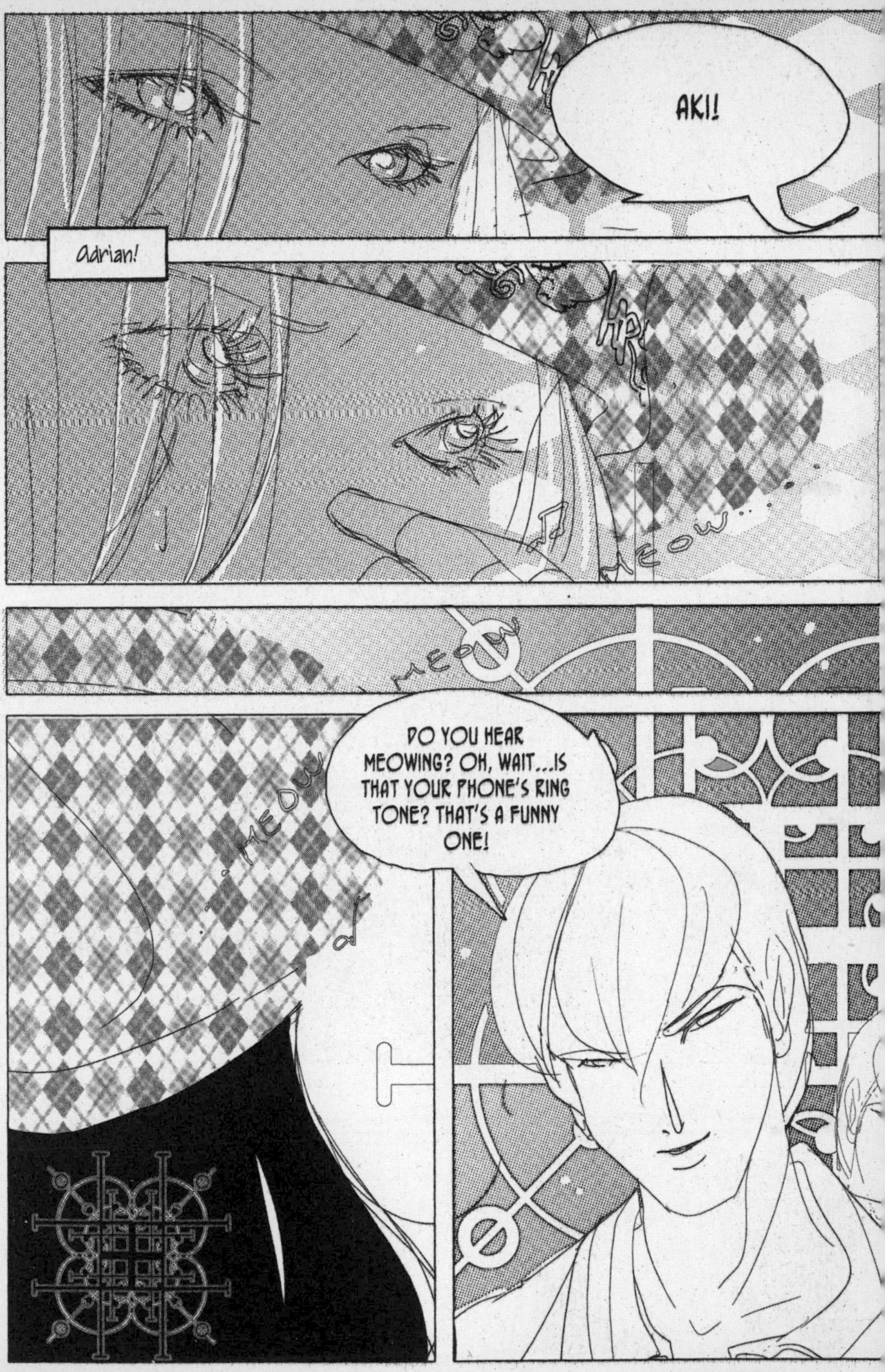
AKI!
Adrian!
MEOW...
MEOW
DO YOU HEAR MEOWING? OH, WAIT...IS THAT YOUR PHONE'S RING TONE? THAT'S A FUNNY ONE!
MEOW

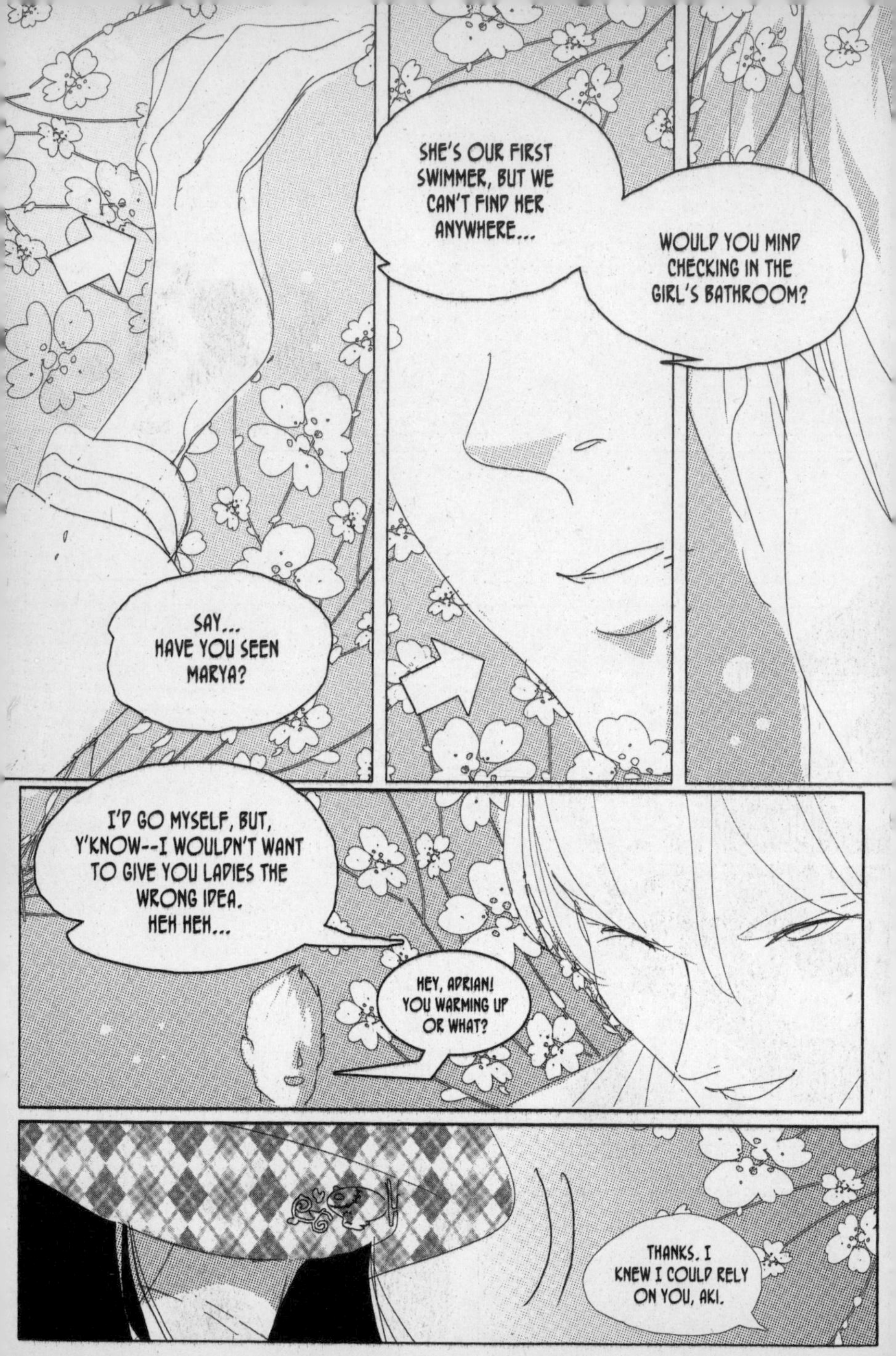
SAY... HAVE YOU SEEN MARYA?
SHE'S OUR FIRST SWIMMER, BUT WE CAN'T FIND HER ANYWHERE...
WOULD YOU MIND CHECKING IN THE GIRL'S BATHROOM?
I'D GO MYSELF, BUT, Y'KNOW--I WOULDN'T WANT TO GIVE YOU LADIES THE WRONG IDEA. HEH HEH...
HEY, ADRIAN! YOU WARMING UP OR WHAT?
THANKS. I KNEW I COULD RELY ON YOU, AKI.

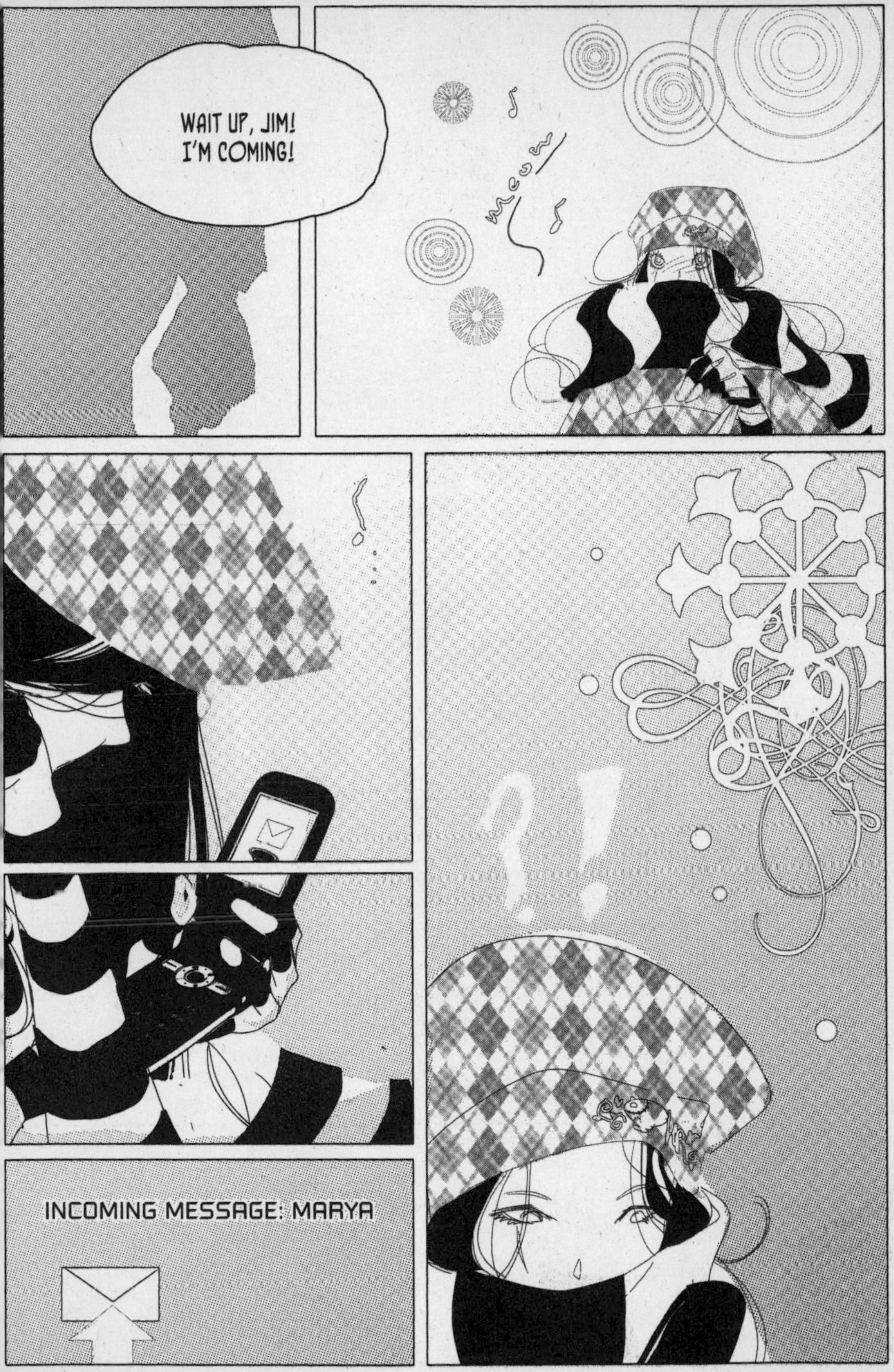
WAIT UP, JIM!
I'M COMING!
INCOMING MESSAGE: MARYA

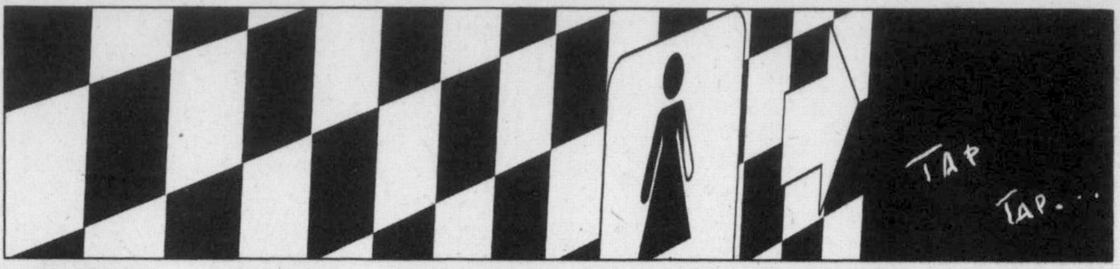
TAP
TAP...
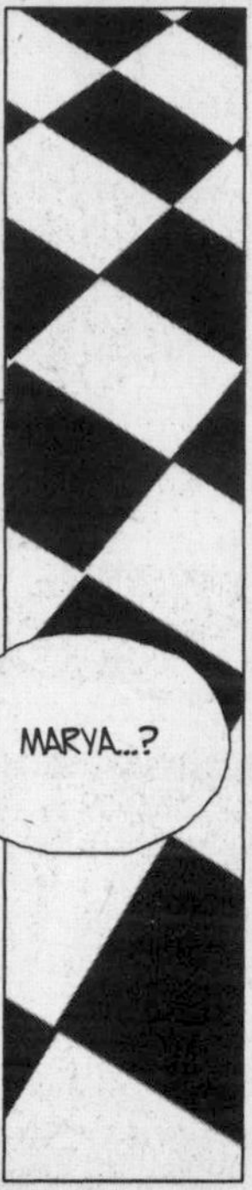
MARYA...?
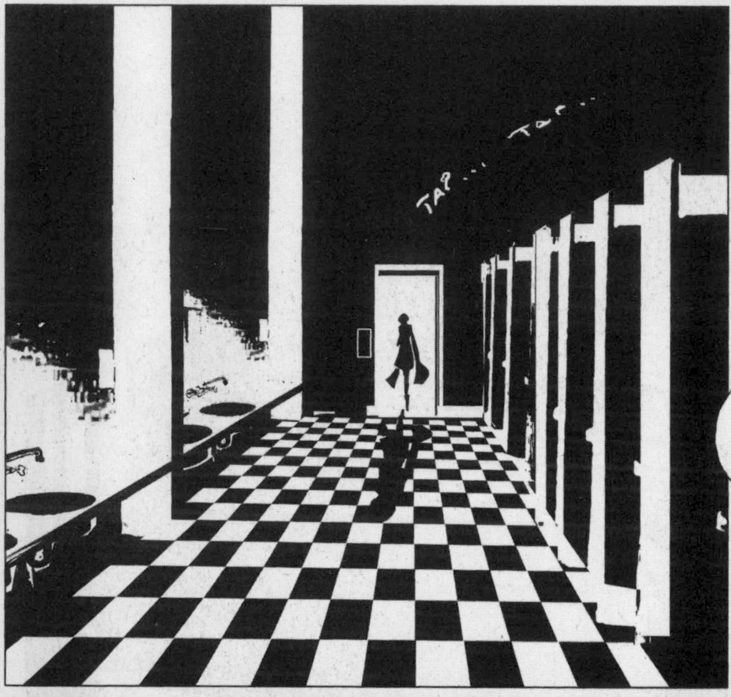
TAP...
TAP...
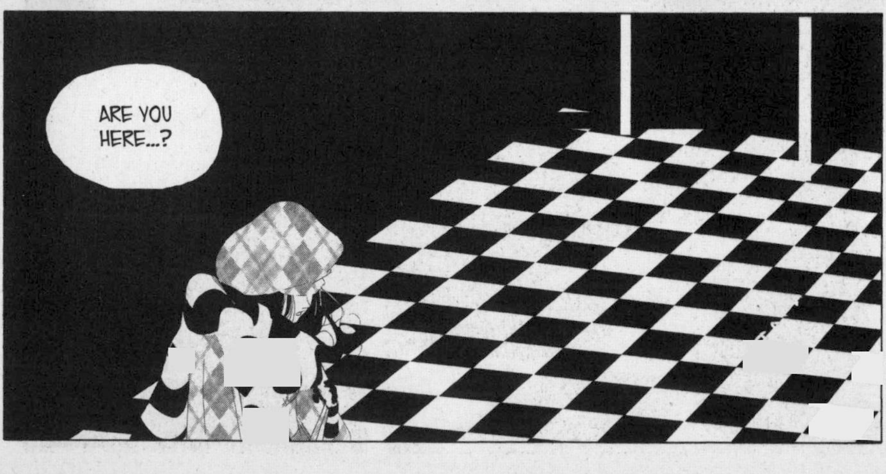
ARE YOU HERE...?

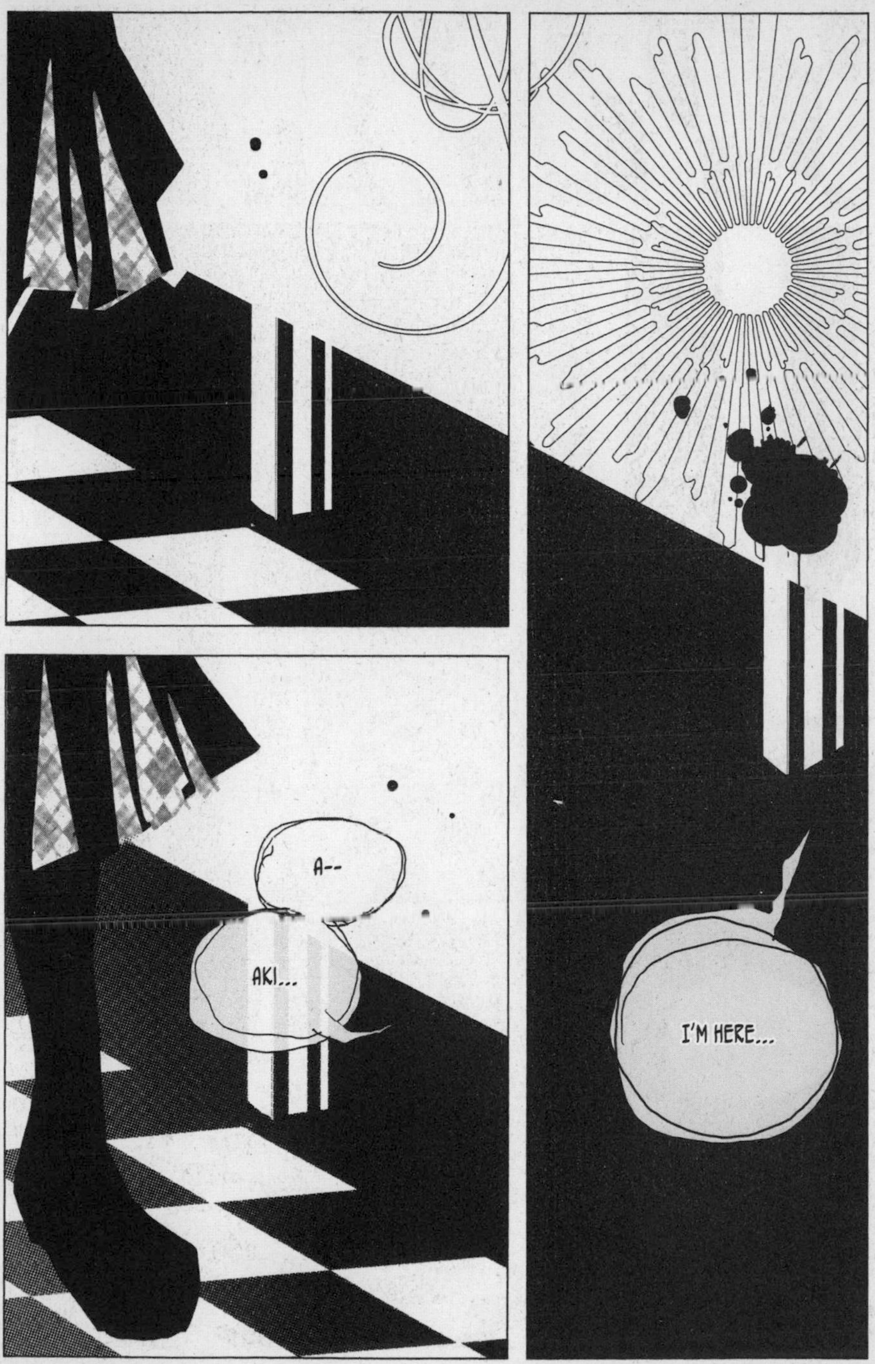
A--
AKI...
I'M HERE...

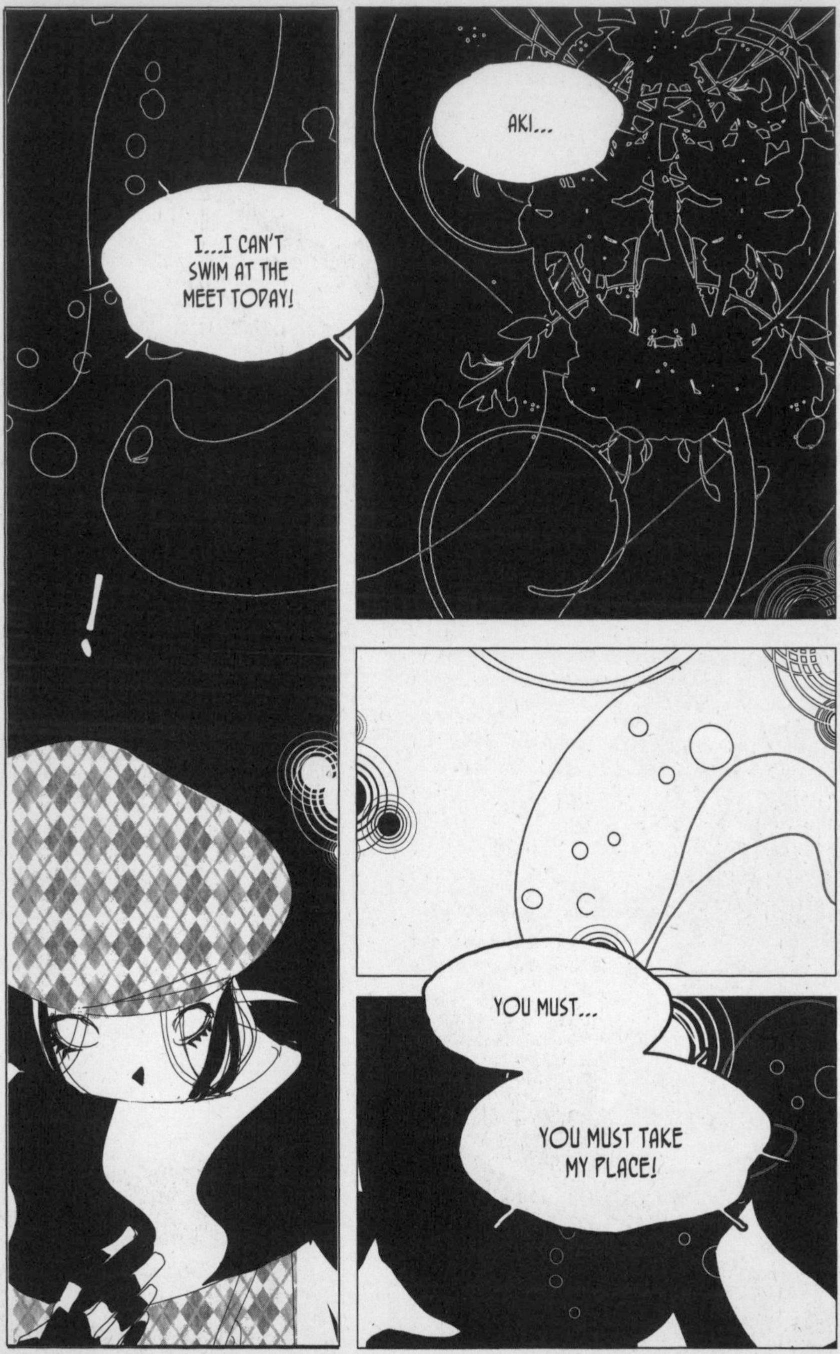
AKI...
I...I CAN'T SWIM AT THE MEET TODAY!
!
YOU MUST...
YOU MUST TAKE MY PLACE!

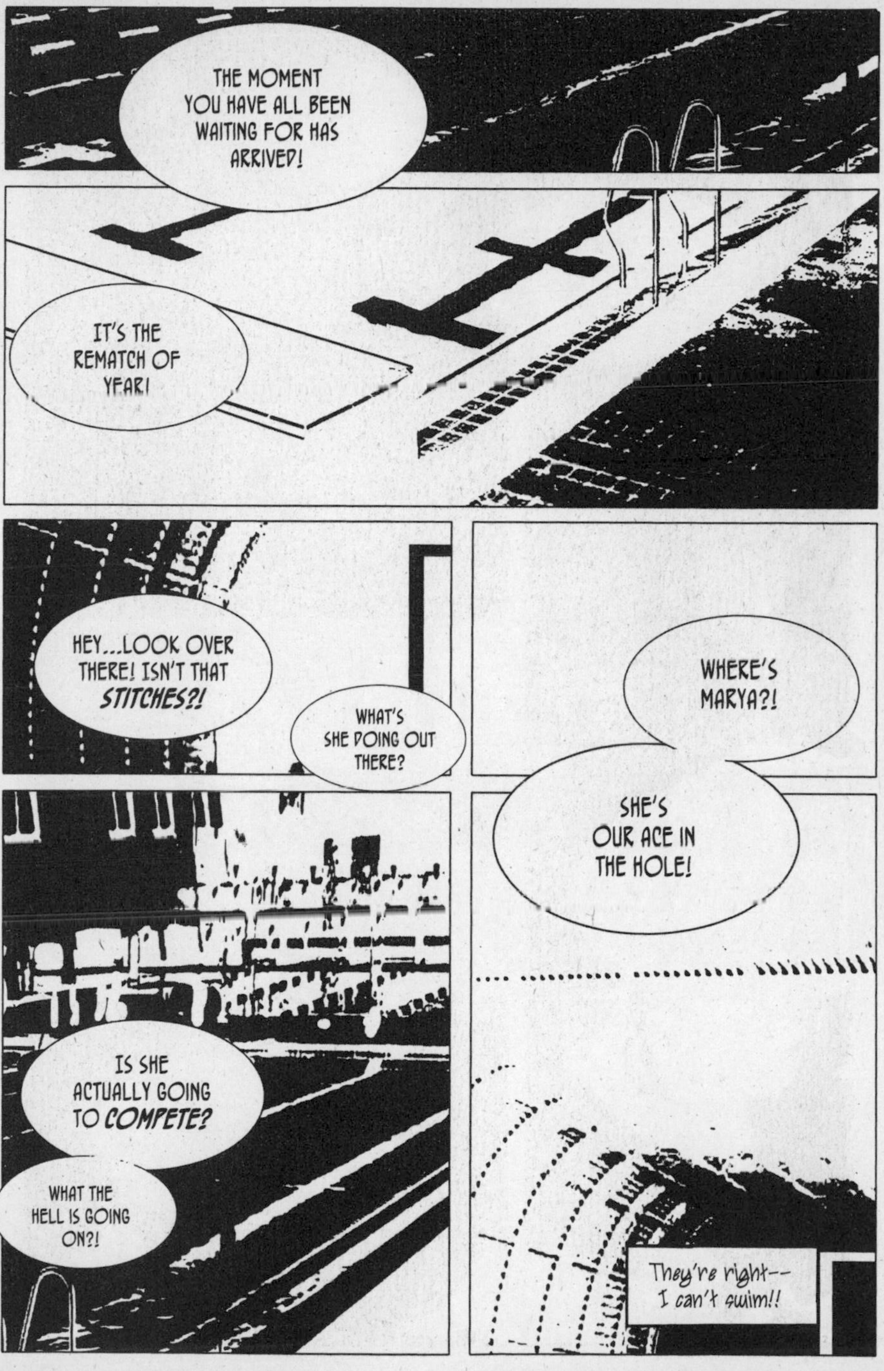
THE MOMENT YOU HAVE ALL BEEN WAITING FOR HAS ARRIVED!
IT'S THE REMATCH OF YEAR!
HEY...LOOK OVER THERE! ISN'T THAT *STITCHES?!*
WHAT'S SHE DOING OUT THERE?
WHERE'S MARYA?!
SHE'S OUR ACE IN THE HOLE!
IS SHE ACTUALLY GOING TO *COMPETE?*
WHAT THE HELL IS GOING ON?!
They're right-- I can't swim!!

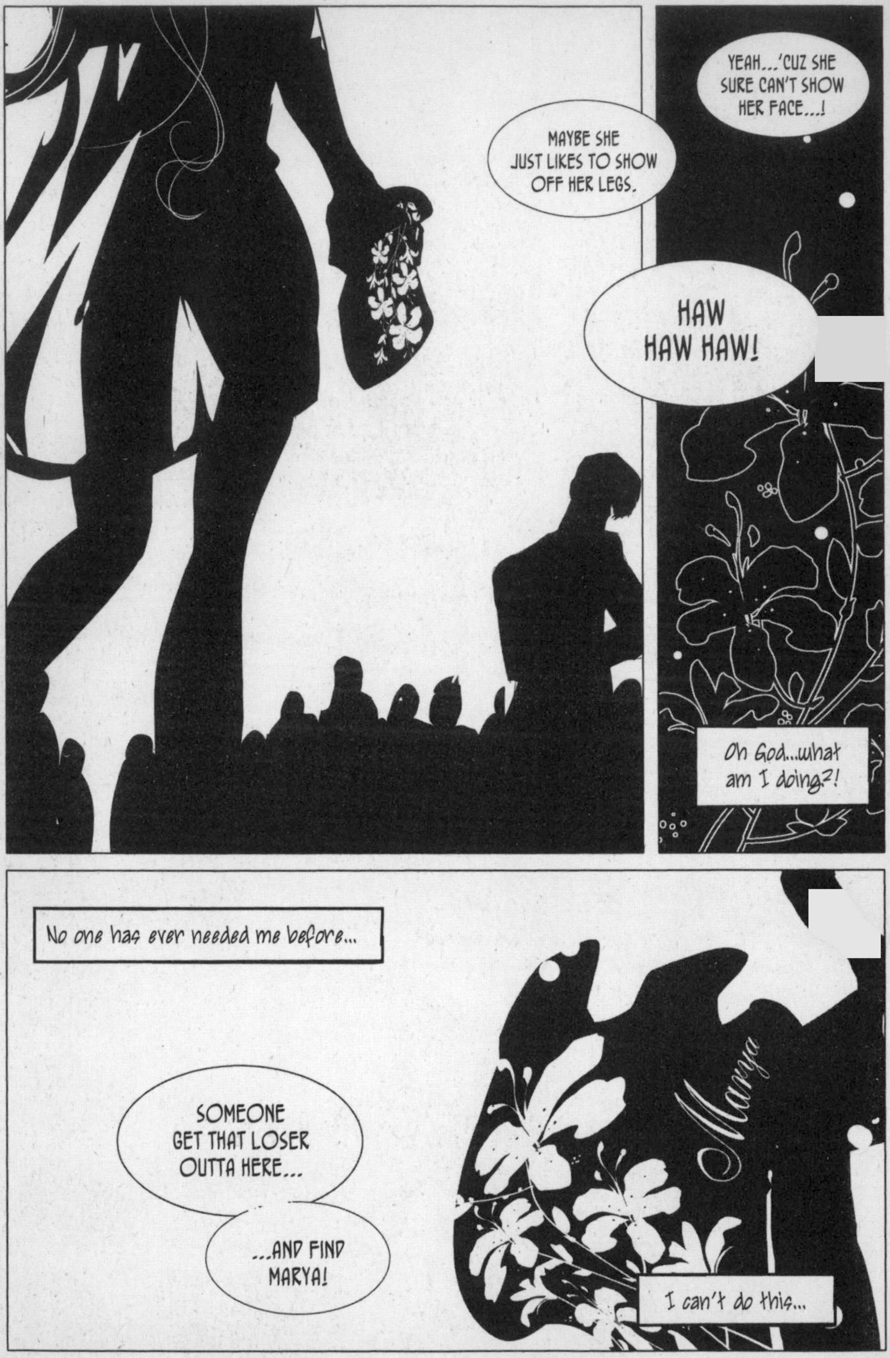
MAYBE SHE JUST LIKES TO SHOW OFF HER LEGS.
YEAH...'CUZ SHE SURE CAN'T SHOW HER FACE...!
HAW HAW HAW!
Oh God...what am I doing?!
No one has ever needed me before...
SOMEONE GET THAT LOSER OUTTA HERE...
...AND FIND MARYA!
Marya
I can't do this...

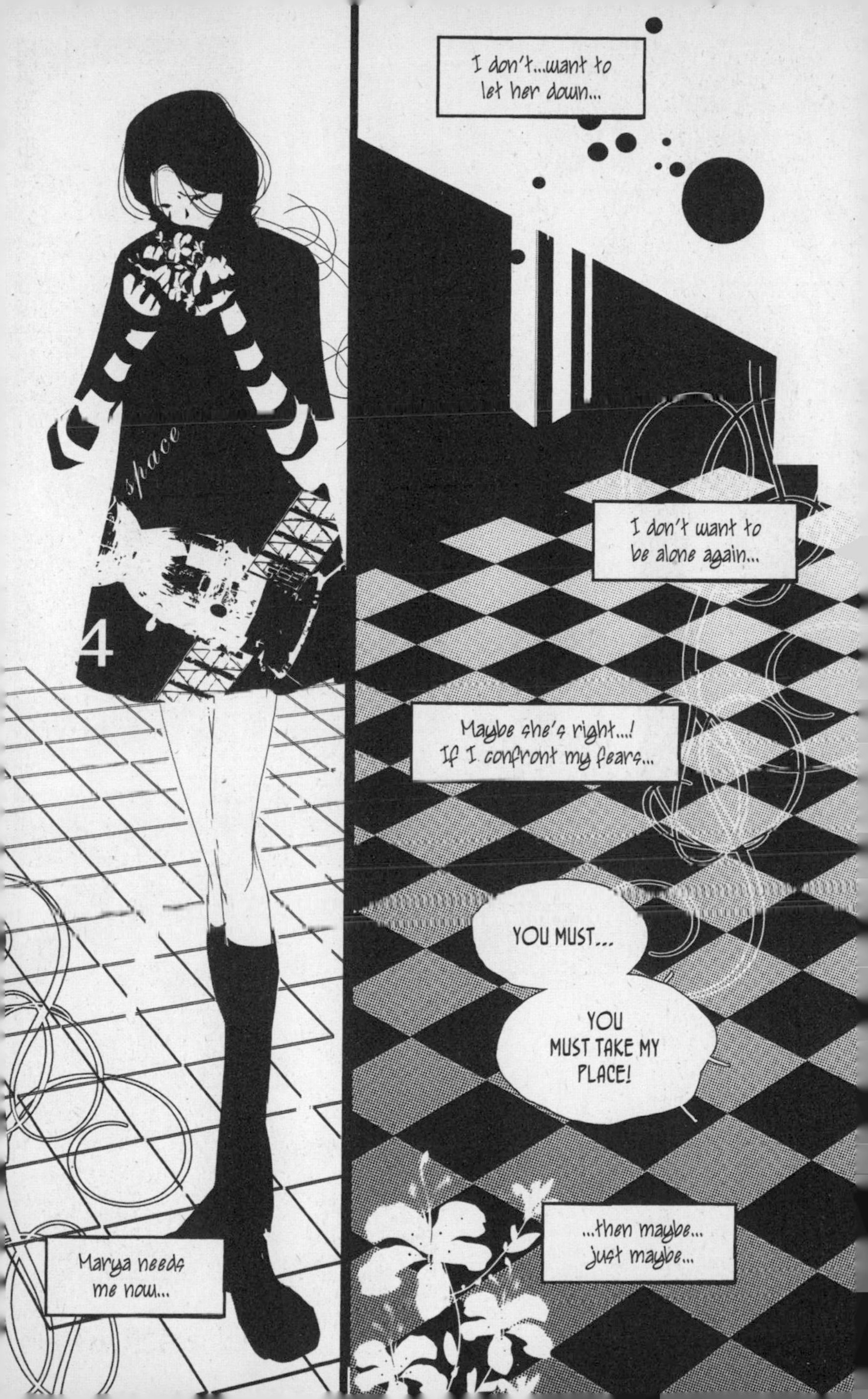
I don't...want to let her down...
I don't want to be alone again...
Maybe she's right...! If I confront my fears...
YOU MUST...
YOU MUST TAKE MY PLACE!
...then maybe... just maybe...
Marya needs me now...

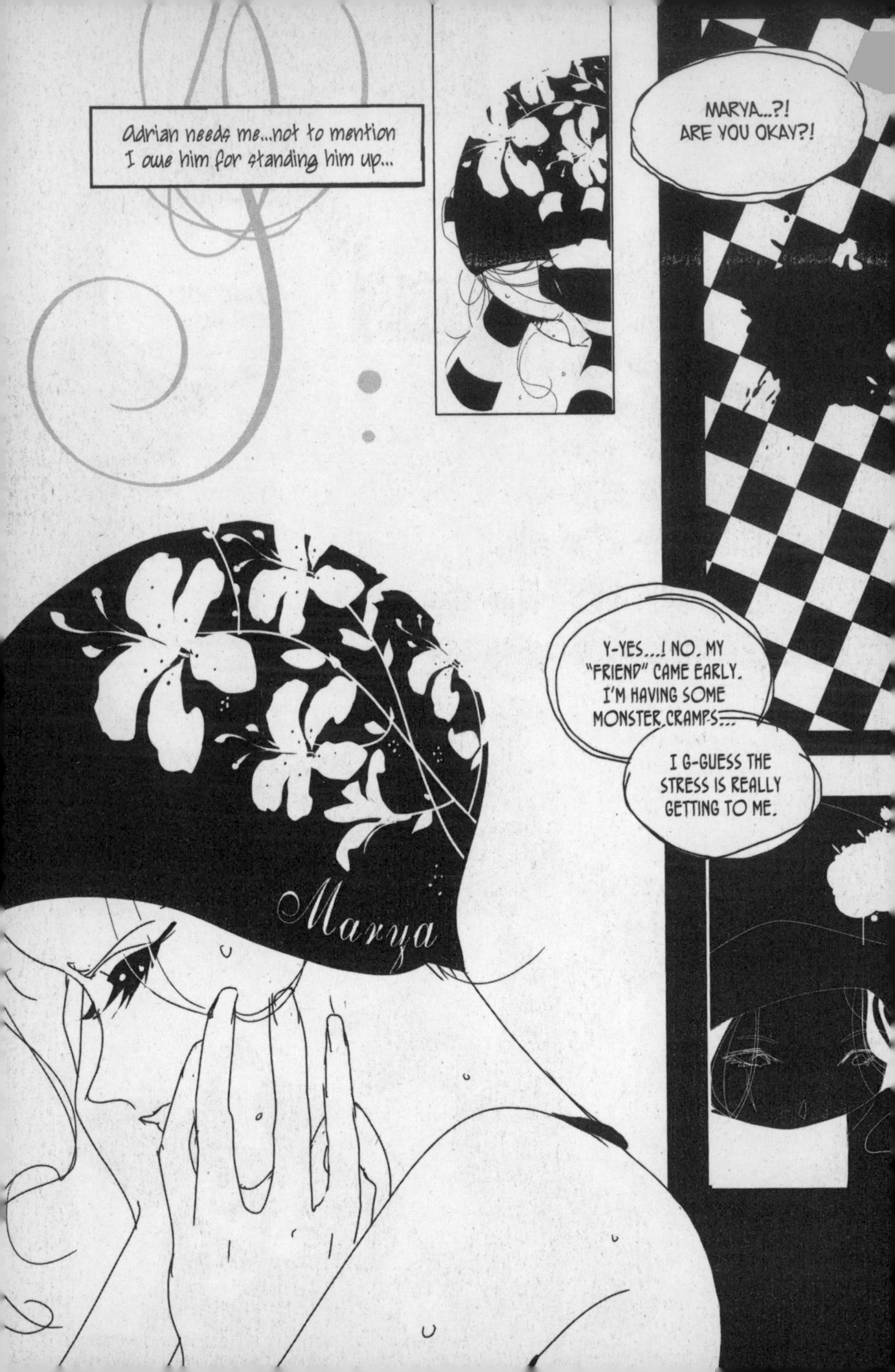
MARYA...?! ARE YOU OKAY?!
Adrian needs me...not to mention I owe him for standing him up...
Y-YES...! NO. MY "FRIEND" CAME EARLY. I'M HAVING SOME MONSTER CRAMPS...
I G-GUESS THE STRESS IS REALLY GETTING TO ME.
Marya

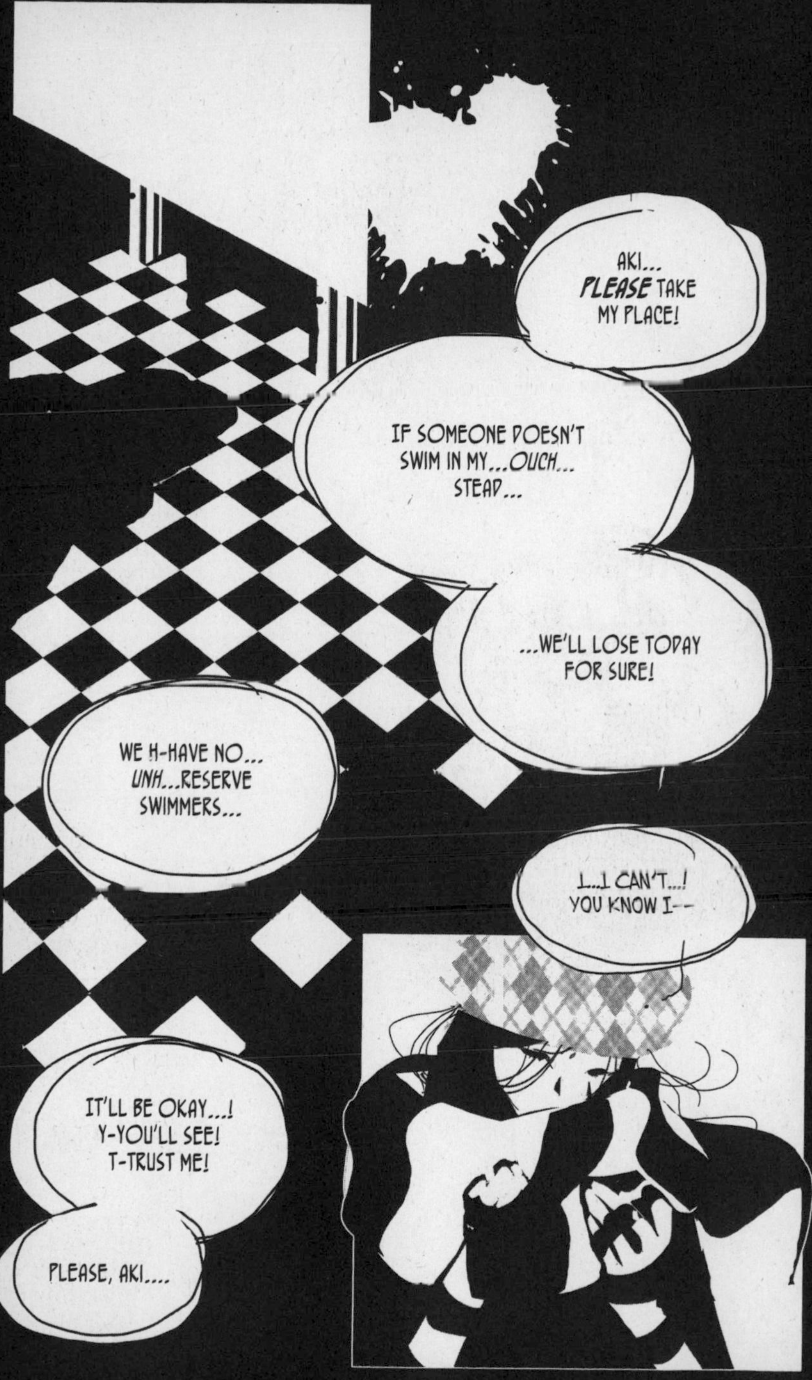
AKI... PLEASE TAKE MY PLACE!
IF SOMEONE DOESN'T SWIM IN MY...OUCH... STEAD...
...WE'LL LOSE TODAY FOR SURE!
WE H-HAVE NO... UNH...RESERVE SWIMMERS...
I...I CAN'T...! YOU KNOW I--
IT'LL BE OKAY...! Y-YOU'LL SEE! T-TRUST ME!
PLEASE, AKI....

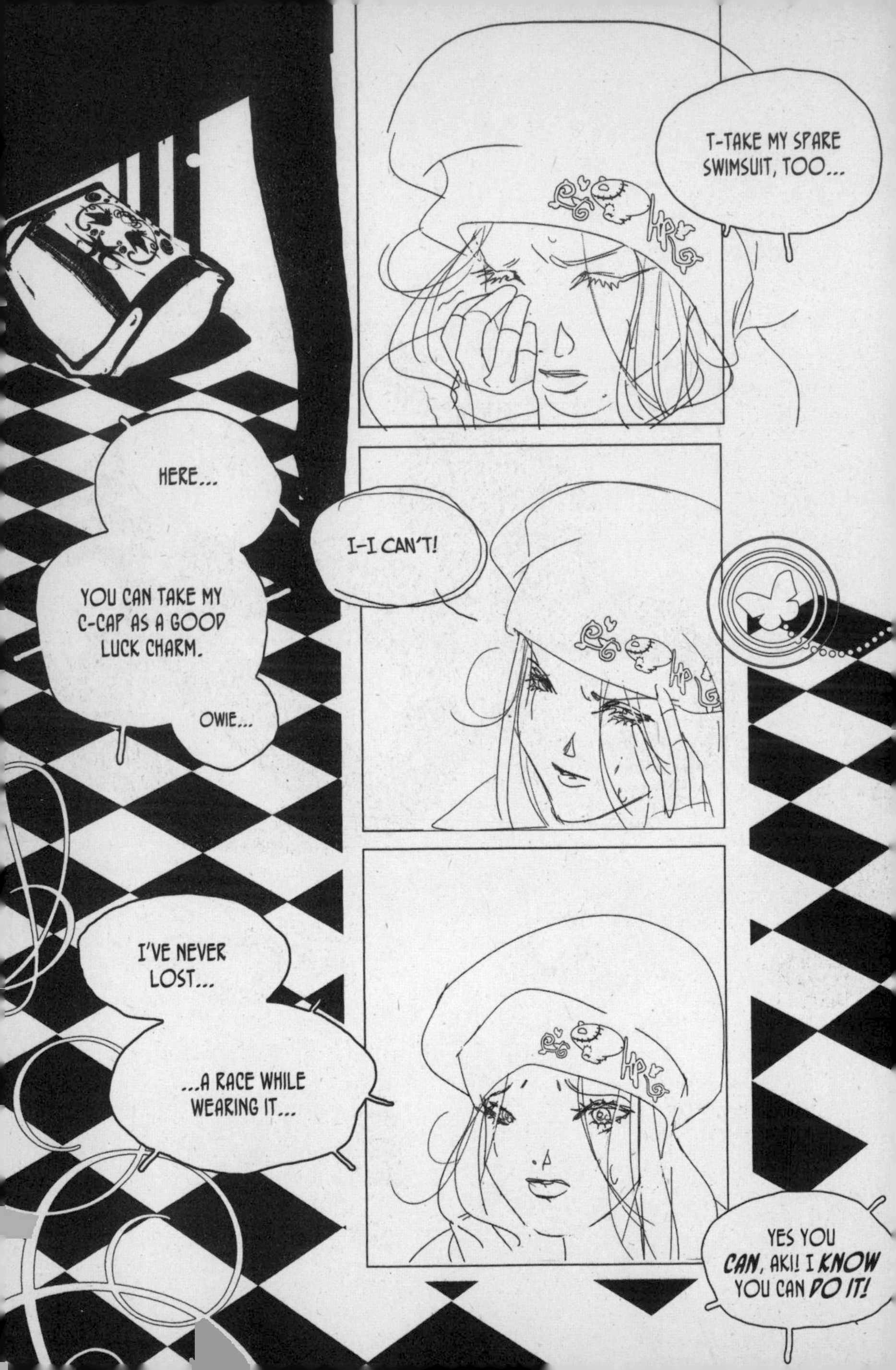

T-TAKE MY SPARE SWIMSUIT, TOO...
HERE...
YOU CAN TAKE MY C-CAP AS A GOOD LUCK CHARM.
OWIE...
I-I CAN'T!
I'VE NEVER LOST...
...A RACE WHILE WEARING IT...
YES YOU ***CAN***, AKI! I ***KNOW*** YOU CAN ***DO IT!***

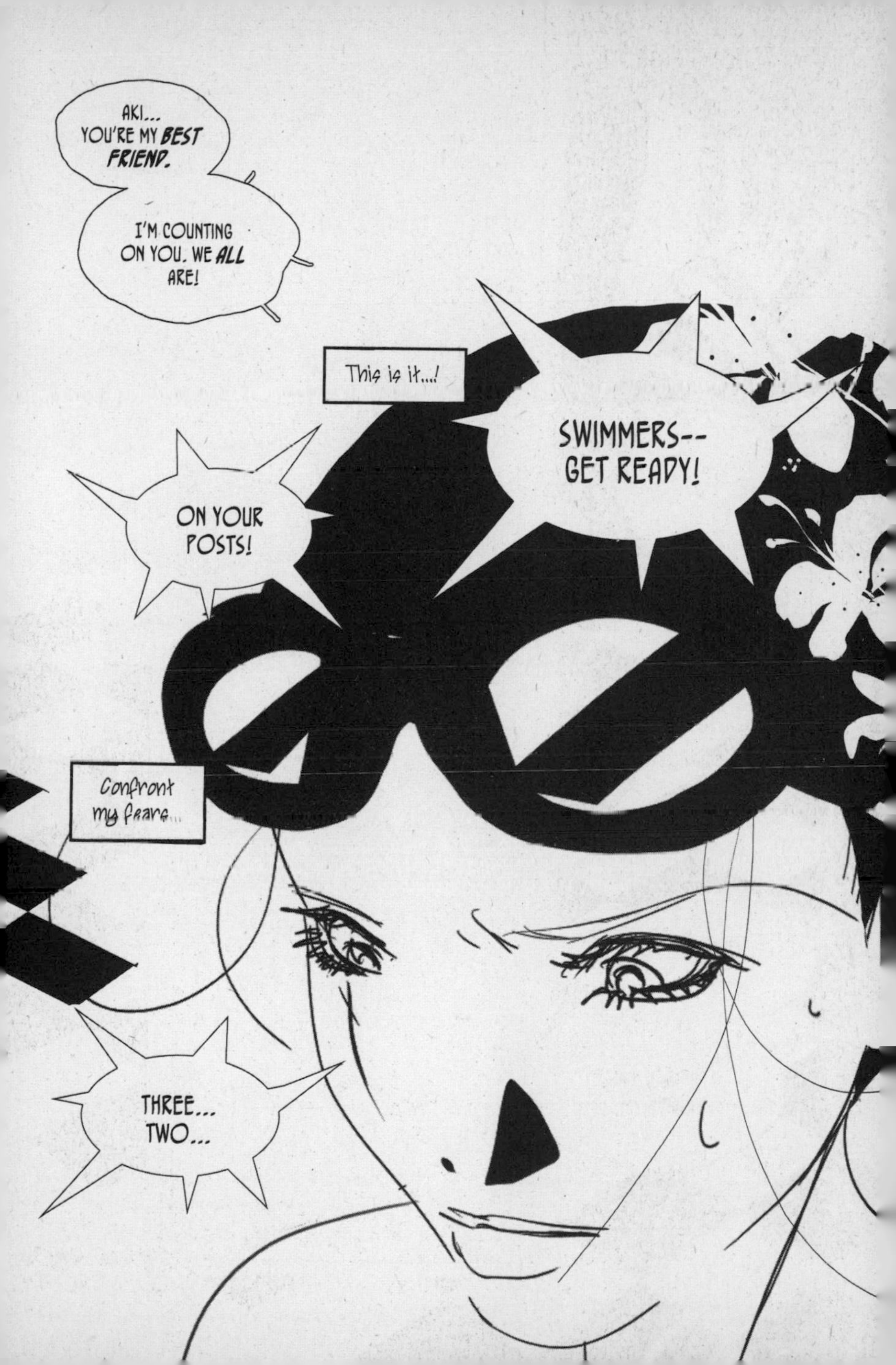
AKI... YOU'RE MY BEST FRIEND.
I'M COUNTING ON YOU. WE ALL ARE!
This is it...!
SWIMMERS-- GET READY!
ON YOUR POSTS!
Confront my fears...
THREE... TWO...

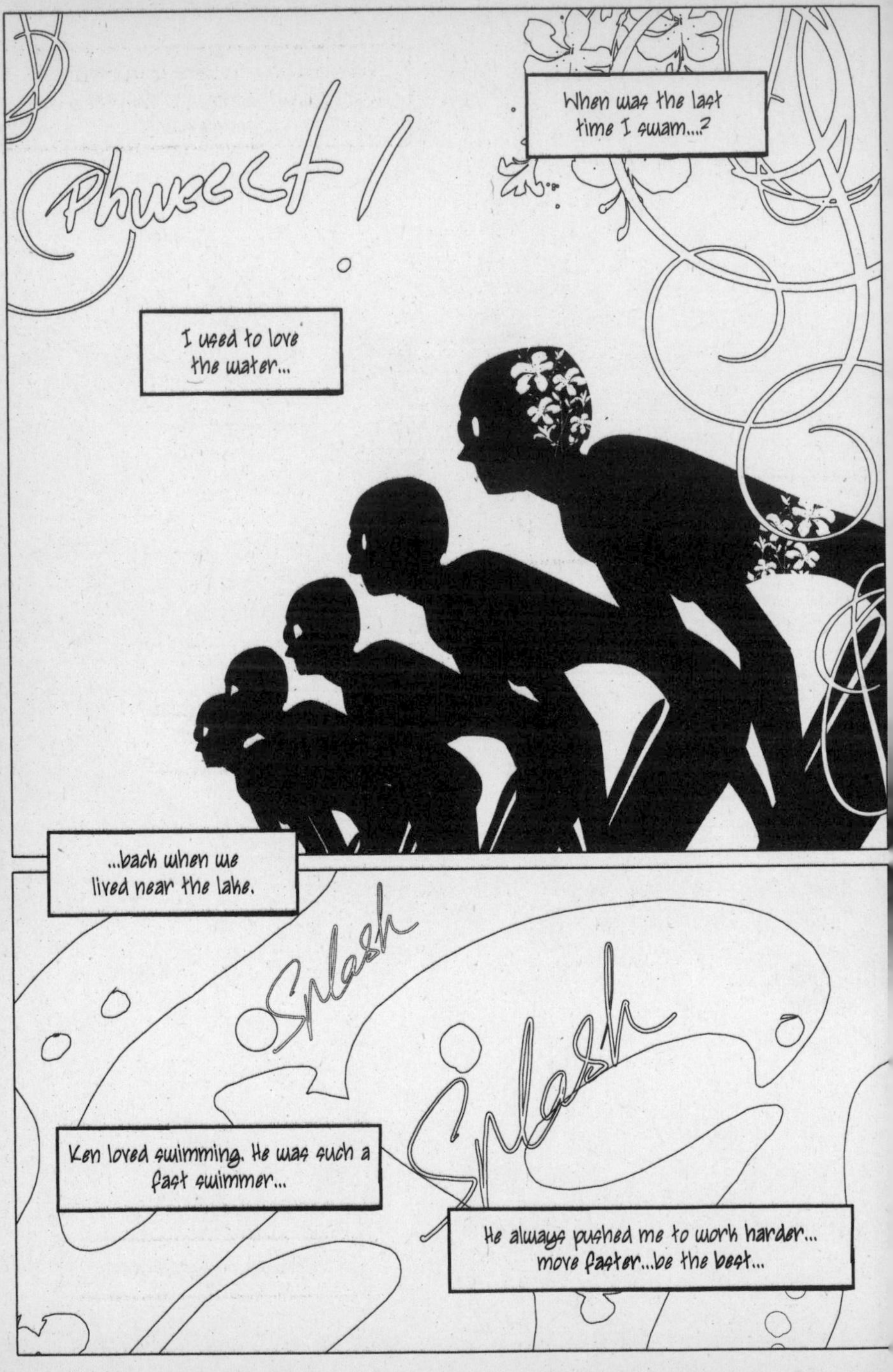
Phuket 1
When was the last time I swam...?
I used to love the water...
...back when we lived near the lake.
Splash
Splash
Ken loved swimming. He was such a fast swimmer...
He always pushed me to work harder... move faster...be the best...

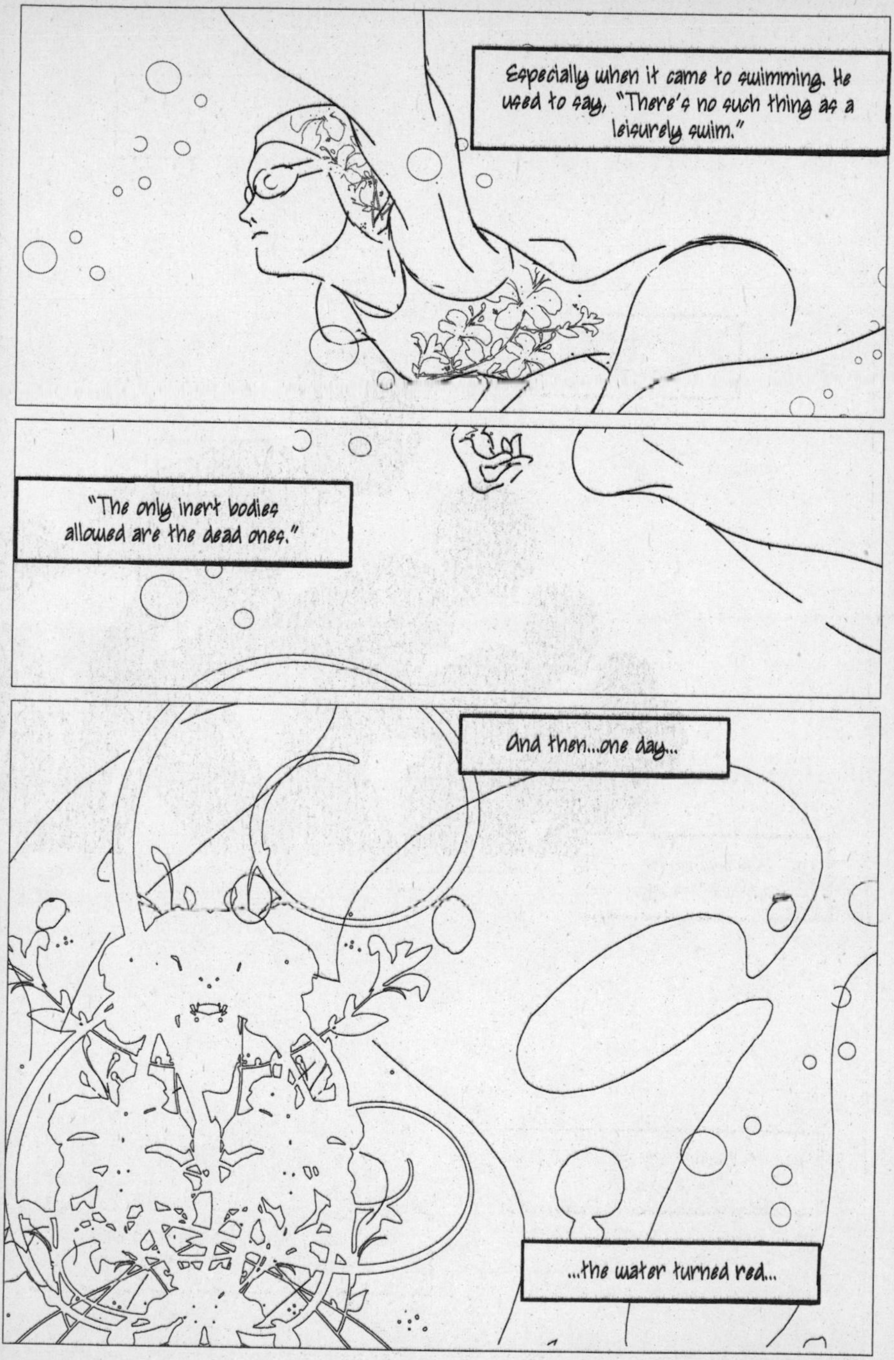
Especially when it came to swimming. He used to say, "There's no such thing as a leisurely swim."
"The only inert bodies allowed are the dead ones."
And then...one day...
...the water turned red...

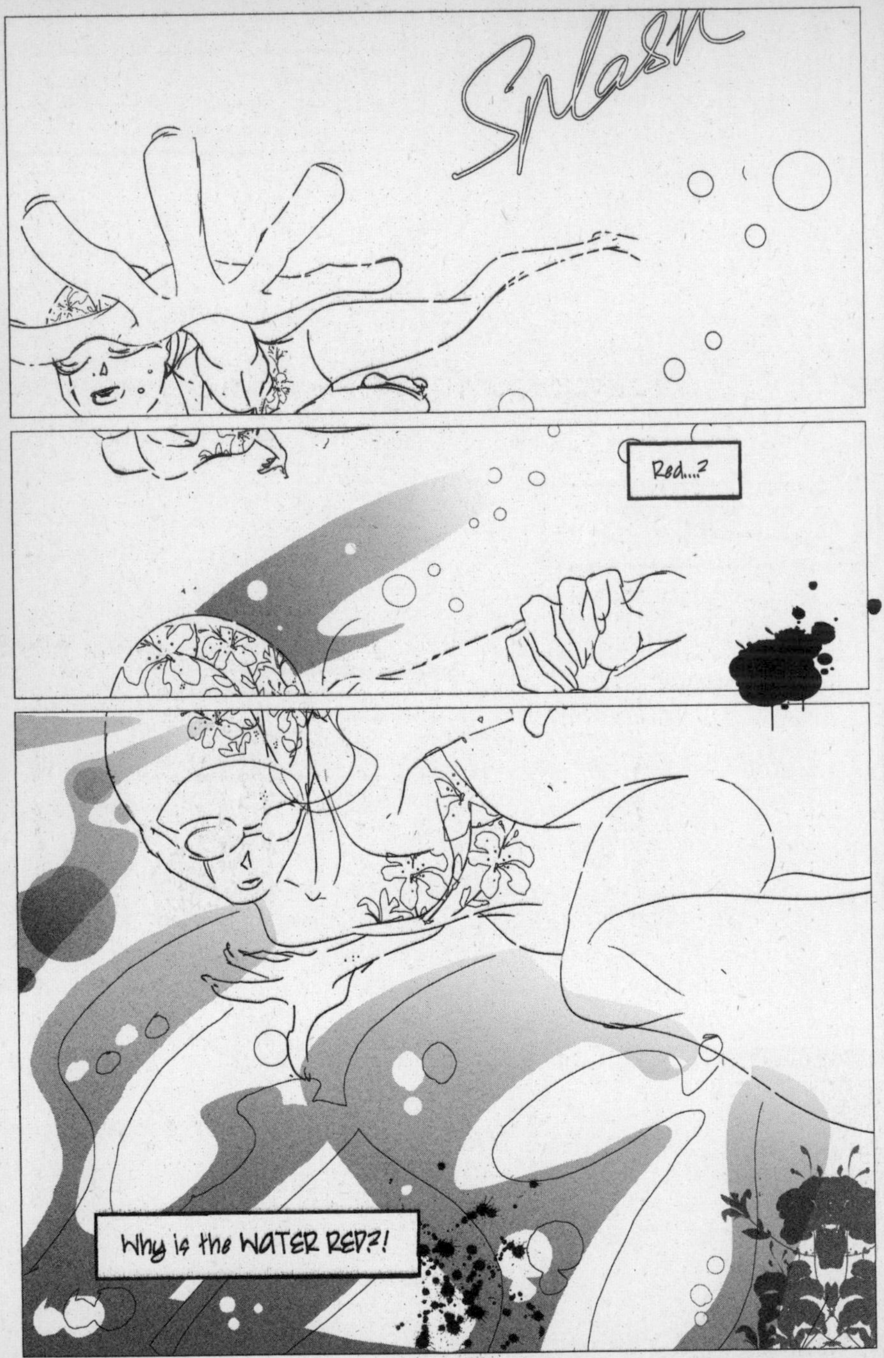
Splash
Red...?
Why is the WATER RED?!

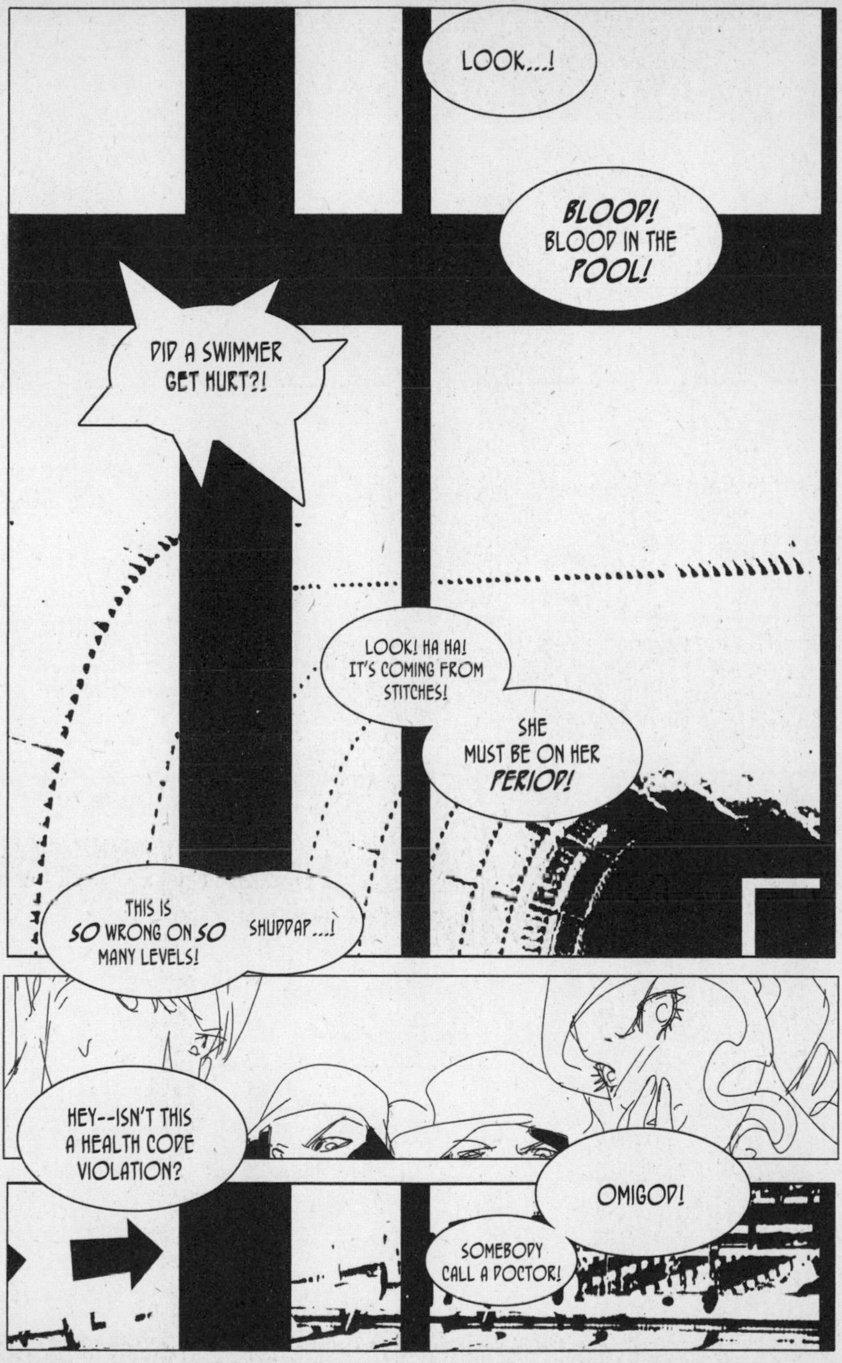
LOOK...!
BLOOD! BLOOD IN THE POOL!
DID A SWIMMER GET HURT?!
LOOK! HA HA! IT'S COMING FROM STITCHES!
SHE MUST BE ON HER PERIOD!
THIS IS SO WRONG ON SO MANY LEVELS!
SHUDDAP...!
HEY--ISN'T THIS A HEALTH CODE VIOLATION?
OMIGOD!
SOMEBODY CALL A DOCTOR!

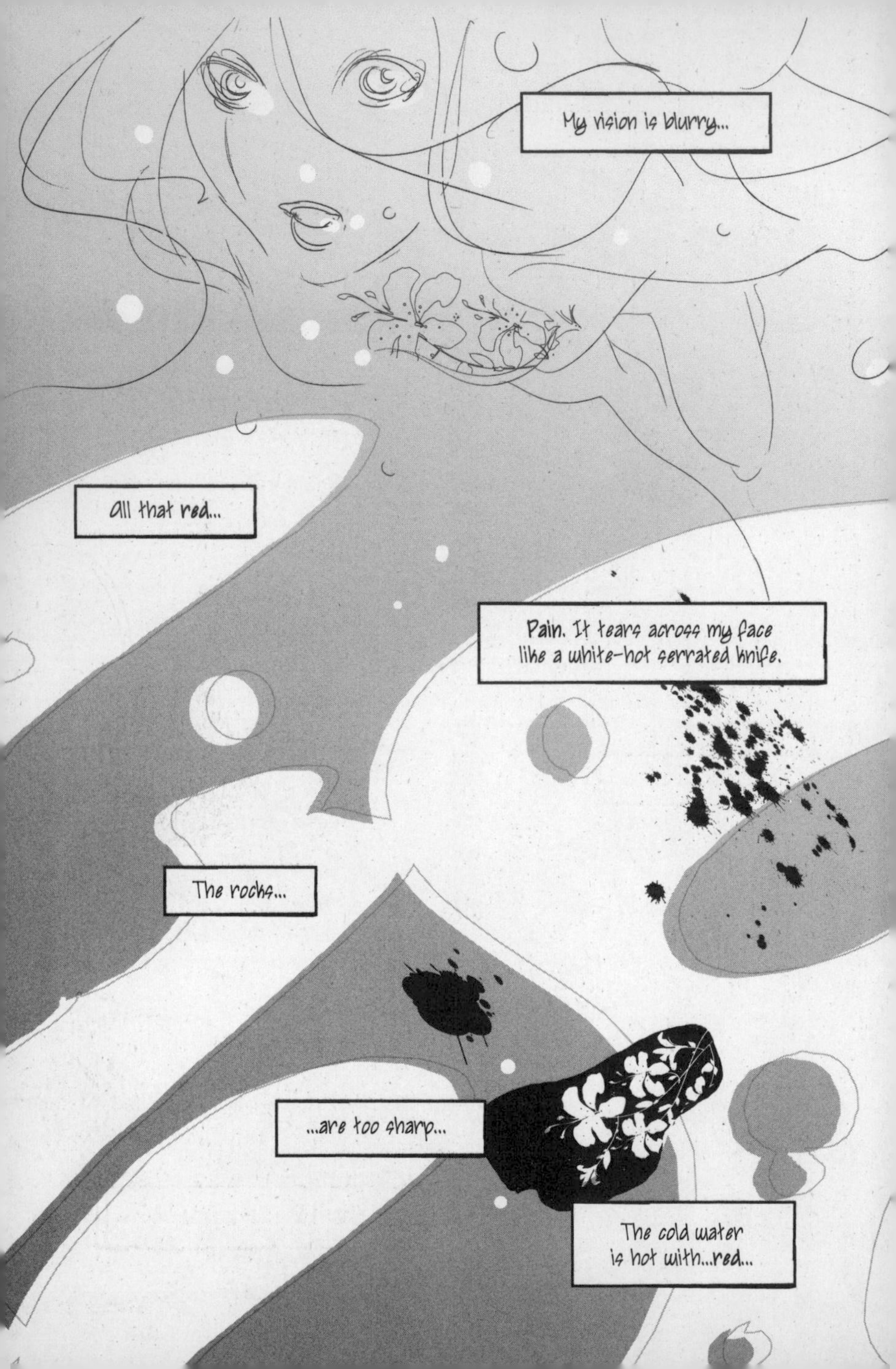
My vision is blurry...
All that red...
Pain. It tears across my face like a white-hot serrated knife.
The rocks...
...are too sharp...
The cold water is hot with...red...

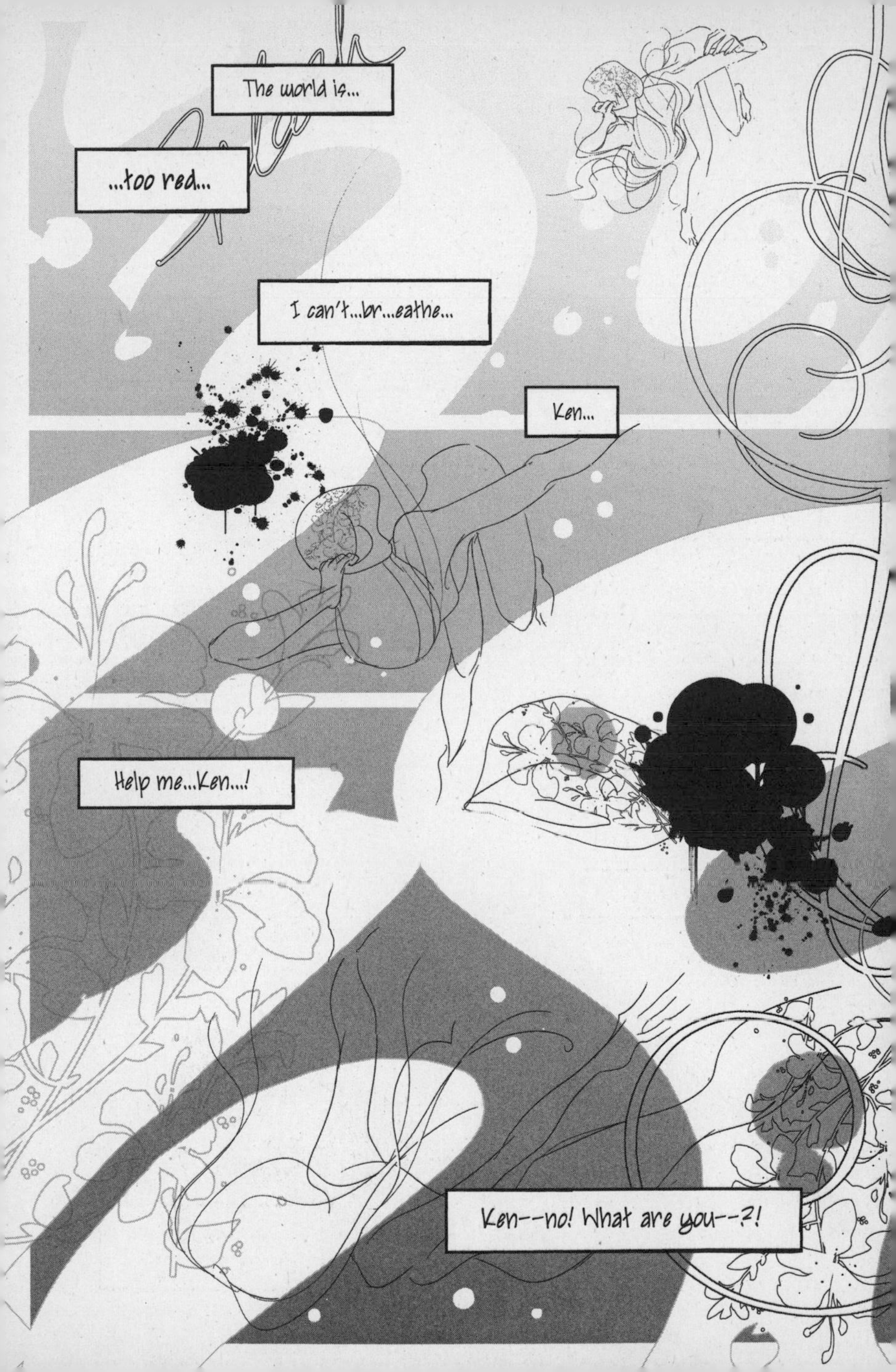
The world is...
...too red...
I can't...br...eathe...
Ken...
Help me...Ken...!
Ken--no! What are you--?!

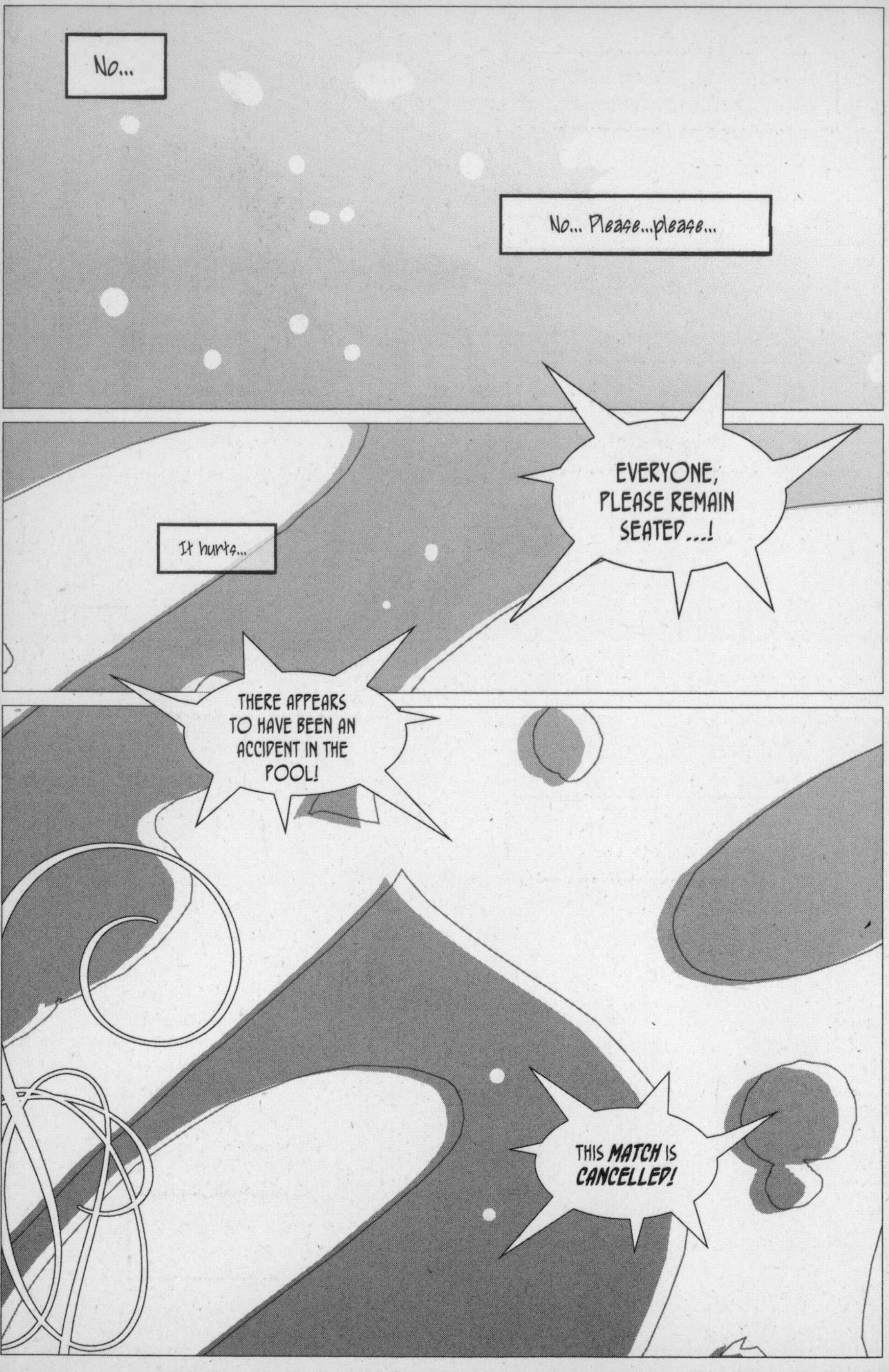
No...
No... Please...please...
EVERYONE, PLEASE REMAIN SEATED...!
It hurts...
THERE APPEARS TO HAVE BEEN AN ACCIDENT IN THE POOL!
THIS *MATCH* IS *CANCELLED!*

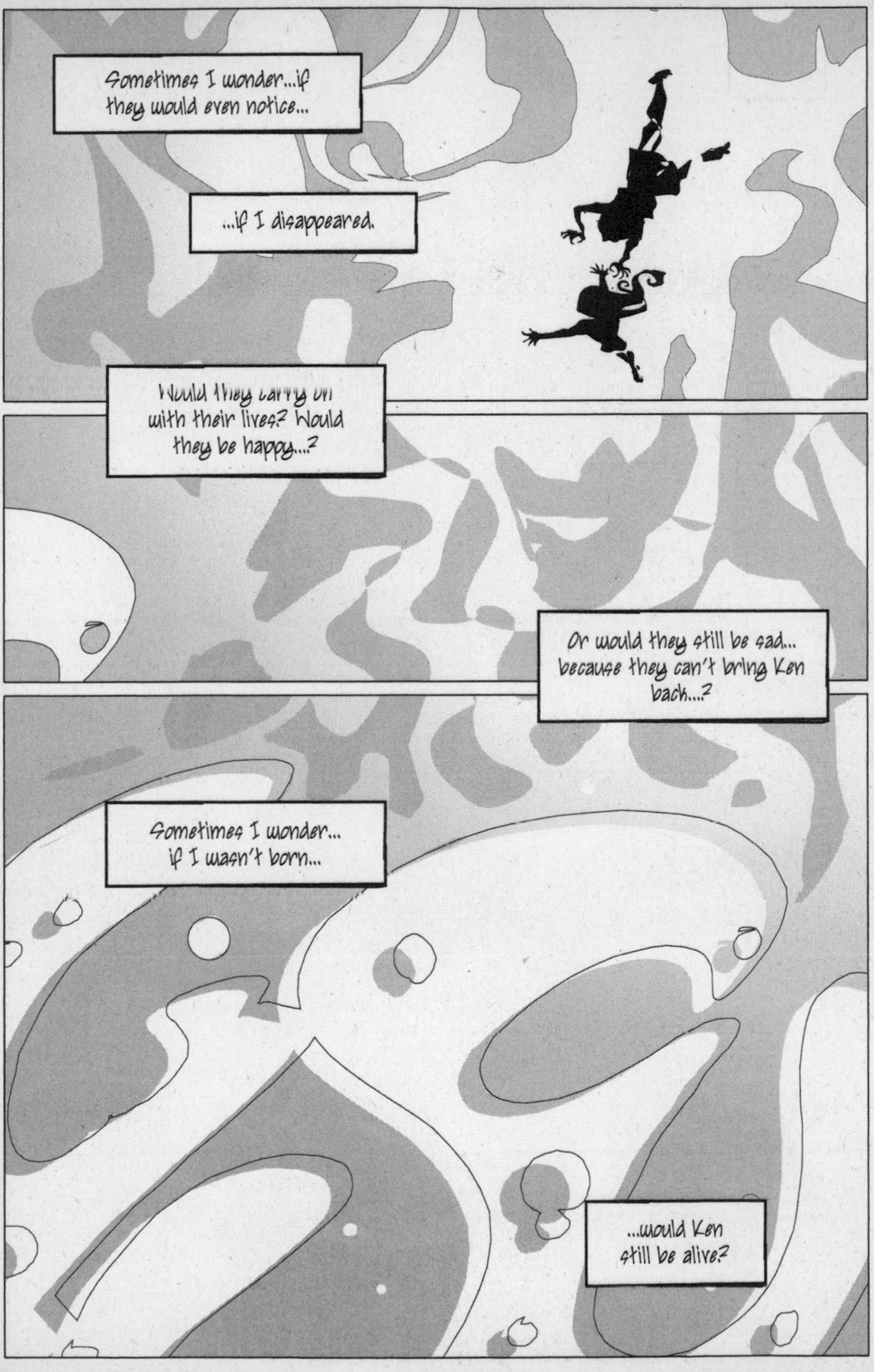
Sometimes I wonder...if they would even notice...
...if I disappeared.
Would they carry on with their lives? Would they be happy...?
Or would they still be sad... because they can't bring Ken back....?
Sometimes I wonder... if I wasn't born...
...would Ken still be alive?

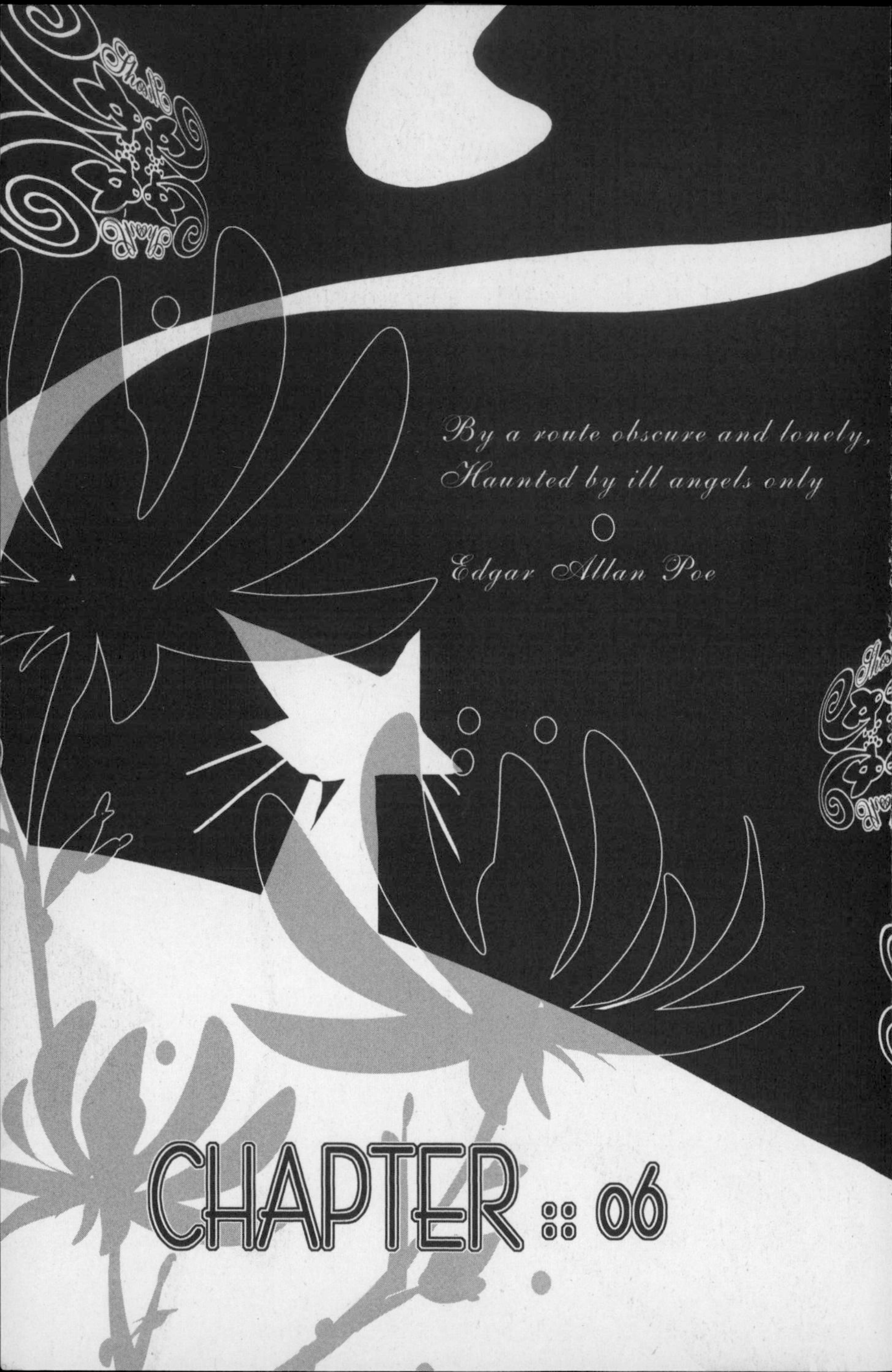
By a route obscure and lonely,
Haunted by ill angels only
Edgar Allan Poe
CHAPTER :: 06

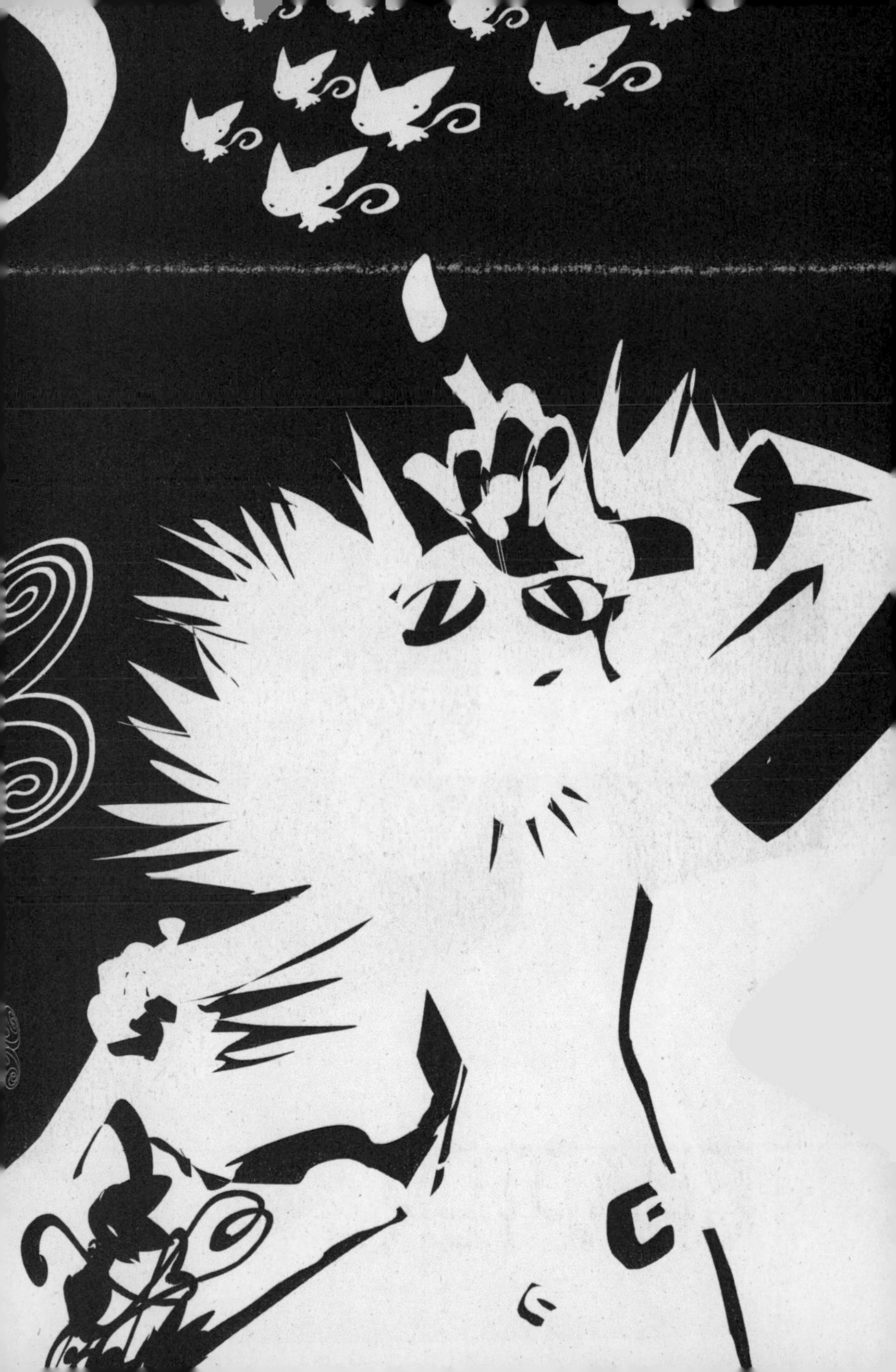

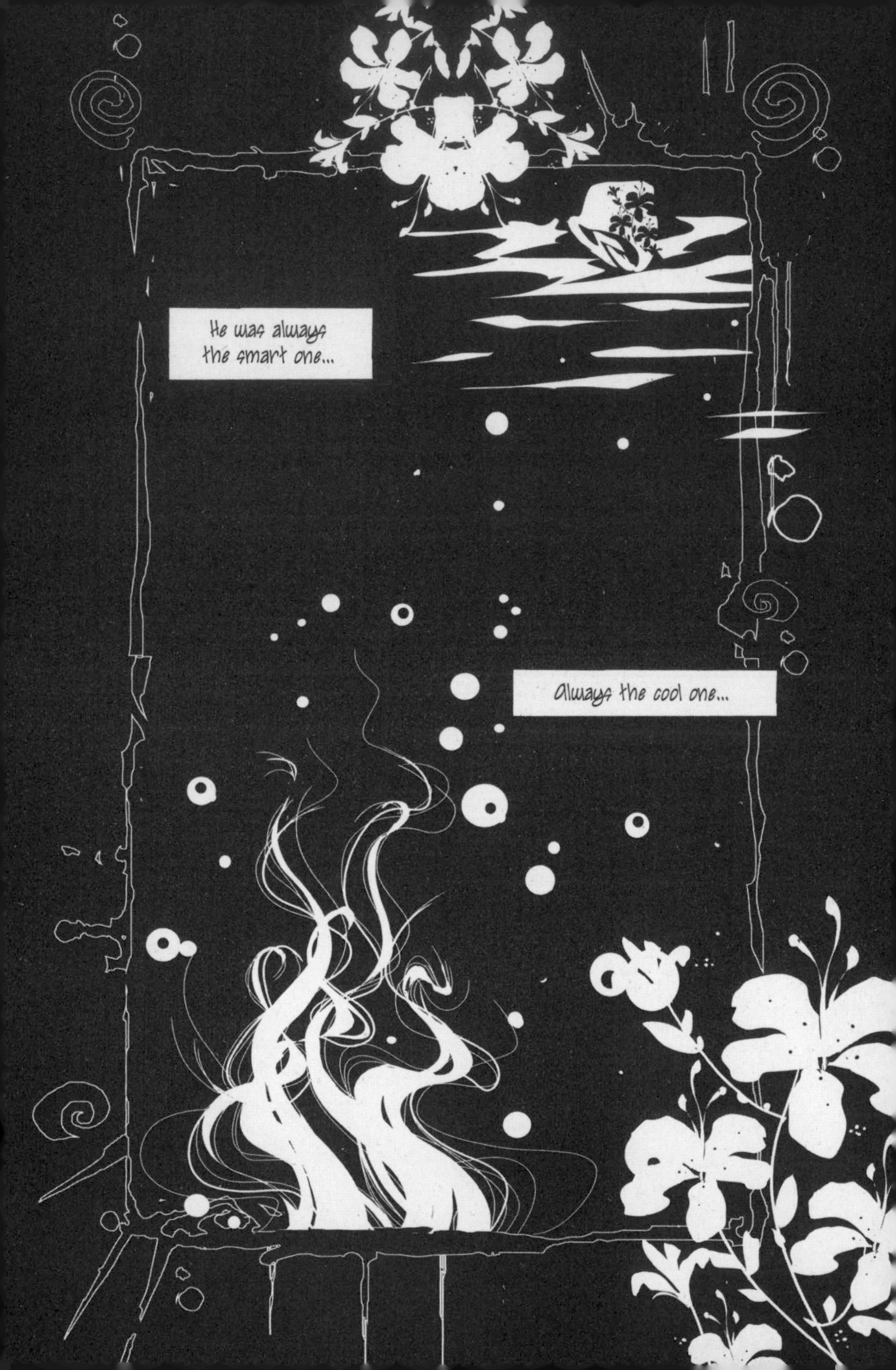
He was always the smart one...
Always the cool one...

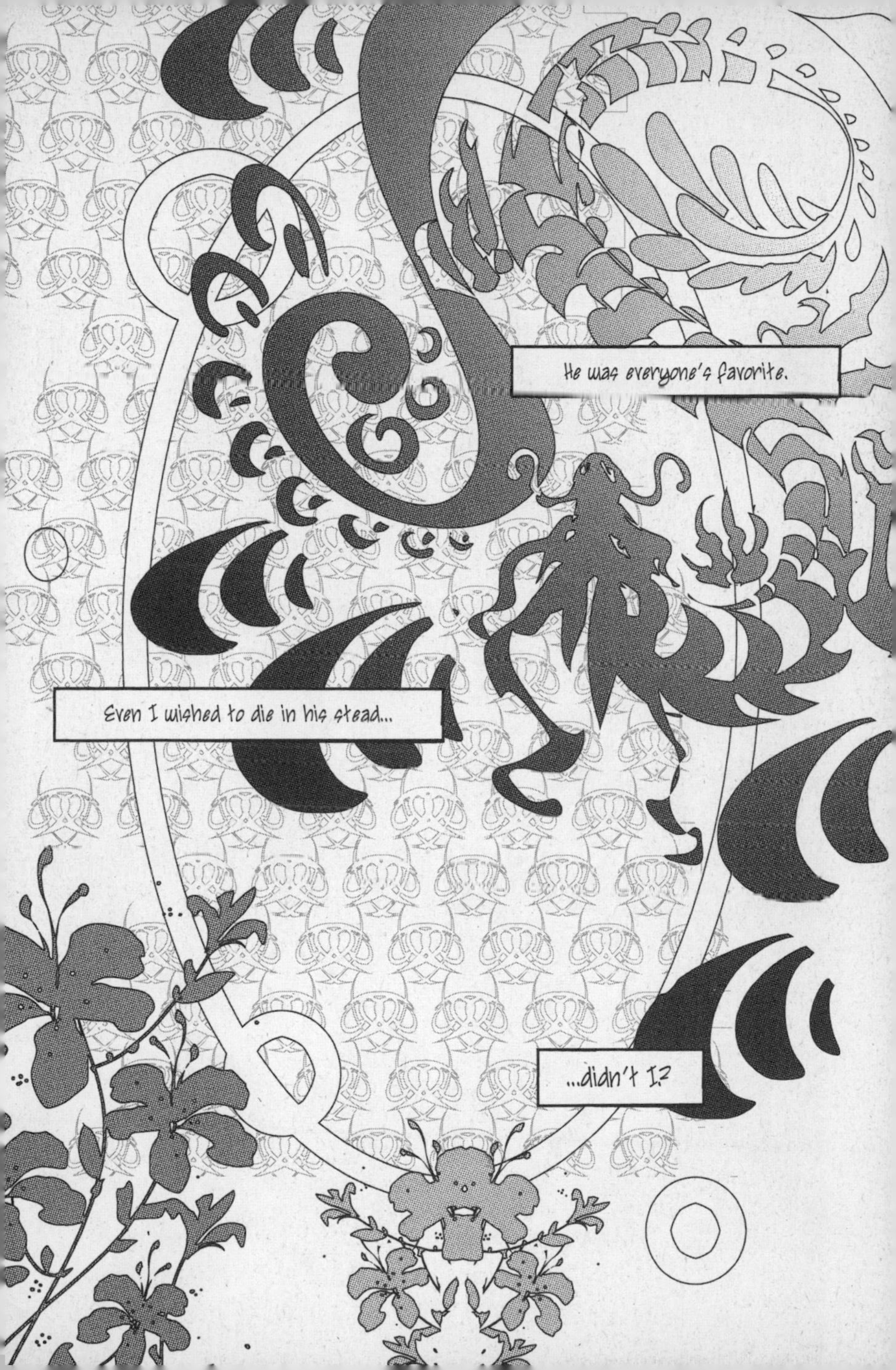
He was everyone's favorite.
Even I wished to die in his stead...
...didn't I?

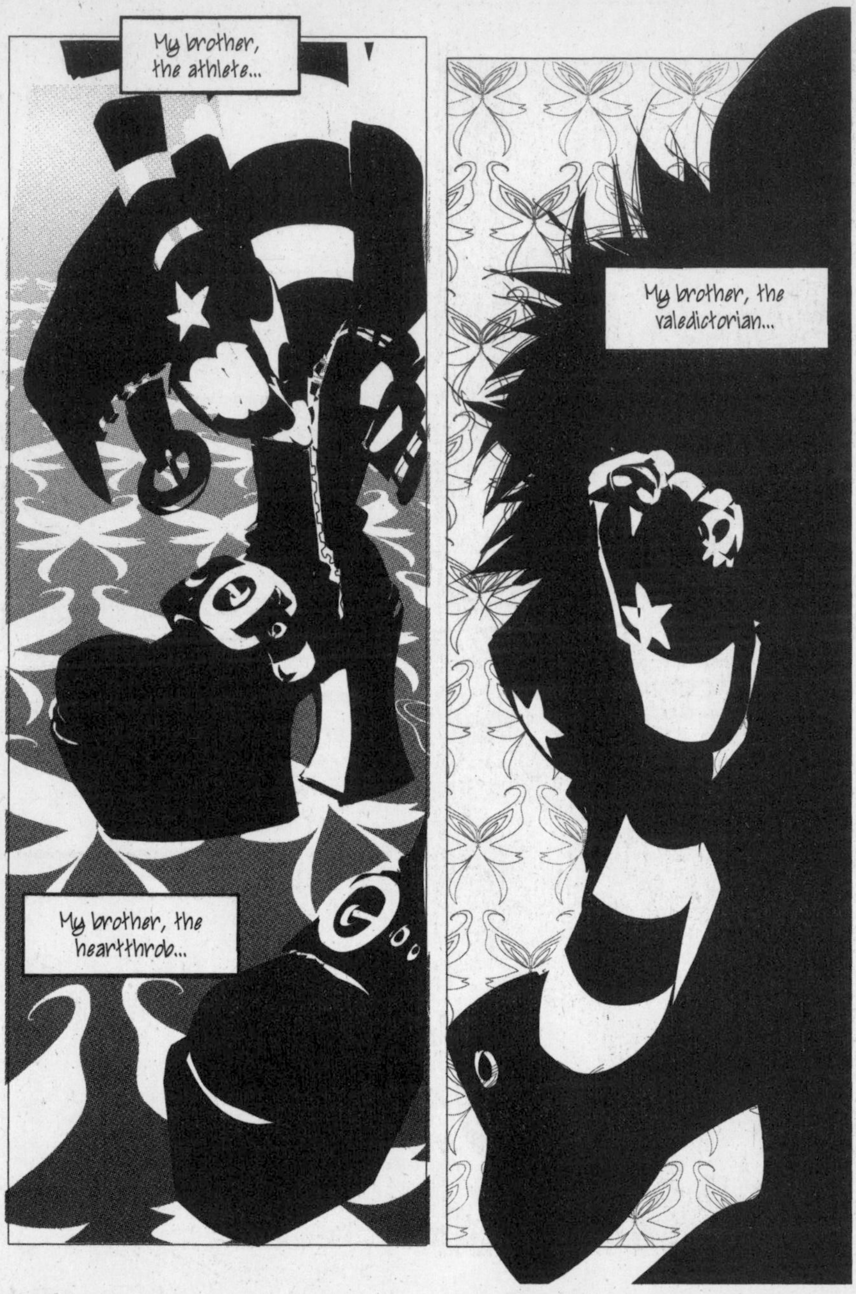
My brother, the athlete...
My brother, the heartthrob...
My brother, the valedictorian...

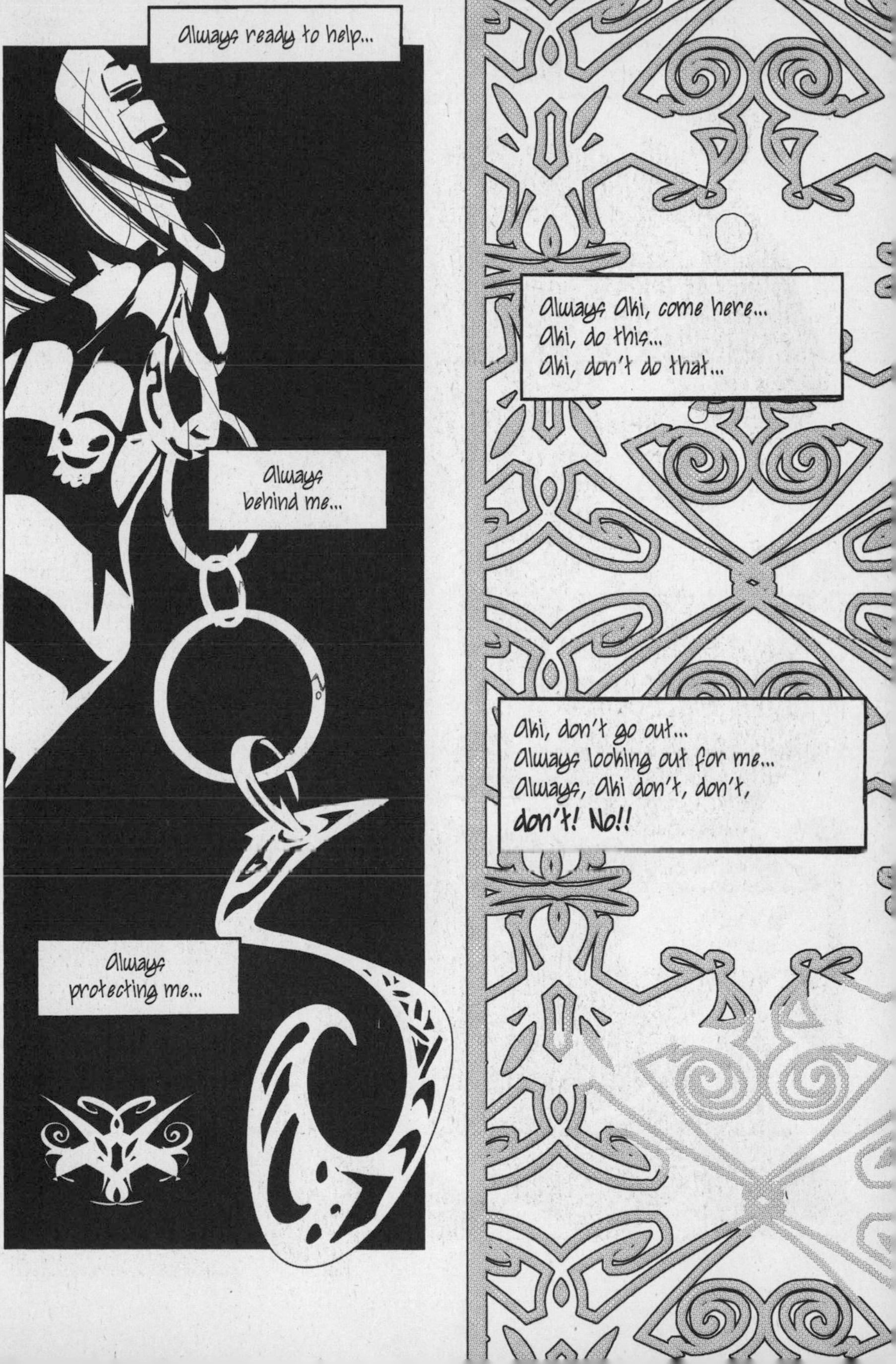
always ready to help...
always behind me...
always protecting me...
always aki, come here...
aki, do this...
aki, don't do that...
aki, don't go out...
always looking out for me...
always, aki don't, don't,
don't! No!!

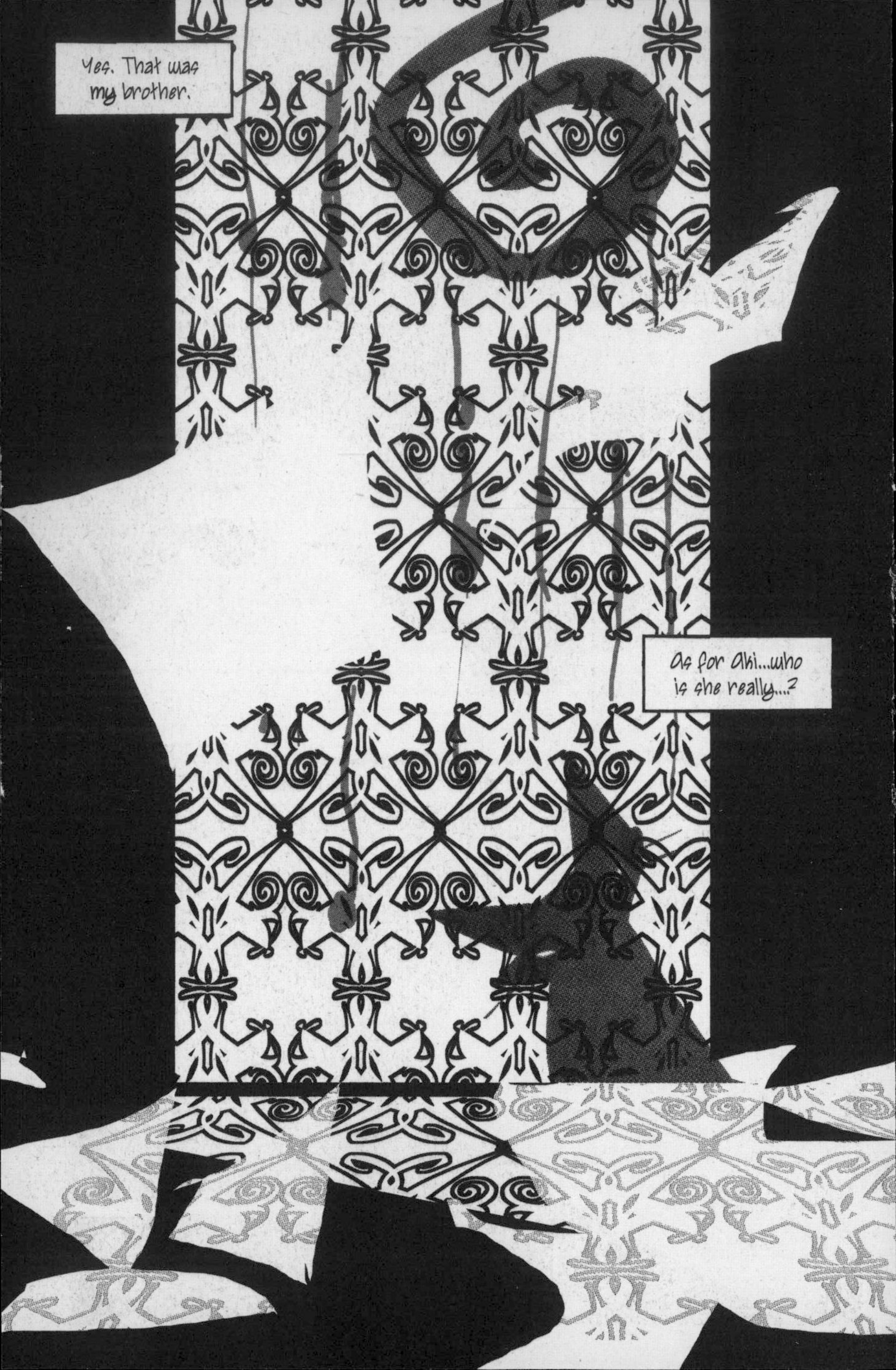
Yes. That was my brother.
As for Aki...who is she really...?

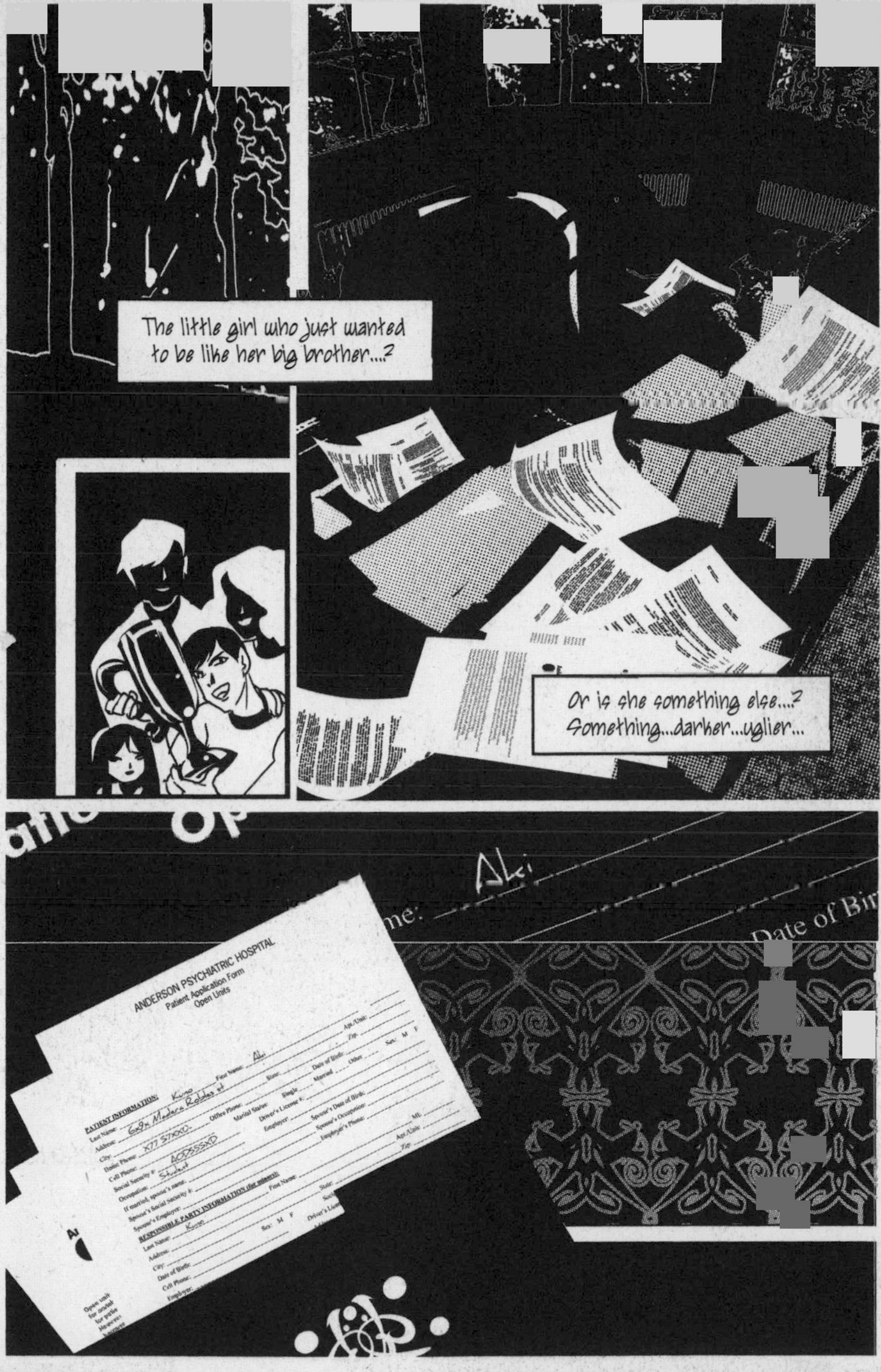
The little girl who just wanted to be like her big brother...?
Or is she something else...? Something...darker...uglier...
Aki
ANDERSON PSYCHIATRIC HOSPITAL
Patient Application Form
Open Units
PATIENT INFORMATION:
RESPONSIBLE PARTY INFORMATION (for minors):

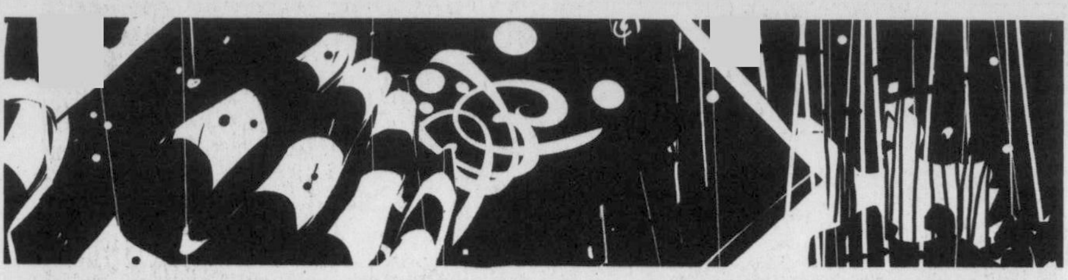
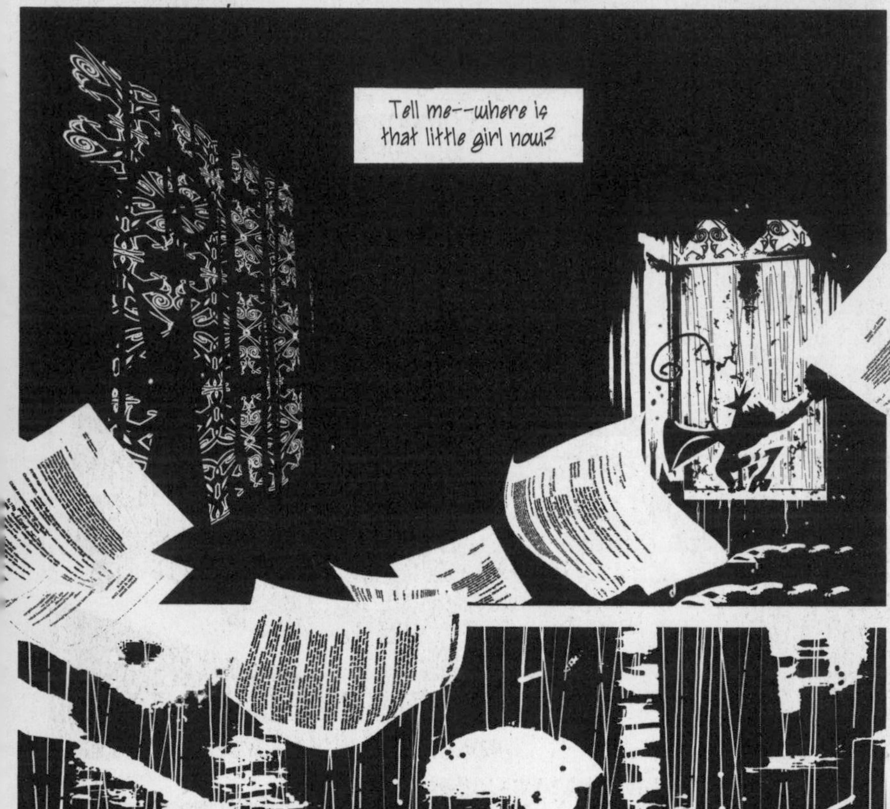
Tell me--where is
that little girl now?
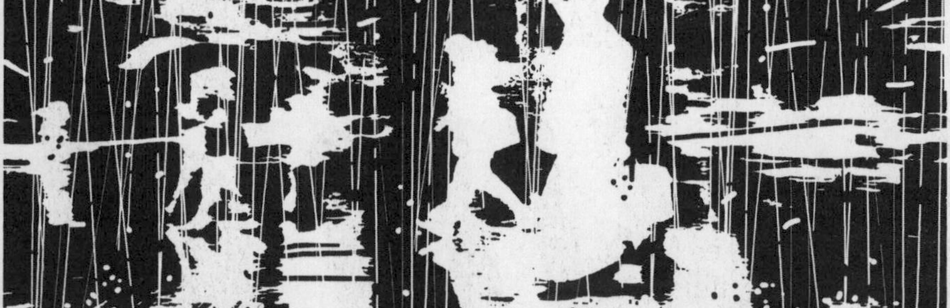

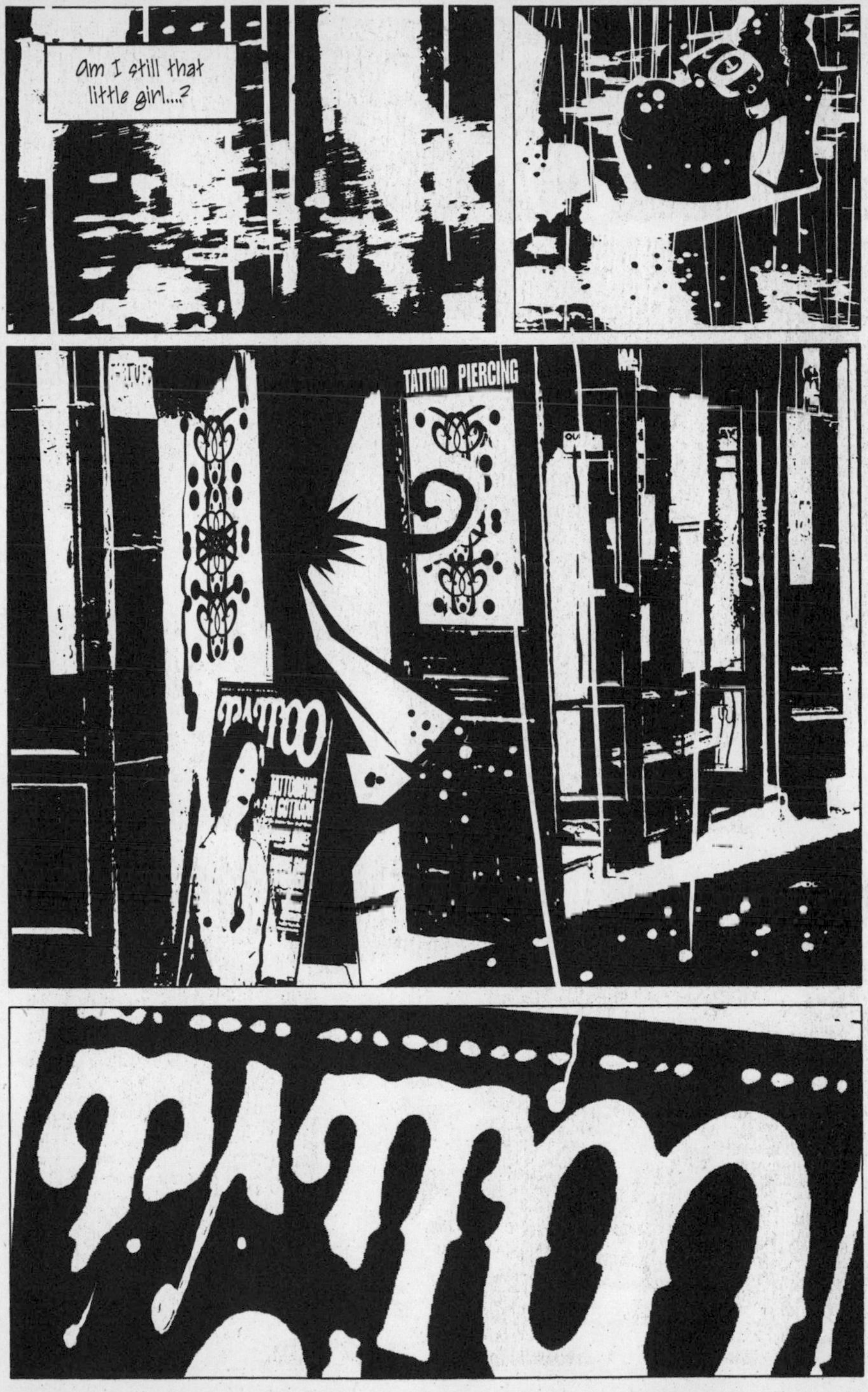
am I still that little girl...?
TATTOO PIERCING
TATTOO

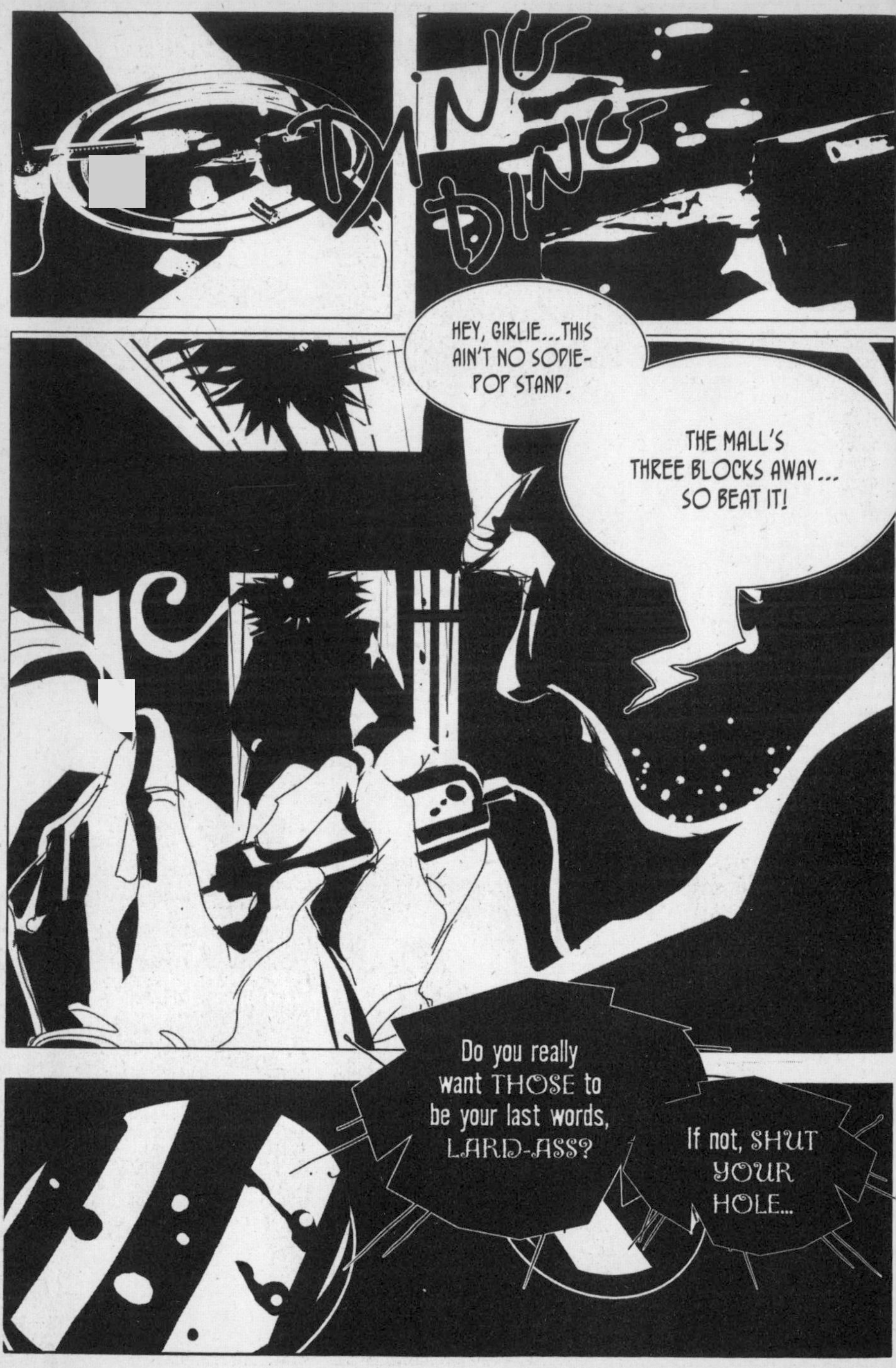
DING DING
HEY, GIRLIE...THIS AIN'T NO SODIE-POP STAND.
THE MALL'S THREE BLOCKS AWAY... SO BEAT IT!
Do you really want THOSE to be your last words, LARD-ASS?
If not, SHUT YOUR HOLE...

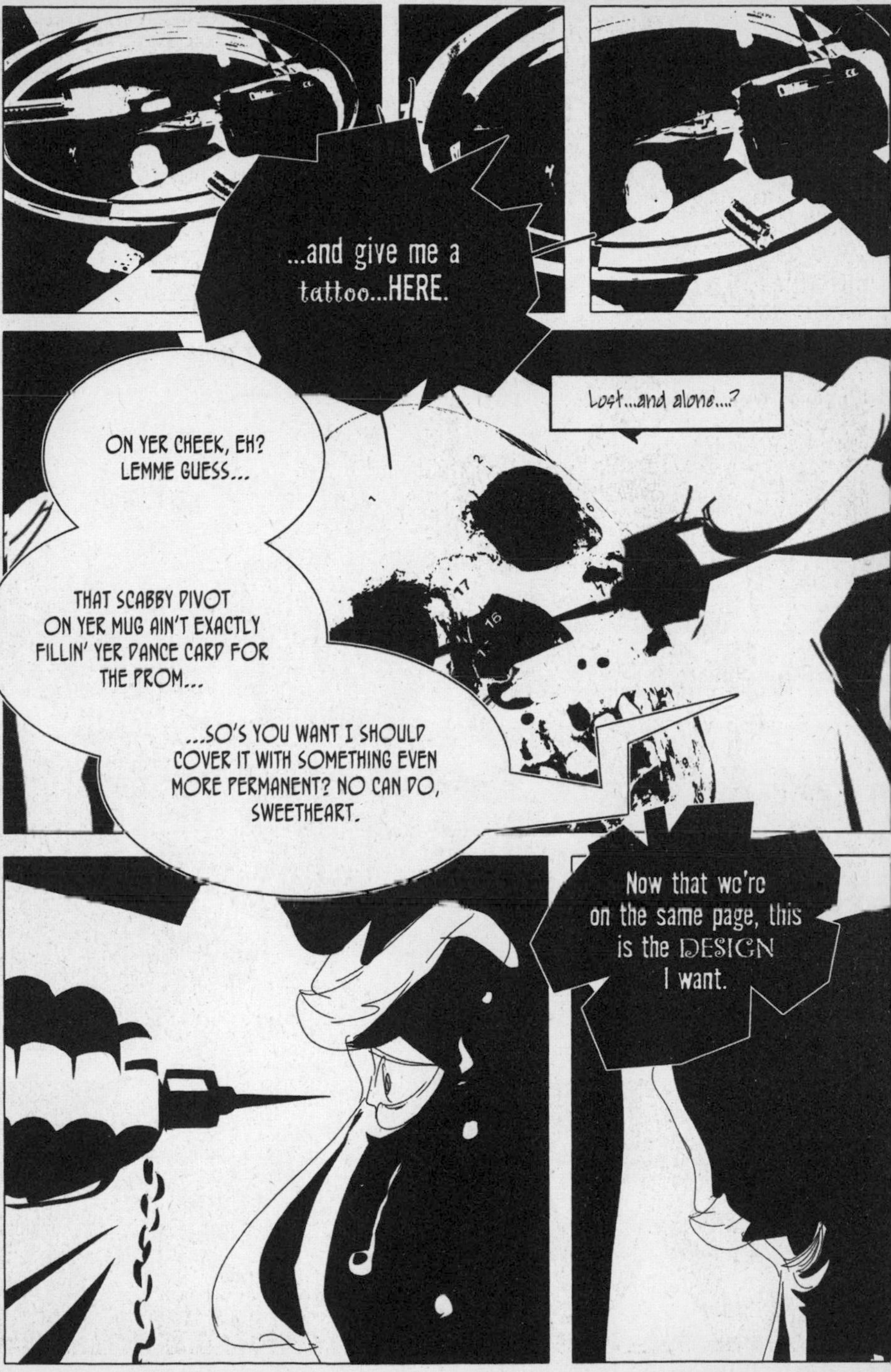

...and give me a tattoo...HERE.
Lost...and alone...?
ON YER CHEEK, EH? LEMME GUESS...
THAT SCABBY DIVOT ON YER MUG AIN'T EXACTLY FILLIN' YER DANCE CARD FOR THE PROM...
...SO'S YOU WANT I SHOULD COVER IT WITH SOMETHING EVEN MORE PERMANENT? NO CAN DO, SWEETHEART.
Now that we're on the same page, this is the DESIGN I want.

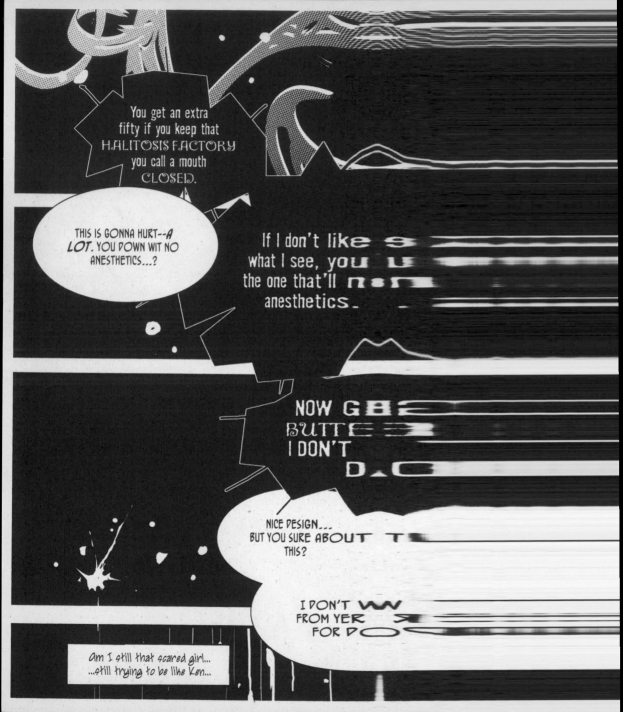

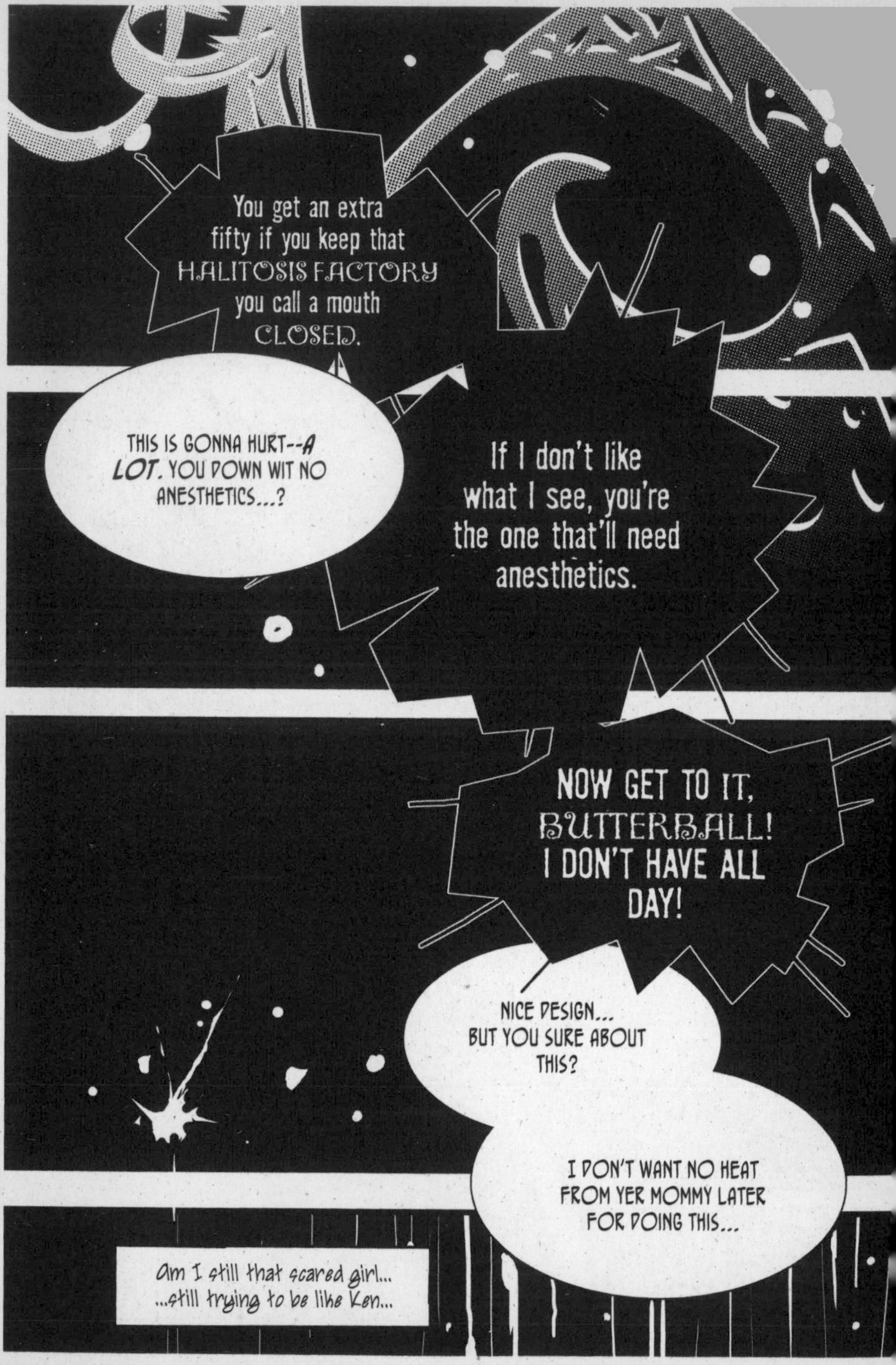

You get an extra fifty if you keep that HALITOSIS FACTORY you call a mouth CLOSED.
THIS IS GONNA HURT--A LOT. YOU DOWN WIT NO ANESTHETICS...?
If I don't like what I see, you're the one that'll need anesthetics.
NOW GET TO IT, BUTTERBALL! I DON'T HAVE ALL DAY!
NICE DESIGN... BUT YOU SURE ABOUT THIS?
I DON'T WANT NO HEAT FROM YER MOMMY LATER FOR DOING THIS...
Am I still that scared girl... ...still trying to be like Ken...

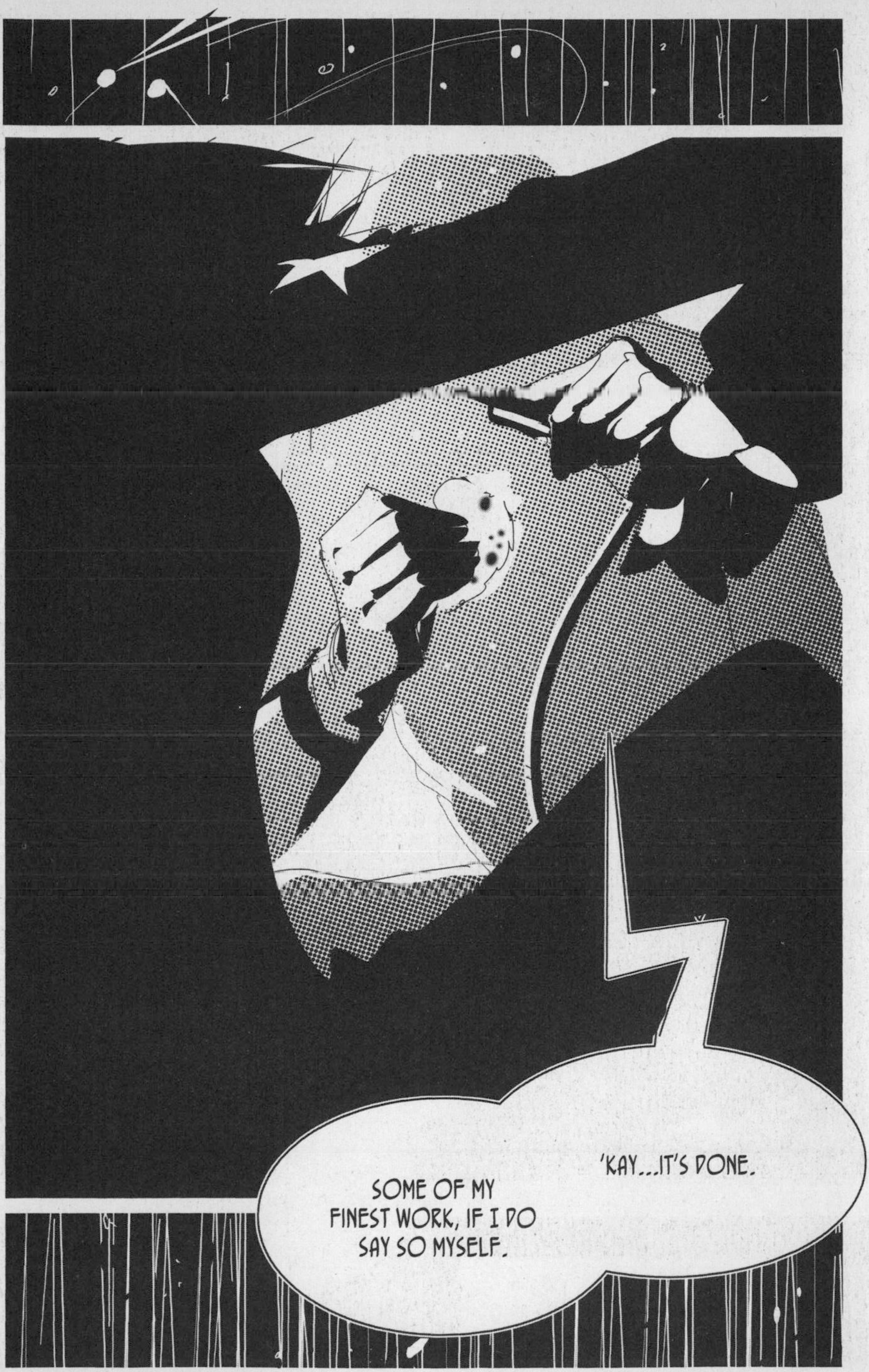
'KAY...IT'S DONE.
SOME OF MY FINEST WORK, IF I DO SAY SO MYSELF.

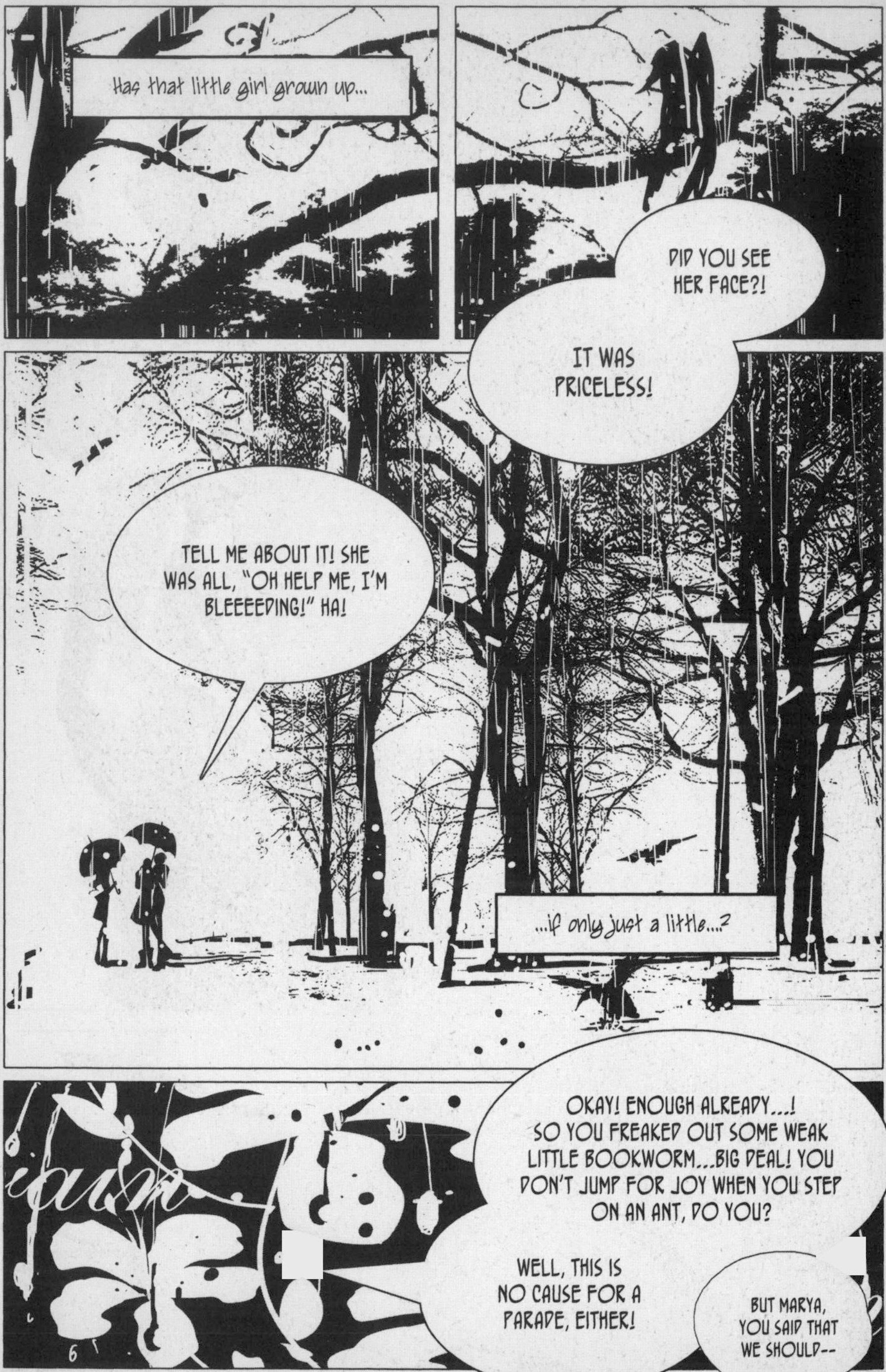

Has that little girl grown up...
DID YOU SEE HER FACE?! IT WAS PRICELESS!
TELL ME ABOUT IT! SHE WAS ALL, "OH HELP ME, I'M BLEEEEDING!" HA!
...if only just a little...?
OKAY! ENOUGH ALREADY...! SO YOU FREAKED OUT SOME WEAK LITTLE BOOKWORM...BIG DEAL! YOU DON'T JUMP FOR JOY WHEN YOU STEP ON AN ANT, DO YOU?
WELL, THIS IS NO CAUSE FOR A PARADE, EITHER!
BUT MARYA, YOU SAID THAT WE SHOULD--

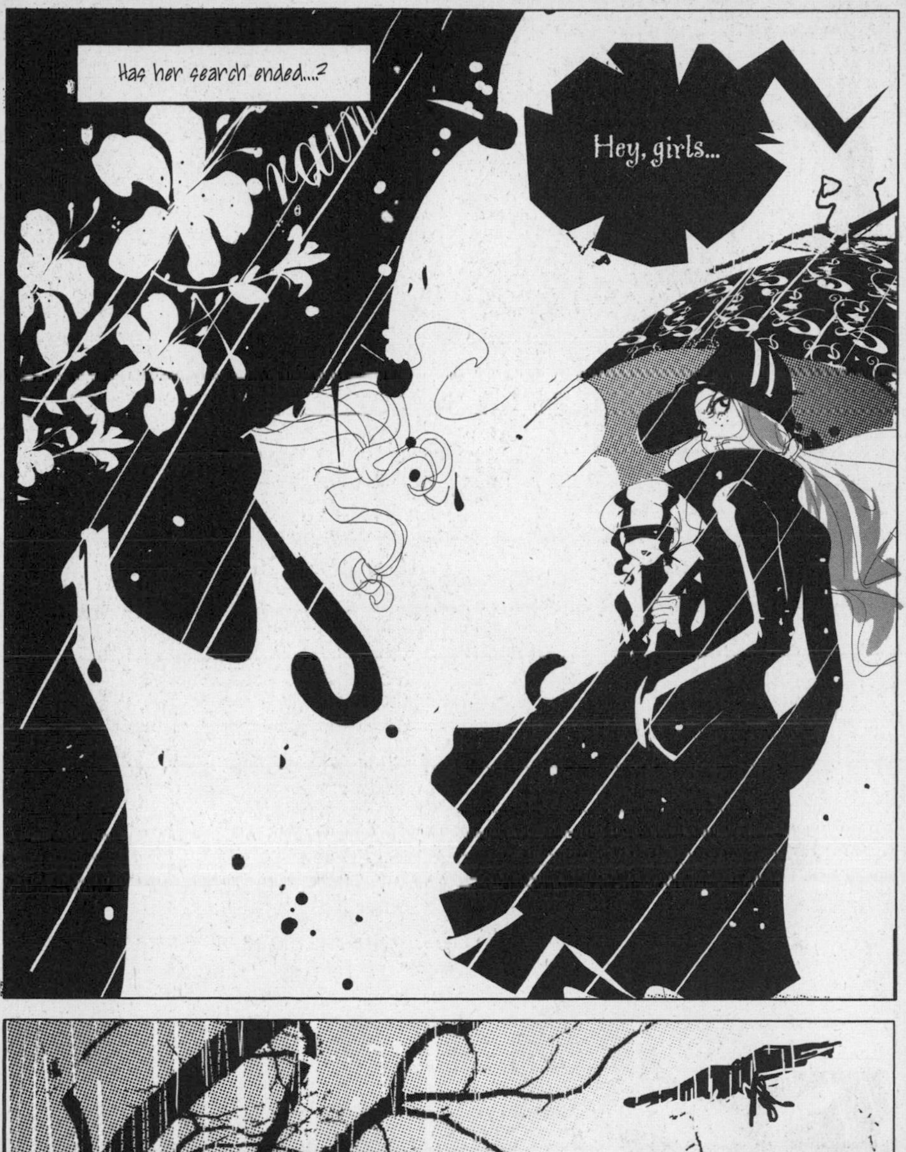
Has her search ended...?
Hey, girls...

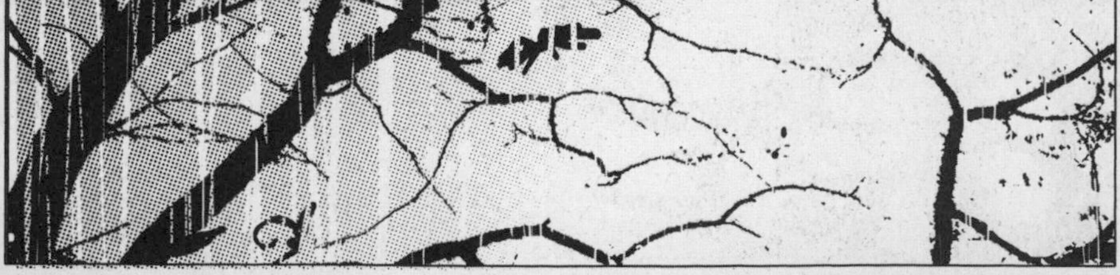

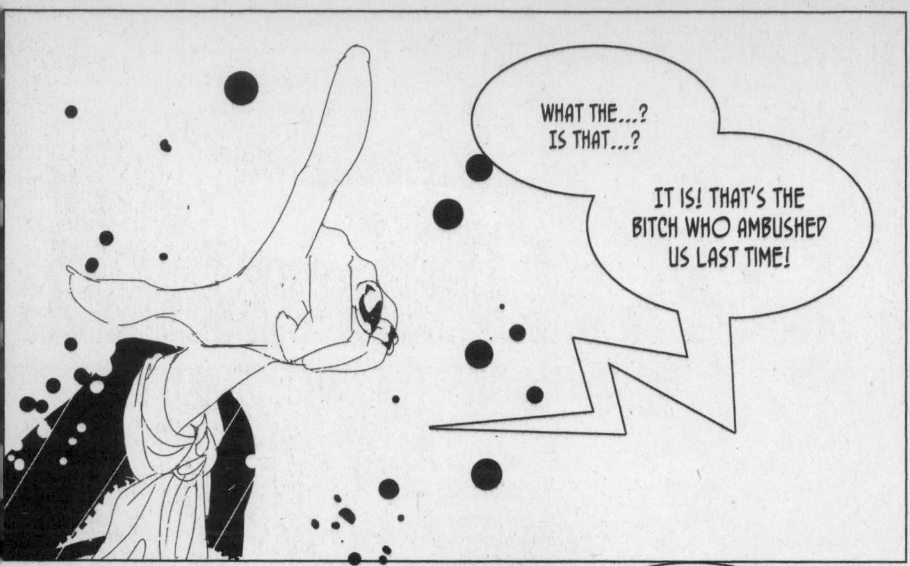
WHAT THE...? IS THAT...?
IT IS! THAT'S THE BITCH WHO AMBUSHED US LAST TIME!

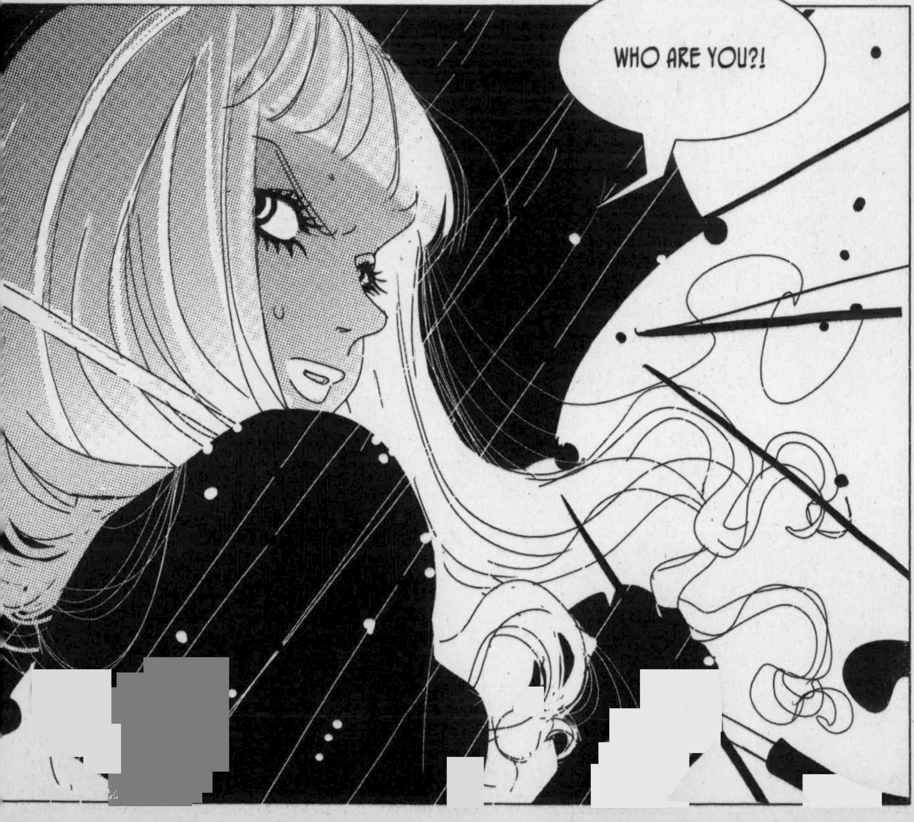
WHO ARE YOU?!

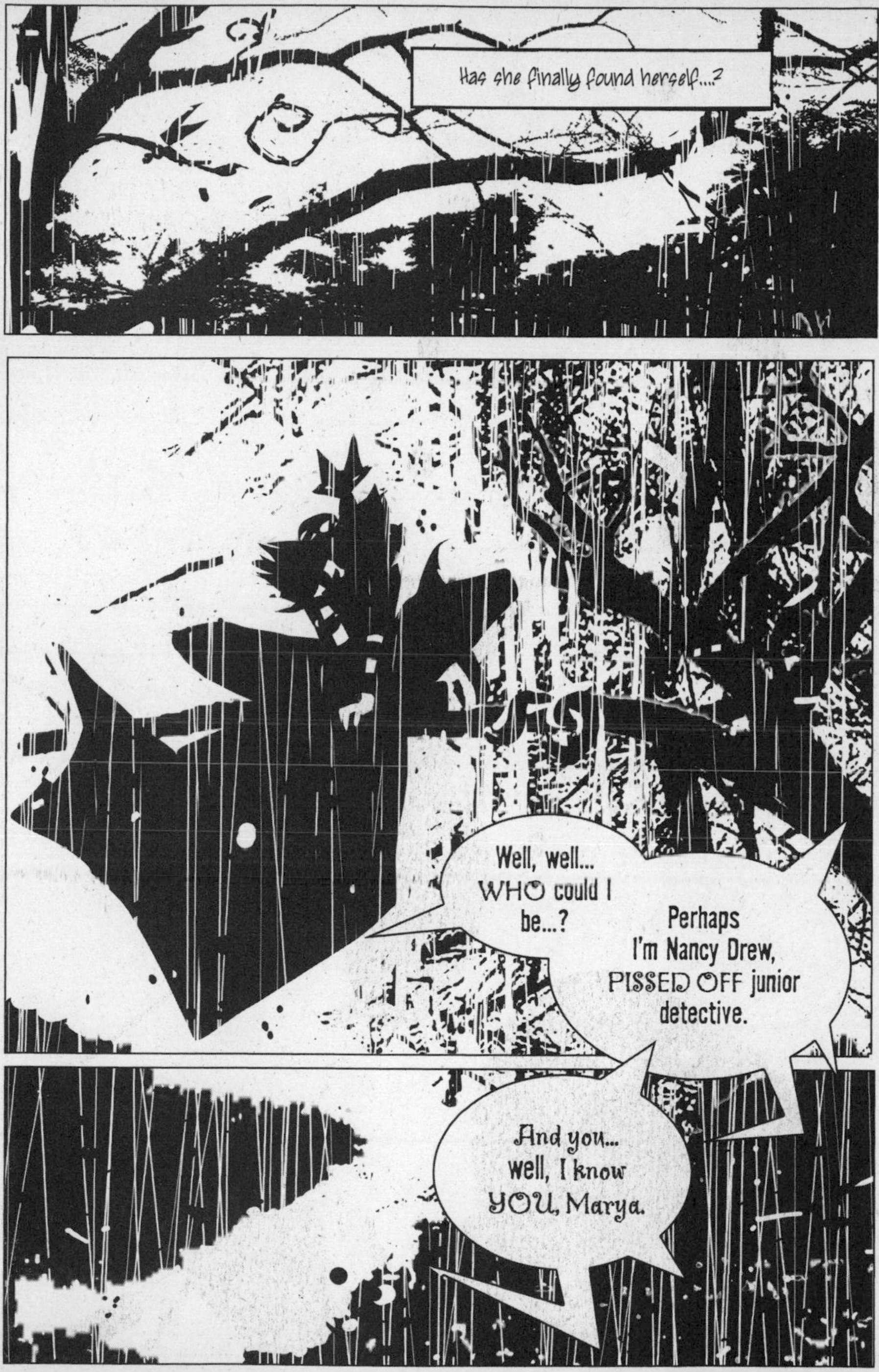
Has she finally found herself...?
Well, well... WHO could I be...?
Perhaps I'm Nancy Drew, PISSED OFF junior detective.
And you... well, I know YOU, Marya.

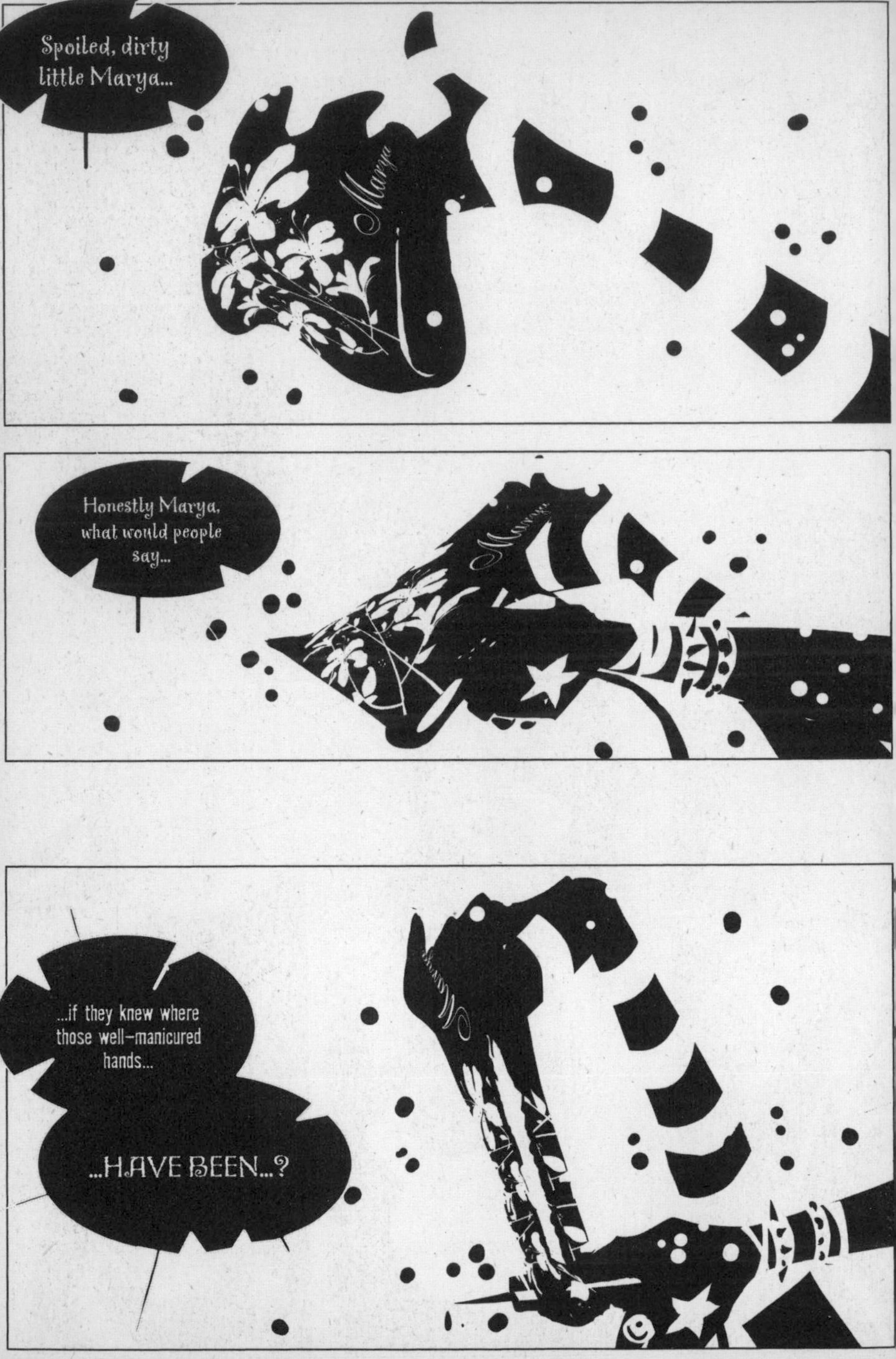
Spoiled, dirty little Marya...
Honestly Marya, what would people say...
...if they knew where those well-manicured hands...
...HAVE BEEN...?

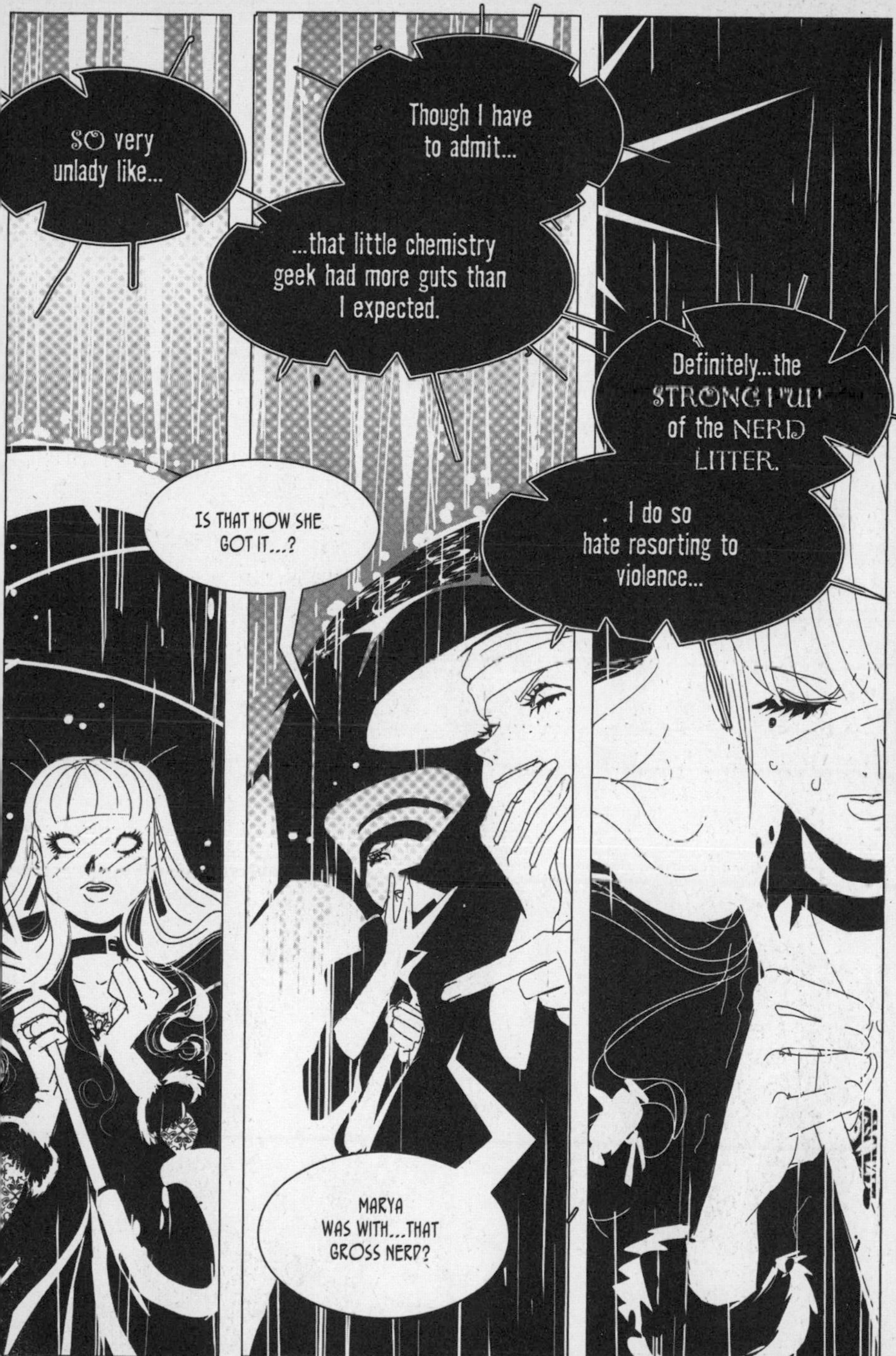
SO very unlady like...
Though I have to admit...
...that little chemistry geek had more guts than I expected.
IS THAT HOW SHE GOT IT...?
MARYA WAS WITH...THAT GROSS NERD?
Definitely...the STRONG PUP of the NERD LITTER.
I do so hate resorting to violence...

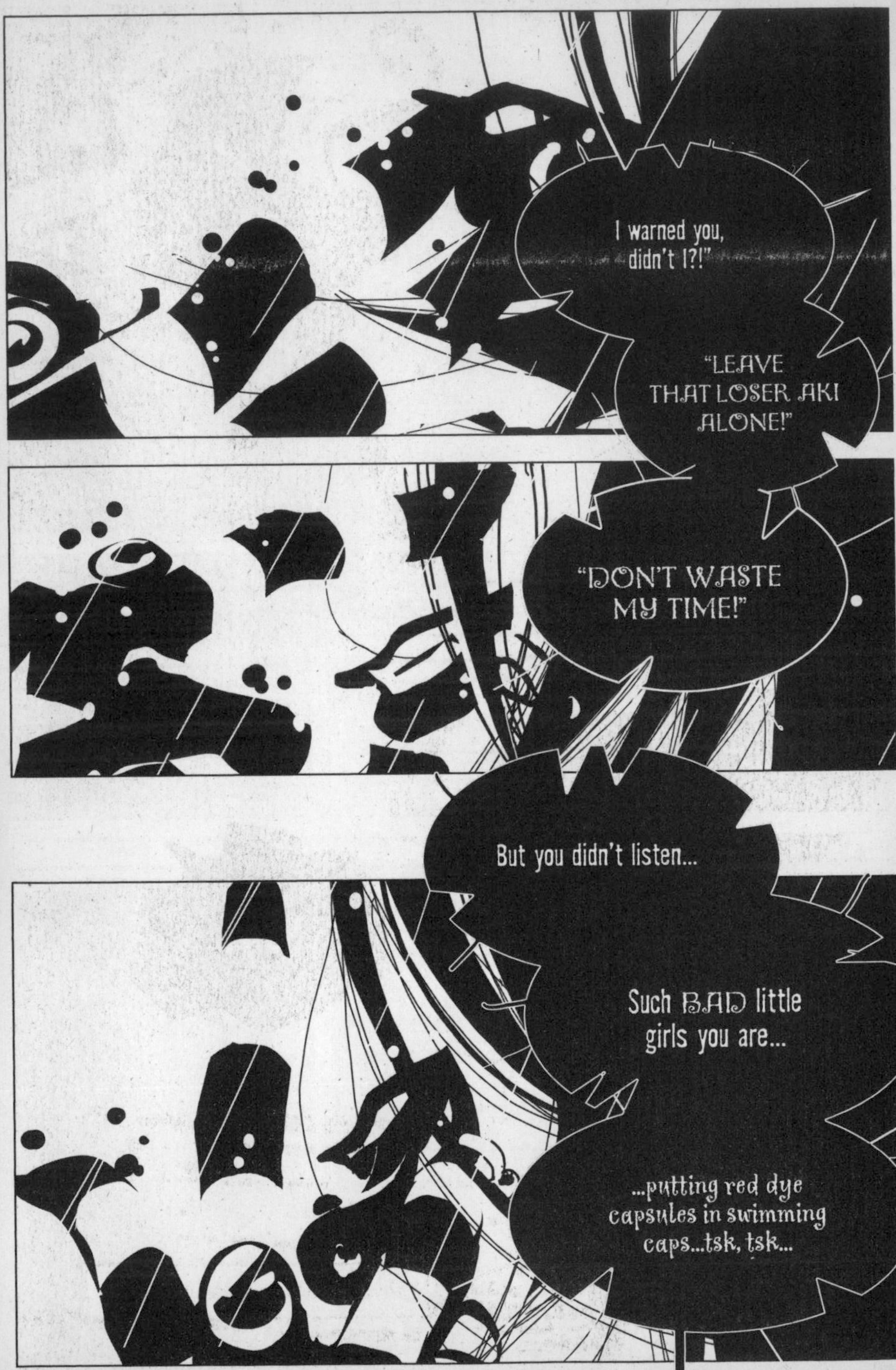
I warned you, didn't I?!"
"LEAVE THAT LOSER AKI ALONE!"
"DON'T WASTE MY TIME!"
But you didn't listen...
Such BAD little girls you are...
...putting red dye capsules in swimming caps...tsk, tsk...

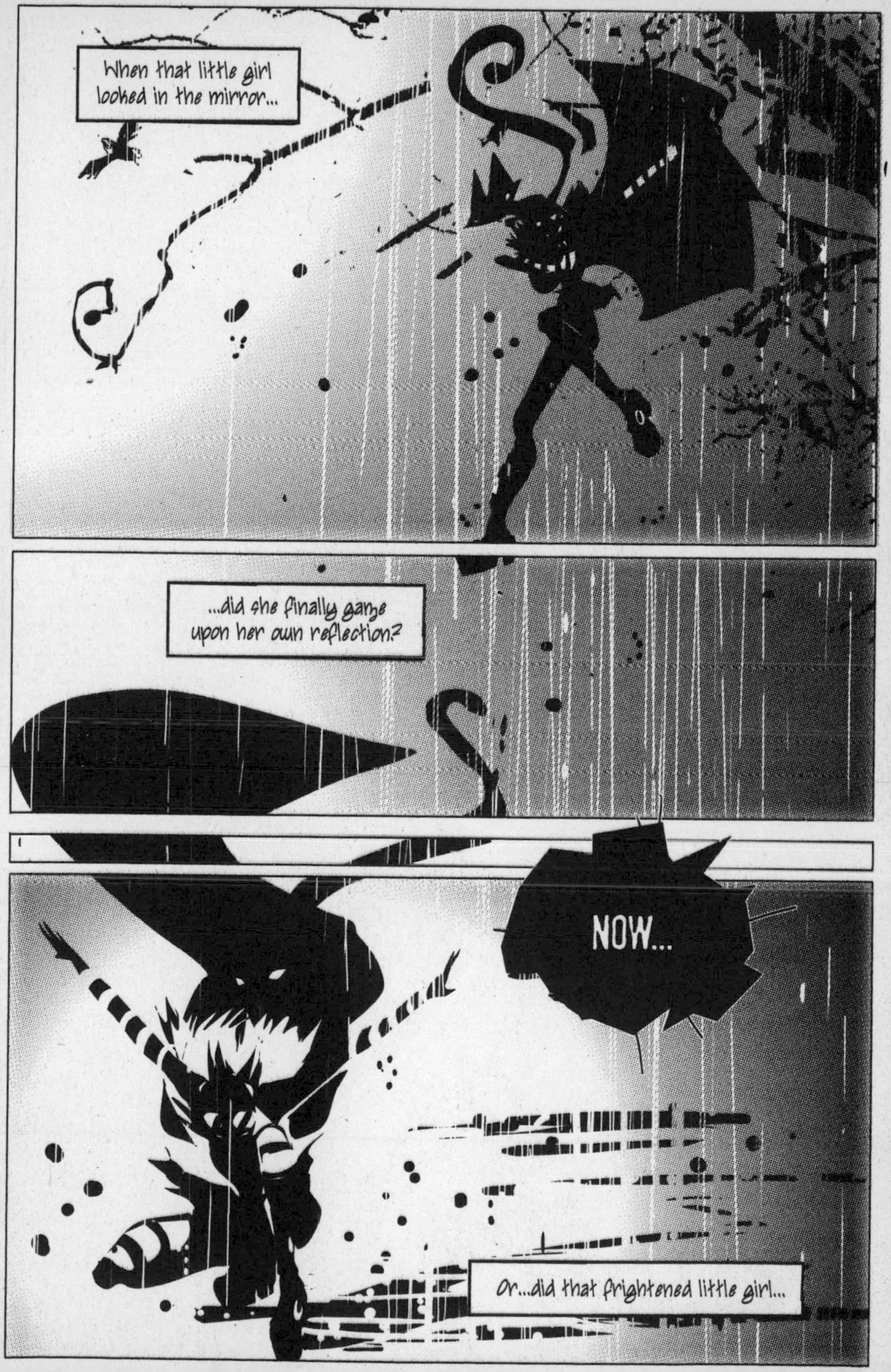
When that little girl looked in the mirror...
...did she finally gaze upon her own reflection?
NOW...
Or...did that frightened little girl...

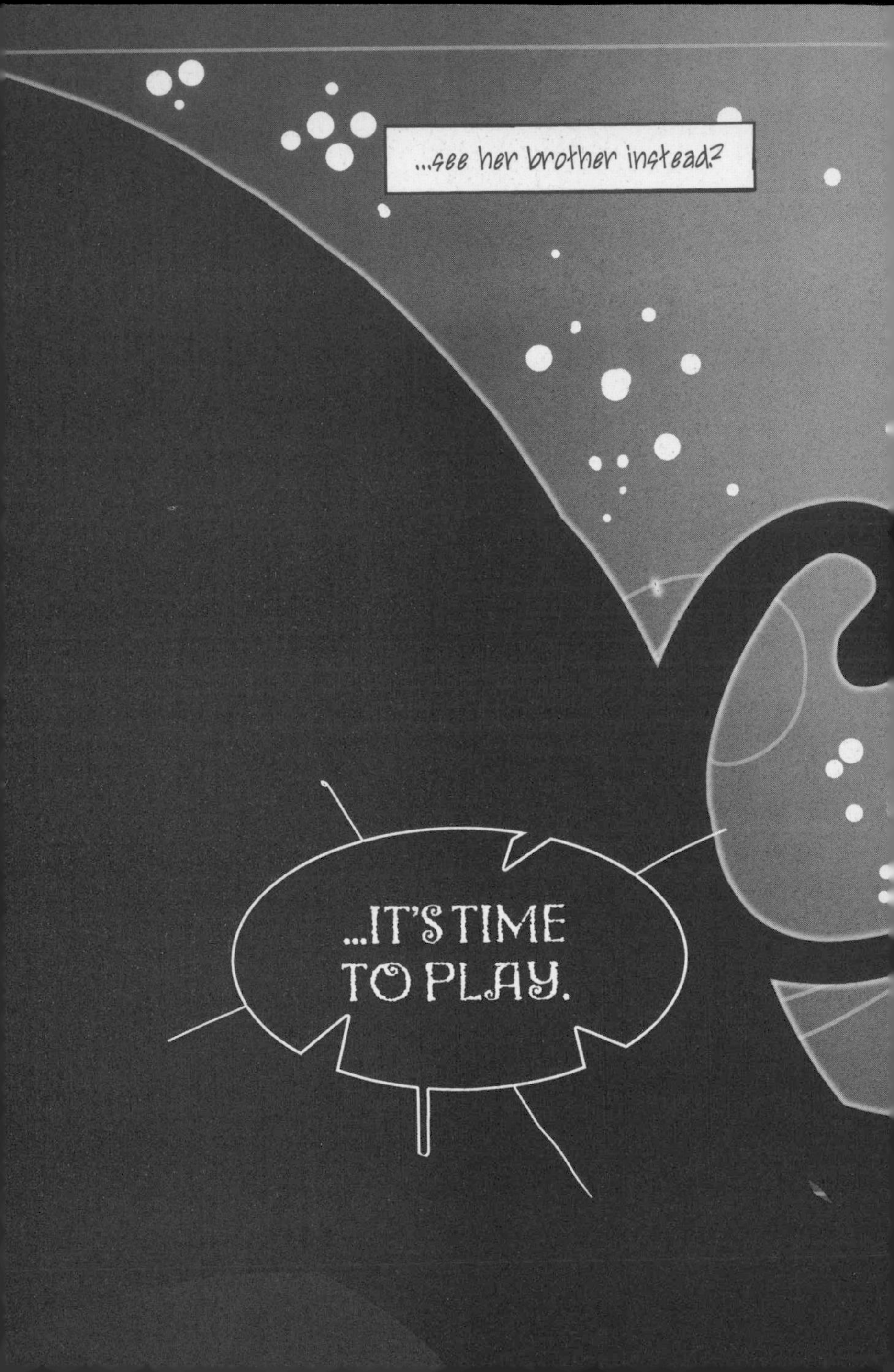
...see her brother instead?
...IT'S TIME TO PLAY.

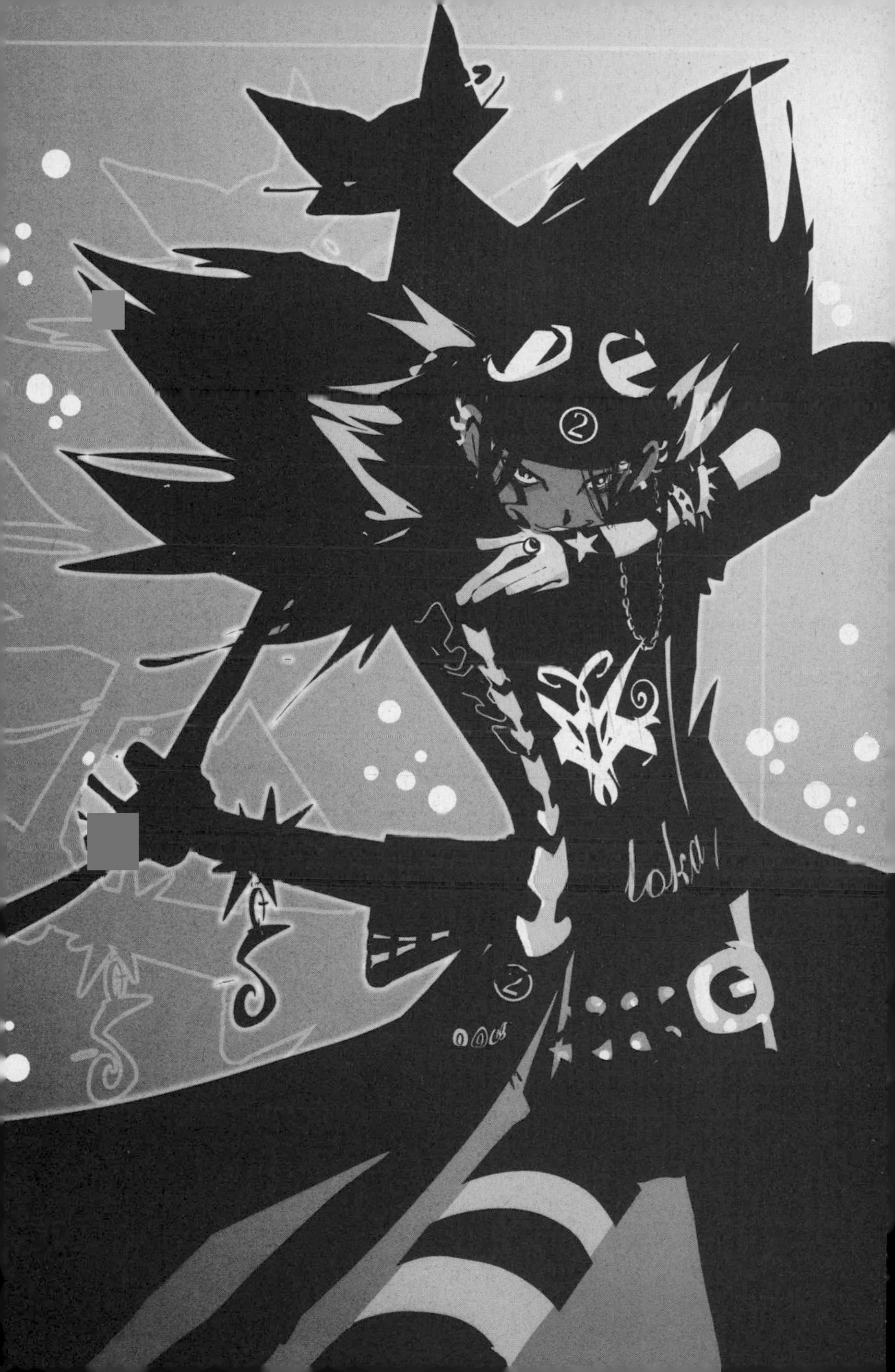

To be continued.....

In the next volume of ME2 ::

Aki's grasp on reality continues to slip, causing her to further alienate the ones close to her, including Adrian. But while her world crumbles, her alter-ego Kia continues to pick up the shards and hold Aki hostage in her own mind. Kia wants to get to the bottom of Ken's death... and her investigation reveals some shocking truths about not only that fateful night, but Ken as well.

However, as this psychosomatic tug-of-war wages, the biggest casualty may be Aki herself. Can she navigate the dark forest that is Kia? Or will she forever tumble down this mental rabbit hole?

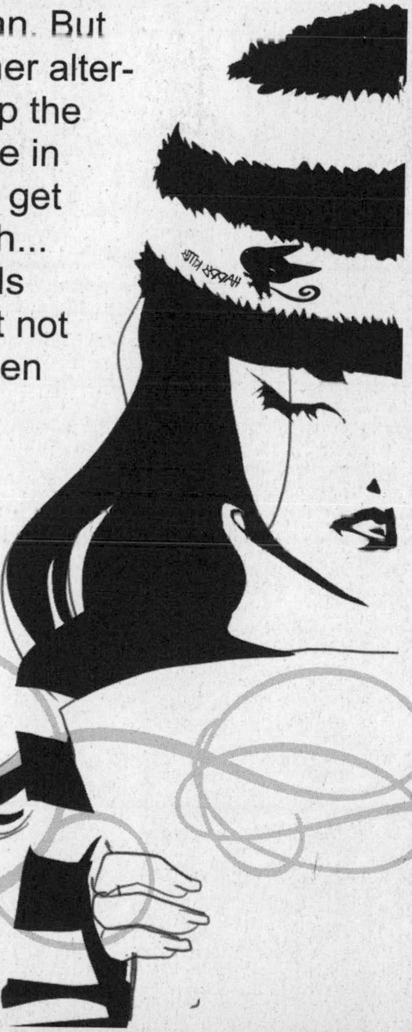

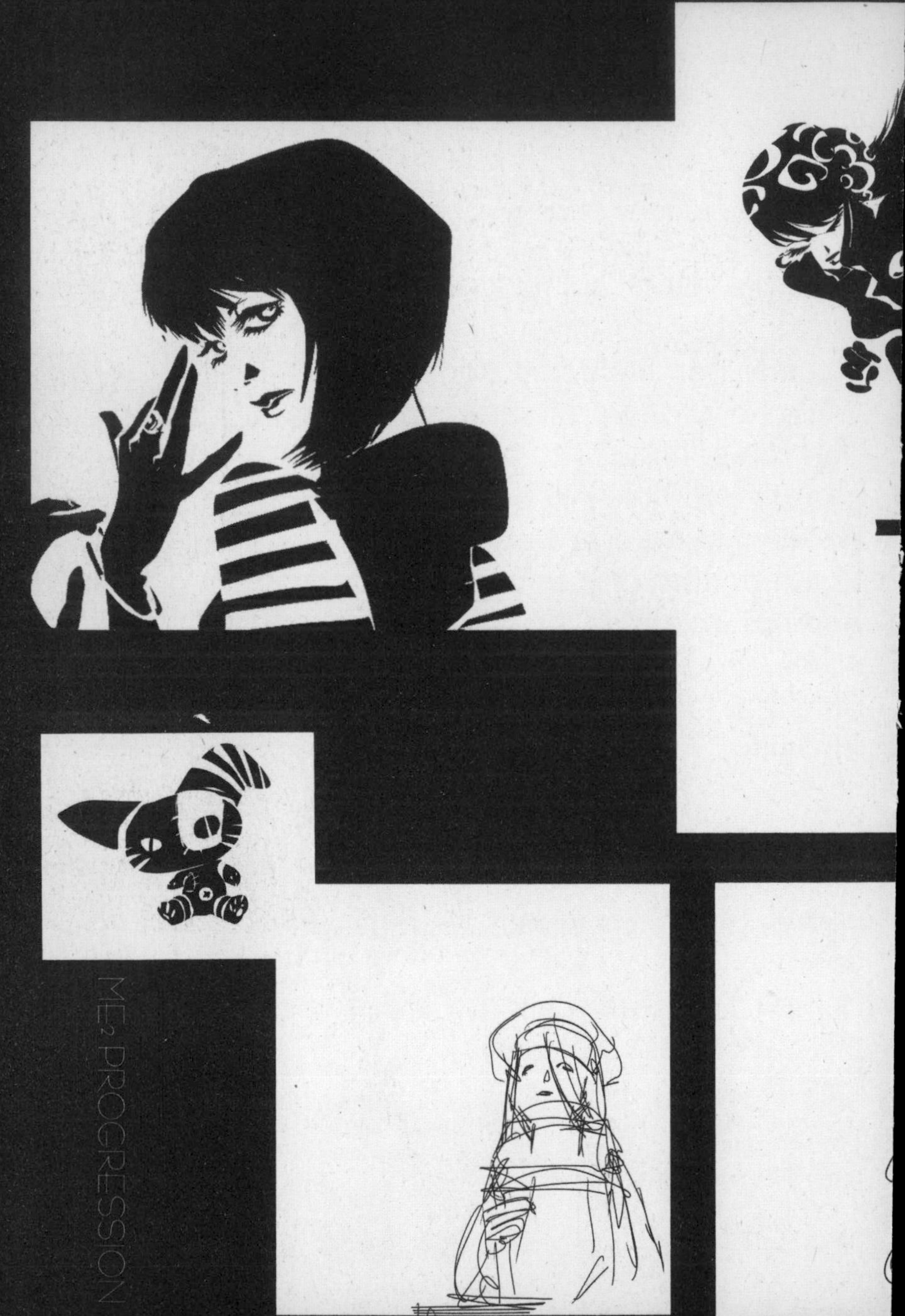
ME2 PROGRESSION

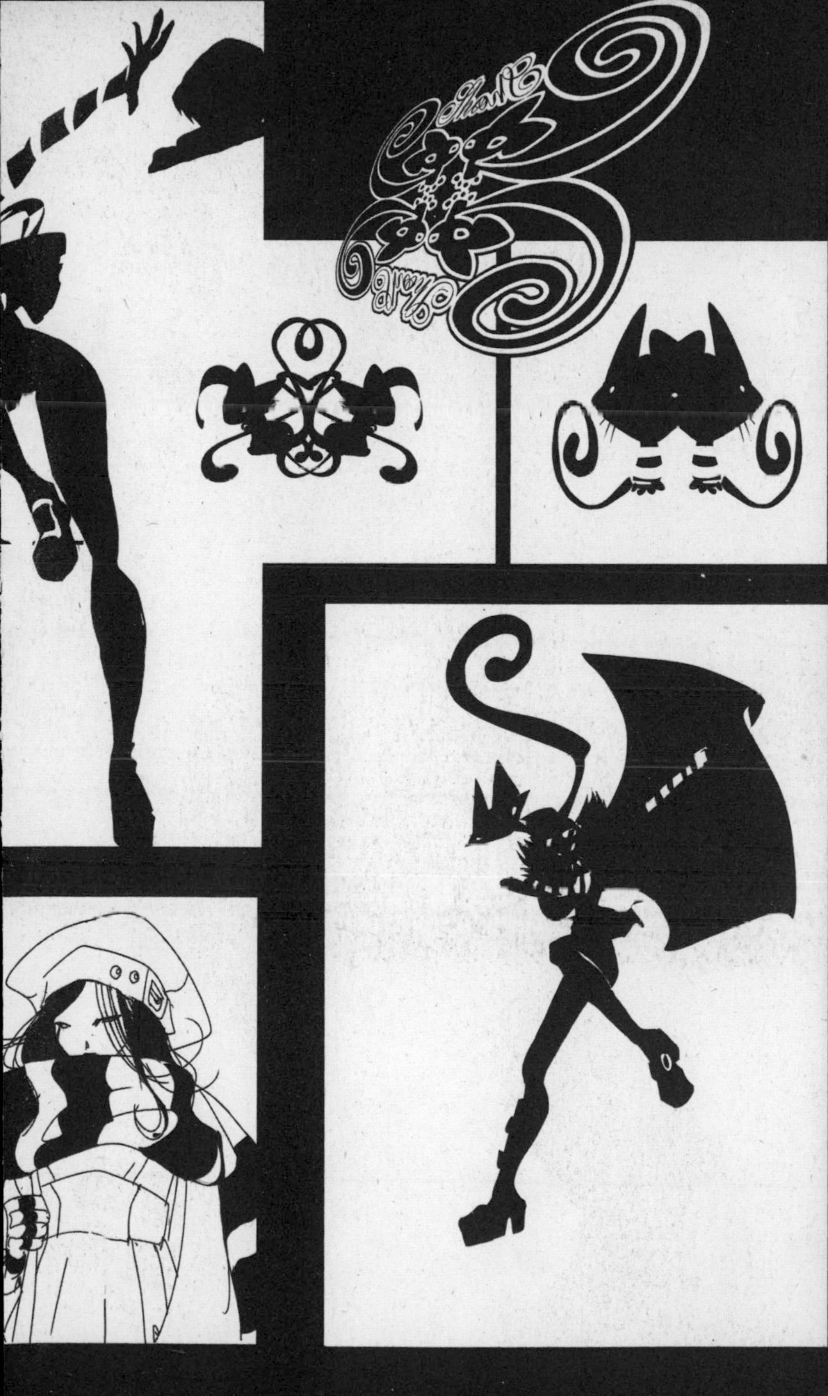

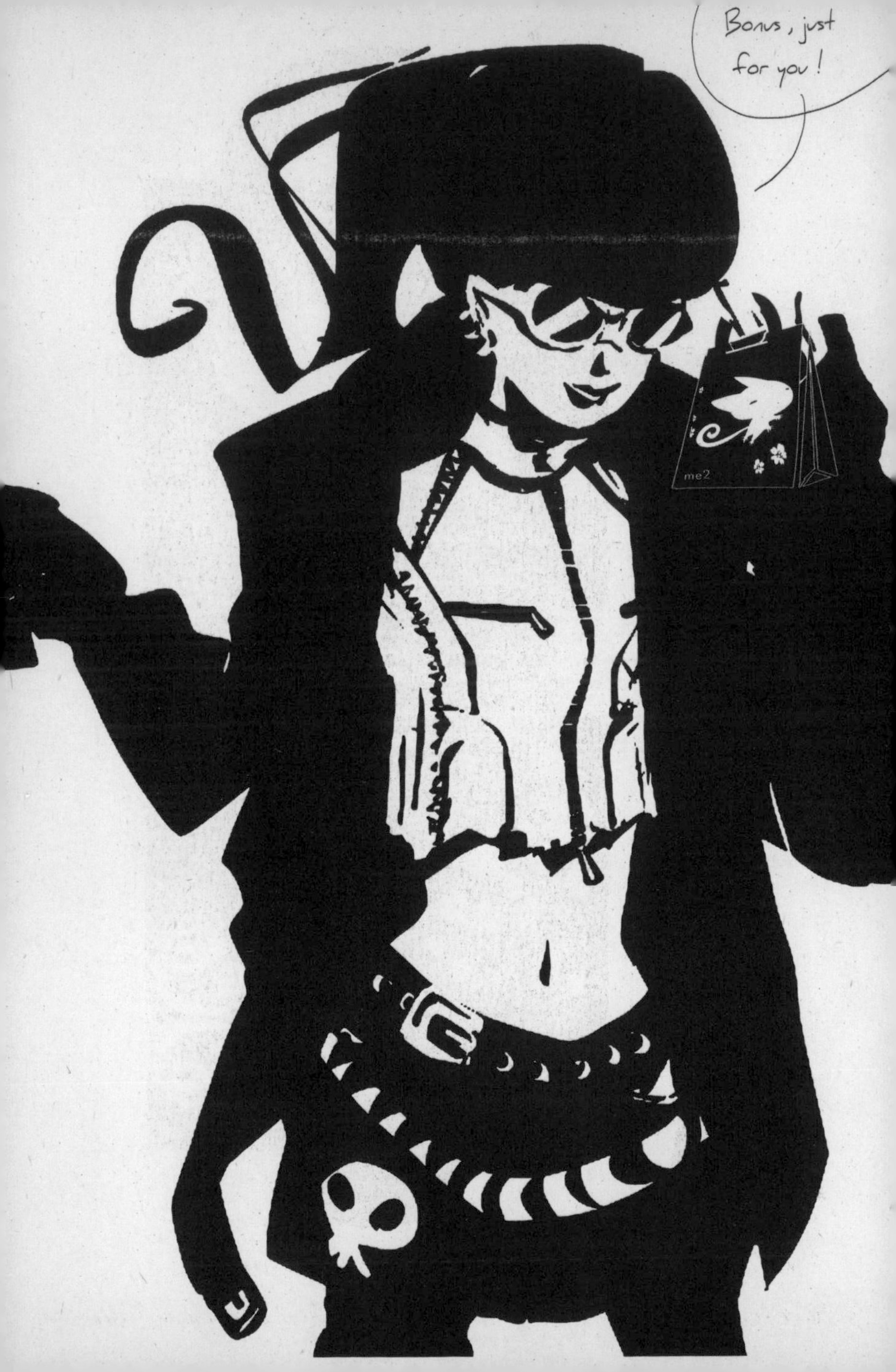
Bonus, just for you!
me2

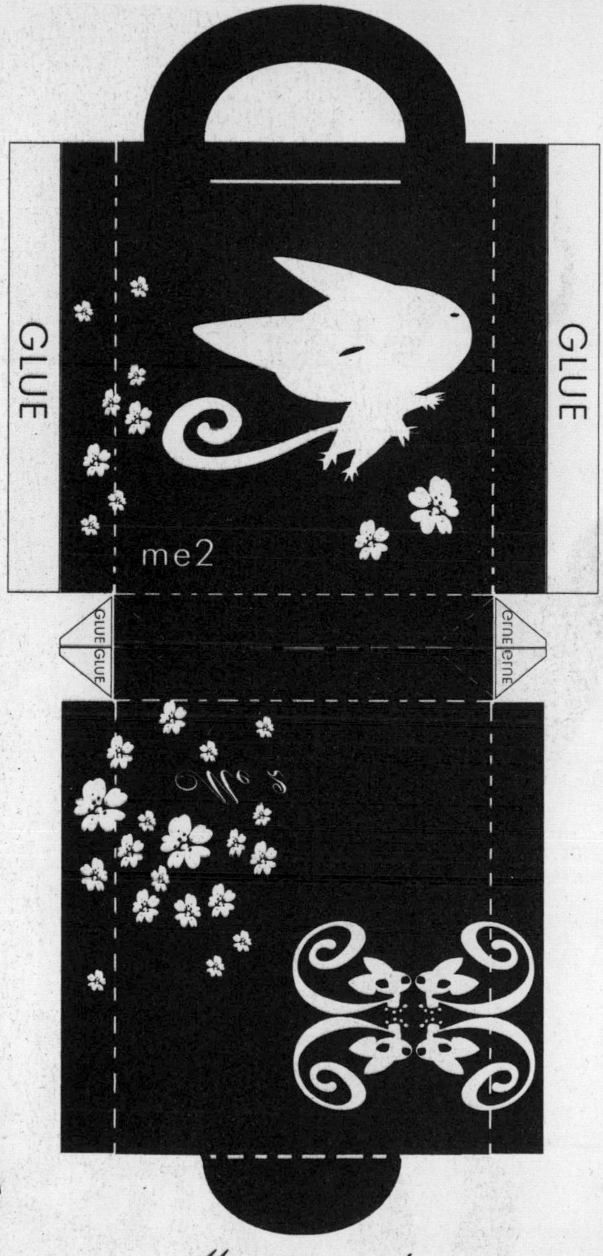
GLUE
GLUE
me2
GLUE
GLUE
GLUE
GLUE

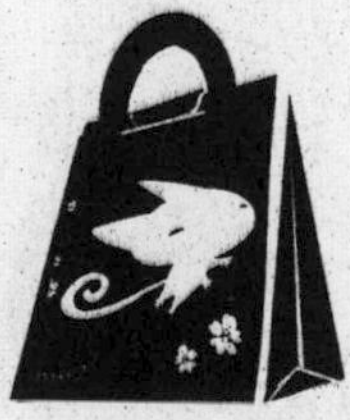

Make your own Me2 paper bag

Cut it, fold it according to dotted guides , and glue where indicated.

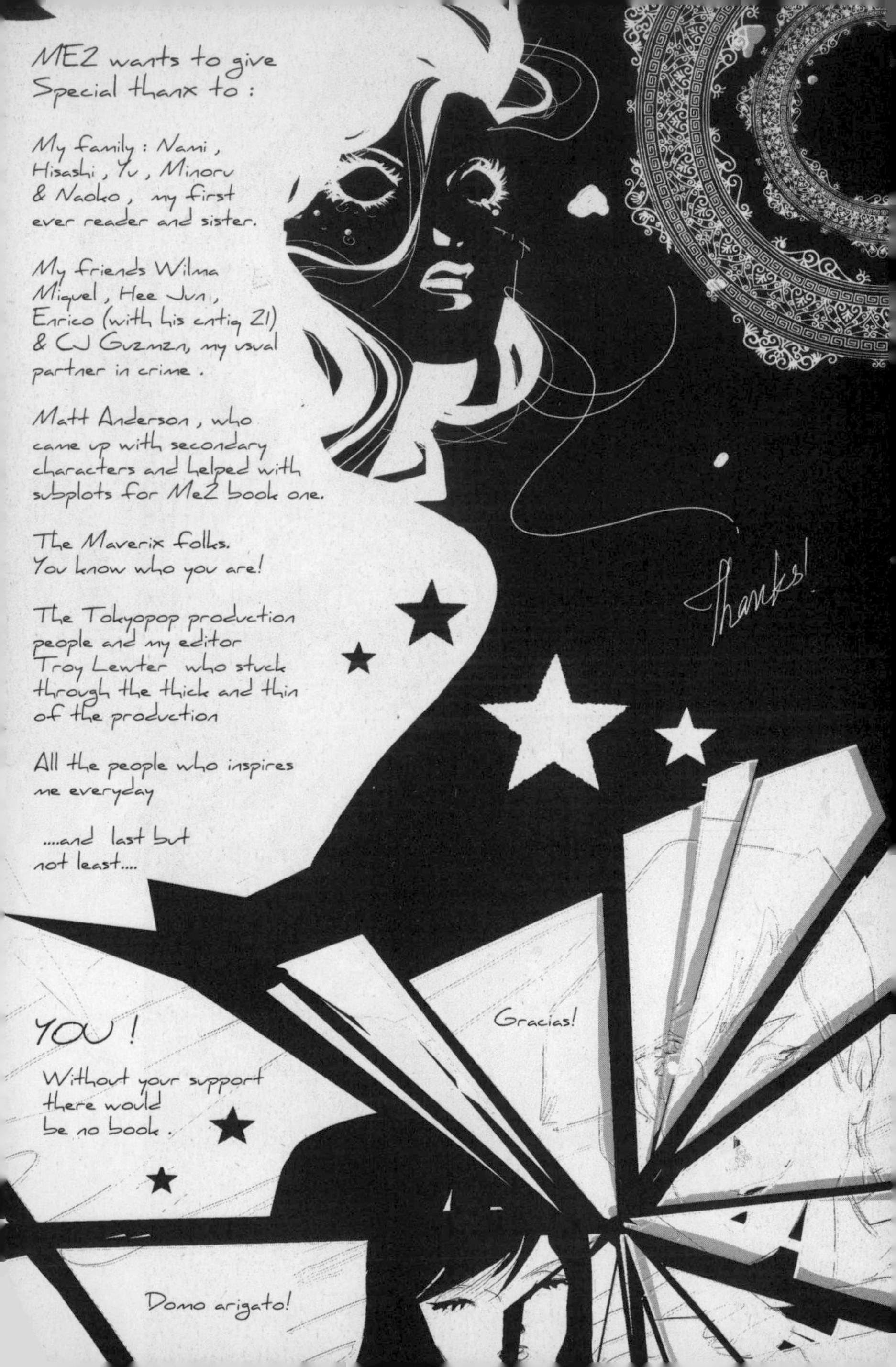
ME2 wants to give Special thanx to :
My family : Nami , Hisashi , Yu , Minoru & Naoko , my first ever reader and sister.
My friends Wilma Miquel , Hee Jun , Enrico (with his entiq 21) & CJ Guzman, my usual partner in crime .
Matt Anderson , who came up with secondary characters and helped with subplots for MeZ book one.
The Maverix folks. You know who you are!
The Tokyopop production people and my editor Troy Lewter who stuck through the thick and thin of the production
All the people who inspires me everyday
....and last but not least....
Thanks!
YOU !
Without your support there would be no book .
Gracias!
Domo arigato!

Rant or Rave :

via email ;
raisedbyberries@gmail.com

website:
http://doublekia.moonfruit.com/
http://shomurase.com/

through blog
http://trozos.blogspot.com/

through myspace
http://www.myspace.com/tokyopop__me2

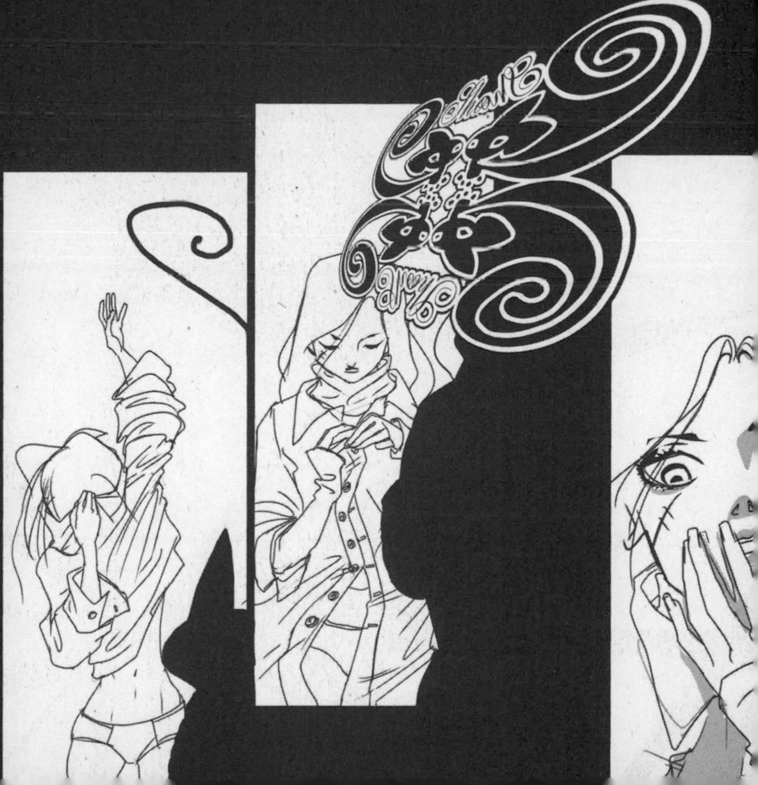

Every morning I wake up tired...
I don't know why those bags under my eyes
get deeper the more I sleep...

Everyone thinks I am weird. Even my parents...

WWW.SHOMURASE.COM

A SPECIAL SNEAK PREVIEW OF

UNDERTOWN

WRITTEN BY

JIM PASCOE

ILLUSTRATED BY

JAKE MYLER

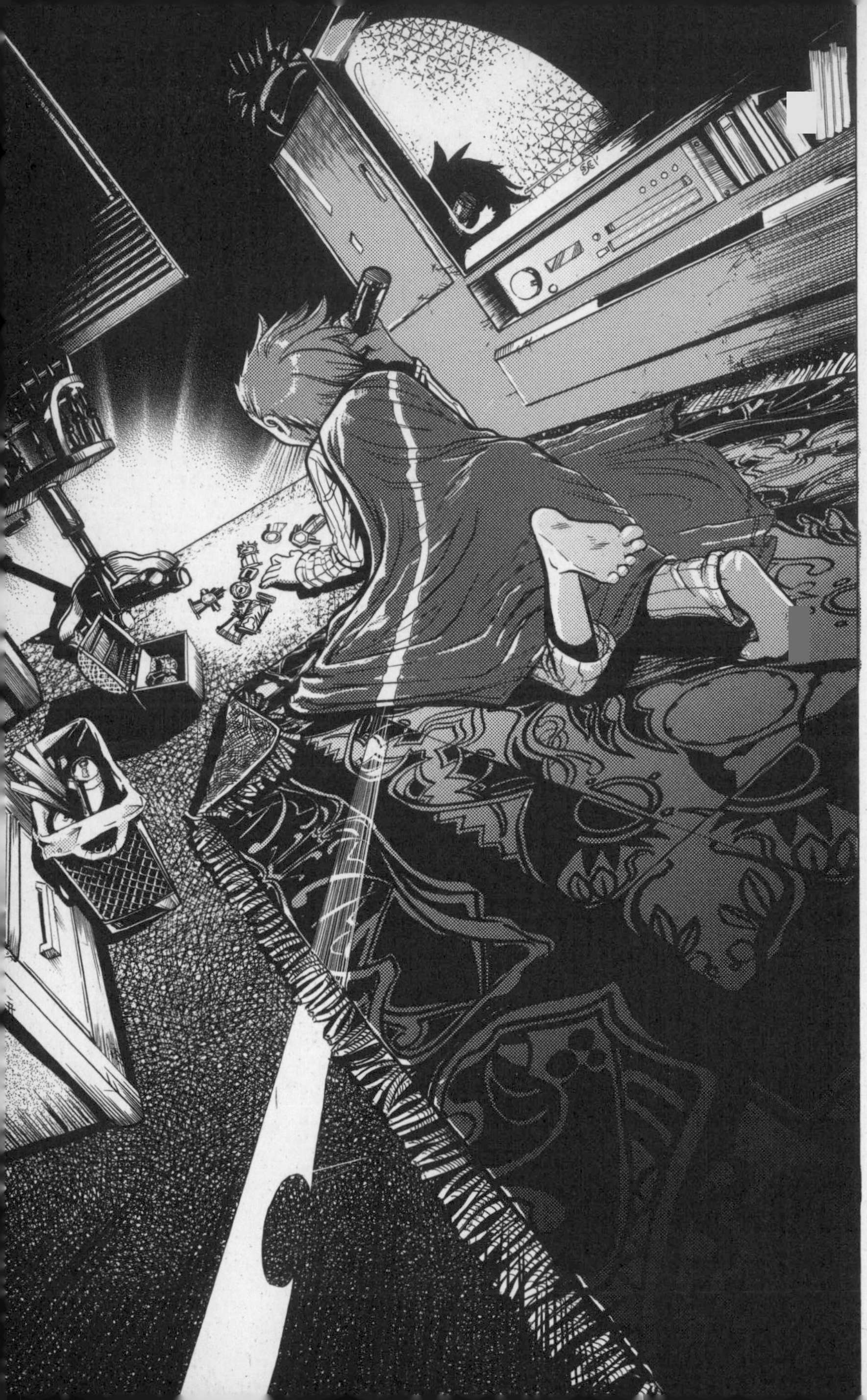

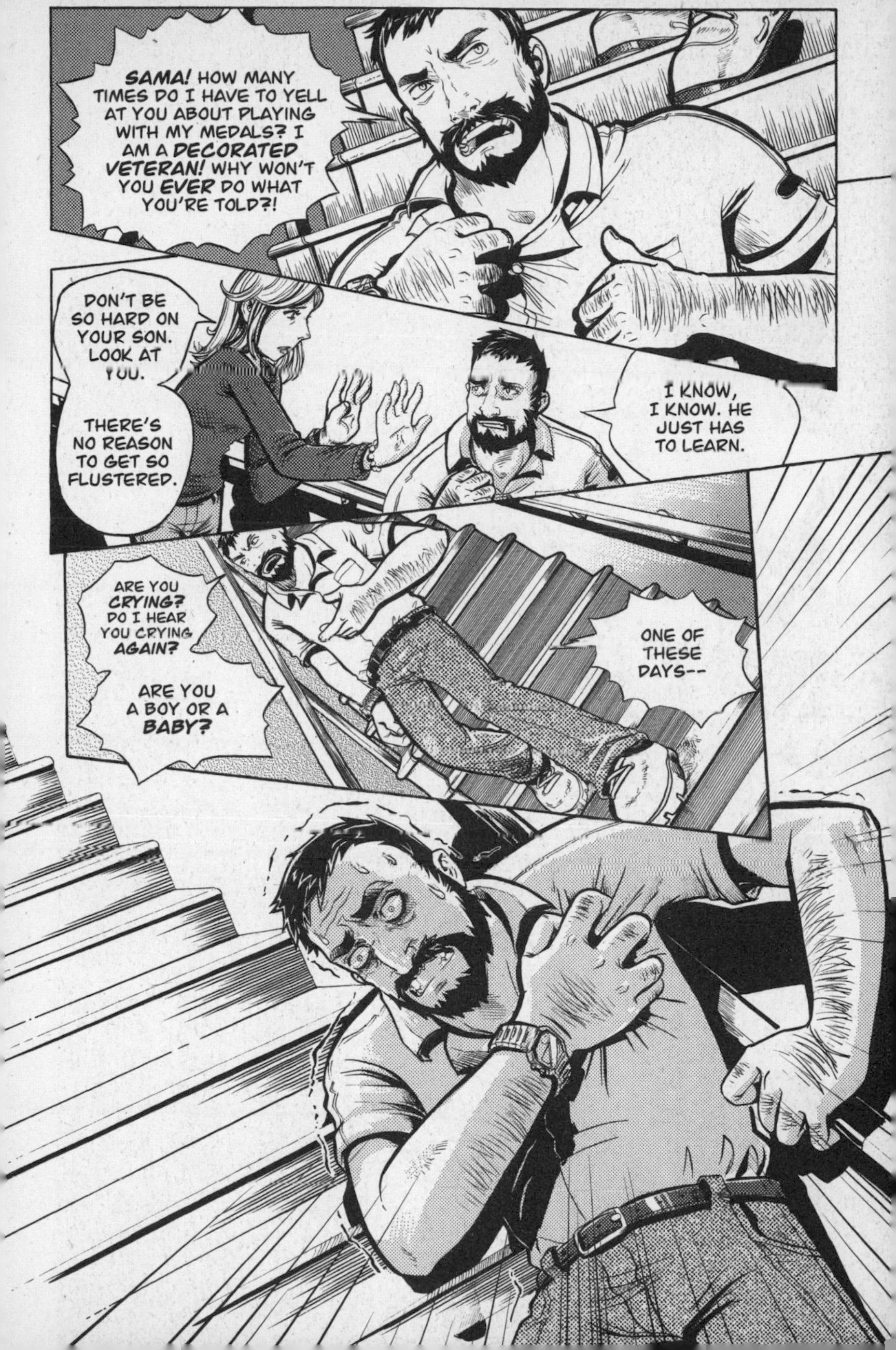
SAMA! HOW MANY TIMES DO I HAVE TO YELL AT YOU ABOUT PLAYING WITH MY MEDALS? I AM A DECORATED VETERAN! WHY WON'T YOU EVER DO WHAT YOU'RE TOLD?!
DON'T BE SO HARD ON YOUR SON. LOOK AT YOU.
THERE'S NO REASON TO GET SO FLUSTERED.
I KNOW, I KNOW. HE JUST HAS TO LEARN.
ARE YOU CRYING? DO I HEAR YOU CRYING AGAIN?
ARE YOU A BOY OR A BABY?
ONE OF THESE DAYS--

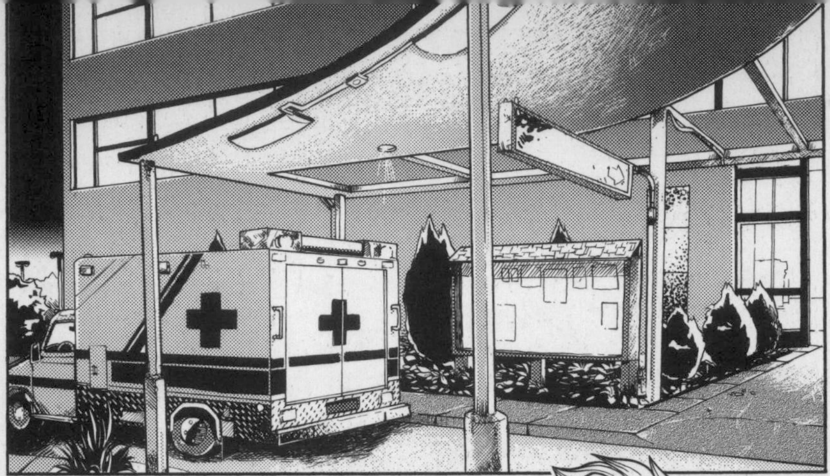
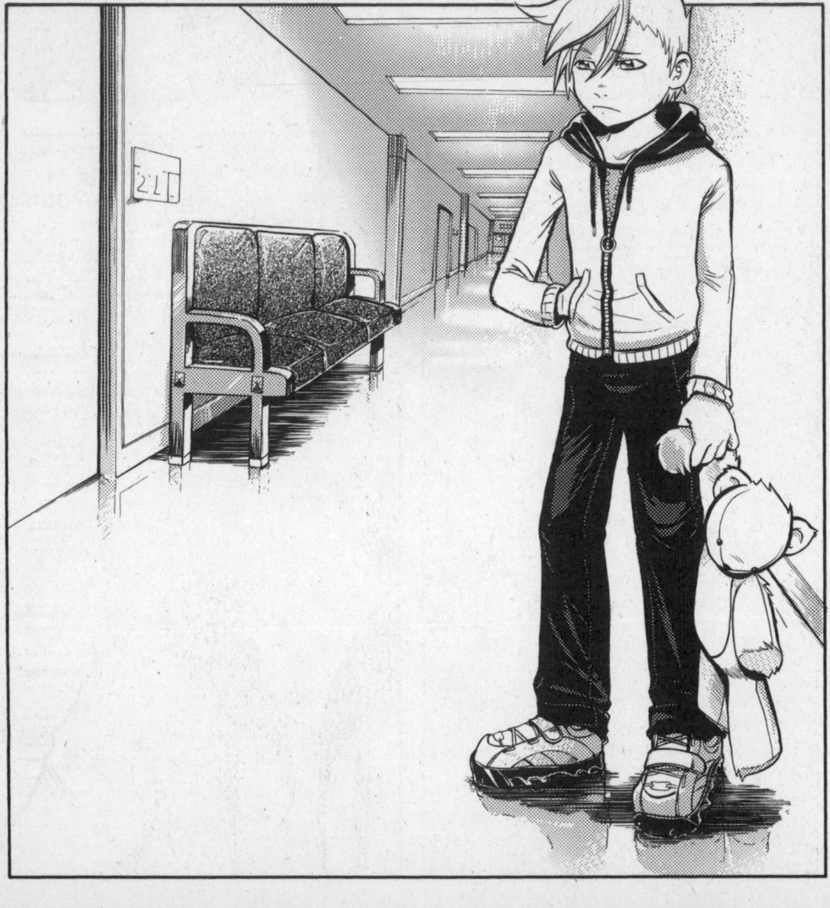

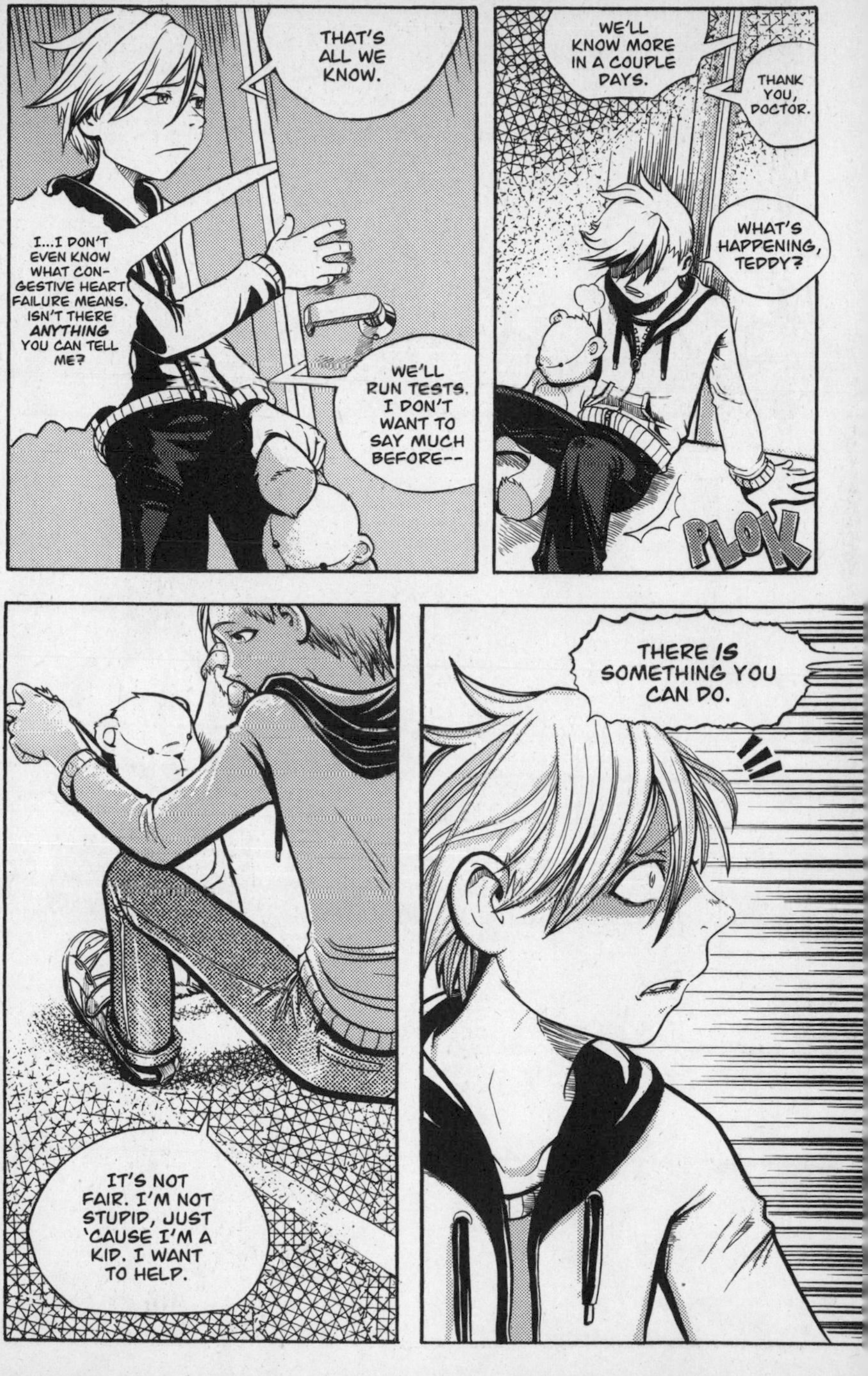
THAT'S ALL WE KNOW.
I...I DON'T EVEN KNOW WHAT CON-GESTIVE HEART FAILURE MEANS. ISN'T THERE *ANYTHING* YOU CAN TELL ME?
WE'LL RUN TESTS. I DON'T WANT TO SAY MUCH BEFORE--
WE'LL KNOW MORE IN A COUPLE DAYS.
THANK YOU, DOCTOR.
WHAT'S HAPPENING, TEDDY?
PLOK
IT'S NOT FAIR. I'M NOT STUPID, JUST 'CAUSE I'M A KID. I WANT TO HELP.
THERE *IS* SOMETHING YOU CAN DO.

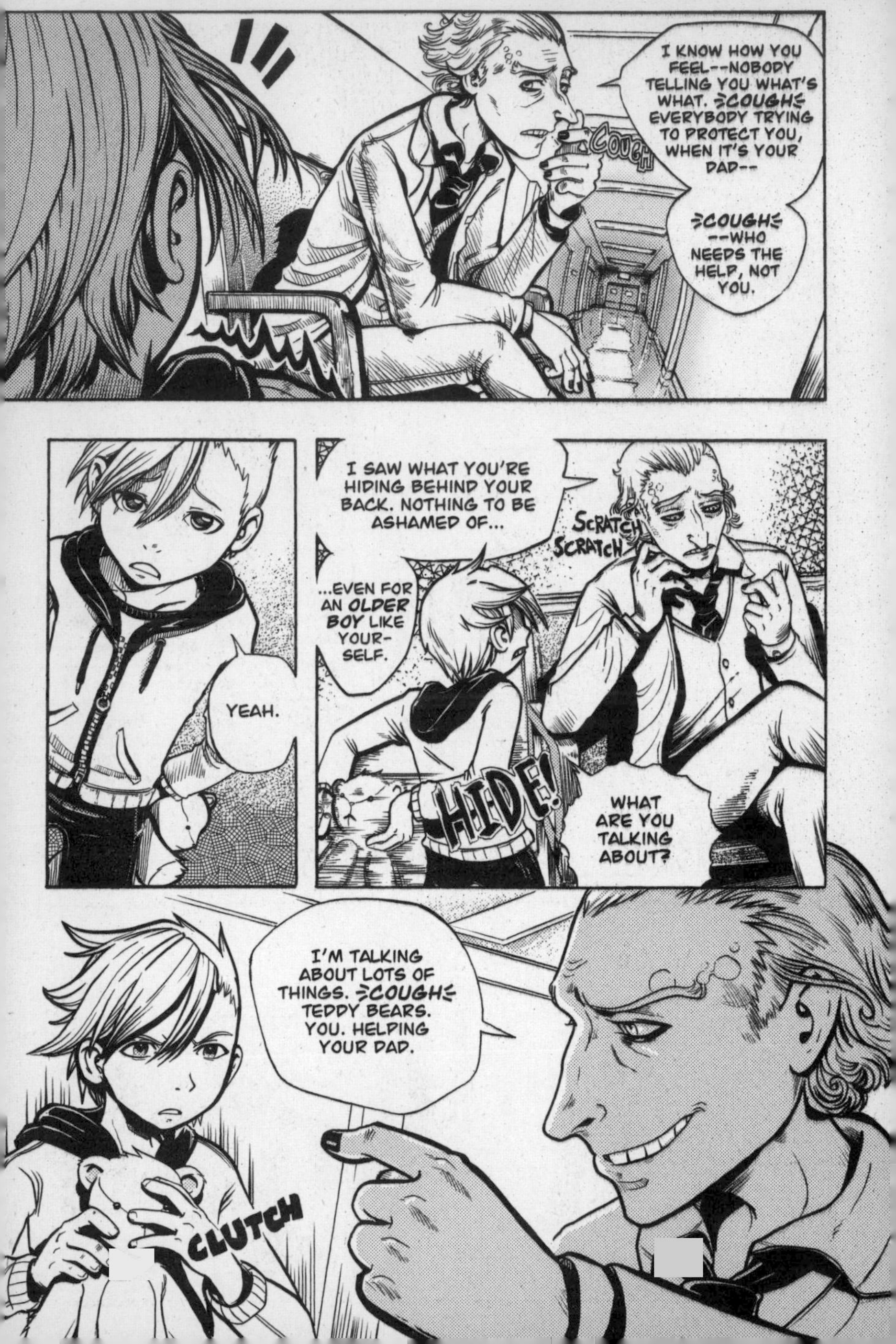
I KNOW HOW YOU FEEL--NOBODY TELLING YOU WHAT'S WHAT. ⩶COUGH⩶ EVERYBODY TRYING TO PROTECT YOU, WHEN IT'S YOUR DAD--
COUGH
⩶COUGH⩶ --WHO NEEDS THE HELP, NOT YOU.
YEAH.
I SAW WHAT YOU'RE HIDING BEHIND YOUR BACK. NOTHING TO BE ASHAMED OF...
...EVEN FOR AN *OLDER BOY* LIKE YOURSELF.
SCRATCH SCRATCH
HIDE!
WHAT ARE YOU TALKING ABOUT?
I'M TALKING ABOUT LOTS OF THINGS. ⩶COUGH⩶ TEDDY BEARS. YOU. HELPING YOUR DAD.
CLUTCH

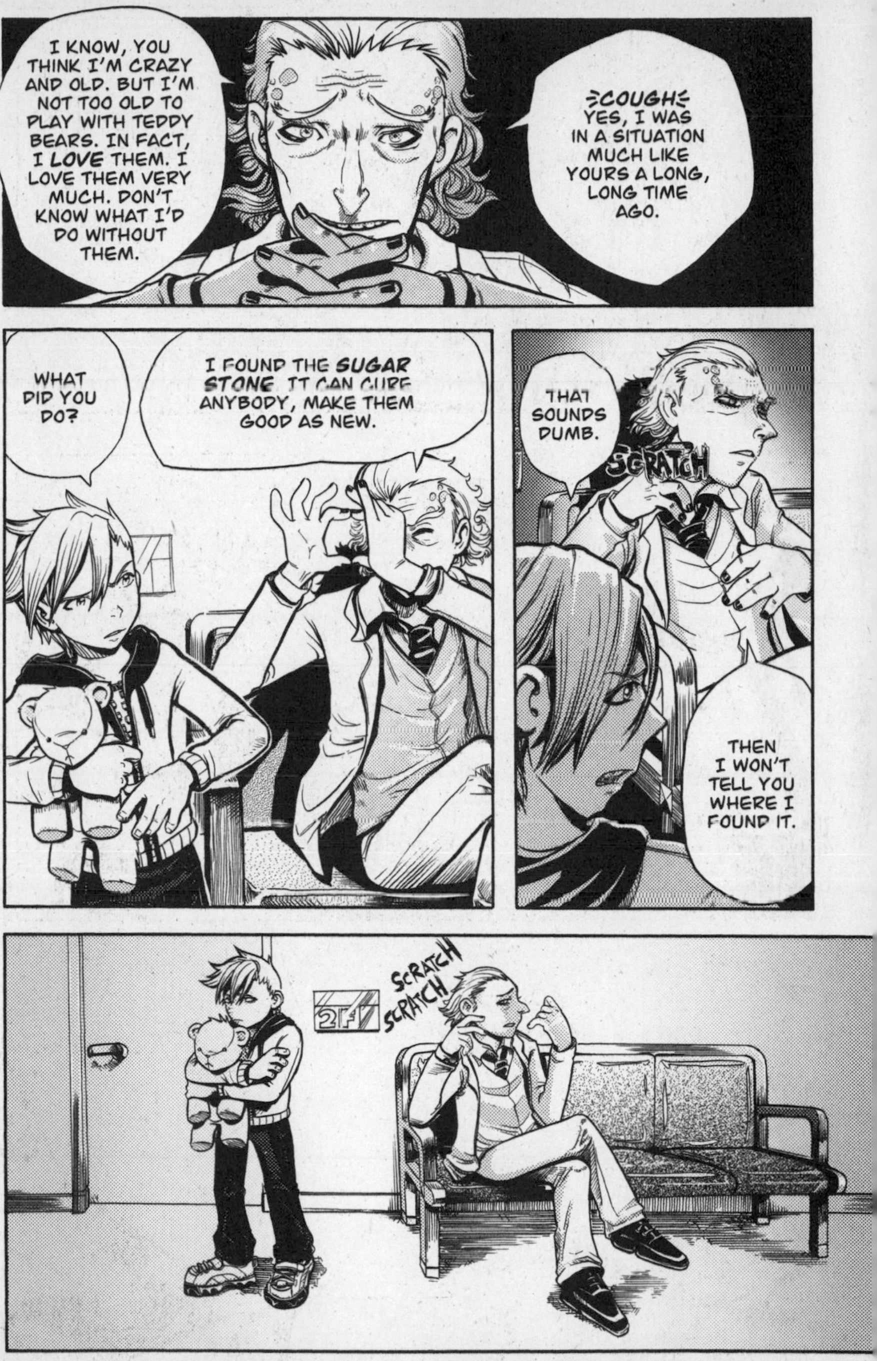
I KNOW, YOU THINK I'M CRAZY AND OLD. BUT I'M NOT TOO OLD TO PLAY WITH TEDDY BEARS. IN FACT, I **LOVE** THEM. I LOVE THEM VERY MUCH. DON'T KNOW WHAT I'D DO WITHOUT THEM.
COUGH YES, I WAS IN A SITUATION MUCH LIKE YOURS A LONG, LONG TIME AGO.
WHAT DID YOU DO?
I FOUND THE **SUGAR STONE**. IT CAN CURE ANYBODY, MAKE THEM GOOD AS NEW.
THAT SOUNDS DUMB.
SCRATCH
THEN I WON'T TELL YOU WHERE I FOUND IT.
2F
SCRATCH
SCRATCH

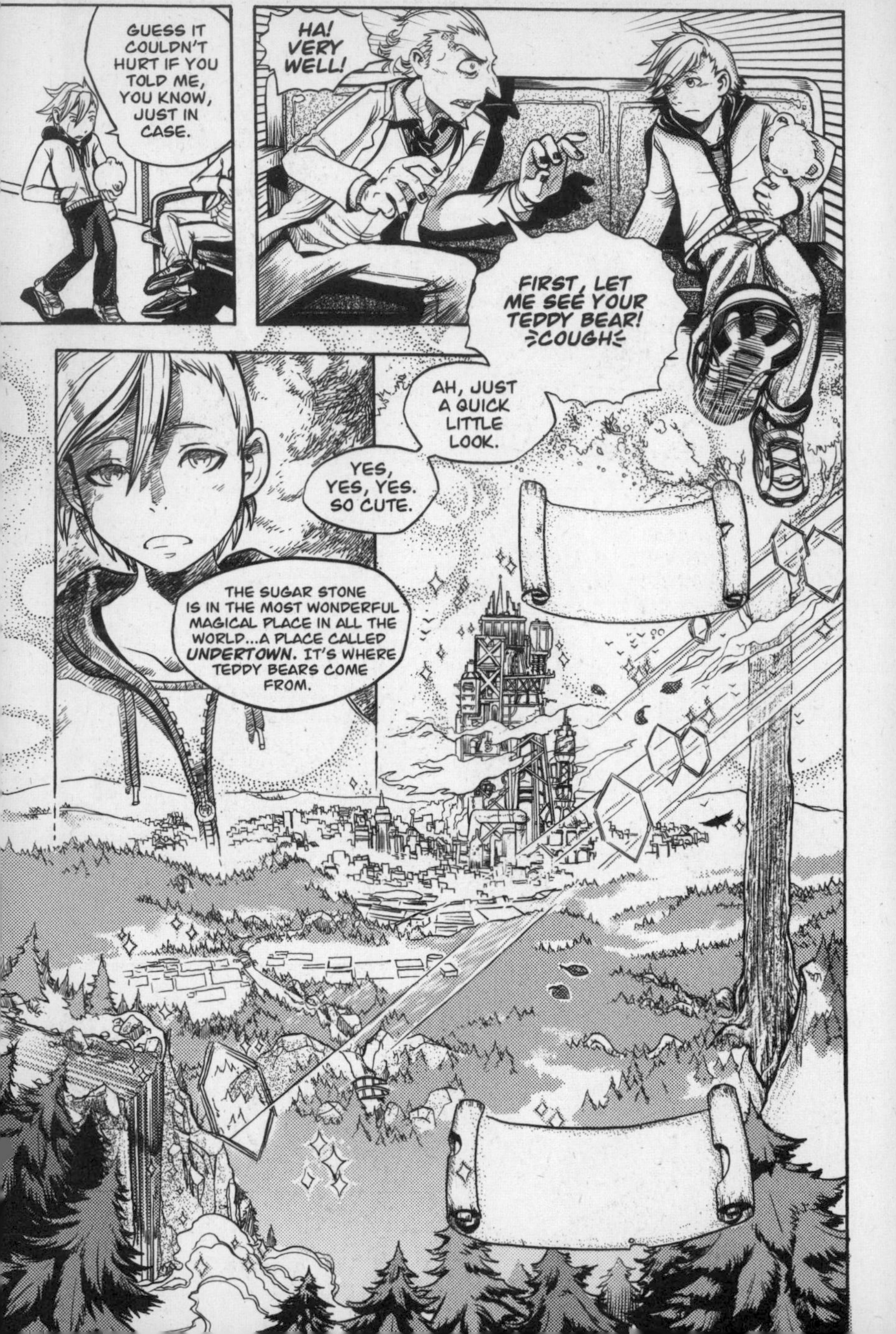
GUESS IT COULDN'T HURT IF YOU TOLD ME, YOU KNOW, JUST IN CASE.
HA! VERY WELL!
FIRST, LET ME SEE YOUR TEDDY BEAR! COUGH
AH, JUST A QUICK LITTLE LOOK.
YES, YES, YES. SO CUTE.
THE SUGAR STONE IS IN THE MOST WONDERFUL MAGICAL PLACE IN ALL THE WORLD...A PLACE CALLED UNDERTOWN. IT'S WHERE TEDDY BEARS COME FROM.

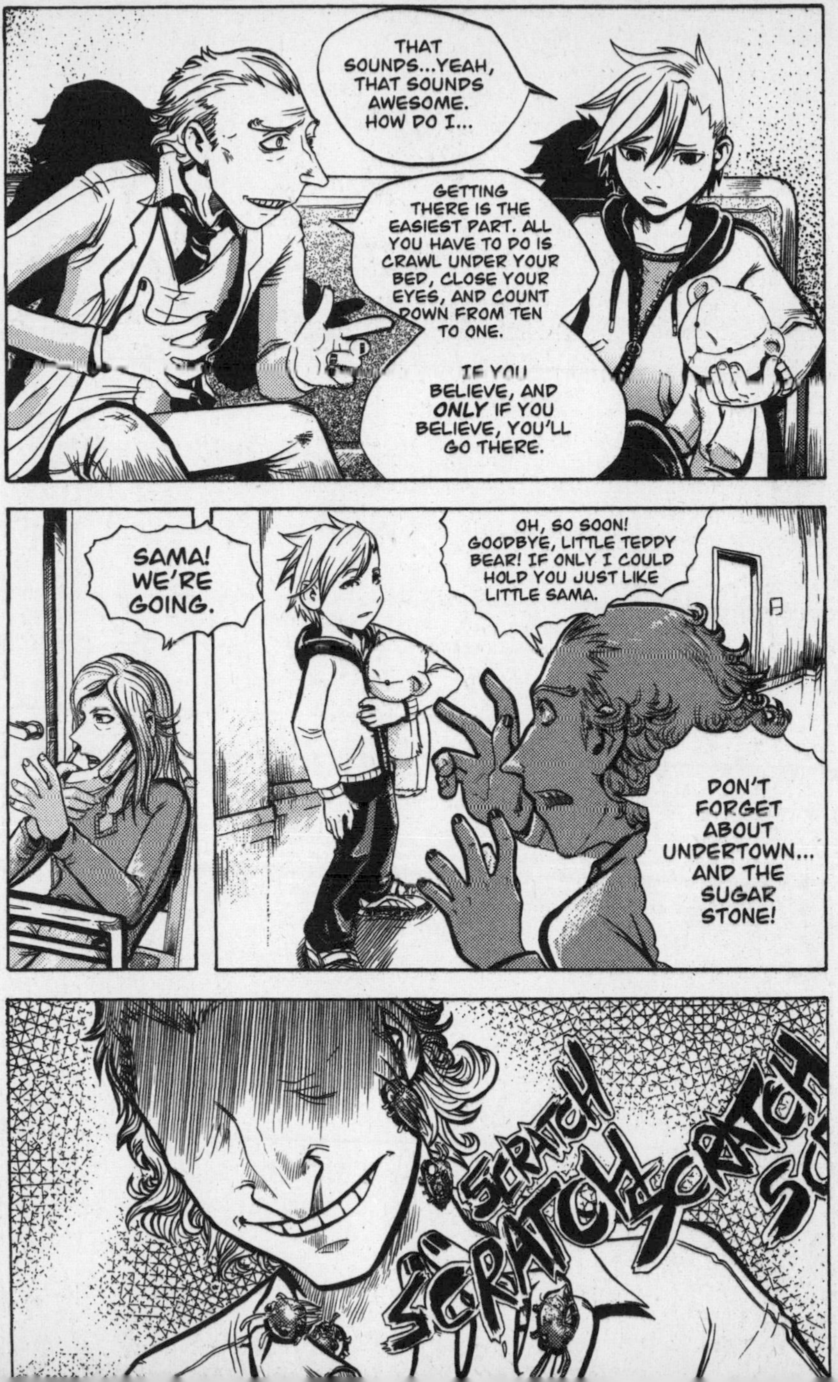
THAT SOUNDS...YEAH, THAT SOUNDS AWESOME. HOW DO I...
GETTING THERE IS THE EASIEST PART. ALL YOU HAVE TO DO IS CRAWL UNDER YOUR BED, CLOSE YOUR EYES, AND COUNT DOWN FROM TEN TO ONE.
IF YOU BELIEVE, AND ONLY IF YOU BELIEVE, YOU'LL GO THERE.
SAMA! WE'RE GOING.
OH, SO SOON! GOODBYE, LITTLE TEDDY BEAR! IF ONLY I COULD HOLD YOU JUST LIKE LITTLE SAMA.
DON'T FORGET ABOUT UNDERTOWN... AND THE SUGAR STONE!
SCRATCH
SCRATCH
SCRATCH

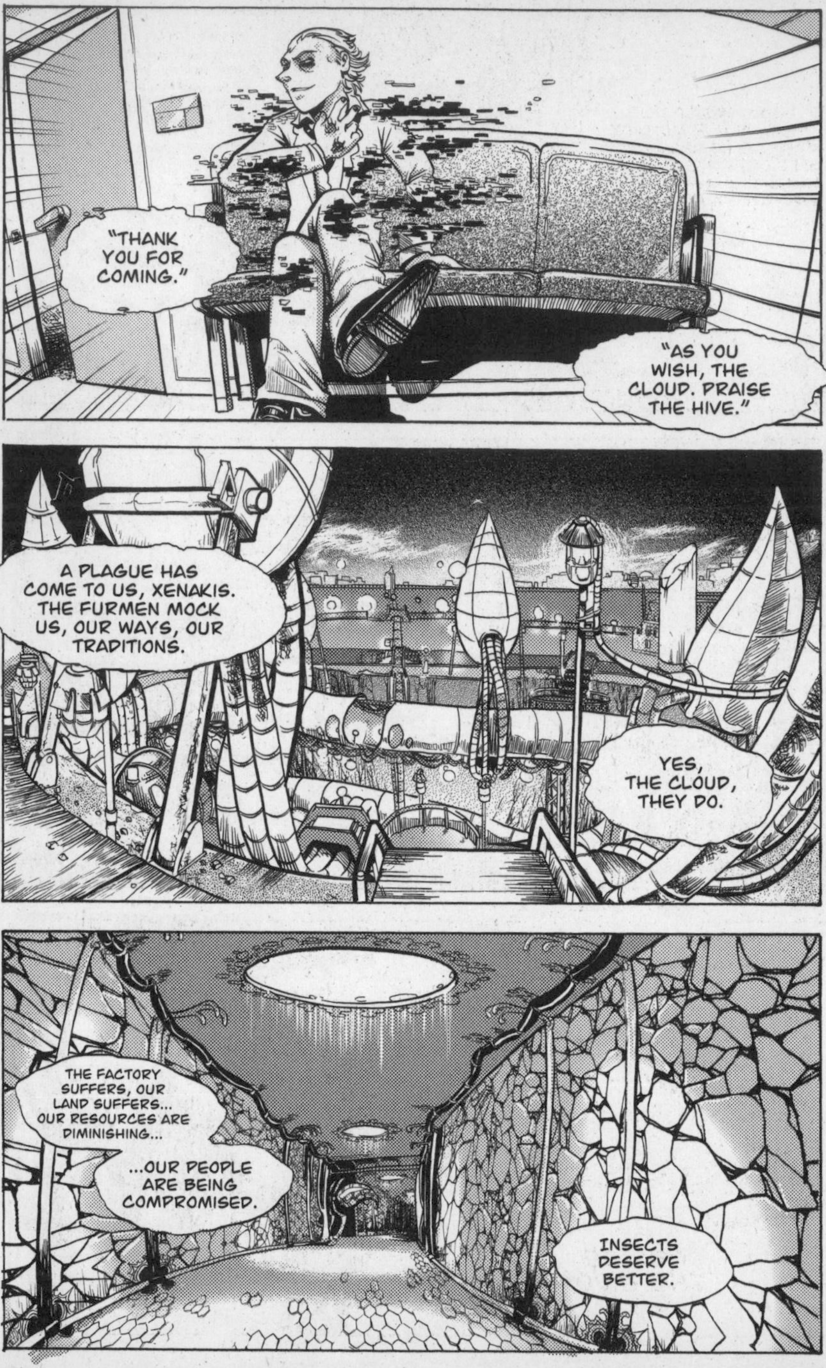
"THANK YOU FOR COMING."
"AS YOU WISH, THE CLOUD. PRAISE THE HIVE."
A PLAGUE HAS COME TO US, XENAKIS. THE FURMEN MOCK US, OUR WAYS, OUR TRADITIONS.
YES, THE CLOUD, THEY DO.
THE FACTORY SUFFERS, OUR LAND SUFFERS... OUR RESOURCES ARE DIMINISHING...
...OUR PEOPLE ARE BEING COMPROMISED.
INSECTS DESERVE BETTER.

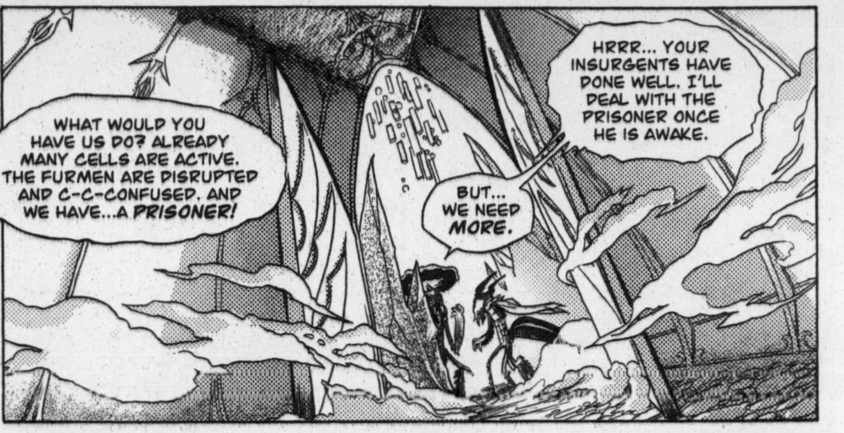
WHAT WOULD YOU HAVE US DO? ALREADY MANY CELLS ARE ACTIVE. THE FURMEN ARE DISRUPTED AND C-C-CONFUSED. AND WE HAVE...A *PRISONER!*
HRRR... YOUR INSURGENTS HAVE DONE WELL. I'LL DEAL WITH THE PRISONER ONCE HE IS AWAKE.
BUT... WE NEED *MORE.*

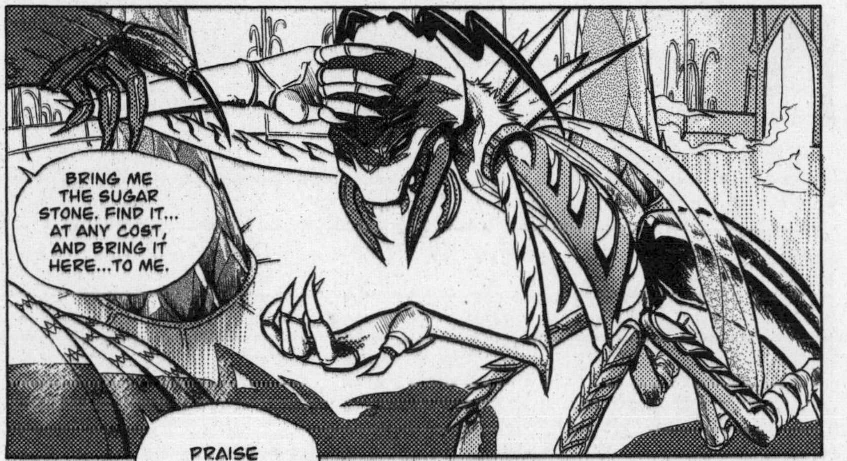
BRING ME THE SUGAR STONE. FIND IT... AT ANY COST, AND BRING IT HERE...TO ME.
PRAISE THE HIVE.

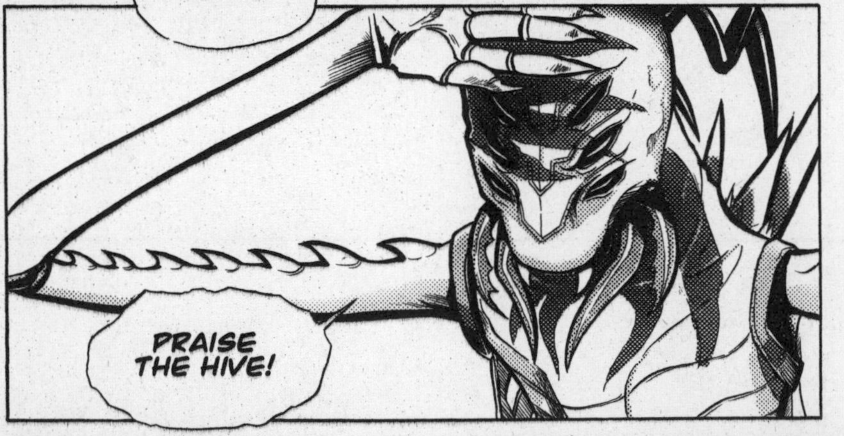
PRAISE THE HIVE!

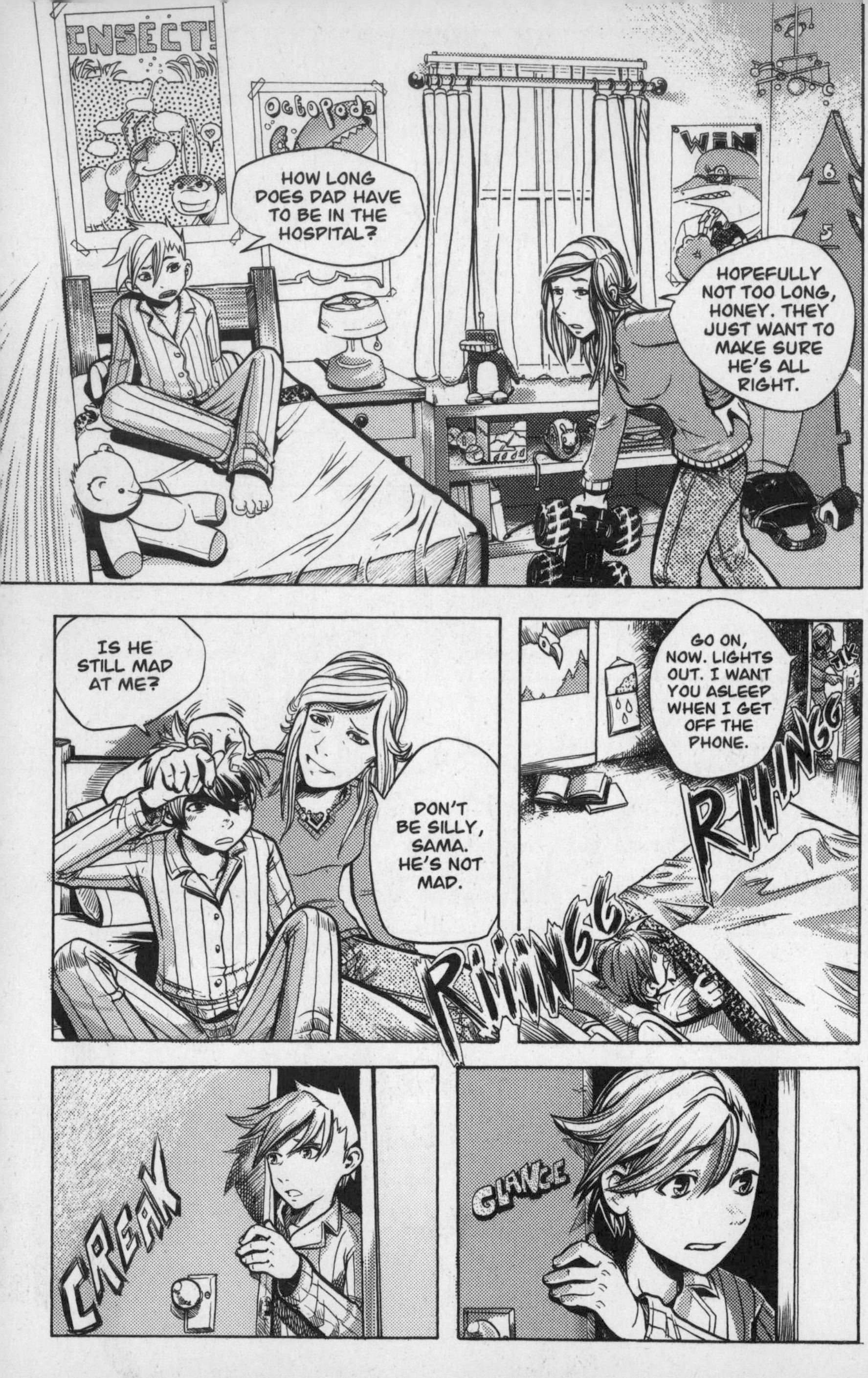

INSECT!
HOW LONG DOES DAD HAVE TO BE IN THE HOSPITAL?
HOPEFULLY NOT TOO LONG, HONEY. THEY JUST WANT TO MAKE SURE HE'S ALL RIGHT.
IS HE STILL MAD AT ME?
DON'T BE SILLY, SAMA. HE'S NOT MAD.
GO ON, NOW. LIGHTS OUT. I WANT YOU ASLEEP WHEN I GET OFF THE PHONE.
RIIINGG
RIIINGG
CREAK
GLANCE

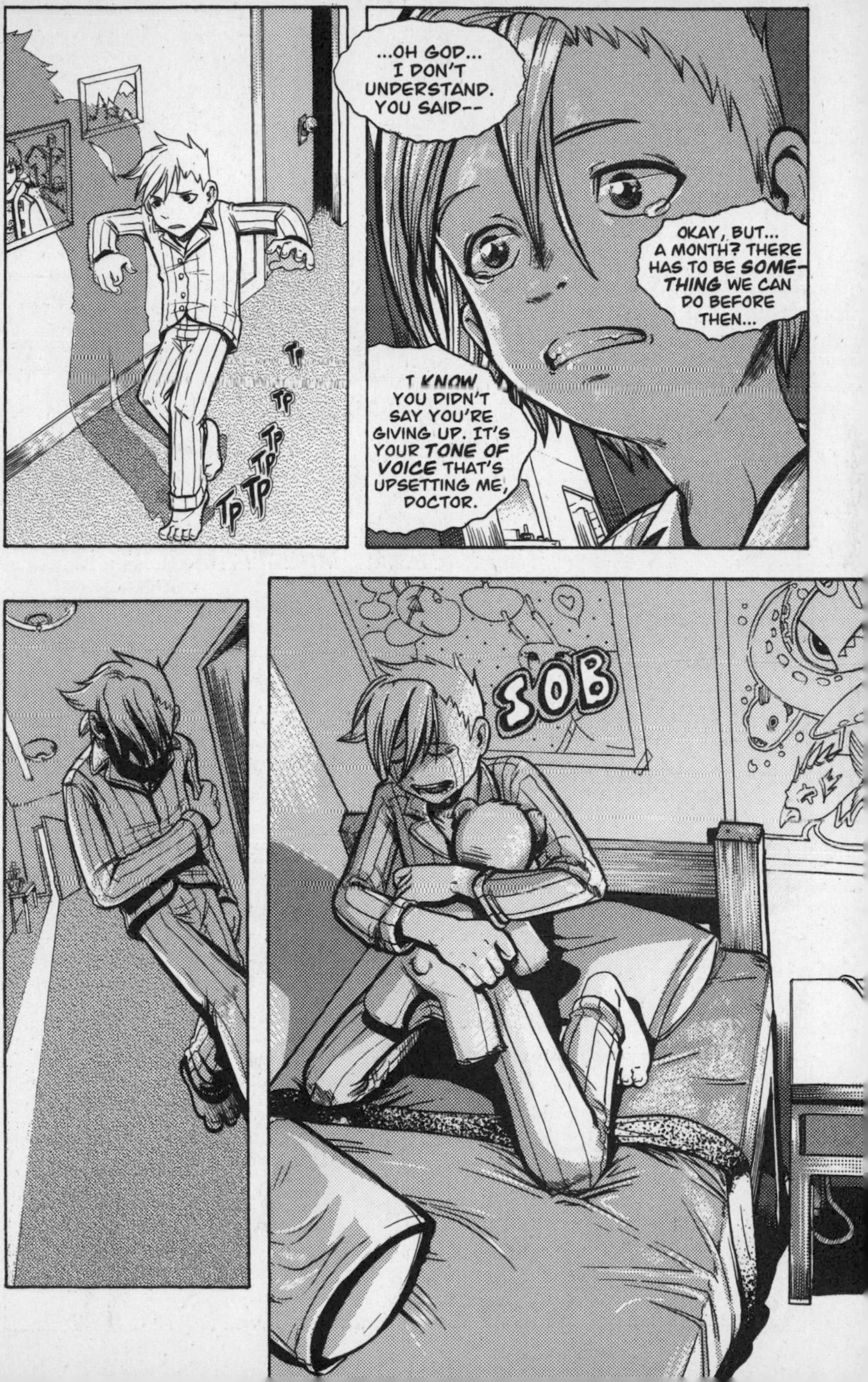
Tp
Tp
Tp
Tp
Tp
Tp
...OH GOD... I DON'T UNDERSTAND. YOU SAID--
I KNOW YOU DIDN'T SAY YOU'RE GIVING UP. IT'S YOUR TONE OF VOICE THAT'S UPSETTING ME, DOCTOR.
OKAY, BUT... A MONTH? THERE HAS TO BE SOMETHING WE CAN DO BEFORE THEN...
SOB

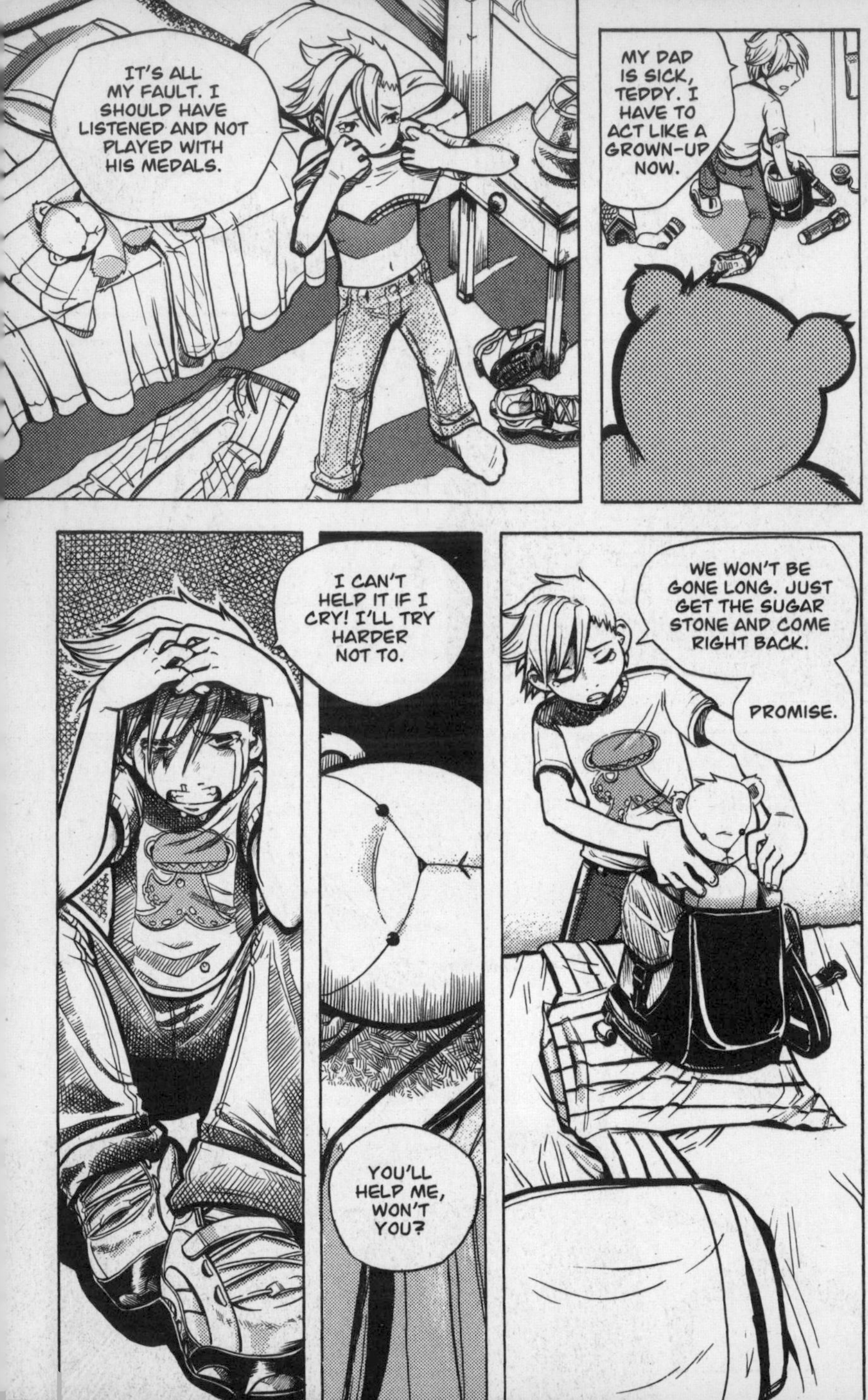
IT'S ALL MY FAULT. I SHOULD HAVE LISTENED AND NOT PLAYED WITH HIS MEDALS.
MY DAD IS SICK, TEDDY. I HAVE TO ACT LIKE A GROWN-UP NOW.
I CAN'T HELP IT IF I CRY! I'LL TRY HARDER NOT TO.
YOU'LL HELP ME, WON'T YOU?
WE WON'T BE GONE LONG. JUST GET THE SUGAR STONE AND COME RIGHT BACK.
PROMISE.

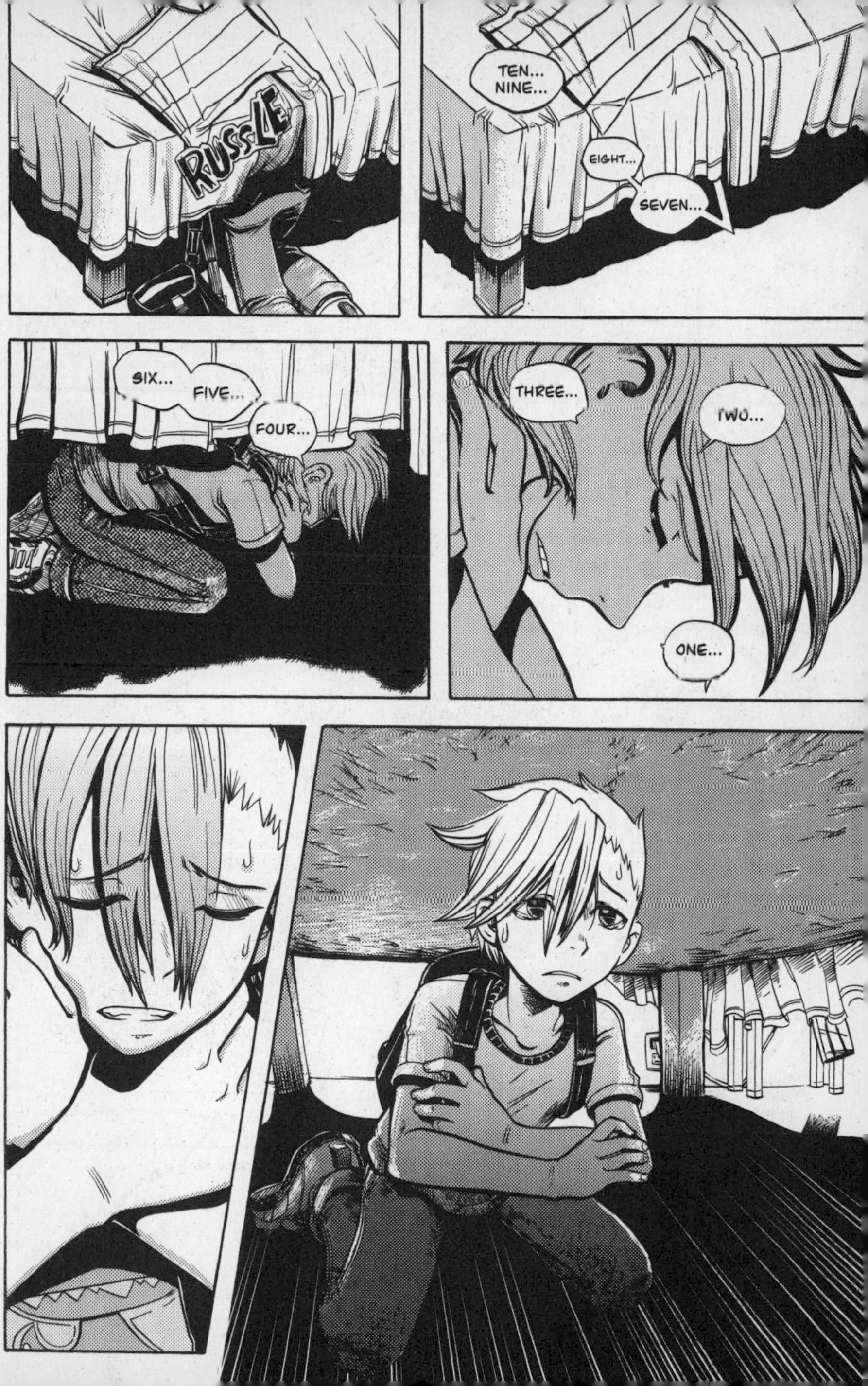
RUSSLE
TEN... NINE...
EIGHT...
SEVEN...
SIX...
FIVE...
FOUR...
THREE...
TWO...
ONE...

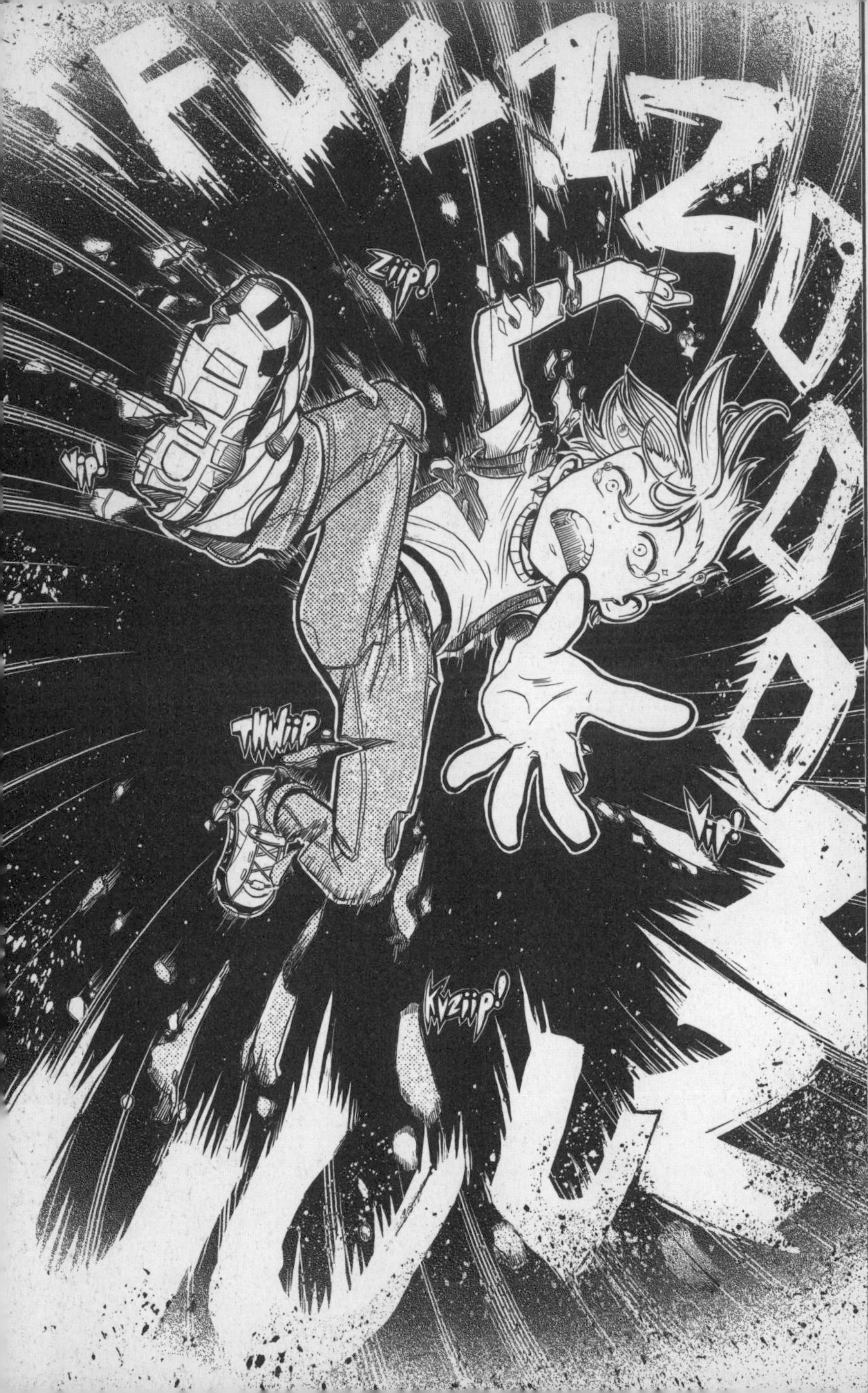
Ziip!
Vip!
THWiiP
ViP!
Kvziip!

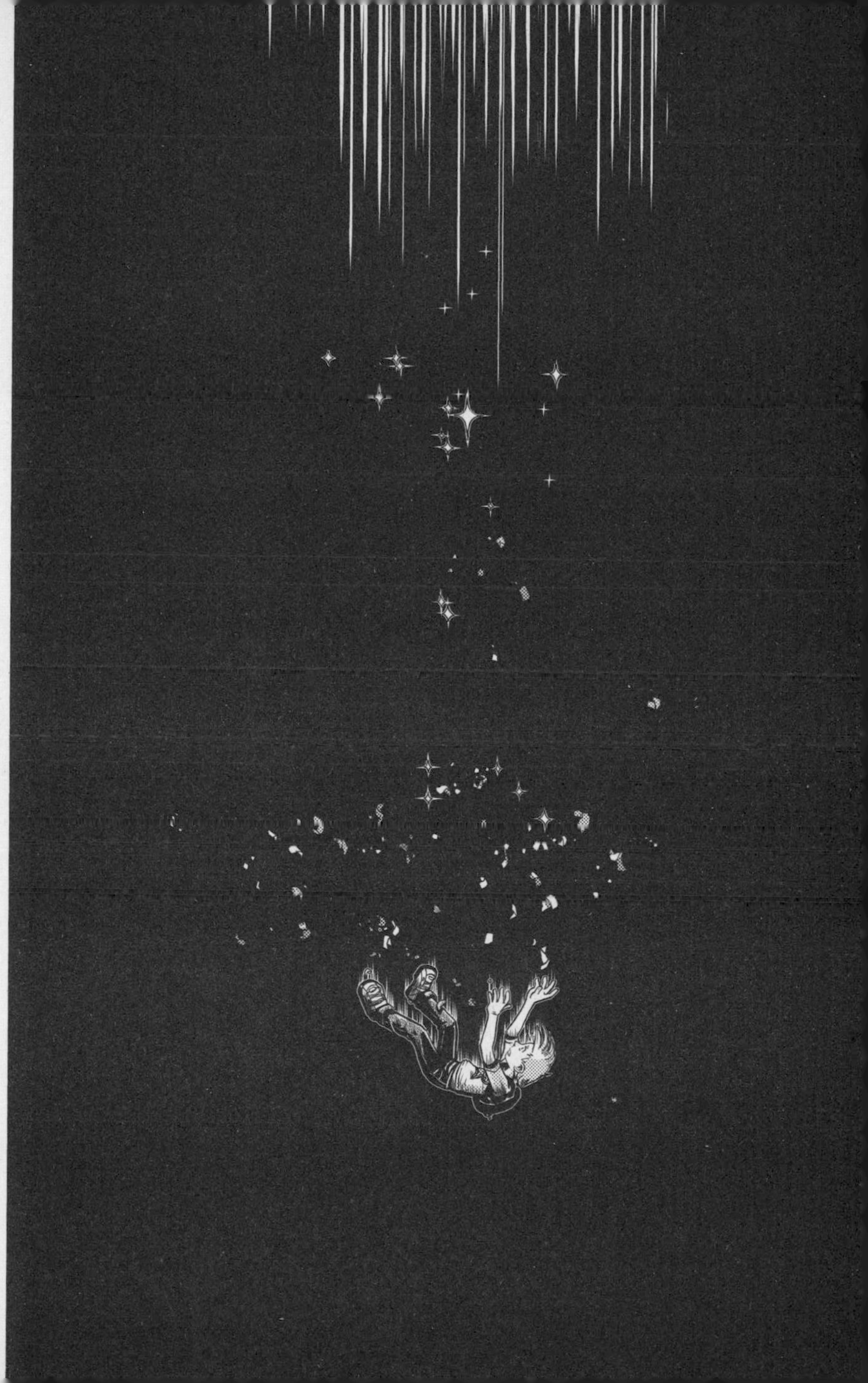

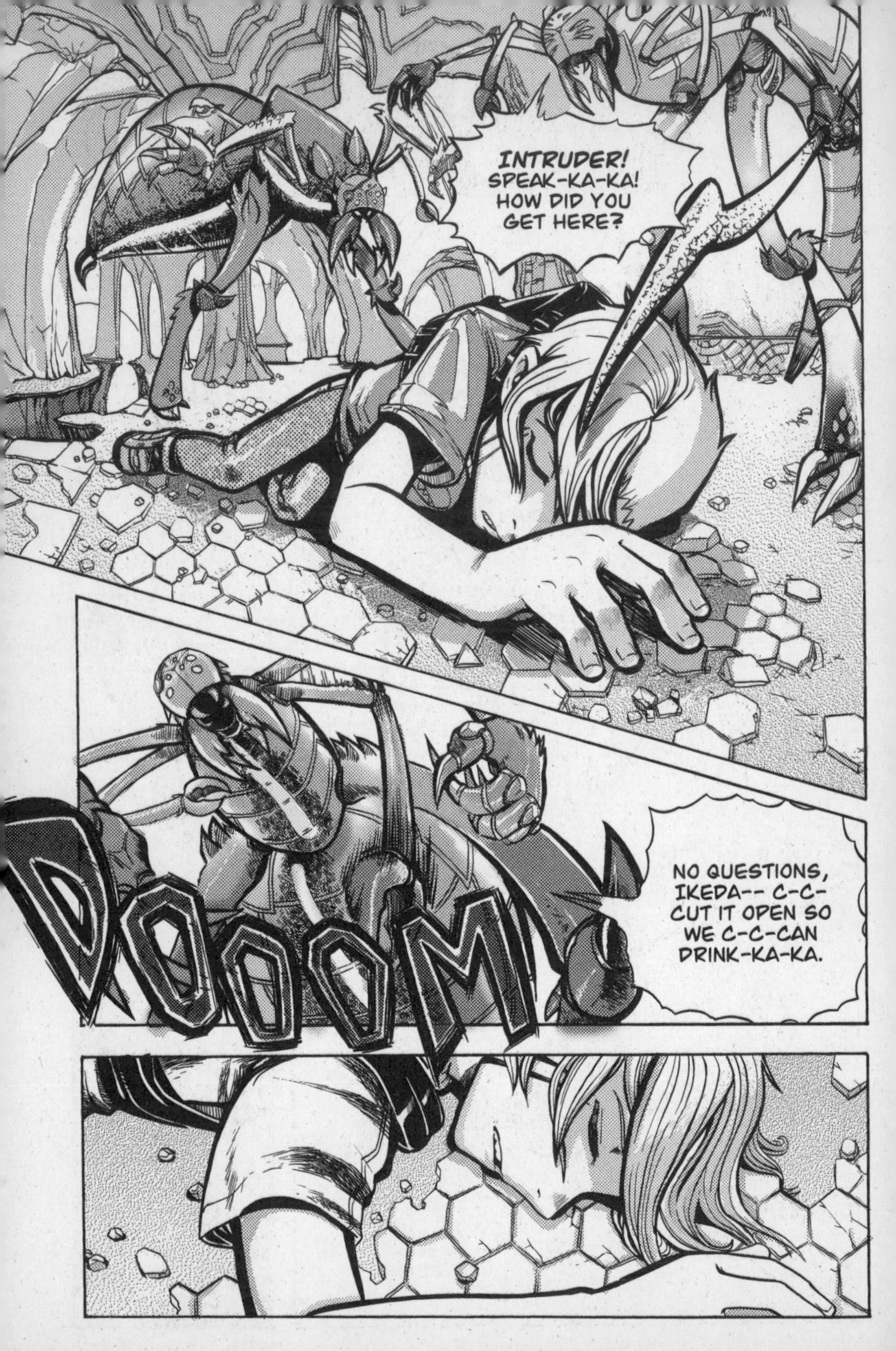
INTRUDER! SPEAK-KA-KA! HOW DID YOU GET HERE?
DOOOOM
NO QUESTIONS, IKEDA-- C-C-CUT IT OPEN SO WE C-C-CAN DRINK-KA-KA.

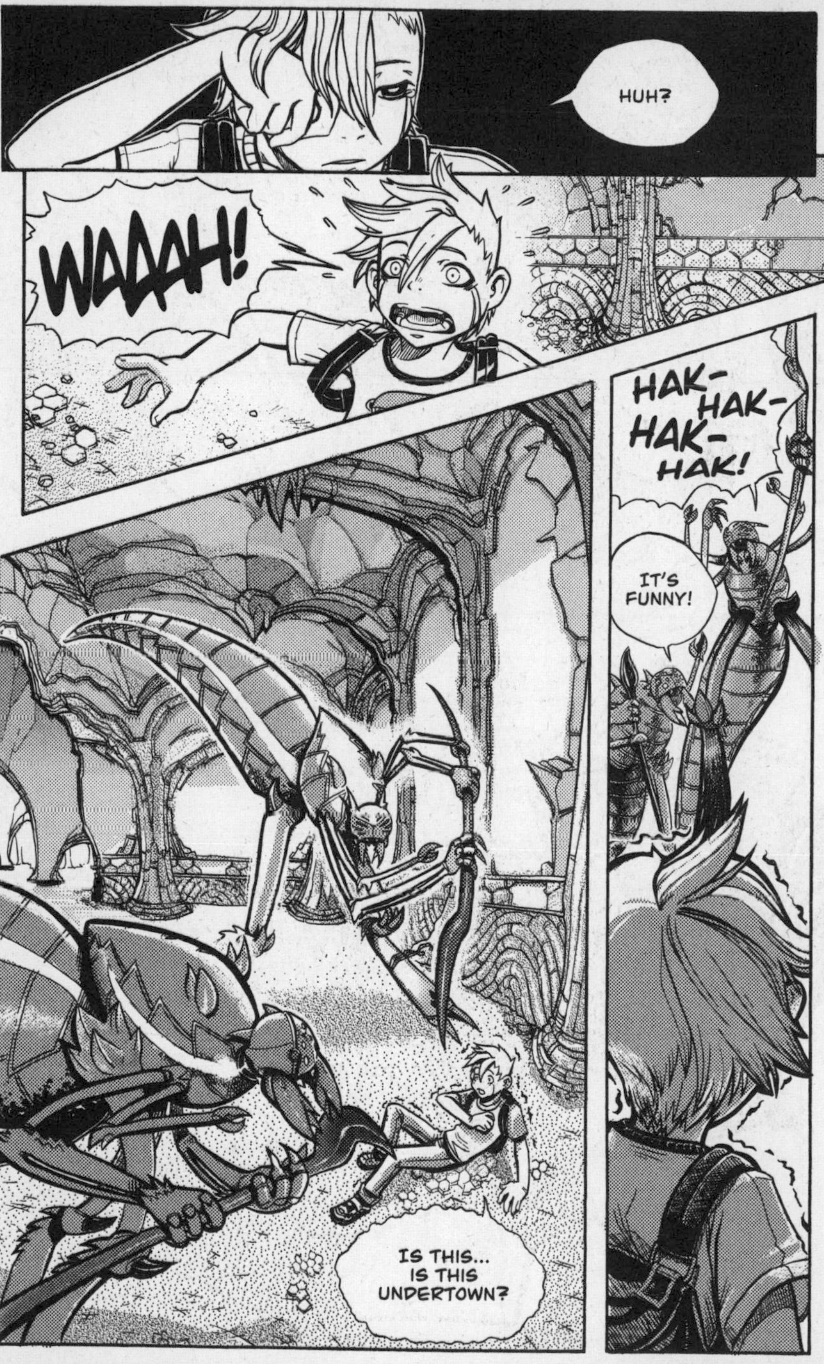
HUH?
WAAAH!
IS THIS... IS THIS UNDERTOWN?
HAK- HAK- HAK- HAK!
IT'S FUNNY!

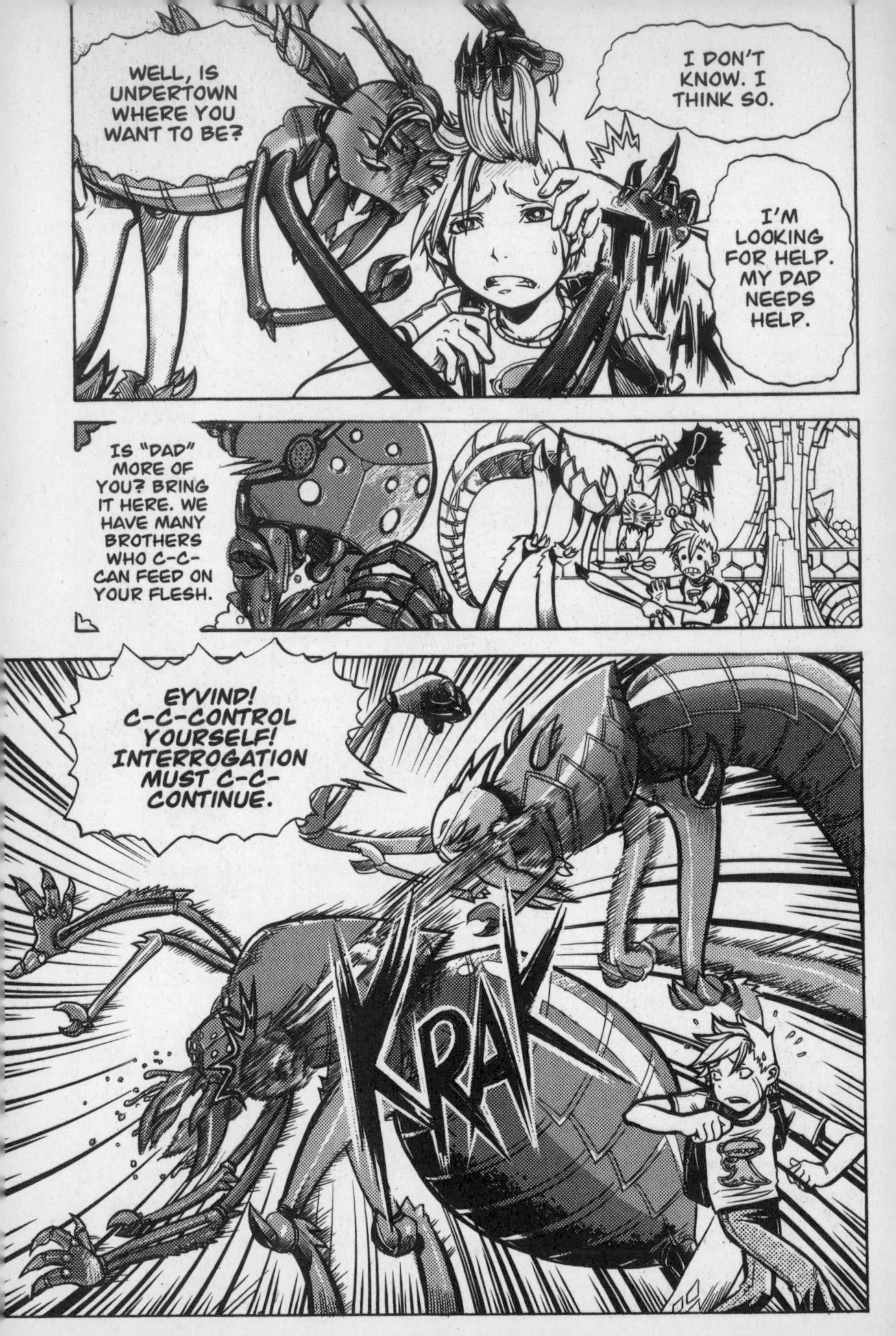

WELL, IS UNDERTOWN WHERE YOU WANT TO BE?
I DON'T KNOW. I THINK SO.
I'M LOOKING FOR HELP. MY DAD NEEDS HELP.
IS "DAD" MORE OF YOU? BRING IT HERE. WE HAVE MANY BROTHERS WHO C-C-CAN FEED ON YOUR FLESH.
!
EYVIND! C-C-CONTROL YOURSELF! INTERROGATION MUST C-C-CONTINUE.

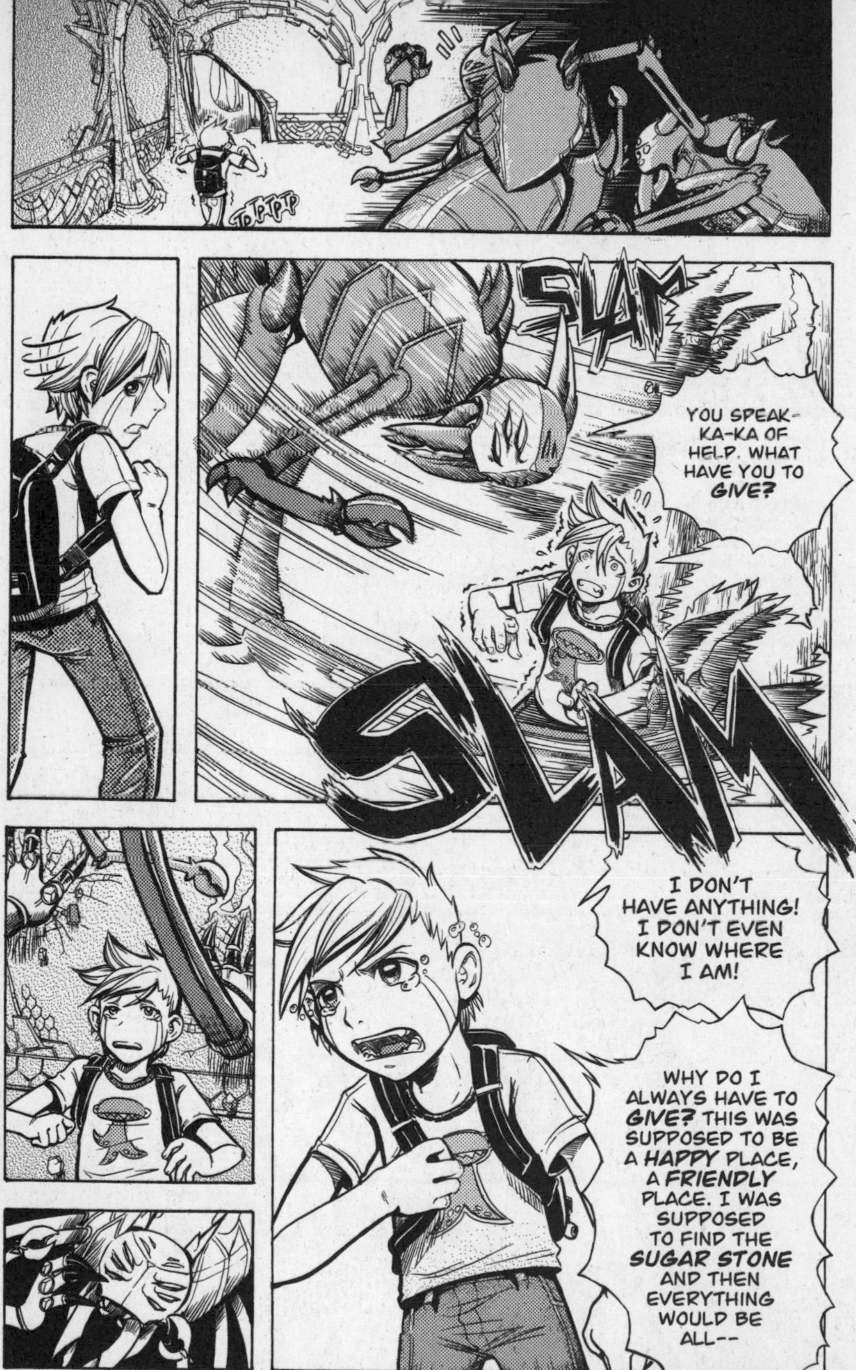
TPTPTPTP
SLAM
YOU SPEAK-KA-KA OF HELP. WHAT HAVE YOU TO GIVE?
SLAM
I DON'T HAVE ANYTHING! I DON'T EVEN KNOW WHERE I AM!
WHY DO I ALWAYS HAVE TO GIVE? THIS WAS SUPPOSED TO BE A HAPPY PLACE, A FRIENDLY PLACE. I WAS SUPPOSED TO FIND THE SUGAR STONE AND THEN EVERYTHING WOULD BE ALL--

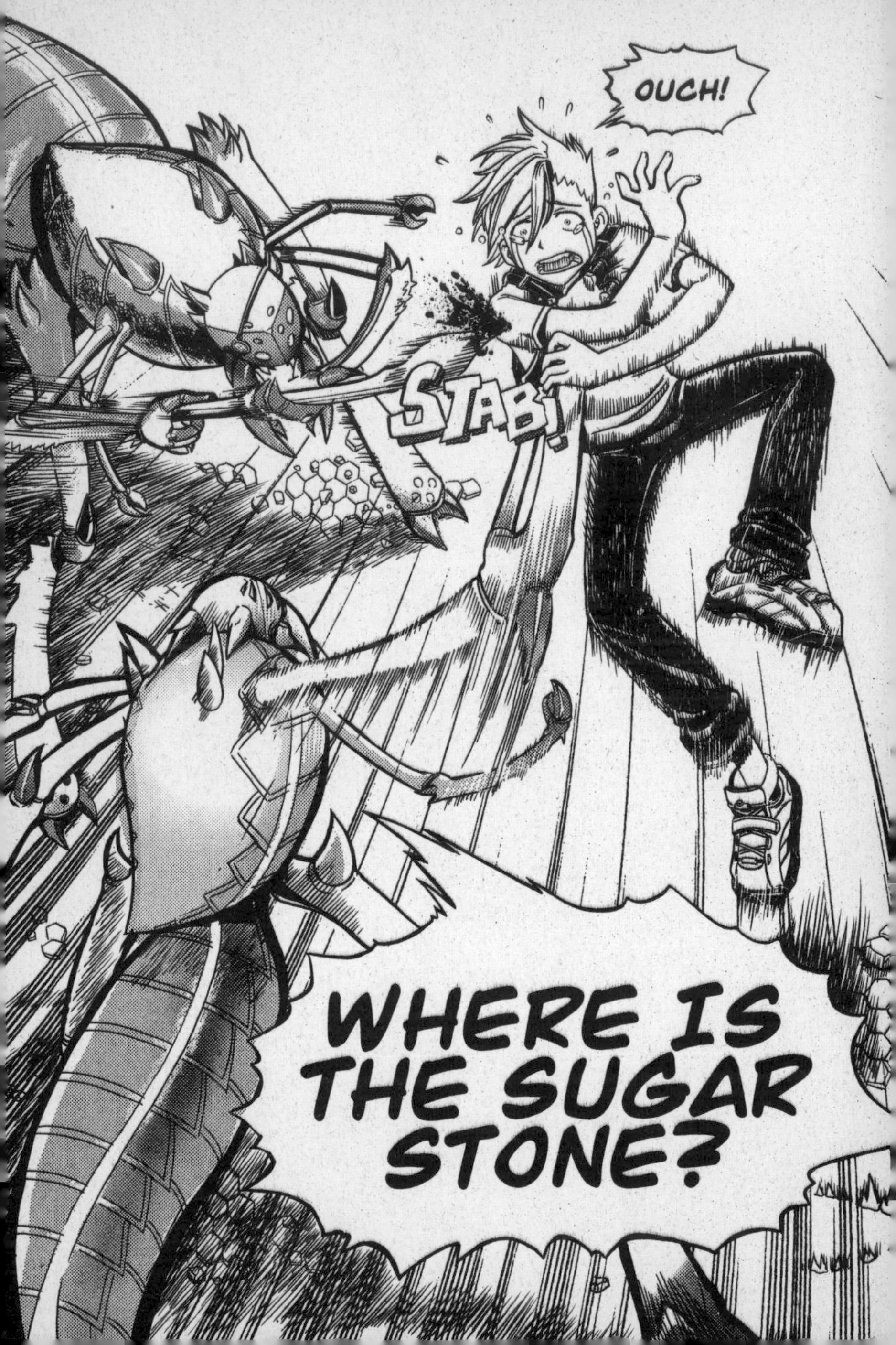
OUCH!
STAB!
WHERE IS THE SUGAR STONE?

TOKYOPOP® PRESENTS

UNDERTOWN™

AVAILABLE AUGUST 2007!